Ha
at
his
in
Lai
His
by
Sul
ma
Bre
Co
Alb
Boo
Tin
coll
nov
nov
Gol
pre
of s
fou
Dre
His
in 2
mer

ny
or
er
ul
ly.
ed
of
as
of
re
k
er
ie
at
d
e
e
e
n
s
d
2.
d
a
d

and the Bomb, followed in 2005. His screenplay *Venus* was directed by Roger Michell in 2006. His latest novel, *Something to Tell You*, was published to great critical acclaim in 2008. In 2009 the National Theatre staged an adaptation of his strikingly prescient and acclaimed novel, *The Black Album*. His *Collected Stories* were published in 2010.

He has been awarded the Chevalier de l'Ordre des Arts des Lettres and a CBE for services to literature and his work has been translated into thirty-six languages. He was awarded the PEN/Pinter Prize in 2010.

Collected Essays

HANIF KUREISHI

ff

faber and faber

First published in 2011
by Faber and Faber Ltd
Bloomsbury House
74–77 Great Russell Street
London WC1B 3DA

Typeset by RefineCatch Ltd
Printed in England by CPI Group (UK), Croydon

A CIP record for this book
is available from the British Library

ISBN 978–0–571–24983–1

2 4 6 8 10 9 7 5 3

Contents

CONTENTS

Introduction: The Writer's Time

This collection begins in the mid-1980s, and as far as I can recall, 'The Rainbow Sign' was the first essay I ever wrote. My then editor at Faber, Robert McCrum, had approached me about publishing the screenplay of *My Beautiful Laundrette* and suggested I write an introduction to it, since it might seem thin on its own.

I'm not keen on reading screenplays myself; I can't recall wanting to read one purely for pleasure, except for *The Third Man*. Certainly, when I write a screenplay, how it reads is not primary. A screenplay is more of a map than a work of art, and should show the director how he might get from here to there, while telling the actors what they should say.

In the 1980s Faber began to sell a lot of screenplays, especially Tarantino's. 'The Rainbow Sign' was an opportunity for me to think more about some of the issues raised in *My Beautiful Laundrette* and in the plays I'd written before that, which were concerned with race, class, sexuality and so on, questions provoked by my childhood and family situation, and which I couldn't help continuing to try to formulate and think around. These were questions – particularly the ones around race – which, it seemed to me, contemporary artists were reluctant to engage with, as if they didn't know where to begin.

Although I'd enjoyed the new extravagant and wild American journalism, a written version of rock 'n' roll, where, mostly, the writer appeared as a character and, inevitably, as the headline – Mailer, Wolfe, Hunter Thompson – I can't say they set a good example. You couldn't see the story for the star.

I preferred the modest intensity of James Baldwin's work. It seemed to me that he had more to say than the others, particularly about what it is to live in a society where one's identity is always in doubt, if not under attack. (If other people have too many ideas about you it's impossible for them to see you. You are both over-scrutinised and ignored.)

And anyhow, whatever else other writers were doing, what I wanted was to describe myself in terms of the country I lived in, Britain. Adolescents read partly to find others who understand their situation, who suffer as they do, and have similar sexual experiences to them. But I had found very little in contemporary British writing which spoke for me. Immigration and social change were mostly off the agenda as subjects, and I was yet to begin my own account of being of mixed race, *The Buddha of Suburbia*.

'The Rainbow Sign', then, was an opportunity for me to con-sider some of these things, and to see if I could use the essay form expressively. After all, the writers I'd admired as a young man wrote essays as well as novels, stories, plays; it was part of the writer's work to use forms which tested and extended him. He was a different kind of writer according to what he was attempt-ing; he could say different things. The theatre I came from, and where I'd worked since I was eighteen, and whose tradition of acting, directing and writing I admired – the Royal Court in Sloane Square – had been committed since the mid-50s to exploring Britain's post-war decline and the effects of the end of the empire, and what sort of renewal might be possible. It wanted to put the contemporary on stage. It recognised that without lively new voices the culture died.

I have wanted, too, to write about London, as so many others have done, and its fascination for me as a young man, particularly areas which were once considered louche, bohemian and 'mixed', and where, for a time after the war, the most lively people gathered: Chelsea, Notting Hill and Soho. These places have now become expensive and bland. Since the mid-80s and the con-struction of Canary Wharf, the centre of gravity of the city has shifted to the East, and it seems to me that I am once more living in a suburb. Luckily, there's no community spirit or noticeable identity in Hammersmith, just immigrants moving in and out. People live here mainly because of its proximity to other places. But it's as good a point as any in which to take the temperature of this massive, diverse city.

I had wanted to be a writer – to devote myself to words and storytelling – from the age of fourteen. I can remember the moment it occurred to me, one day at school, and how differently I felt about the world after, the door to the future opening. But I hadn't given much thought as to how I would support myself, and later, a family. I seemed to believe that I'd get by somehow. The details didn't matter, particularly since I made the decision to write in 1968 – a time when creativity rather than 'bread' was the key. And the writers I'd admired – Kafka, Beckett, Kerouac, Henry Miller, amongst others – hardly had 'professional writer' on their passports. They were artists, which was different, and none of them, to my knowledge, seemed concerned about the price of prams, or had children at private school – both of which, according to a rather arch idea of Cyril Connolly's, were lethal for writers: 'There is no more sombre enemy of good art than the pram in the hallway.'

Perhaps, for some people, becoming an artist implies abandoning ordinary life for the excitement of bohemianism, but I can't say I know many writers like that. Writing is as steady a job as any job can be. Routine makes the imagination possible. 'Acting in', you could call it, as opposed to acting out. Writers are envied because writing, or perhaps any form of art, is the most gratifying sublimation of all; it is one thing you don't have to leave the house to do – warm but not impressive underwear being the only requirement, apart from some talent.

I guess I inherited the idea of 'professionalism' from my father, who is referred to often in this collection, as well as in my memoir *My Ear at His Heart.* His deepest wish was to write for a living rather than work as a clerk in an embassy, and he thought that being paid was a higher accolade, and a more dependable and useful form of praise, than a good review, something any writer would agree with.

When I dropped out of the first university I attended, and my father was ill – and things were beginning to fall apart for me, almost before they'd begun – someone suggested they might be able to get me work in Fleet Street. I considered this, but knew even then that I could never be a journalist. Journalism didn't resemble in any way what I wanted to do. It was too functional; I thought it would dilute my style; and it was too quick for me. Later, newspapers would call up with a request for a piece, often about a fascinating subject, and they'd want it overnight or in two and a half hours. I can write fast; I like to, it's sometimes the best way, charging ahead without hesitation or inhibition. But I have no interest in being continually under that kind of pressure; I panic, freeze and head for the pub.

The piece of writing I usually most enjoy doing is inevitably the thing I'm not supposed to be doing, so it can seem illicit. I like to work on something over a long period, returning to it repeatedly, adding, subtracting and altering, and taking advice from editors and friends, until I can't bear to look at it, which is when I guess it's done. Writing is highly labour intensive. It takes a lot of time – and much patient toleration of boredom, frustration and self-loathing – to achieve anything. Then you try to sell something to the world it doesn't know it needs.

George Orwell writes, with some baffled amusement, about people who just decide to write, without quite knowing what they might write about. No writer knows this, or would want to. He or she will probably be aware of some sort of impulse to speak, and will begin writing to explore, to discover – to create a self; it is a form of play more like a conversation than a programme. For me, the occasion of an essay is the opportunity to walk and think and dip into my library. It is an opportunity to continue to be a student – the finest thing in the world – and to try to find out if I have something to say. Writers often think of themselves, and are often characterised, as idlers, loafers or bums, since much of what we do takes place when we're not working, in the unconscious, and in cafés. I can't begin to tell you what hard work it is looking out of the window and wondering about your favourite pen, and which colour ink you prefer that day, but few will be convinced.

Nevertheless, loafing is always more generative than obsessive concentration. It wouldn't be as if I knew in advance what I thought, particularly about the important subjects – writing, teaching, liberalism, and so-called religious fundamentalism. But I know I'm interested in the area where philosophy, literature and psychoanalysis cross over – the mind in the world. And I want to take the essential strangeness of the human being – both to himself and to others – as my subject.

At school in the 1950s and 1960s, the system wanted you to shut up; they had no desire to hear from you. Creativity in the young, and their engagement with the new Pop, existed only in spite of the authorities. More or less the whole of my formal education was concerned with enforced inhibition and constraint. I had to unfetter my imagination myself and learn to let it run. It sounds awkward to say that you might train your imagination, but you might learn, at least, to hear what it has to say, and to respond. Since a period in the early 1980s when I found I couldn't move forward with my work, I have used, in the morning, Freud's method of free association, which he himself discovered, oddly enough, in a wonderfully titled writing manual by Ludwig Borne: *The Art of Becoming an Original Writer in Three Days.* I found I could create ideas and avoid anxiety by throwing words at the page at random – putting down whatever occurred to me – the same way I used dreams as a way of uncovering ideas and connections. My unconscious might know more than I did – it was quicker, funnier and more economical – but its emanations, which could be prolific, had to be organised and considered.

I was always aware that I wanted to make a living as a writer, since it implied a level of commitment and seriousness which were crucial to me. For a start, I wouldn't have to wonder about what else I might like to do. It was the end of a certain kind of doubt. And vocational choices in the suburbs were limited, mostly to crime or clerking. I knew that the desire to make art and the desire to make money are only sometimes compatible. Oddly, the curious public is often more concerned about the writer's routine than they are about how he actually gets food on his table, which is his major concern.

When I first began to write plays I was on the dole, and earned little money. Eight years after leaving university, I wrote a hit film and began to be surprised and a little overwhelmed at the number of cheques which turned up at my council flat. After all, I had nothing but myself to spend it on, and I wasted months wondering if I deserved it, or had truly earned it. If writing is, finally, a pleasure, and if you find that people envy you your vocation, you might wonder if you should be financially rewarded. But at last I decided to buy the most valuable commodity there is for a writer – time. I began the novel I'd always wanted to write. Being a screenwriter is always uncomfortable: the real artist in film is the director and, if you're lucky, the actors will make the dialogue sound good. The novelist works alone. It's all his responsibility.

However, I recall a morning, ten years after this, when my eldest sons were babies. They were playing with their au pair; an underpaid illegal immigrant was cleaning the house. Later, a no-doubt ruinously expensive man was coming to fix the central heating, and I was working on a dull short story for which I'd earn a hundred pounds, if I were lucky – and anyway I was blocked on that. I wondered if we'd ever survive. (We did, but I had to concentrate, particularly in the afternoons.)

Since then, as with most writers, there have been numerous dips and surges, and, I guess, it'll continue that way. I've written at least one book, my first novel *The Buddha of Suburbia*, which has remained in print worldwide for twenty years and provided a steady if not spectacular income. (An author should write at least one work the title of which the general public will remember and associate with him.) However, it's almost impossible for most writers to predict what they will earn in a year's time, let alone in five years. Perhaps this is a common writer's fear and wish, that he'll run out of money and will have to do something else. I have many fears, among them that I will run out of paper, and also that I'll never finish anything, my computer being filled with incompleted pieces.

The position of the writer has altered a lot during the period I've been writing. In the 1980s small, individual publishing houses were bought by conglomerates, and advances increased hugely for some writers. Where before publishers could only afford relatively modest advances, some became extravagant and, luckily for some writers, even foolish. The publisher might have justified having the writer on their list in order to add weight, or respectability, or excitement. But the problem with a large advance is how much publicity and press the writer might have to do attempting to pay it off – not that he would be compelled to. However, next time the advance could well be lower.

I must give at least one interview a week, and I don't mind it much, unless the journalist calls me irritable, or diminutive. It does mean that the questions and the answers will always seem pre-packaged, although they may appear to be new to someone somewhere. If you are asked the same question repeatedly, you either sulkily refuse to answer it, or you are forced to find ways to make it appear interesting – mostly to yourself. Over a period of time, in interviews, you work up an account of yourself, then you develop it and one day you find you even believe it; finally it has become the story of your life.

The problem with being interviewed is that, on the whole, the two people are at cross-purposes. One wants to flog a few copies of their new book at full price and escape without personal injury, while the other wants to find out something new, and perhaps shocking, about the subject, which they will then inform the world about under a lurid headline. Fortunately both are usually disappointed. At the end, you always ask yourself, how many people are there who can only sell their product by also selling a part of themselves?

These days you can't put a cigarette paper between a writer and a performing flea. There is far more publicity, and more media, than before. Critics and reviewers have less influence, as do individual newspapers. Every year there are new festivals, and occasions for writers, accompanied by an army of PR girls with clipboards, to display their work and their bodies, meeting readers and scratching in the front of their books. For a writer there are few sights more heartening than that of a long line at a book signing, and few experiences worse than sharing a table with a writer whose queue stretches outside the tent. Writing has almost become part of light entertainment, a form of cabaret. Some writers are good at this form of speaking, being adaptable and cheap – I have come to enjoy it. But many writers don't. There's no connection between being able to write and being able to explain your work in a rain-swept tent to an audience staring at you like hungry animals contemplating a suspect steak. Listening and reading are different experiences. Reading, writing for a reader, and being read, are intimate acts, and there's something about trying to articulate what you've done that can flatten and reduce it, horrifyingly so. Some writers choose the written word because they find it difficult to speak directly; many writers are in love with solitude. Whichever it is, good writing should resist interpretation, summary and the need for applause.

A lot of writers, of course, work as teachers, for money, pleasure and distraction, and I write in this collection about the importance and place of teaching, how useful it is and what idiocy it can encourage. It has been said that at least 2 per cent of the population is writing a novel; apparently that number is rising. There's been a gigantic increase in the number of writing courses available, both in universities and other institutions. Many of these students can only become teachers themselves, and I am sceptical of professional creative writing teachers. The most helpful teachers are usually 'real' writers who see working with students as part of their work. Scarcer is practical and realistic advice for young writers, particularly about how difficult it is to make a consistent living. Any artist has to exist in some functional relation to the real world. Of my students, the film students are the most knowing and pragmatic, since to work in film at all is to be faced continuously with questions of budgets and time.

Writers are mad and promiscuous, if they're lucky; they make people up for a living, give them something to say, enter their minds, toy with them and often ruin their lives. One might like to think of oneself as a realist, but a good proportion of the important world is insubstantial, being made up of dream, fantasy, paranoid projections and the imagination. The only figure which comes close to showing the whole chaotic caboodle is literature.

But if a novel is concerned with numerous voices, and wants to keep them in play until the dispute is done, an essay is a monologue, a form of direct speech, and a whisper at that. The essay is as flexible a form as a story or novel; it is amenable to most forms of content. It can be as intellectual as Roland Barthes, Adam Phillips or Susan Sontag, as informal and casual as Max Beerbohm, or as cool and minimalist as Joan Didion. Unlike academic writing, the essay is usually written for the general or 'common' reader rather than for experts or students; for someone in a deck chair rather than at a desk. There should neither be footnotes nor much information in an essay; as a form, it is a meditation rather than an act of persuasion – though Robert Louis Stevenson's fine essay 'An Apology for Idlers' has encouraged me, as it should, towards a greater indolence: 'Perpetual devotion to what a man calls his business, is only to be sustained by perpetual neglect of many other things.'

Idleness may be the midwife of art, but the desire to write has not diminished in me over the years. If anything, it has increased. There is still that daily pressure to achieve something true, or at least put down a few words. Or, best of all, to have a good idea before bedtime which takes the work forward. I like to be surprised by what I write, and sometimes I even laugh at what comes out. I am my own first reader, and if I enjoy something, the reader might too.

I often wonder if I haven't said it all by now; I'd be happy to say it all again at half the price, but one doesn't stop developing, burying old selves, seeking new difficulty and resistances in the material, and wanting to pin words to things. I'm not sure any writer gets over feeling clumsy, or, at times, over-facile. There are things he will never be able to get right, things he'll want to work on. Ageing writers slow down, they read more, and struggle with despair. But there are few artists who have the desire to give up their creativity as they decline. It is always exciting to have a good idea. The end of a life is as interesting as the beginning. If anyone asks a writer which of their pieces is their favourite, the answer can only be the one to come.

Hanif Kureishi, August 2010

POLITICS AND CULTURE

The Rainbow Sign

First published with the screenplay of *My Beautiful Laundrette*, 1986

'God gave Noah the rainbow sign,
No more water, the fire next time!'

ONE: ENGLAND

I was born in London of an English mother and Pakistani father. My father, who lives in London, came to England from Bombay in 1947 to be educated by the old colonial power. He married here and never went back to India. The rest of his large family, his brothers, their wives, his sisters, moved from Bombay to Karachi, in Pakistan, after partition.

Frequently during my childhood, I met my Pakistani uncles when they came to London on business. They were important, confident people who took me to hotels, restaurants and Test matches, often in taxis. But I had no idea of what the subcontinent was like or how my numerous uncles, aunts and cousins lived there. When I was nine or ten a teacher purposefully placed some pictures of Indian peasants in mud huts in front of me and said to the class: Hanif comes from India. I wondered: did my uncles ride on camels? Surely not in their suits? Did my cousins, so like me in other ways, squat down in the sand like little Mowglis, half-naked and eating with their fingers?

In the mid-1960s, Pakistanis were a risible subject in England, derided on television and exploited by politicians. They had the worst jobs, they were uncomfortable in England, some of them had difficulties with the language. They were despised and out of place.

From the start I tried to deny my Pakistani self. I was ashamed. It was a curse and I wanted to be rid of it. I wanted to be like everyone else. I read with understanding a story in a newspaper about a black boy who, when he noticed that burnt skin turned white, jumped into a bath of boiling water.

At school, one teacher always spoke to me in a 'Peter Sellers' Indian accent. Another refused to call me by my name, calling me Pakistani Pete instead. So I refused to call the teacher by *his* name and used his nickname instead. This led to trouble; arguments, detentions, escapes from school over hedges, and eventually suspension. This played into my hands; this couldn't have been better.

With a friend I roamed the streets and fields all day; I sat beside streams; I stole yellow lurex trousers from a shop and smuggled them out of the house under my school trousers; I hid in woods reading hard books; and I saw the film *Zulu* several times.

This friend, who became Johnny in my film, *My Beautiful Laundrette*, came one day to the house. It was a shock.

He was dressed in jeans so tough they almost stood up by themselves. These were suspended above his boots by Union Jack braces of 'hangman's strength', revealing a stretch of milk-bottle white leg. He seemed to have sprung up several inches because of his Dr Martens boots, which had steel caps and soles as thick as cheese sandwiches. His Ben Sherman shirt with a pleat down the back was essential. And his hair, which was only a quarter of an inch long all over, stuck out of his head like little nails. This unmoving creation he concentratedly touched up every hour with a sharpened steel comb that also served as a dagger.

He soon got the name Bog Brush, though this was not a moniker you would use to his face. Where before he was an angel-boy with a blond quiff flattened down by his mother's loving spit, a clean handkerchief always in his pocket, as well as being a keen cornet player for the Air Cadets, he'd now gained a brand-new truculent demeanour.

My mother was so terrified by this stormtrooper dancing on her doorstep to the 'Skinhead Moonstomp', which he moaned to himself continuously, that she had to lie down.

4

I decided to go out roaming with B.B. before my father got home from work. But it wasn't the same as before. We couldn't have our talks without being interrupted. Bog Brush had become Someone. To his intense pleasure, similarly dressed strangers greeted Bog Brush in the street as if they were in a war-torn foreign country and in the same army battalion. We were suddenly banned from cinemas. The Wimpy Bar in which we sat for hours with milkshakes wouldn't let us in. As a matter of pride we now had to go round the back and lob a brick at the rear window of the place.

Other strangers would spot us from the other side of the street. B.B. would yell 'Leg it!' as the enemy dashed through traffic and leapt over the bonnets of cars to get at us, screaming obscenities and chasing us up alleys, across allotments, around reservoirs, and on and on.

And then, in the evening, B.B. took me to meet with the other lads. We climbed the park railings and strolled across to the football pitch, by the goal posts. This is where the lads congregated to hunt down Pakistanis and beat them. Most of them I was at school with. The others I'd grown up with. I knew their parents. They knew my father.

I withdrew, from the park, from the lads, to a safer place, within myself. I moved into what I call my 'temporary' period. I was only waiting now to get away, to leave the London suburbs, to make another kind of life, somewhere else, with better people.

In this isolation, in my bedroom where I listened to Pink Floyd, the Beatles and the John Peel Show, I started to write down the speeches of politicians, the words which helped create the neo-Nazi attitudes I saw around me. This I called 'keeping the accounts'.

In 1965, Enoch Powell said: 'We should not lose sight of the desirability of achieving a steady flow of voluntary repatriation for the elements which are proving unsuccessful or unassimilable.'

In 1967, Duncan Sandys said: 'The breeding of millions of half-caste children would merely produce a generation of misfits and create national tensions.'

I wasn't a misfit; I could join the elements of myself together. It was the others, they wanted misfits; they wanted you to embody within yourself their ambivalence.

Also in 1967, Enoch Powell – who once said he would have loved to have been Viceroy of India – quoted a constituent of his as saying that because of the Pakistanis 'this country will not be worth living in for our children'.

And Powell said, more famously: 'As I look ahead I am filled with foreboding. Like the Roman, "I seem to see the River Tiber foaming with much blood".'

As Powell's speeches appeared in the papers, graffiti in support of him appeared in the London streets. Racists gained confidence. People insulted me in the street. Someone in a café refused to eat at the same table with me. The parents of a girl I was in love with told her she'd get a bad reputation by going out with darkies.

Powell allowed himself to become a figurehead for racists. He helped create racism in Britain and was directly responsible not only for the atmosphere of fear and hatred but, through his influence, for individual acts of violence against Pakistanis.

Television comics used Pakistanis as the butt of their humour. Their jokes were highly political: they contributed to a way of seeing the world. The enjoyed reduction of racial hatred to a joke did two things: it expressed a collective view (which was sanctioned by its being on the BBC), and it was a celebration of contempt in millions of living rooms in England. I was afraid to watch TV because of it; it was too embarrassing, too degrading.

Parents of my friends, both lower-middle-class and working-class, often told me they were Powell supporters. Sometimes I heard them talking, heatedly, violently, about race, about 'the Pakis'. I was desperately embarrassed and afraid of being identified with these loathed aliens. I found it almost impossible to answer questions about where I came from. The word 'Pakistani' had been made into an insult. It was a word I didn't want used about myself. I couldn't tolerate being myself.

The British complained incessantly that the Pakistanis wouldn't assimilate. This meant they wanted the Pakistanis to be exactly like them. But of course even then they would have rejected them.

The British were doing the assimilating: they assimilated Pakistanis to their world view. They saw them as dirty, ignorant and less than human – worthy of abuse and violence.

At this time I found it difficult to get along with anyone. I was frightened and hostile. I suspected that my white friends were capable of racist insults. And many of them did taunt me, innocently. I reckoned that at least once every day since I was five years old I had been racially abused. I became incapable of distinguishing between remarks that were genuinely intended to hurt and those intended as 'humour'.

I became cold and distant. I began to feel I was very violent. But I didn't know how to be violent. If I had known, if that had come naturally to me, or if there'd been others I could follow, I would have made my constant fantasies of revenge into realities, I would have got into trouble, willingly hurt people, or set fire to things.

But I mooched around libraries. There, in an old copy of *Life* magazine, I found pictures of the Black Panthers. It was Eldridge Cleaver, Huey Newton, Bobby Seale and their confederates in black vests and slacks, with Jimi Hendrix haircuts. Some of them were holding guns, the Army .45 and the 12-gauge Magnum shotgun with 18-inch barrel that Huey specified for street fighting.

I tore down my pictures of the Rolling Stones and Cream and replaced them with the Panthers. I found it all exhilarating. These people were proud and they were fighting. To my knowledge, no one in England was fighting.

There was another, more important picture.

On the cover of the Penguin edition of *The Fire Next Time* was James Baldwin holding a child, his nephew. Baldwin, having suffered, having been there, was all anger and understanding. He was intelligence and love combined. As I planned my escape I read Baldwin all the time, I read Richard Wright and I admired Muhammad Ali.

A great moment occurred when I was in a sweet shop. I saw through to a TV in the back room on which was showing the 1968 Olympic Games in Mexico. Tommie Smith and John Carlos were raising their fists on the victory rostrum, giving the Black Power salute as 'The Star Spangled Banner' played. The white shopkeeper was outraged. He said to me: they shouldn't mix politics and sport.

During this time there was always Muhammad Ali, the former Cassius Clay, a great sportsman become black spokesman. Now a Muslim, millions of fellow Muslims all over the world prayed for his victory when he fought.

And there was the Nation of Islam movement to which Ali belonged, led by the man who called himself the Messenger of Islam and wore a gold-embroidered fez, Elijah Muhammad.

Elijah was saying in the mid-1960s that the rule of the white devils would end in fifteen years. He preached separatism, separate development for black and white. He ran his organisation by charisma and threat, claiming that anyone who challenged him would be chastened by Allah. Apparently Allah also turned the minds of defectors into a turmoil.

Elijah's disciple Malcolm X, admirer of Gandhi and self-confirmed anti-Semite, accepted in prison that 'the key to a Muslim is submission, the attunement of one towards Allah'. That this glorious resistance to the white man, the dismissal of Christian meekness, was followed by submission to Allah and worse, to Elijah Muhammad, was difficult to take.

I saw racism as unreason and prejudice, ignorance and a failure of sense; it was Fanon's 'incomprehension'. That the men I wanted to admire had liberated themselves only to take to unreason, to the abdication of intelligence, was shocking to me. And the separatism, the total loathing of the white man as innately corrupt, the 'All whites are devils' view, was equally unacceptable. I had to live in England, in the suburbs of London, with whites. My mother was white. I wasn't ready for separate development. I'd had too much of that already.

8

Luckily James Baldwin wasn't too keen either. In *The Fire Next Time* he describes a visit to Elijah Muhammad. He tells of how close he feels to Elijah and how he wishes to be able to love him. But when he tells Elijah that he has many white friends, he receives Elijah's pity. For Elijah the whites' time is up. It's no good Baldwin telling him he has white friends with whom he'd entrust his life.

As the evening goes on, Baldwin tires of the sycophancy around Elijah. He and Elijah would always be strangers and 'possibly enemies'. Baldwin deplores the black Muslims' turning to Africa and to Islam, this turning away from the reality of America and 'inventing' the past. Baldwin also mentions Malcolm X and the chief of the American Nazi party saying that racially speaking they were in complete agreement: they both wanted separate development. Baldwin adds that the debasement of one race and the glorification of another in this way inevitably leads to murder.

After this the Muslims weren't too keen on Baldwin, to say the least. Eldridge Cleaver, who once raped white women 'on principle', had a picture of Elijah Muhammad, the great strength-giver, on his prison wall. Later he became a devoted supporter of Malcolm X.

Cleaver says of Baldwin: 'There is in James Baldwin's work the most gruelling, agonising, total hatred of the blacks, particularly of himself, and the most shameful, fanatical, fawning, sycophantic love of the white that one can find in the writing of any black American writer of note in our time.'

How strange it was to me, this worthless abuse of a writer who could enter the minds and skins of both black and white, and the good just anger turning to passionate Islam as a source of pride instead of to a digested political commitment to a different kind of whole society. And this easy thrilling talk of 'white devils' instead of close analysis of the institutions that kept blacks low.

I saw the taking up of Islam as an aberration, a desperate fantasy of worldwide black brotherhood; it was a symptom of extreme alienation. It was also an inability to seek a wider political view or cooperation with other oppressed groups – or with the working class as a whole – since alliance with white groups was necessarily out of the question.

I had no idea what an Islamic society would be like, what the application of the authoritarian theology Elijah preached would mean in practice. I forgot about it, fled the suburbs, went to university, got started as a writer and worked as an usher at the Royal Court Theatre. It was over ten years before I went to an Islamic country.

TWO: PAKISTAN

The man had heard that I was interested in talking about his country, Pakistan, and that this was my first visit. He kindly kept trying to take me aside to talk. But I was already being talked to.

I was at another Karachi party, in a huge house, with a glass of whisky in one hand, and a paper plate in the other. Casually I'd mentioned to a woman friend of the family that I wasn't against marriage. Now this friend was earnestly recommending to me a young woman who wanted to move to Britain, with a husband. To my discomfort this go-between was trying to fix a time for the three of us to meet and negotiate.

I went to three parties a week in Karachi. This time, when I could get away from this woman, I was with landowners, diplomats, businessmen and politicians: powerful people. This pleased me. They were people I wouldn't have been able to get to in England and I wanted to write about them.

They were drinking heavily. Every liberal in England knows you can be lashed for drinking in Pakistan. But as far as I could tell, none of this English-speaking international bourgeoisie would be lashed for anything. They all had their favourite trusted bootleggers who negotiated the potholes of Karachi at high speed on disintegrating motorcycles, with the hooch stashed on the back. Bad bootleggers passed a hot needle through the neck of your bottle and drew your whisky out. Stories were told of guests politely sipping ginger beer with their ice and soda, glancing at other guests to see if they were drunk and wondering if their own alcohol tolerance had miraculously increased.

I once walked into a host's bathroom to see the bath full of floating whisky bottles being soaked to remove the labels, a servant sitting on a stool serenely poking at them with a stick.

So it was all as tricky and expensive as buying cocaine in London, with the advantage that as the hooch market was so competitive, the 'leggers delivered video tapes at the same time, dashing into the room towards the TV with hot copies of *The Jewel in the Crown*, *The Far Pavilions*, and an especially popular programme called *Mind Your Language*, which represented Indians and Pakistanis as ludicrous caricatures.

Everyone, except the mass of the population, had videos. And I could see why, since Pakistan TV was so peculiar. On my first day I turned it on and a cricket match was taking place. I settled in my chair. But the English players, who were on tour in Pakistan, were leaving the pitch. In fact, Bob Willis and Ian Botham were running towards the dressing rooms surrounded by armed police and this wasn't because Botham had made derogatory remarks about Pakistan. (He said it was a country to which he'd like to send his mother-in-law.) In the background a section of the crowd was being tear-gassed. Then the screen went blank.

Stranger still, and more significant, was the fact that the news was now being read in Arabic, a language few people in Pakistan understood. Someone explained to me that this was because the Koran was in Arabic, but everyone else said it was because General Zia wanted to kiss the arses of the Arabs.

The man at the party, who was drunk, wanted to tell me something and kept pulling at me. The man was worried. But wasn't I worried too? I was trapped with this woman and the marriage proposal.

I was having a little identity crisis. I'd been greeted so warmly in Pakistan, I felt so excited by what I saw, and so at home with all my uncles, I wondered if I were not better off here than there. And when I said, with a little unnoticed irony, that I was an Englishman, people laughed. They fell about. Why would anyone with a brown face, Muslim name and large well-known family in Pakistan want to lay claim to that cold little decrepit island off Europe where you always had to spell your name? Strangely, anti-British remarks made me feel patriotic, though I only felt patriotic when I was away from England.

But I couldn't allow myself to feel too Pakistani. I didn't want to give in to that falsity, that sentimentality. As someone said to me at a party, provoked by the fact I was wearing jeans: we are Pakistanis, but you, you will always be a Paki – emphasising the slang derogatory name the English used against Pakistanis, and therefore the fact that I couldn't rightfully lay claim to either place.

In England I was a playwright. In Karachi this meant little. There were no theatres; the arts were discouraged by the state – music and dancing are un-Islamic – and ignored by practically everyone else. So despite everything I felt pretty out of place.

The automatic status I gained through my family obtained for me such acceptance, respect and luxury that for the first time I could understand the privileged and their penchant for marshalling ridiculous arguments to justify their delicious and untenable position as an élite. But as I wasn't a doctor, businessman or military person, people suspected that this writing business I talked about was a complicated excuse for idleness, uselessness and general bumming around. In fact, as I proclaimed an interest in the entertainment business, and talked much and loudly about how integral the arts were to a society, moves were being made to set me up in the amusement arcade business, in Shepherd's Bush.

Finally the man got me on my own. His name was Rahman. He was a friend of my intellectual uncle. I had many uncles, but Rahman preferred the intellectual one who understood Rahman's particular sorrow and like him considered himself to be a marginal man.

In his fifties, a former Air Force officer, Rahman was liberal, well travelled and married to an Englishwoman who now had a Pakistani accent.

He said to me: 'I tell you, this country is being sodomised by religion. It is even beginning to interfere with the making of money. And now we are embarked on this dynamic regression, you must know, it is obvious, Pakistan has become a leading country to go away from. Our patriots are abroad. We despise and envy them. For the rest of us, our class, your family, we are in Hobbes's state of nature: insecure, frightened. We cling together out of necessity.' He became optimistic. 'We could be like Japan, a tragic oriental country that is now progressive, industrialised.' He laughed and then said, ambiguously: 'But only God keeps this country together. You must say this around the world: we are taking a great leap backwards.'

The bitterest blow for Rahman was the dancing. He liked to waltz and foxtrot. But now the expression of physical joy, of sensuality and rhythm, was banned. On TV you could see where it had been censored. When couples in Western programmes got up to dance there'd be a jerk in the film, and they'd be sitting down again. For Rahman it was inexplicable, an unnecessary cruelty that was almost more arbitrary than anything else.

Thus the despair of Rahman and my uncles' 'high and dry' generation. Mostly educated in Britain, like Jinnah, the founder of Pakistan – who was a smoking, drinking, non-Urdu-speaking lawyer and claimed that Pakistan would never be a theocracy ('that Britisher', he was sometimes called) – their intellectual mentors were Tawney, Shaw, Russell, Laski. For them the new Islamisation was the negation of their lives.

It was a lament I heard often. This was the story they told. Karachi was a goodish place in the 1960s and 1970s. Until about 1977 it was lively and vigorous. You could drink and dance in the Raj-style clubs (providing you were admitted) and the atmosphere was liberal – as long as you didn't meddle in politics, in which case you'd probably be imprisoned. Politically there was Bhutto: urbane, Oxford-educated, considering himself to be a poet and revolutionary, a veritable Chairman Mao of the subcontinent. He said he would fight obscurantism and illiteracy, ensure the equality of men and women, and increase access to education and medical care. The desert would bloom.

Later, in an attempt to save himself, appease the mullahs and rouse the dissatisfied masses behind him, he introduced various Koranic injunctions into the constitution and banned alcohol, gambling, horse-racing. The Islamisation had begun, and was fervently continued after his execution.

Islamisation built no hospitals, no schools, no houses; it cleaned no water and installed no electricity. But it was direction, identity. The country was to be in the hands of the divine, or rather, in the hands of those who elected themselves to interpret the single divine purpose. Under the tyranny of the priesthood, with the cooperation of the army, Pakistan would embody Islam in itself.

There would now be no distinction between ethical and religious obligation; there would now be no areas in which it was possible to be wrong. The only possible incertitude was of interpretation. The theory would be the written eternal and universal principles which Allah created and made obligatory for men; the model would be the first three generations of Muslims; and the practice would be Pakistan.

As a Professor of Law at the Islamic University wrote: 'Pakistan accepts Islam as the basis of economic and political life. We do not have a single reason to make any separation between Islam and Pakistan society. Pakistanis now adhere rigorously to Islam and cling steadfastly to their religious heritage. They never speak of these things with disrespect. With an acceleration in the process of Islamisation, governmental capabilities increase and national identity and loyalty become stronger. Because Islamic civilisation has brought Pakistanis very close to certainty, this society is ideally imbued with a moral mission.'

This moral mission and the over-emphasis on dogma and punishment resulted in the kind of strengthening of the repressive, militaristic and nationalistically aggressive state seen all over the world in the authoritarian 1980s. With the added bonus that in Pakistan, God was always on the side of the government.

But despite all the strident nationalism, as Rahman said, the patriots were abroad; people were going away: to the West, to Saudi Arabia, anywhere. Young people continually asked me about the possibility of getting into Britain and some thought of taking some smack with them to bankroll their establishment. They had what was called the Gulf Syndrome, a condition I recognised from my time living in the suburbs. It was a dangerous psychological cocktail consisting of ambition, suppressed excitement, bitterness and sexual longing.

Then a disturbing incident occurred which seemed to encapsulate the going-away fever. An eighteen-year-old girl from a village called Chakwal dreamed that the villagers walked across the Arabian Sea to Karbala where they found money and work. Following this dream the village set off one night for the beach which happened to be near my uncle's house, in fashionable Clifton. Here lived politicians and diplomats in LA-style white bungalows with sprinklers on the lawn, a Mercedes in the drive and dogs and watchmen at the gates.

Here Benazir Bhutto was under house arrest. Her dead father's mansion was patrolled by the army who boredly nursed machine-guns and sat in tents beneath the high walls.

On the beach, the site of barbecues and late-night parties, the men of the Chakwal village packed the women and children into trunks and pushed them into the Arabian Sea. Then they followed them into the water, in the direction of Karbala. All but twenty of the potential émigrés were drowned. The survivors were arrested and charged with illegal emigration.

It was the talk of Karachi. It caused much amusement but people like Rahman despaired of a society that could be so confused, so advanced in some respects, so very naive in others.

And all the (more orthodox) going away disturbed and confused the family set-up. When the men who'd been away came back, they were different, they were dissatisfied, they had seen more, they wanted more. Their neighbours were envious and resentful. Once more the society was being changed by outside forces, not by its own volition.

About twelve people lived permanently in my uncle's house, plus servants who slept in sheds at the back, just behind the chickens and dogs. Relatives sometimes came to stay for months. New bits had to be built on to the house. All day there were visitors; in the evenings crowds of people came over; they were welcome, and they ate and watched videos and talked for hours. People weren't so protective of their privacy as they were in London.

This made me think about the close-bonding within the families and about the intimacy and interference of an extended family and a more public way of life. Was the extended family worse than the little nuclear family because there were more people to dislike? Or better because relationships were less intense?

Strangely, bourgeois-bohemian life in London, in Notting Hill and Islington and Fulham, was far more formal. It was frozen dinner parties and the division of social life into the meeting of couples with other couples, to discuss the lives of other coupling couples. Months would pass, then this would happen again.

In Pakistan, there was the continuity of the various families' knowledge of each other. People were easy to place; your grandparents and theirs were friends. When I went to the bank and showed the teller my passport, it turned out he knew several of my uncles, so I didn't receive the usual perfunctory treatment. This was how things worked.

I compared the collective hierarchy of the family and the performance of my family's circle with my feckless, rather rootless life in London, in what was called 'the inner city'. There I lived alone, and lacked any long connection with anything. I'd hardly known anyone for more than eight years, and certainly not their parents. People came and went. There was much false intimacy and forced friendship. People didn't take responsibility for each other.

Many of my friends lived alone in London, especially the women. They wanted to be independent and to enter into relationships – as many as they liked, with whom they liked – out of choice. They didn't merely want to reproduce the old patterns of living. The future was to be determined by choice and reason, not by custom. The notions of duty and obligation barely had positive meaning for my friends; they were loaded, Victorian words, redolent of constraint and grandfather clocks, the antithesis of generosity in love, the new hugging, and the transcendence of the family. The ideal of the new relationship was no longer the S and M of the old marriage – it was F and C, freedom plus commitment.

In the large, old families where there was nothing but the old patterns, disturbed only occasionally by the new ways, this would have seemed a contrivance, a sort of immaturity, a failure to understand and accept the determinacies that life necessarily involved.

So there was much pressure to conform, especially on the women.

'Let these women be warned,' said a mullah to the dissenting women of Rawalpindi. 'We will tear them to pieces. We will give them such terrible punishments that no one in future will dare to raise a voice against Islam.'

I remember a woman saying to me at dinner one night: 'We know at least one thing. God will never dare to show his face in this country – the women will tear him apart!'

The family scrutiny and criticism was difficult to take, as was all the bitching and gossip. But there was warmth and continuity for a large number of people; there was security and much love. Also there was a sense of duty and community – of people's lives genuinely being lived together, whether they liked each other or not – that you didn't get in London. There, those who'd eschewed the family hadn't succeeded in creating some other form of supportive common life. In Pakistan there was that supportive common life, but at the expense of movement and change.

In the 1960s of Enoch Powell and graffiti, the Black Muslims and Malcolm X gave needed strength to the descendants of slaves by 'taking the wraps off the white man'; Eldridge Cleaver was yet to be converted to Christianity and Huey P. Newton was toting his Army ·45. A boy in a bedroom in a suburb, who had the King's

Road constantly on his mind and who changed the picture on his wall from week to week, was unhappy, and separated from the 1960s as by a thick glass wall against which he could only press his face. But bits of the 1960s were still around in Pakistan: the liberation rhetoric, for example, the music, the clothes, the drugs, not as the way of life they were originally intended to be, but as appendages to another, stronger tradition.

As my friends and I went into the Bara Market near Peshawar, close to the border with Afghanistan, in a rattling motorised rickshaw, I became apprehensive. There were large signs by the road telling foreigners that the police couldn't take responsibility for them: beyond this point the police would not go. Apparently the Pathans there, who were mostly refugees from Afghanistan, liked to kidnap foreigners and extort ransoms. My friends, who were keen to buy opium, which they'd give to the rickshaw driver to carry, told me everything was all right, because I wasn't a foreigner. I kept forgetting that.

The men were tough, martial, insular and proud. They lived in mud houses and tin shacks built like forts for shooting from. They were inevitably armed, with machine-guns slung over their shoulders. In the street you wouldn't believe women existed here, except you knew they took care of the legions of young men in the area who'd fled from Afghanistan to avoid being conscripted by the Russians and sent to Moscow for re-education.

Ankle deep in mud, I went round the market. Pistols, knives, Russian-made rifles, hand grenades and large lumps of dope and opium were laid out on stalls like tomatoes and oranges. Everyone was selling heroin.

The Americans, who had much money invested in Pakistan, in this compliant right-wing buffer-zone between Afghanistan and India, were furious that their children were being destroyed by a flourishing illegal industry in a country they financed. But the Americans sent to Pakistan could do little about it. Involvement in the heroin trade went right through Pakistan society: the police, the judiciary, the army, the landlords, the customs officials were all involved. After all, there was nothing in the Koran about heroin, nothing specific. I was even told that its export made ideological sense. Heroin was anti-Western; addiction in Western children was a deserved symptom of the moral vertigo of godless societies. It was a kind of colonial revenge. Reverse imperialism, the Karachi wits called it, inviting nemesis. The reverse imperialism was itself being reversed.

In a flat high above Karachi, an eighteen-year-old kid strung-out on heroin danced cheerfully around the room in front of me and pointed to an erection in the front of his trousers, which he referred to as his Imran Khan, the name of the handsome Pakistan cricket captain. More and more of the so-called multinational kids were taking heroin now. My friends who owned the flat, journalists on a weekly paper, were embarrassed.

But they always had dope to offer their friends. These laid-back people were mostly professionals: lawyers, an inspector in the police who smoked what he confiscated, a newspaper magnate, and various other journalists. Heaven it was to smoke at midnight on the beach, as local fishermen, squatting respectfully behind you, fixed fat joints; and the 'erotic politicians' themselves, the Doors, played from a portable stereo while the Arabian Sea rolled on to the beach. Oddly, since heroin and dope were both indigenous to the country, it took the West to make them popular in the East.

In so far as colonisers and colonised engage in a relationship with the latter aspiring to be like the former, you wouldn't catch anyone of my uncle's generation with a joint in their mouth. It was *infra dig* – for the peasants. Shadowing the British, they drank whisky and read *The Times*; they praised others by calling them 'gentlemen'; and their eyes filled with tears at old Vera Lynn records.

But the kids discussed yoga exercises. You'd catch them standing on their heads. They even meditated. Though one boy who worked at the airport said it was too much of a Hindu thing for Muslims to be doing; if his parents caught him chanting a mantra he'd get a backhander across the face. Mostly the kids listened to the Stones,

Van Morrison and Bowie as they flew over ruined roads to the beach in bright red and yellow Japanese cars with quadraphonic speakers, past camels and acres of wasteland.

Here, all along the railway track, the poor and diseased and hungry lived in shacks and huts; the filthy poor gathered around rusty standpipes to fetch water; or ingeniously they resurrected wrecked cars, usually Morris Minors; and here they slept in huge sewer pipes among buffalo, chickens and wild dogs. Here I met a policeman who I thought was on duty. But the policeman lived here, and hanging on the wall of his falling-down shed was his spare white police uniform, which he'd had to buy himself.

If not to the beach, the kids went to the Happy Hamburger to hang out. Or to each other's houses to watch Clint Eastwood tapes and giggle about sex, of which they were so ignorant and deprived. I watched a group of agitated young men in their mid-twenties gather around a 1950s medical book to look at the female genitalia. For these boys, who watched Western films and mouthed the lyrics of pop songs celebrating desire ('come on, baby, light my fire'), life before marriage could only be like spending years and years in a single-sex public school; for them women were mysterious, unknown, desirable and yet threatening creatures of almost another species, whom you had to respect, marry and impregnate but couldn't be friends with. And in this country where the sexes were usually strictly segregated, the sexual tension could be palpable. The men who could afford to, flew to Bangkok for relief. The others squirmed and resented women. The kind of sexual openness that was one of the few real achievements of the 1960s, the discussion of contraception, abortion, female sexuality and prostitution which some women were trying to advance, received incredible hostility. But women felt it was only a matter of time before progress was made; it was much harder to return to ignorance than the mullahs thought.

A stout intense lawyer in his early thirties of immense extrovert charm – with him it was definitely the 1980s, not the 1960s. His father was a judge. He himself was intelligent, articulate and fiercely representative of the other 'new spirit' of Pakistan. He didn't drink, smoke or fuck. Out of choice. He prayed five times a day. He worked all the time. He was determined to be a good Muslim, since that was the whole point of the country existing at all. He wasn't indulgent, except religiously, and he lived in accordance with what he believed. I took to him immediately.

We had dinner in an expensive restaurant. It could have been in London or New York. The food was excellent, I said. The lawyer disagreed, with his mouth full, shaking his great head. It was definitely no good, it was definitely meretricious rubbish. But for ideological reasons only, I concluded, since he ate with relish. He was only in the restaurant because of me, he said.

There was better food in the villages; the new food in Pakistan was, frankly, a tribute to chemistry rather than cuisine. Only the masses had virtue, they knew how to live, how to eat. He told me that those desiccated others, the marginal men I associated with and liked so much, were a plague class with no values. Perhaps, he suggested, eating massively, this was why I liked them, being English. Their education, their intellectual snobbery, made them un-Islamic. They didn't understand the masses and they spoke in English to cut themselves off from the people. Didn't the best jobs go to those with a foreign education? He was tired of those Westernised elders denigrating their country and its religious nature. They'd been contaminated by the West, they didn't know their own country, and the sooner they got out and were beaten up by racists abroad the better.

The lawyer and I went out into the street. It was busy, the streets full of strolling people. There were dancing camels and a Pakistan trade exhibition. The lawyer strode through it all, yelling. The exhibition was full of Pakistan-made imitations of Western goods: bathrooms in chocolate and strawberry, TVs with stereos attached; fans, air-conditioners, heaters; and an arcade full of space-invaders. The lawyer got agitated.

These were Western things, of no use to the masses. The masses didn't have water, what would they do with strawberry bathrooms?

The masses wanted Islam, not space-invaders or . . . or elections. Are elections a Western thing? I asked. Don't they have them in India too? No, they're a Western thing, the lawyer said. How could they be required under Islam? There need only be one party – the party of the righteous.

This energetic lawyer would have pleased and then disappointed Third World intellectuals and revolutionaries from an earlier era, people like Fanon and Guevara. This talk of liberation – at last the acknowledgement of the virtue of the toiling masses, the struggle against neo-colonialism, its bourgeois stooges, and American interference – the entire recognisable rhetoric of freedom and struggle, ends in the lawyer's mind with the country on its knees, at prayer. Having started to look for itself it finds itself . . . in the eighth century.

Islam and the masses. My numerous meetings with scholars, revisionists, liberals who wanted the Koran 'creatively' interpreted to make it compatible with modern science. The many medieval monologues of mullahs I'd listened to. So much talk, theory and Byzantine analysis.

I strode into a room in my uncle's house. Half-hidden by a curtain, on a verandah, was an aged woman servant wearing my cousin's old clothes, praying. I stopped and watched her. In the morning as I lay in bed, she swept the floor of my room with some twigs bound together. She was at least sixty. Now, on the shabby prayer mat, she was tiny and around her the universe was endless, immense, but God was above her. I felt she was acknowledging that which was larger than her, humbling herself before the infinite, knowing and feeling her own insignificance. It was a truthful moment, not empty ritual. I wished I could do it.

I went with the lawyer to the Mosque in Lahore, the largest in the world. I took off my shoes, padded across the immense court-yard with the other men – women were not allowed – and got on my knees. I banged my forehead on the marble floor. Beside me a man in a similar posture gave a world-consuming yawn. I waited but could not lose myself in prayer. I could only travesty the woman's prayer, to whom it had a world of meaning.

Perhaps she did want a society in which her particular moral and religious beliefs were mirrored, and no others, instead of some plural, liberal mélange; a society in which her own cast of mind, her customs, way of life and obedience to God were established with full legal and constituted authority. But it wasn't as if anyone had asked her.

In Pakistan, England just wouldn't go away. Despite the Lahore lawyer, despite everything, England was very much on the minds of Pakistanis. Relics of the Raj were everywhere: buildings, monuments, Oxford accents, libraries full of English books, and newspapers. Many Pakistanis had relatives in England; thousands of Pakistani families depended on money sent from England. Visiting a village, a man told me through an interpreter that when his three grandchildren visited from Bradford, he had to hire an interpreter to speak to them. It was happening all the time – the closeness of the two societies, and the distance.

Although Pakistanis still wanted to escape to England, the old men in their clubs and the young eating their hamburgers took great pleasure in England's decline and decay. The great master was fallen. Now it was seen as strikebound, drug-ridden, riot-torn, inefficient, disunited, a society which had moved too suddenly from puritanism to hedonism and now loathed itself. And the Karachi wits liked to ask me when I thought the Americans would decide the British were ready for self-government.

Yet people like Rahman still clung to what they called British ideals, maintaining that it is a society's ideals, its conception of human progress, that define the level of its civilisation. They regretted, under the Islamisation, the repudiation of the values which they said were the only positive aspect of Britain's legacy to the subcontinent. These were: the idea of secular institutions based on reason, not revelation or scripture; the idea that there were no final solutions to human problems; and the idea that the health and vigour of a society was bound up with its ability to tolerate and express a plurality of views on all issues, and that these views would be welcomed.

But England as it is today, the ubiquity of racism and the suffering of Pakistanis because of it, was another, stranger subject. When I talked about it, the response was unexpected. Those who'd been to England often told of being insulted, or beaten up, or harassed at the airport. But even these people had attitudes similar to those who hadn't been there.

It was that the English misunderstood the Pakistanis because they saw only the poor people, those from the villages, the illiterates, the peasants, the Pakistanis who didn't know how to use toilets, how to eat with knives and forks because they were poor. If the British could only see *them*, the rich, the educated, the sophisticated, they wouldn't be so hostile. They'd know what civilised people the Pakistanis really were. And then they'd like them.

The implication was that the poor who'd emigrated to the West to escape the strangulation of the rich in Pakistan deserved the racism they received in Britain because they really were contemptible. The Pakistani middle class shared the disdain of the British for the émigré working class and peasantry of Pakistan.

It was interesting to see that the British working class (and not only the working class, of course) used the same vocabulary of contempt about Pakistanis – the charges of ignorance, laziness, fecklessness, uncleanliness – that their own, British middle class used about them. And they weren't able to see the similarity.

Racism goes hand-in-hand with class inequality. Among other things, racism is a kind of snobbery, a desire to see oneself as superior culturally and economically, and a desire to actively experience and enjoy that superiority by hostility or violence. And when that superiority of class and culture is unsure or not acknowledged by the Other – as it would be acknowledged by the servant and master in class-stable Pakistan – but is in doubt, as with the British working class and Pakistanis in England, then it has to be demonstrated physically. Everyone knows where they stand then –

the class inequality is displayed, just as any other snob demonstrates superiority by exhibiting wealth or learning or ancestry.

So some of the middle class of Pakistan, who also used the familiar vocabulary of contempt about their own poor (and, incidentally, about the British poor), couldn't understand when I explained that British racists weren't discriminating in their racial discrimination: they loathed all Pakistanis and kicked whoever was nearest. To the English all Pakistanis were the same; racists didn't ask whether you had a chauffeur, TV and private education before they set fire to your house. But for some Pakistanis, it was their own poor who had brought this upon them.

THREE: ENGLAND

It has been an arduous journey. Since Enoch Powell in the 1960s, there have been racist marches through south London approved by the Labour Home Secretary; attacks by busloads of racists on Southall, which the Asians violently and successfully repelled; and the complicated affair of young Asians burned to death and Asian shops razed to the ground by young blacks in Handsworth, Birmingham. The insults, the beatings, the murders continue. Although there has been white anger and various race relations legislation, Pakistanis are discriminated against in all areas.

Powell's awful prophecy was fulfilled: the hate he worked to create and the party of which he was a member brought about his prediction. The River Tiber has indeed overflowed with much blood – Pakistani blood. And seventeen years later Powell has once more called for repatriation, giving succour to those who hate.

The fight back is under way. The defence committees, vigilante groups, study groups, trade union and women's groups are flourishing. People have changed, become united, through struggle and self-defence. My white friends, like Bog Brush, didn't enjoy fighting Pakistanis. They had a reputation for premature sobbing and cowardice. You didn't get your money's worth fighting a Paki. That's quite different now.

The fierce truculent pride of the Black Panthers is here now, as is the separatism, the violence, the bitterness and pathetic elevation of an imaginary homeland. This is directly spawned by racism.

Our cities are full of Asian shops. Where one would want black united with black, there are class differences as with all groups. Those Pakistanis who have worked hard to establish businesses now vote Tory and give money to the Conservative Party. Their interests are the same as those of middle-class business people everywhere, though they are subject to more jealousy and violence. They have wanted to elevate themselves out of the maelstrom and by gaining economic power and the opportunity and dignity it brings, they have made themselves safe – safer. They have taken advantage of England.

But what is the Conservative view of them? Roger Scruton in his book *The Meaning Of Conservatism* sets out the case against mutual respect and understanding.

Firstly he deplores all race relations legislation and tries to justify certain kinds of racism by making it seem a harmless preference for certain kinds of people. He calls this preference a 'natural offshoot' of allegiance. Secondly, and more tellingly, he says that 'illiberal sentiments . . . arise inevitably from social consciousness: they involve natural prejudice, and a desire for the company of one's kind. That is hardly sufficient ground to condemn them as "racist".'

The crucial Conservative idea here is Scruton's notion of 'the company of one's kind'. What is the company of one's kind? Who exactly is of one's kind and what kind of people are they? Are they only those of the same 'nation', of the same colour, race and background? I suspect that that is what Scruton intends. But what a feeble, bloodless, narrow conception of human relationships and the possibilities of love and communication that he can only see 'one's kind' in this exclusive and complacent way!

One does seek the company of one's kind, of those in the same street, in the same club, in the same office. But the idea that these are the only people one can get along with or identify with, that one's humanity is such a held-back thing that it can't extend beyond this, leads to the denigration of those unlike oneself. It leads to the idea that others have less humanity than oneself or one's own group or 'kind'; and to the idea of the Enemy, of the alien, of the Other. As Baldwin says: 'this inevitably leads to murder', and of course it has often done so in England recently.

Scruton quotes approvingly those who call this view 'death camp chic'. He would argue, I suppose, that loyalty and allegiance to one's kind doesn't necessarily lead to loathing of those not of one's kind. But Scruton himself talks of the 'alien wedge' and says that 'immigration cannot be an object of merely passive contemplation on the part of the present citizenship'.

The evil of racism is that it is a violation not only of another's dignity, but also of one's own person or soul; the failure of connection with others is a failure to understand or feel what it is one's own humanity consists in, what it is to be alive, and what it is to see both oneself and others as being ends not means, and as having souls. However much anodyne talk there is of 'one's kind', a society that is racist is a society that cannot accept itself, that hates parts of itself so deeply that it cannot see, does not want to see – because of its spiritual and political nullity and inanition – how much people have in common with each other. And the whole society and every element in it is reduced and degraded because of it. This is why racism isn't a minor or sub-problem: it reflects on the whole and weighs the entire society in the balance.

Therefore, in the end, one's feeling for others, one's understanding of their humanity cannot be anything to do with their being of 'one's kind' in the narrow way Scruton specifies. It can't be to do with others having any personal qualities at all. For paradoxically, as Simone Weil says: 'So far from its being his person, what is sacred in a human being is the impersonal in him. Everything which is impersonal in man is sacred, and nothing else.'

What of Labour?

The Pakistani working class is as unprotected politically as it has ever been. Despite various paternalistic efforts and an attempt at a kind of 'Raj decency', racism is the Trojan horse within the Labour movement. The Labour Party has failed to show that it is serious about combating racism and serious in representing the black working class. There are few black councillors, few black Parliamentary candidates, few blacks on the General Management Committees of Constituency Labour Parties, no blacks on the NEC and so on, right through the Labour and trade union movement.

In my own ward and management committee, I have seen racist attitudes that would shame some Tories. People have stood up at Labour Party meetings I have attended and delivered racist diatribes. I have seen blacks discouraged from joining the Labour Party, and when they have joined, actively discouraged from canvassing in case they discouraged white racists from voting Labour.

The Labour Party wishes to be egalitarian and liberal on the race issue but knows that vast numbers of its voters are neither. The party is afraid – in some parts consciously and in other parts unconsciously – that blacks and black issues are a vote loser. If the Labour Party occasionally wishes blacks to serve it, it does not desire to serve blacks. Hence it acknowledges that thousands of its supporters are racist. It refuses to confront that.

Others in the party believe that racism is a sub-issue which has to be subordinate to the class issues of the time: housing, unemployment, education, maintenance of the social services and so on. They believe that winning elections and representing the mass of the working class in Parliament is more important than giving office or power to blacks. This is the choice it has made. This is the kind of party it is, and in so far as this is true, the Labour Party is a truly representative party, representing inequality and racism.

Coming back to England was harder than going. I had culture shock in reverse. Images of plenty yelled at me. England seemed to be overflowing with . . . things. Things from all over the world. Things and information. Information, though, which couldn't bite through the profound insularity and indifference.

In Pakistan people were keen to know: not only about Asia and the Middle East, but about Europe and the United States. They sought out information about the whole world. They needed it. They ordered books from Europe, listened to international radio and chewed up visiting academics like pieces of orange.

In Britain today, among the middle class, thinking and argument are almost entirely taboo. The other taboo, replacing death in its unacceptability, is money. As our society has become more divided, the acknowledgement of that division – which is a financial division, a matter of economic power – is out of the question. So money is not discussed. It is taken for granted that you have it; that you have means of obtaining it; that you are reasonably well off and gain status and influence over others because of it.

Accompanying this financial silence, and shoring up both the social division and the taboo, is the prohibition on thought. The discussion of a serious subject to a conclusion using logic, evidence and counter-evidence is an unacceptable social embarrassment. It just isn't done to argue: it is thought to be the same as rowing. One has opinions in England, but they are formed in private and clung to in public despite everything, despite their often being quite wrong.

There is real defensiveness and insecurity, a Victorian fear of revealing so much as a genital of an idea, the nipple of a notion or the sex of a syllogism. Where sexual exhibitionism and the discussion of positions and emissions is fashionable, indeed orthodox, thinking and argument are avoided.

In Pakistan it was essential to have knowledge because political discussion was serious. It mattered what you thought. People put chairs in a circle, sat down, and *talked*. What was said to each other was necessary. Intellectual dignity was maintained, earned anxiety was expressed; you weren't alone; ideas and feelings were shared. These things had to be said, even in low voices, because absolute silence was intolerable, absolute silence was the acceptance of isolation and division. It was a relief to argue, to exercise intelligence in a country where intelligence was in itself a weapon and a threat.

I will never forget the hospitality, warmth and generosity of the people of Pakistan; the flowers on the lawn of the Sind Club, the sprawling open houses, full of air and people and the smell of spices; the unbelievable brightness of the light shining through a dust haze; the woman walking perfectly straight-backed along a street with an iron balanced on her head; the open-air typists outside the law courts; butterflies as big as clock faces; the man who slept with a chicken in his bed; my uncle's library, bought in the 1940s in Cambridge, where he was taught by Russell – though when I opened the books after being given the library, they were rotten with worms, the pitted pages falling apart just as I stood there. And the way the men shake hands. This is worth going into.

First you offer them your hand and they grasp it. The clasped hands are slapped then with their spare hand as an affirmation of initial contact. This is, as it were, the soup. Now they pull you to them for the main course, the full embrace, the steak. As you look over their shoulder, your bodies thrust together, your heat intermingled, they crack you on the back at least three times with their open palm. These are not negligible taps, but good healthy whacks, demonstrating equality and openness. Depending on the nature of the friendship, these whacks could go on a considerable time and may debilitate the sick or weak. But they must be reciprocated. This done, they will let you move away from them, but still holding your right hand. You are considered fully, with affection overbrimming, as they regard all of you, as they seem to take in your entire being from top to toe, from inside to out. At last, after complete contact has been made, all possibility of concealment or inhibition banished, they carefully let go of your hand as if it were a delicate object. *That is a greeting.*

And there was the photograph of my father in my uncle's room, in which he must have been about the same age as me. A picture in a house that contained fragments of my past: a house full of stories, of Bombay, Delhi, China; of feuds, wrestling matches, adulteries, windows, broken with hands, card games, impossible loves, and magic spells. Stories to help me see my place in the world and give me a sense of the past which could go into making a life in the present and the future. This was surely part of the way I could understand myself. This knowledge, garnered in my mid-twenties, would help me form an image of myself: I'd take it back to England where I needed it to protect myself. And it would be with me in London and the suburbs, making me stronger.

When I considered staying in Pakistan to regain more of my past and complete myself with it, I had to think that that was impossible. Didn't I already miss too much of England? And wasn't I too impatient with the illiberalism and lack of possibility of Pakistan?

So there was always going to be the necessary return to England. I came home . . . to my country.

This is difficult to say. 'My country' isn't a notion that comes easily. It is still difficult to answer the question, where do you come from? I have never wanted to identify with England. When Enoch Powell spoke for England I turned away in final disgust. I would rather walk naked down the street than stand up for the National Anthem. The pain of that period of my life, in the mid-1960s, is with me still. And when I originally wrote this piece I put it in the third person: Hanif saw this, Hanif felt that, because of the difficulty of directly addressing myself to what I felt then, of not wanting to think about it again. And perhaps that is why I took to writing in the first place, to make strong feelings into weak feelings.

But despite all this, some kind of identification with England remains.

It is strange to go away to the land of your ancestors, to find out how much you have in common with people there, yet at the same time to realise how British you are, the extent to which, as Orwell says: 'the suet puddings and the red pillar boxes have entered into your soul'. It isn't *that* you wanted to find out. But it is part of what you do find out. And you find out what little choice you have in the matter of your background and where you belong. You look forward to getting back; you think often of England and what it means to you – and you think often of what it means to be British.

Two days after my return I took my washing to a laundrette and gave it to the attendant only to be told she didn't touch the clothes of foreigners: she didn't want me anywhere near her blasted laundrette. More seriously: I read in the paper that a Pakistani family in the East End had been firebombed. A child was killed. This, of course, happens frequently. It is the pig's head through the window, the spit in the face, the children with the initials of racist organisations tattooed into their skin with razor blades, as well as the more polite forms of hatred.

I was in a rage. I thought: who wants to be British anyway? Or as a black American writer said: who wants to be integrated into a burning house anyway?

And indeed I know Pakistanis and Indians born and brought up here who consider their position to be the result of a diaspora: they are in exile, awaiting return to a better place, where they belong, where they are welcome. And there this 'belonging' will be total. This will be home, and peace.

It is not difficult to see how much illusion and falsity there is in this view. How much disappointment and unhappiness might be involved in going 'home', only to see the extent to which you have been formed by England and the depth of attachment you feel to the place, despite everything.

It isn't surprising that some people believe in this idea of 'home'. The alternative to believing it is more conflict here; it is more self-hatred; it is the continual struggle against racism; it is the continual adjustment to life in Britain. And blacks in Britain know they have made more than enough adjustments.

So what is it to be British?

In his 1941 essay 'England Your England' Orwell says: 'the gentleness of the English civilisation is perhaps its most marked characteristic'. He calls the country 'a family with the wrong members in control' and talks of the 'soundness and homogeneity of England'.

Elsewhere he considers the Indian character. He explains the 'maniacal suspiciousness' which, agreeing, he claims, with

E. M. Forster in *A Passage to India*, he calls 'the besetting Indian vice ...' But he has the grace to acknowledge in his essay 'Not Counting Niggers' 'that the overwhelming bulk of the British proletariat [lives] ... in Asia and Africa'.

But this is niggardly. The main object of his praise is British 'tolerance' and he writes of 'their gentle manners'. He also says that this aspect of England 'is continuous, it stretches into the future and the past, there is something in it that persists'.

But does it persist? If this version of England was true then, in the 1930s and 1940s, it is under pressure now. From the point of view of thousands of black people it just does not apply. It is completely without basis.

Obviously tolerance in a stable, confident wartime society with a massive Empire is quite different to tolerance in a disintegrating uncertain society during an economic depression. But surely this would be the test; this would be just the time for this much-advertised tolerance in the British soul to manifest itself as more than vanity and self-congratulation. But it has not. Under real continuous strain it has failed.

Tolerant, gentle British whites have no idea how little of this tolerance is experienced by blacks here. No idea of the violence, hostility and contempt directed against black people every day by state and individual alike in this land once described by Orwell as being not one of 'rubber truncheons' or 'Jew-baiters' but of 'flower-lovers' with 'mild knobbly faces'. But in parts of England the flower-lovers are all gone, the rubber truncheons and Jew-baiters are at large, and if any real contemporary content is to be given to Orwell's blind social patriotism, then clichés about 'tolerance' must be seriously examined for depth and weight of substantial content.

In the mean time it must be made clear that blacks don't require 'tolerance' in this particular condescending way. It isn't this particular paternal tyranny that is wanted, since it is major adjustments to British society that have to be made.

I stress that it is the British who have to make these adjustments.

It is the British, the white British, who have to learn that being British isn't what it was. Now it is a more complex thing, involving new elements. So there must be a fresh way of seeing Britain and the choices it faces: and a new way of being British after all this time. Much thought, discussion and self-examination must go into seeing the necessity for this, what this 'new way of being British' involves and how difficult it might be to attain.

The failure to grasp this opportunity for a revitalised and broader self-definition, in the face of a real failure to be human, will be more insularity, schism, bitterness and catastrophe.

The two countries, Britain and Pakistan, have been part of each other for years, usually to the advantage of Britain. They cannot now be wrenched apart, even if that were desirable. Their futures will be intermixed. What that intermix means, its moral quality, whether it is violently resisted by ignorant whites and character-ised by inequality and injustice, or understood, accepted and humanised, is for all of us to decide.

This decision is not one about a small group of irrelevant people who can be contemptuously described as 'minorities'. It is about the direction of British society. About its values and how humane it can be when experiencing real difficulty and possible breakdown. It is about the respect it accords individuals, the power it gives to groups, and what it really means when it describes itself as 'democratic'. The future is in our hands.

Bradford

First published in *Granta 20*, Winter 1986

Some time ago, I noticed that there was something unusual about the city of Bradford, something that distinguished it from other northern industrial cities.

To begin with, there was Ray Honeyford. Three years ago Honeyford, the headmaster of Bradford's Drummond Middle School, wrote a short, three-page article that was published in the *Salisbury Review*. The *Salisbury Review* has a circulation of about 1,000, but the impact of Honeyford's article was felt beyond the magazine's readership. It was discussed in the *Yorkshire Post* and reprinted in the local *Telegraph and Argus*. A parents' group demanded Honeyford's resignation. His school was then boycotted, and children, instructed by their parents not to attend classes, gathered outside, shouting abuse at the man who weeks before was their teacher. There were fights, sometimes physical brawls, between local leaders and politicians. The 'Honeyford Affair', as it became known, attracted so much attention that it became common every morning to come upon national journalists and television crews outside the school. And when it was finally resolved that Honeyford had to go, the Bradford district council had to pay him over £160,000 to get him to leave: ten times his annual salary.

But there were other things about Bradford. The Yorkshire Ripper was from Bradford. The prostitutes who came down to London on the train on 'cheap day return' tickets were from Bradford. At a time when the game of soccer was threatened by so many troubles, Bradford seemed to have troubles of the most extreme kind. Days after the deaths in Brussels at the Heysel stadium, fifty-six Bradford football supporters were killed in one of the worst fires in the history of the sport. Eighteen months later, there was yet another fire, and a match stopped because of crowd violence.

There was more: there was unemployment in excess of 20 per cent; there was a prominent branch of the National Front; there were regular racial attacks on taxi drivers; there were stories of forced emigration; there was a mayor from a village in Pakistan. Bradford, I felt, was a place I had to see for myself, because it seemed that so many important issues, of race, culture, nationalism, and education, were evident in an extremely concentrated way in this medium-sized city of 400,000 people, situated between the much larger cities of Manchester and Leeds. These were issues that related to the whole notion of what it was to be British and what that would mean in the future. Bradford seemed to be a microcosm of a larger British society that was struggling to find a sense of itself, even as it was undergoing radical change. And it was a struggle not seen by the people governing the country, who, after all, had been brought up in a world far different from today's. In 1945, England ruled over six hundred million people. And there were few black faces on its streets.

The first thing you notice as you get on the Inter-City train to Bradford is that the first three carriages are first class. These are followed by the first-class restaurant car. Then you are free to sit down. But if the train is packed and you cannot find an empty seat, you have to stand. You stand for the whole journey, with other people lying on the floor around you, and you look through at the empty seats in the first-class carriages where men sit in their shirtsleeves doing important work and not looking up. The ticket collector has to climb over us to get to them.

Like the porters on the station, the ticket collector was black, probably of West Indian origin. In other words, black British. Most of the men fixing the railway line, in their luminous orange jackets, with pickaxes over their shoulders, were also black. The guard on the train was Pakistani, or should I say another Briton, probably born here, and therefore 'black'.

When I got to Bradford I took a taxi. It was simple: Bradford is full of taxis. Raise an arm and three taxis rush at you. Like most taxi drivers in Bradford, the driver was Asian and his car had furry, bright purple seats, covered with the kind of material people in the suburbs sometimes put on the lids of their toilets. It smelled of perfume, and Indian music was playing. The taxi driver had a Bradford-Pakistani accent, a cross between the north of England and Lahore, which sounds odd the first few times you hear it. Mentioning the accent irritates people in Bradford. How else do you expect people to talk? they say. And they are right. But hearing it for the first time disconcerted me because I found that I associated northern accents with white faces, with people who eat puddings, with Geoffrey Boycott and Roy Hattersley.

We drove up a steep hill, which overlooked the city. In the distance there were modern buildings and among them the older mill chimneys and factories with boarded-up windows. We passed Priestley Road. J. B. Priestley was born in Bradford, and in the early 1960s both John Braine and Alan Sillitoe set novels here. I wondered what the writing of the next fifteen years would be like. There were, I was to learn, stories in abundance to be told.

The previous day I had watched one of my favourite films, Keith Waterhouse and Willis Hall's *Billy Liar*, also written in the early 1960s. Billy works for an undertaker and there is a scene in which Billy tries to seduce one of his old girlfriends in a graveyard. Now I passed that old graveyard. It was full of monstrous mausoleums, some with spires thirty feet high; others were works of architecture in themselves, with arches, urns and roofs. They dated from the late nineteenth century and contained the bones of the great mill barons and their families. In *The Waste Land* T. S. Eliot wrote of the 'silk hat on a Bradford millionaire'. Now the mills and the millionaires had nearly disappeared. In the cemetery there were some white youths on a Youth Opportunity Scheme, hacking unenthusiastically at the weeds, clearing a path. This was the only work that could be found for them, doing up the cemetery.

I was staying in a house near the cemetery. The houses were of a good size, well-built with three bedrooms and lofts. Their front doors were open and the street was full of kids running in and out. Women constantly crossed the street and stood on each other's doorsteps, talking. An old man with a stick walked along slowly. He stopped to pat a child who was crying so much I thought she would explode. He carried on patting her head, and she carried on crying, until finally he decided to enter the house and fetched the child's young sister.

The houses were overcrowded – if you looked inside you would usually see five or six adults sitting in the front room – and there wasn't much furniture: often the linoleum on the floor was torn and curling, and a bare lightbulb hung from the ceiling. The wallpaper was peeling from the walls.

Each house had a concrete yard at the back, where women and young female children were always hanging out the washing: the cleaning of clothes appeared never to stop. There was one man – his house was especially run-down – who had recently acquired a new car. He walked round and round it; he was proud of his car, and occasionally caressed it.

It was everything I imagined a Bradford working-class community would be like, except that there was one difference. Everyone I'd seen since I arrived was Pakistani. I had yet to see a white face.

The women covered their heads. And while the older ones wore jumpers and overcoats, underneath they, like the young girls, wore *salwar kamiz*, the Pakistani long tops over baggy trousers. If I ignored the dark Victorian buildings around me, I could imagine that everyone was back in their village in Pakistan.

That evening, Jane – the friend I was staying with – and I decided to go out. We walked back down the hill and into the centre of town. It looked like many other town centres in Britain. The subways under the roundabouts stank of urine; graffiti defaced them and lakes of rainwater gathered at the bottom of the stairs. There was a massive shopping centre with unnatural lighting; some kids were rollerskating through it, pursued by three pink-faced security guards in paramilitary outfits. The shops were also the same: Ryman's, Smith's, Dixons, the National Westminster Bank. I hadn't become accustomed to Bradford and found myself making simple comparisons with London. The clothes people wore were shabby and old; they looked as if they'd been bought in jumble sales or second-hand shops. And their faces had an unhealthy aspect: some were malnourished.

As we crossed the city, I could see that some parts looked old-fashioned. They reminded me of my English grandfather and the Britain of my childhood: pigeon-keeping, greyhound racing, roast-beef eating and pianos in pubs. Outside the centre, there were shops you'd rarely see in London now: drapers, ironmongers, fish and chip shops that still used newspaper wrappers, barber's shops with photographs in the window of men with Everly Brothers haircuts. And here, among all this, I also saw the Islamic Library and the Ambala Sweet Centre where you could buy spices: dhaniya, haldi, garam masala, and dhal and ladies' fingers. There were Asian video shops where you could buy tapes of the songs of Master Sajjad, Nayyara, Alamgir, Nazeen and M. Ali Shahaiky.

Jane and I went to a bar. It was a cross between a pub and a nightclub. At the entrance the bouncer laid his hands on my shoulders and told me I could not go in.

'Why not?' I asked.

'You're not wearing any trousers.'

I looked down at my legs in astonishment.

'Are you sure?' I asked.

'No trousers,' he said, 'no entry.'

Jeans, it seems, were not acceptable.

We walked on to another place. This time we got in. It too was very smart and entirely white. The young men had dressed up in open-necked shirts, Topshop grey slacks and Ravel loafers. They stood around quietly in groups. The young women had also gone to a lot of trouble: some of them looked like models, in their extravagant dresses and high heels. But the women and the men were not talking to each other. We had a drink and left. Jane said she wanted me to see a working men's club.

The working men's club turned out to be near an estate, populated, like most Bradford estates, mostly by whites. The Asians tended to own their homes. They had difficulty acquiring council houses or flats, and were harassed and abused when they moved on to white estates.

The estate was scruffy: some of the flats were boarded up, rubbish blew about; the balconies looked as if they were about to crash off the side of the building. The club itself was in a large modern building. We weren't members of course, but the man on the door agreed to let us in.

There were three large rooms. One was like a pub; another was a snooker room. In the largest room at least 150 people sat around tables in families. At one end was a stage. A white man in evening dress was banging furiously at a drum-kit. Another played the organ. The noise was unbearable.

At the bar, it was mostly elderly men. They sat beside each other. But they didn't talk. They had drawn, pale faces and thin, narrow bodies that expanded dramatically at the stomach and then disappeared into the massive jutting band of their trousers. They had little legs. They wore suits, the men. They had dressed up for the evening.

Here there were no Asians either, and I wanted to go to an Asian bar, but it was getting late and the bars were closing, at ten-thirty as they do outside London. We got a taxi and drove across town. The streets got rougher and rougher. We left the main road and suddenly were in a leafy, almost suburban area. The houses here were large, occupied I imagined by clerks, insurance salesmen, business people. We stopped outside a detached three-storey house that seemed to be surrounded by an extraordinary amount of darkness and shadow. There was one light on, in the kitchen, and the woman inside was Sonia Sutcliffe, the wife of the Yorkshire Ripper, an ex-schoolteacher. I thought of Peter Sutcliffe telling his wife he was the Yorkshire Ripper. He had wanted to tell her himself; he insisted on it. Many of his victims had come from the surrounding area.

The surrounding area was mostly an Asian district and here the pubs stayed open late, sometimes until two in the morning. There were no trouser rules.

During the day in this part of town the Asian kids would be playing in the streets. The women, most of them uneducated, illiterate, unable to speak English, would talk in doorways as they did where I was staying.

It was around midnight, and men were only now leaving their houses – the women remaining behind with the children – and walking down the street to the pub. Jane said it stayed open late with police permission. It gave the police an opportunity to find out what was going on: their spies and informers could keep an eye on people. Wherever you went in Bradford, people talked about spies and informers: who was and who wasn't. I'd never known anything like it, but then I'd never known any other city, except perhaps Karachi, in which politics was such a dominant part of daily life. Apparently there was money to be made working for the police and reporting what was going on: what the Asian militants were doing; what the racists were doing; who the journalists were talking to; what attacks or demonstrations were planned; what vigilante groups were being formed.

The pub was packed with Asian men and they still kept arriving. They knew each other and embraced enthusiastically. There were few women and all but three were white. Asian men and white women kissed in corners. As we squeezed in, Jane said she knew several white women who were having affairs with Asian men, affairs that had sometimes gone on for years. The men had married Pakistani women, often out of family pressure, and frequently the women were from the villages. The Asian women had a terrible time in Bradford.

The music was loud and some people were dancing, elbow to elbow, only able in the crush to shake their heads and shuffle their feet. There was a lot of very un-Islamic drinking. I noticed two

Asian girls. They stood out, with their bright jewellery and pretty clothes. They were with Asian men. Their men looked inhibited and the girls left early. Jane, who was a journalist, recognised a number of prostitutes in the pub. She'd interviewed them at the time of the Ripper. One stood by Jane and kept pulling at her jumper. 'Where did you get that jumper? How much was it?' she kept saying. Jane said the prostitutes hadn't stopped work during the time of the Ripper. They couldn't afford to. Instead, they'd worked in pairs, one girl fucking the man, while the other stood by with a knife in her hand.

In 1933, when J. B. Priestley was preparing his *English Journey*, he found three Englands. There was guidebook England, of palaces and forests; nineteenth-century industrial England of factories and suburbs; and contemporary England of bypasses and suburbs. Now, half a century later, there is another England as well: the inner city.

In front of me, in this pub, there were five or six gay men and two lesbian couples. Three white kids wore black leather jackets and had mohicans: their mauve, red and yellow hair stood up straight for a good twelve inches and curved across their heads like a feather glued on its thin edge to a billiard ball. And there were the Asians. This was not one large, solid community with a shared outlook, common beliefs and an established form of life; not Orwell's 'one family with the wrong members in control'. It was diverse, disparate, strikingly various.

Jane introduced me to a young Asian man, an activist and local political star from his time of being on trial as one of the Bradford Twelve. I was pleased to meet him. In 1981, a group of twelve youths, fearing a racial attack in the aftermath of the terrible assault on Asians by skinheads in Southall in London, had made a number of petrol bombs. But they were caught and charged under the Explosives Act with conspiracy – a charge normally intended for urban terrorists. It was eleven months before they were acquitted.

I greeted him enthusiastically. He, with less enthusiasm, asked me if I'd written a film called *My Beautiful Laundrette*. I said yes, I had, and he started to curse me: I was a fascist, a reactionary. He was shouting. Then he seemed to run out of words and pulled back to hit me. But just as he raised his fist, his companions grabbed his arm and dragged him away.

I said to Jane that I thought the next day we should do something less exhausting. We could visit a school.

I had heard that there was to be a ceremony for a new school that was opening, the Zakariya Girls School. The large community hall was already packed with three hundred Asian men when I arrived. Then someone took my arm, to eject me, I thought. But instead I was led to the front row, where I found myself sitting next to three white policemen and assorted white dignitaries, both women and men, in smart Sunday-school clothes.

On the high stage sat local councillors, a white Muslim in white turban and robes, and various Asian men. A white man was addressing the audience, the MP for Scarborough, Sir Michael Shaw. 'You have come into our community,' he was saying, 'and you must become part of that community. All branches must lead to one trunk, which is the British way of life. We mustn't retire to our own communities and shut ourselves out. Yet you have felt you needed schools of your own . . .'

The MP was followed by a man who appeared to be a home-grown Batley citizen. 'As a practising Roman Catholic, I sympathise with you, having had a Catholic education myself,' he said, and went on to say how good he thought the Islamic school would be.

Finally the man from the local mosque read some verses from the Koran. The local policemen cupped their hands and lowered their heads in true multicultural fashion. The other whites near me, frantically looking around at each other, quickly followed suit. Then Indian sweets were brought round, which the polite English ladies picked politely at.

I left the hall and walked up the hill towards the school. The policeman followed me, holding the hands of the six or seven Asian children that surrounded him.

Batley is outside Bradford, on the way to Leeds. It is a small town surrounded by countryside and hills. The view from the hill into the valley and then up into the hills was exquisite. In the town there was a large Asian community. The Zakariya Girls School had actually been started two years ago as a 'pirate' school, not having received approval from the Department of Education until an extension was built. Now it was finished. And today it became the first high school of its kind – an Islamic school for girls – to be officially registered under the Education Act. As a pirate school it had been a large, overcrowded old house on the top of a hill. Now, outside, was a new two-storey building. It was spacious, clean, modern.

I went in and looked around. Most of the books were on the Koran or Islam, on prayer or on the prophet Mohammed. The walls were covered with verses from the Koran. And despite its being a girls' school there were no girls there and no Asian women, just the men and lots of little boys in green, blue and brown caps, running about.

The idea for the school had been the pop star Cat Stevens's, and he had raised most of the money for it privately, it was said, from Saudi Arabia. Stevens, who had changed his name to Yusuf Islam, was quoted as saying that he had tried everything, running the gamut of international novelties to find spiritual satisfaction: materialism, sex, drugs, Buddhism, Christianity and finally Islam. I wondered if it was entirely arbitrary that he'd ended with Islam or whether perhaps today, the circumstances being slightly different, we could as easily have been at the opening of a Buddhist school.

Yusuf Islam was not at the school but his assistant, Ibrahim, was. Ibrahim was the white Muslim in the white robes with the white turban who spoke earlier. There was supposed to be a press conference, but nothing was happening; everything was disorganised. Ibrahim came and sat beside me. I asked him if he'd talk about the school. He was, he said, very keen; the school had been the result of so much effort and organisation, so much goodness. I looked at him. He seemed preternaturally good and calm.

Ibrahim was from Newcastle, and had a long ginger beard. (I remembered someone saying to me in Pakistan that the only growth industry in Islamic countries was in human hair on the face.) Ibrahim's epiphany had occurred on a trip to South Africa. There, seeing black and white men praying together in a mosque, he decided to convert to Islam.

He told me about the way the school worked. The human face, for instance, or the face of any animate being, could not be represented at the school. And dancing would not be encouraged, nor the playing of musical instruments. Surely, he said, looking at me, his face full of conviction, the human voice was expressive enough? When I said this would probably rule out the possibility of the girls taking either art or music O-levels, he nodded sadly and admitted that it would.

And modern literature? I asked.

He nodded sadly again and said it would be studied 'in a critical light'.

I said I was glad to hear it. But what about science?

That was to be studied in a critical light too, since – and here he took a deep breath – he didn't accept Darwinism or any theory of evolution because, well, because the presence of monkeys who hadn't changed into men disproved it all.

I took another close look at him. He obviously believed these things. But why was he being so apologetic?

As I walked back down the hill I thought about the issues raised by the Zakariya Girls School. There were times, I thought, when to be accommodating you had to bend over backwards so far that you fell over. Since the mid-1960s the English liberal has seen the traditional hierarchies and divisions of British life challenged, if not destroyed. Assumptions of irrevocable, useful and moral differences – between classes, men and women, gays and straights, older and younger people, developed and under-developed societies – had changed for good. The commonly made distinction between 'higher' and 'lower' cultures had become suspect. It had become

questionable philosophically to apply criteria of judgement available in one society to events in another: there could not be any
independent or bridging method of evaluation. And it followed
that we should be able, as a broad, humane and pluralistic society,
to sustain a wide range of disparate groups living in their own way.
And if one of these groups wanted halal meat, Islamic schools,
anti-Darwinism and an intimate knowledge of the Koran for its
girls, so be it. As it was, there had been Catholic schools and Jewish
schools for years.

But Islamic schools like the one in Batley appeared to violate
the principles of a liberal education, and the very ideas to which
the school owed its existence. And because of the community's
religious beliefs, so important to its members, the future prospects
for the girls were reduced. Was that the choice they had made? Did
the Asian community really want this kind of separate education
anyway? And if it did, how many wanted it? Or was it only a few
earnest and repressed believers, all men, frightened of England
and their daughters' sexuality?

The house Frederick Delius was born in, in Bradford, was now the
Council of Mosques, which looked after the interests of the
Bradford Muslims. There are sixty thousand Muslims and thirty
Muslim organisations in Bradford. Chowdhury Khan, the
President of the Council, told me about the relations between men
and women in Islam and the problem of girls' schools.

He said there were no women in the Council because 'we respect
them too much'. I mentioned that I found this a little perplexing,
but he ignored me, adding that this is also why women were not
encouraged to have jobs or careers.

'Women's interests', he said confidently, 'are being looked after.'

'And the girls'?'

After the age of twelve, he said, women should not mix with
men. That was why more single-sex schools were required in
Bradford. The local council had agreed that this was desirable and
would provide more single-sex schools when resources were

available. He added that despite the Labour manifesto, Neil Kinnock approved of this.

I said I doubted this.

Anyway, he continued, the local Labour Party was lobbying for more single-sex schools after having tried, in the 1960s, to provide mixed-sex schools. But – and this he emphasised – the Council of Mosques wanted single-sex schools, *not* Islamic ones or racially segregated schools. He banged on his desk, No, no, no! No apartheid!

He wanted the state to understand that, while Muslim children would inevitably become Westernised – they were reconciled to that – they still wanted their children to learn about Islam at school, to learn subcontinental languages and be taught the history, politics and geography of India, Pakistan and Bangladesh. Surely, he added, the white British would be interested in this too. After all, the relations between England and the subcontinent had always been closer than those between Britain and France, say.

I found Chowdhury Khan to be a difficult and sometimes strange man. But his values, and the values of the Council he represented, are fairly straightforward. He believes in the pre-eminent value of the family and, for example, the importance of religion in establishing morality. He also believes in the innately inferior position of women. He dislikes liberalism in all its forms, and is an advocate of severe and vengeful retribution against law-breakers.

These are extremely conservative and traditional views. But they are also, isolated from the specifics of their subcontinental context, the values championed by Ray Honeyford, among others. There were a number of interesting ironies developing.

I sought out the younger, more militant section of the community. How did its members see their place in Britain?

When I was in my teens, in the mid-1960s, there was much talk of the 'problems' that kids of my colour and generation faced in Britain because of our racial mix or because our parents were immigrants. We didn't know where we belonged, it was said; we were neither fish nor fowl. I remember reading that kind of thing in the newspaper. We were frequently referred to as 'second-generation immigrants' just so there was no mistake about our not really belonging in Britain. We were 'Britain's children without a home'. The phrase 'caught between two cultures' was a favourite. It was a little too triumphant for me. Anyway, this view was wrong. It has been easier for us than for our parents. For them Britain really had been a strange land and it must have been hard to feel part of a society if you had spent a good deal of your life elsewhere and intended to return: most immigrants from the Indian subcontinent came to Britain to make money and then go home. Most of the Pakistanis in Bradford had come from one specific district, Mirpur, because that was where the Bradford mill-owners happened to look for cheap labour twenty-five years ago. And many, once here, stayed for good; it was not possible to go back. Yet when they got older the immigrants found they hadn't really made a place for themselves in Britain. They missed the old country. They'd always thought of Britain as a kind of long stopover rather than the final resting place it would turn out to be.

But for me and the others of my generation born here, Britain was always where we belonged, even when we were told – often in terms of racial abuse – that this was not so. Far from being a conflict of cultures, our lives seemed to synthesise disparate elements: the pub, the mosque, two or three languages, rock 'n' roll, Indian films. Our extended family and our British individuality commingled.

Tariq was twenty-two. His office was bare in the modern style: there was a desk; there was a computer. The building was paid for by the EEC and Bradford Council. His job was to advise on the setting-up of businesses and on related legal matters. He also advised the Labour Party on its economic policy. In fact, although so young, Tariq had been active in politics for a number of years: at the age of sixteen, he had been chairman of the Asian Youth Movement, which was founded in 1978 after the National Front began marching on Bradford. But few of the other young men I'd met in Bradford had Tariq's sense of direction or ambition, including the young activists known as the Bradford Twelve. Five years after their acquittal, most of them were, like Tariq, very active – fighting deportations, monitoring racist organisations, advising on multicultural education – but, like other young people in Bradford, they were unemployed. They hung around the pubs; their politics were obscure; they were 'anti-fascist' but it was difficult to know what they were for. Unlike their parents, who'd come here for a specific purpose, to make a life in the affluent West away from poverty and lack of opportunity, they, born here, had inherited only pointlessness and emptiness. The emptiness, that is, derived not from racial concerns but economic ones.

Tariq took me to a Pakistani café. Bradford was full of them. They were like English working men's cafés, except the food was Pakistani, you ate with your fingers and there was always water on the table. The waiter spoke to us in Punjabi and Tariq replied. Then the waiter looked at me and asked a question. I looked vague, nodded stupidly and felt ashamed. Tariq realised I could only speak English.

How many languages did he speak?

Four: English, Malay, Urdu and Punjabi.

I told him about the school I'd visited.

Tariq was against Islamic schools. He thought they made it harder for Asian kids in Britain to get qualifications than in ordinary, mixed-race, mixed-sex schools. He said the people who wanted such schools were not representative; they just made a lot of noise and made the community look like it was made up of separatists, which it was not.

He wasn't a separatist, he said. He wanted the integration of all into the society. But for him the problem of integration was adjacent to the problem of being poor in Britain: how could people feel themselves to be active participants in the life of a society when they were suffering all the wretchedness of bad housing, poor insulation and the indignity of having their gas and electricity disconnected; or when they were turning to loan sharks to pay their bills; or when they felt themselves being dissipated by unemployment; and when they weren't being properly educated, because the resources for a proper education didn't exist.

There was one Asian in Bradford it was crucial to talk to. He'd had political power. For a year he'd been mayor, and as Britain's first Asian or black mayor he'd received much attention. He'd also had a terrible time.

I talked to Mohammed Ajeeb in the nineteenth-century town hall. The town hall was a monument to Bradford's long-gone splendour and pride. Later I ran into him at Bradford's superb Museum of Film, Television and Photography, where a huge photo of him and his wife was unveiled. Ajeeb is a tall, modest man, sincere, sometimes openly uncertain and highly regarded for his tenacity by the Labour leader Neil Kinnock. Ajeeb is careful in his conversation. He lacks the confident politician's polish: from him, I heard no well-articulated banalities. He is from a small village in the Punjab. When we met at the Museum, we talked about the differences between us, and he admitted that it had been quite a feat for someone like him to have got so far in Britain. In Pakistan, with its petrified feudal system, he would never have been able to transcend his background.

During his time in office, a stand at the Valley Parade football ground had burned down, killing fifty-six people and injuring three hundred others. There was the Honeyford affair, about which he had been notoriously outspoken ('I cannot see', he said in a speech that contributed to Honeyford's removal, 'the unity of our great city being destroyed by one man'). As mayor, Ajeeb moved through areas of Bradford society to which he never had access before, and the racism he experienced, both explicit and covert, was of a viciousness he hadn't anticipated. And it was relentless. His house was attacked, and he, as mayor, was forced to move; and at Grimsby Town football ground, when he presented a cheque to the families of those killed in the fire, the crowd abused him with racist slogans; finally, several thousand football supporters started chanting Honeyford's name so loudly that Ajeeb was unable to complete his speech. He received sackfuls of hate mail and few letters of support.

Ajeeb said that no culture could remain static, neither British nor Pakistani. And while groups liked to cling to the old ways and there would be conflict, eventually different groups would intermingle. For him the important thing was that minorities secure political power for themselves. At the same time, he said that, although he wanted to become a Parliamentary candidate, no one would offer him a constituency where he could stand. This was, he thought, because he was Asian and the Labour Party feared that the white working class wouldn't vote for him. He could stand as Parliamentary candidate only in a black area, which seemed fine to him for the time being; he was prepared to do that.

There were others who weren't prepared to put up with the racism in the trade union movement and in the Labour Party itself in the way Ajeeb had. I met a middle-aged Indian man, a tax inspector, who had been in the Labour Party for at least ten years. He had offered to help canvass during the local council elections – on a white council estate. He was told that it wouldn't be to the party's advantage for him to help in a white area. He was so offended that he offered his services to the Tories. Although he hated Margaret Thatcher, he found the Tories welcomed him. He started to lecture on the subject of Asians in Britain to various Tory groups and Rotary Club dinners, until he found himself talking at the Wakefield Police College. At the Wakefield Police College he encountered the worst racists he had ever seen in his life.

He did not need to go into details. Only a few months before, at an anti-apartheid demonstration outside South Africa House in London, I'd been standing by a police line when a policeman started to talk to me. He spoke in a low voice, as if he were telling me about the traffic in Piccadilly. 'You bastards,' he said. 'We hate you, we don't want you here. Everything would be all right, there'd be none of this, if you pissed off home.' And he went on like that, fixing me with a stare. 'You wogs, you coons, you blacks, we hate you all.'

Ajeeb said that if there was anything he clung to when things became unbearable, it was the knowledge that the British electorate always rejected the far right. They had never voted in significant numbers for neo-fascist groups like the National Front and the British National Party. Even the so-called New Right, a prominent and noisy group of journalists, lecturers and intellectuals, had no great popular following. People knew what viciousness underlay their ideas, he said.

Some of the views of the New Right, Ajeeb believed, had much in common with proletarian far-right organisations like the National Front: its members held to the notion of white racial superiority, they believed in repatriation and they argued that the mixing of cultures would lead to the degeneration of British culture. Ajeeb argued that they used the rhetoric of 'culture' and 'religion' and 'nationhood' as a fig-leaf; in the end they wished to defend a mythical idea of white culture. Honeyford was associated with the New Right, and what he and people like him wanted, Ajeeb said, was for Asians to behave exactly like the whites. And if they didn't do this, they should leave.

This movement known as the New Right is grouped around the Conservative Philosophy Group and the *Salisbury Review*, the magazine that published Honeyford's article. The group is a loose affiliation of individuals with similar views. A number of them are graduates of Peterhouse, Cambridge. These include John Vincent, Professor of History at Bristol University, who writes a weekly column for the *Sun*, and Colin Welch, a columnist for the *Spectator*.

Like a lot of people in Bradford, Ajeeb became agitated on the subject of the New Right and Honeyford's relationship with it. But how important was it? What did the views of a few extremists really matter? So what if they wrote for influential papers? At least they weren't on the street wearing boots. But the ideas expressed by Honeyford had split Bradford apart. These ideas were alive and active in the city, entering into arguments about education, housing, citizenship, health, food and politics. Bradford was a city in which ideas carried knives.

Ray Honeyford went to Bradford's Drummond Middle School as headmaster in January 1980. The children were aged between nine and thirteen. At the time the school was 50 per cent Asian. When he left last spring it was 95 per cent.

Honeyford is from a working-class background. He failed his exams for grammar school, and from the age of fifteen worked for ten years for a company that makes desiccated coconut. In his late twenties, he attended a two-year teacher-training course at Didsbury College, and later got further degrees from the universities of Lancaster and Manchester. He described himself as a Marxist, and was a member of the Labour Party. But all that changed when he began teaching at a mixed-race school. He submitted an unsolicited article to the *Salisbury Review*, and the article, entitled 'Education and Race – An Alternative View', was accepted.

The article is a polemic. It argues that the multi-racial policies endorsed by various members of the teaching establishment are damaging the English way of life, and that proper English people should resist these assaults on the 'British traditions of understatement, civilised discourse and respect for reason'. It wasn't too surprising that a polemic of this sort written by the headmaster of a school made up almost entirely of Asian children was seen to be controversial.

But the real problem wasn't the polemic but the rhetorical asides and parentheticals. Honeyford mentions the 'hysterical political temperament of the Indian subcontinent', and describes Asians as 'these people' (in an earlier article, they are 'settler children'). A Sikh is 'half-educated and volatile', and black intellectuals are 'aggressive'. Honeyford then goes on to attack Pakistan itself, which in a curious non-sequitur seems to be responsible for British drug problems:

Pakistan is a country which cannot cope with democracy; under martial law since 1977, it is ruled by a military tyrant who, in the opinion of at least half his countrymen, had his predecessor judicially murdered. A country, moreover, which despite disproportionate western aid because of its important strategic position, remains for most of its people obstinately backward.

Corruption at every level combines with unspeakable treatment not only of criminals, but of those who dare to question Islamic orthodoxy as interpreted by a despot. Even as I write, wounded dissidents are chained to hospital beds awaiting their fate. Pakistan, too, is the heroin capital of the world. (A fact which is now reflected in the drug problems of English cities with Asian populations.)

It is perhaps not unreasonable that some people felt the article was expressing more than merely an alternative view on matters of education.

Honeyford wrote a second piece for the *Salisbury Review*, equally 'tolerant', 'reasonable' and 'civilised', but this one was noticed by someone in Bradford's education department, and then the trouble started – the protests, the boycott, the enormous publicity. A little research revealed that Honeyford's asides were a feature of most of his freelance journalism, his most noteworthy being his reference in the *Times Educational Supplement* to an Asian parent who visited him wanting to talk about his child's education: his accent, it seems, was 'like that of Peter Sellers's Indian doctor on an off day'.

The difficulty about the 'Honeyford Affair' was that it did not involve only Honeyford. His views are related to the much larger issue of what it is to be British, and what Britain should be in the future. And these views are, again, most clearly stated by the New Right, with which Honeyford closely identified himself. 'He is', Honeyford said of Roger Scruton, the high Tory editor of the *Salisbury Review*, 'the most brilliant man I have ever met.'

It would be easy to exaggerate the influence of the New Right. It would be equally easy to dismiss it. But it is worth bearing in mind that shortly after Honeyford was dismissed, he was invited to 10 Downing Street to help advise Margaret Thatcher on Tory education policy. Thatcher has also attended New Right 'think tanks', organised by the Conservative Philosophy Group. So too have Paul Johnson, Tom Stoppard, Hugh Trevor-Roper and Enoch Powell.

The essential tenet of the New Right is expressed in the editorial of the first issue of the *Salisbury Review*: 'the consciousness of nationhood is the highest form of political consciousness.' For Maurice Cowling, Scruton's tutor at Peterhouse in Cambridge, the consciousness of nationhood requires 'a unity of national sentiment'. Honeyford's less elegant phrase is the 'unity notion of culture'. The real sense underlying these rather abstract phrases is expressed in the view the New Right holds of people who are British but not white: as Ajeeb pointed out, Asians are acceptable as long as they behave like whites; if not, they should leave. This explains why anti-racism and multi-racial policies in education are, for the New Right, so inflammatory: they erode the 'consciousness of nationhood'. For Scruton, anti-racism is virtually treason. In 1985, he wrote that

> Those who are concerned about racism in Britain, that call British society 'racist', have no genuine attachment to British customs and institutions, or any genuine allegiance to the Crown.

The implications are fascinating to contemplate. John Casey is a Fellow of Caius College, Cambridge, and co-founded the Conservative Philosophy Group with Scruton. Four years ago, in a talk entitled 'One Nation – The Politics of Race', delivered to the same Conservative Philosophy Group attended by the Prime Minister, Casey proposed that the legal status of Britain's black community be altered retroactively, 'so that its members became guest workers . . . who would eventually, over a period of years, return to their countries of origin. The great majority of people', Casey added, dissociating himself from the argument, 'are actually or potentially hostile to the multi-racial society which all decent persons are supposed to accept.'

This 'great majority' excludes, I suppose, those who brought over the Afro-Caribbean and Asian workers – encouraged by the British government – to work in the mills, on the railways and in the hospitals. These are the same workers who, along with their children, are now part of the 'immigrant and immigrant-descended population' which, according to Casey, should be repatriated. It is strange how the meaning of the word 'immigrant' has changed. Americans, Australians, Italians, and Irish are not immigrants. It isn't Rupert Murdoch, Clive James or Kiri Te Kanawa who will be on their way: it is black people.

There is a word you hear in Bradford all the time, in pubs, shops, discos, schools and on the streets. The word is 'culture'. It is a word often used by the New Right, who frequently cite T. S. Eliot: that culture is a whole way of life, manifesting itself in the individual, in the group and in the society. It is everything we do and the particular way in which we do it. For Eliot culture 'includes all the characteristic activities of the people: Derby Day, Henley regatta, Cowes, the Twelfth of August, a cup final, the dog races, the pin-table, Wensleydale cheese, boiled cabbage cut into sections, beet-root in vinegar, nineteenth-century gothic churches and the music of Elgar'.

If one were compiling such a list today there would have to be numerous additions to the characteristic activities of the British people. They would include: yoga exercises, going to Indian restaurants, the music of Bob Marley, the novels of Salman Rushdie, Zen Buddhism, the Hare Krishna Temple, as well as the films of Sylvester Stallone, therapy, hamburgers, visits to gay bars, the dole office and the taking of drugs.

Merely by putting these two, rather arbitrary, lists side by side, it is possible to see the kinds of changes that have occurred in Britain since the end of the war. It is the first list, Eliot's list, that represents the New Right's vision of England. And for them unity can only be maintained by opposing those seen to be outside the culture. In an Oxbridge common-room, there is order, tradition, a settled way of doing things. Outside there is chaos: there are the barbarians and philistines.

Among all the talk of unity on the New Right, there is no sense of the vast differences in attitude, lifestyle and belief, or in class, race and sexual preference, that *already* exist in British society: the differences between those in work and those out of it; between those who have families and those who don't; and, importantly, between those who live in the North and those in the South. Sometimes, especially in the poor white areas of Bradford where there is so much squalor, poverty and manifest desperation, I could have been in another country. This was not anything like the south of England.

And of course from the New Right's talk of unity, we get no sense of the racism all black people face in Britain: the violence, abuse and discrimination in jobs, housing, policing and political life. In 1985 in Bradford there were 111 recorded incidents of racist attacks on Asians, and in the first three months of 1986 there were 79.

But how cold they are, these words: 'in the first three months of 1986 there were 79'. They describe an Asian man being slashed in a pub by a white gang. Or they describe a Friday evening last April when a taxi company known to employ Asian drivers received a 'block booking' for six cabs to collect passengers at the Jack and Jill Nightclub. Mohammed Saeed was the first to arrive. He remembers nothing from then on until he woke seven hours later in the intensive care ward of the hospital. This is because when he arrived, his windscreen and side window were smashed and he drove into a wall. And because he was then dragged from the car, kicked and beaten on the head with iron bars, and left on the pavement unconscious. He was left there because by then the second taxi had arrived, but Mohammed Suleiman, seeing what lay ahead, reversed his car at high speed – but not before the twenty or thirty whites rushing towards him had succeeded in smashing his windows with chair legs and bats. His radio call, warning the other drivers, was received too late by Javed Iqbal. 'I was', he told the *Guardian* later, 'bedridden for nearly a fortnight and I've still got double vision. I can't go out on my own.'

Wild Women, Wild Men

First published in *Granta 39*, Spring 1992

When I saw them waiting beside their car, I said, 'You must be freezing.' It was cold and foggy, the first night of winter, and the two women had matching short skirts and skimpy tops; their legs were bare.

'We wear what we like,' Zarina said.

Zarina was the elder of the pair, at twenty-four. For her this wasn't a job; it was an uprising, mutiny. She was the one with the talent for anarchy and unpredictability that made their show so wild. Qumar was nineteen and seemed more tired and wary. The work could disgust her. And unlike Zarina she did not enjoy the opportunity for mischief and disruption. Qumar had run away from home – her father was a barrister – and worked as a stripper on the Soho circuit, pretending to be Spanish. Zarina had worked as a kissogram. Neither had made much money until they identified themselves as Pakistani Muslims who stripped and did a lesbian double-act. They'd discovered a talent and an audience for it.

The atmosphere was febrile and overwrought. The two women's behaviour was a cross between a pop star's and a fugitive's; they were excited by the notoriety, the money and the danger of what they did. They'd been written up in the *Sport* and the *News of the World*. They wanted me and others to write about them. But everything could get out of hand. The danger was real. It gave their lives an edge, but of the two of them only Qumar knew they were doomed. They had excluded themselves from their community and been condemned. And they hadn't found a safe place among other men and women. Zarina's temperament wouldn't allow her to accept this, though she appeared to be the more nervous. Qumar just knew it would end badly but didn't know how to stop it, perhaps because Zarina didn't want it to stop. And Qumar was, I think, in love with Zarina.

We arrived – in Ealing. A frantic Asian man had been waiting in the drive of a house for two and a half hours. 'Follow my car,' he said. We did: Zarina started to panic.

'We're driving into Southall!' she said. Southall is the heart of southern England's Asian community, and the women had more enemies here than anywhere else. The Muslim butchers of Southall had threatened their lives and, according to Zarina, had recently murdered a Muslim prostitute by hacking her up and letting her bleed to death, halal style. There could be a butcher concealed in the crowd, Zarina said; and we didn't have any security. It was true: in one car there was the driver and me, and in another there was a female Indian journalist, with two slight Pakistani lads who could have been students.

We came to a row of suburban semi-detached houses with gardens: the street was silent, frozen. If only the neighbours knew. We were greeted by a buoyant middle-aged Muslim man with a round, smiling face. He was clearly anxious but relieved to see us, as he had helped to arrange the evening. It was he, presumably, who had extracted the £30 a head, from which he would pay the girls and take his own cut.

He shook our hands and then, when the front door closed behind us, he snatched at Qumar's arse, pulled her towards him and rubbed his crotch against her. She didn't resist or flinch but she did look away, as if wishing she were somewhere else, as if this wasn't her.

The house was not vulgar, only dingy and virtually bare, with white walls, grimy white plastic armchairs, a brown fraying carpet and a wall-mounted gas fire. The ground floor had been knocked into one long, narrow, over-lit room. This unelaborated space was where the women would perform. The upstairs rooms were rented to students.

The men, a third of them Sikh and the rest Muslim, had been waiting for hours and had been drinking. But the atmosphere was benign. No one seemed excited as they stood, many of them in suits and ties, eating chicken curry, black peas and rice from plastic plates. There was none of the aggression of the English lad.

Zarina was the first to dance. Her costume was green and gold, with bells strapped to her ankles; she had placed the big tape-player on the floor beside her. If it weren't for the speed of the music and her jerky, almost inelegant movements, we might have been witnessing a cultural event at the Commonwealth Institute. But Zarina was tense, haughty, unsmiling. She feared Southall. The men stood inches from her, leaning against the wall. They could touch her when they wanted to. And from the moment she began they reached out to pinch or stroke her. But they didn't know what Zarina might do in return.

At the end of the room stood a fifty-year-old six-foot Sikh, an ecstatic look on his face, swaying to the music, wiggling his hips at Zarina. Zarina, who was tiny but strong and fast, suddenly ran at the Sikh, threateningly, as if she were going to tackle him. She knocked into him, but he didn't fall, and she then appeared to be climbing up him. She wrestled off his tweed jacket and threw it down. He complied. He was enjoying this. He pulled off his shirt and she dropped to her knees, jerking down his trousers and pants. His stomach fell out of his clothes – suddenly, like a suitcase falling off the top of a wardrobe. The tiny button of his penis shrank. Zarina wrapped her legs around his waist and beat her hands on his shoulders. The Sikh danced, and the others clapped and cheered. Then he plucked off his turban and threw it into the air, a balding man with his few strands of hair drawn into a frizzy bun.

Zarina was then grabbed from behind. It was the mild, buoyant man who had greeted us at the door. He pulled his trousers off and stood in his blue and white spotted boxer shorts. He began to gyrate against Zarina.

And then she was gone, slipping away as if greased from the bottom of the scrum, out of the door and upstairs to Qumar. The music ended, and the big Sikh, still naked, was putting his turban back on. Another Sikh looked at him disapprovingly; a younger one laughed. The men fetched more drinks. They were pleased and exhilarated, as if they'd survived a fight. The door-greeter walked around in his shorts and shoes.

After a break, Zarina and Qumar returned for another set, this time in black bra and pants. The music was even faster. I noticed that the door-greeter was in a strange state. He had been relaxed, even a little glazed, but now, as the women danced, he was rigid with excitement, chattering to the man next to him, and then to himself, until finally his words became a kind of chant. 'We are hypocrite Muslims,' he was saying. 'We are hypocrite Muslims' – again and again, causing the man near him to move away.

Zarina's assault on the Sikh and on some of the other, more reluctant men had broken that line that separated spectator from performer. The men had come to see the women. They hadn't anticipated having their pants pulled around their ankles and their cocks revealed to other men. But it was Zarina's intention to round on the men, not turn them on – to humiliate and frighten them. This was part of the act.

The confirmed spectators were now grouped in the kitchen behind a table: the others joined in on the floor. Qumar and Zarina removed their tops. The young and friendly man who owned the house was sitting next to me, exultant. He thought I was the women's manager and he said in my ear: 'They are fantastic, this is out of this world! I have never seen anything like this before – what a beef! Get me two more girls for Wednesday and four for Saturday.' But things were getting out of hand. The centre of the room was starting to resemble a playground fight, a bundle, a children's party. The landlord, panicking, was attempting to separate the men and the two women. He told me to help.

An older man, another Sikh, the oldest man in the room, had been sitting in an armchair from which he reached out occasionally to nip Zarina's breasts. But now he was on the floor – I don't know how – and Zarina was on his head, Qumar was squatting on his stomach with her hand inside his trousers. It didn't seem like a game any more, and people were arguing. The landlord was saying to me, 'This man, he's a respectable man, he's the richest man, one of the best known in Southall, he's an old man . . .' Zarina and Qumar were stripping him. Other men, having lost their tempers, were attempting to drag the women away.

The old man was helped to his feet. He was breathing heavily, as if about to have a seizure. He was trying to stop himself from crying. His turban had been dislodged and chicken curry and rice had been smeared over him, which he was trying to brush off.

There was still the final part of the show. For this, the men sat cross-legged on the floor to watch the women pretend to have sex with each other. One man got down on his knees as if he were checking his car exhaust-pipe – and peered up Zarina's cunt. Beside me, the landlord was passing comment once more. Our Muslim girls don't usually shave themselves, he said. He disapproved of the neatly trimmed black strip of hair over Zarina's cunt.

The show lasted over two hours. 'It wasn't difficult,' Qumar said. They were exhausted. They would ache and be covered in bruises. They did two shows a week.

Finishing the Job

First published in *New Statesman & Society*, October 1988

It was time for an adventure; I'd been stifling indoors for three months, just writing, which can make you forget the world. I'd escape, go to Brighton where our governing party were having their annual conference. I wanted to see their faces. I'd get in amongst them. In four days perhaps a look, a word, anything, might help me steal a clue to what our leaders and their supporters were like. To learn that, I'd have to look them in the eye, smell them, be there. Anyhow, I was sick of seeing history on television. The camera was always aimed at the prepared centre of things: I inclined towards the edges, details, irrelevancies.

Friends said there should be a decompression chamber; the shock of arriving directly amongst them would jar. This seemed good advice. The decompressant would be the south London suburb of Bromley, where I was born and brought up. Bromley (once Macmillan's constituency) was quintessential Thatcherland. Perched between London and Kent, it was affluent, white, Jew-free, lower-middle-class England. If Margaret Thatcher had supporters this was where they lived and shopped.

Bromley had changed in the ten years since I'd fled to London. It was now a minor business centre: glass blocks, reflecting other glass blocks into oblivion, had been built around the High Street.

Walking past the houses of my childhood I noticed how, in an orgy of alteration they had been 'done up'. One house had a new porch; another double-glazing, 'Georgian' windows or a new door with brass fittings. Kitchens had been extended, lofts converted, walls excised, garages inserted.

This ersatz creativity is truly the English passion. Look into the centre of the suburban soul and you see double-glazing. It was DIY they loved in Thatcherland, not self-improvement or culture or food, but property, bigger and better homes complete with every mod-con – the concrete display of hard-earned cash. Display was the game.

On the day I went back, a Saturday, there were manic shoppers in Bromley High Street. It was like edging through the centre of a carnival; it was like Christmas with the same desperation, as the shops were raped. But I was struck by something. These frantic crowds on heat for 'nests' of tables, these consumers who camped for two days outside Debenhams before the Christmas sales – they hadn't voted for acid rain; they hadn't voted for the police to punish the miners, or for unemployment, or for the SAS, or for the police to enter the BBC and confiscate programmes; they hadn't voted for the closing down of hospitals. It was simpler than that. Thatcher, rising out of the ashes of the late 1970s unemployment and insecurity, had done this for the suburbs: she'd given them money and she'd freed them from the nightmare of a collective life they'd never wanted. She'd freed them for Do It Yourself.

In Brighton, up around the railway station where the Regency façade doesn't extend, there were pubs barely altered since the 1930s. There were Christmas lights around the windows and kids with pink hair, sleeveless leather jackets and grown-out mohicans lying in fat ripped armchairs. In the afternoons the pubs, full of the unemployed, were like leisure centres.

Further down, as I walked towards the front, my first sight was of a police helicopter hovering over the beach, lifting what looked like a tin workman's hut on to the concrete bunker of the conference centre itself. Nearby, an old man with horn-rimmed glasses was holding up a cardboard sign advertising Esperanto. Looking closer at this odd figure I realised he had been my maths teacher in Bromley. He gave me a leaflet which included a number of exercises to translate into Esperanto. ('Use ballpen, write clearly,' it instructed. Translate 'the men sold cakes' and 'the teacher sees a boy' and then 'send this completed sheet with SAE for free correction'.)

There were police every ten yards and everyone staying in a hotel was interviewed by the police. Even the pier was patrolled; speedboats roared through the water; out to sea a Royal Navy minesweeper circled. Obviously the Tories didn't want a bunch of Irishmen blowing them out of their beds again; but there was also a strong element of militaristic exhibitionism in all the security. Nevertheless the pier was flourishing. There were two Victorian-style restaurants with furniture in pastel shades and waitresses in Victorian costume. (As it happens, the pier is owned by the Labour council; the other pier, privately owned, is disintegrating in the sea like a drowning chandelier.)

On Tuesday morning I entered the conference hall. It smelled of woodshaving and paint. The organist was playing 'An English Country Garden'. At the rear of the platform was a light blue wall which resembled an early 1960s BBC test card, consisting of three panels with three eyes in them: the centre eye had embossed on it 'Leading Britain into the 1990s'. Squarely in the centre of the other two eyes were video screens on which were projected the speakers' faces and 'visual aids': if there was talk of a butter mountain then we would see a cartoon of a mountain made out of butter. At the end of the platform was a Union Jack.

The press sat at six long tables below the edge of the platform along which were yards of fresh flowers. The photographers clustered around the journalists, their cameras on adjustable poles, with lenses as long and thick as marrows.

When I looked up I suddenly saw Thatcher in the flesh for the first time. She was ten yards away in a black two-piece with a wide white collar and white earrings. She looked softer than in her photographs. I could see that her throat and neck had gone; below the golden swept-back hair and mask of make-up she was loose, baggy and wrinkled.

I had spoken to Neil Kinnock on a few occasions and he said to me once that seeing Thatcher at the opening of Parliament last year she'd seemed worn out, withered, a shell. But today neither she nor her government seemed desiccated. Recently I'd been to a party attended by many of the Kinnock camp. They were not happy. It was Kinnock who had not grown in stature with the job; he was too strong to resign, too weak to win, they said; he also knew this. And there was a depressing thing I heard them say again and again about him: he couldn't cope on television. They would be glad when he resigned after losing the next election. So there was no talk of policy now, just of television; and Thatcher appeared odious on television. Later, I spoke to one of Thatcher's speechwriters, who said she was not exhausted in the least. Most leaders, he said, took power when they were old and tired. But Thatcher was only fifty-four when she took power in 1979.

There were hymns. The journalists, who had already attended three party conferences this year, were like irritable teenagers, and gazed boredly out at the sanitary, dead hall, only half full. There were a few old women in hats; there were many young people – some young men were without ties, in white T-shirts. The Tories were definitely becoming less patrician, more a mass party of the working class. The journalist next to me was reading a paperback which had a blurb saying: 'David Profit is a coke dealer with a dream.' Another young journalist in a smart suit and yellow socks giggled to himself as he scribbled. I went through the conference motions printed in the handbook. Most of them began with: 'This conference congratulates the Chancellor of the Exchequer.' One motion, from Liverpool, stated that 'The BBC does not always give fair and balanced views when reporting on Israel and South African affairs.'

Staring at Thatcher and considering her unexhausted and un-English sense of mission, I began to think of something which couldn't possibly be said of any other successful British politician. It was that in some aspects of herself Thatcher embodied some of Nietzsche's ideas. I mean the scorn for weakness, the basic belief in inequality and the passion for overcoming. Nietzsche, who hated free thinkers, humanitarians and socialism (which he saw as an ill-applied Christian ideal), also dismissed compassion: it sapped vitality and led to feebleness, dependency and decadence. Compassionate ones opposed the natural and impetuous urges of those sovereign ones, those 'supermen' who lived great lives beyond the begging fingers of mediocrities and failures.

So yes, as expected, there was complacency, indifference, triumphalism in the faces I examined as they sang 'King of glory, king of peace, I will love thee'. But they were not a party rotten with the assumptions of power, slow, bored, eager to dispense a little late and guilty generosity. No, because Thatcher is a revolutionary in a democracy; and she is tireless and will not rest until England, Britain even, is made in her image. In that sense she has a totalitarian aspect. I'd often wondered why, after nearly ten years in power, and with negligible opposition and a cooperative media, the Conservatives were still so angry. It was, I could see now, looking at Thatcher, that there was not a scrap of liberalism in her; everything had to be as she wanted it; the job had to be finished.

At last the Mayor of Brighton, Patricia Hawkes, started to speak. There were banalities. Thatcher stared at her, blinking at a tremendous rate, as if Hawkes had started to read from the Kama Sutra. Later I realised Thatcher wasn't listening at all; this was her serious and concentrating look. But Patricia Hawkes, a Labour mayor, had good courage. It was the sentence 'power must bring responsibility and compassion' that first had eyes opening and then widening in the hall of the Worker's Party. Hawkes hit her stride as the audience listened carefully. 'Think not just of those with wealth, but those living in bedsitting squalor, those waiting and hoping for a job, and our pensioners living close to the margin.' Now they knew they'd been slapped in the face, squirted in the eye, in the opening minutes of their rally, their celebration of power. They jeered and brayed, they slow-handclapped and yelled and their anger was genuine. The giggling journalist beside me was ecstatic; he said it would be the only dissent all week, apart from when they'd abuse the Home Secretary, Douglas Hurd. That did indeed seem likely: Hurd's combination of brains, breeding and a refusal to vote for the reintroduction of hanging would not stimulate the dull palate of the Worker's Party.

That evening I went off eagerly to my first fringe meeting, to be addressed by John Biffen. The room, which had a plaque on the wall saying 'Paganini played here, 9 December 1831', was full of men in dark woollen suits. Biffen, a mild-looking man, a doctor perhaps, disappointed the audience with his good sense. People attending the conference craved phrases to applaud or jeer; they wanted a Tom Jones concert, not a reading of 'Dover Beach'. Later in the week I'd come and hear Enoch Powell in this room. Perhaps the temperature would rise then. Perhaps Wolverhampton's clearest thinker would earn a plaque on the wall, too.

Biffen said that Kinnock reminded him of Gaitskell, heaving the Labour Party towards the centre of British politics. The left of the party would soon be irrelevant. The fact that Benn, Livingstone and Heffer opposed Kinnock was good publicity for him, this is how he would prove himself. What a shame, Biffen added, that the press caricatured the Labour Party, making it difficult for interested people to see it clearly. Biffen then warned the audience: 'We are a party which favours the up and running. But we do not want to be seen as the party which made a country fit for yuppies.' People started to leave. He went on: 'We have to be a thinking party. Where are we weak? The NHS is underfunded.' Finally, after saying the Poll Tax wasn't worth it in terms of social division, he talked of the Soviet Union, saying that in an altered politics of Europe, Russia would cease to be a global power and become more of a European one.

Next morning I went back to the conference hall. Outside were a middle-aged couple with a banner saying 'Our children were murdered – bring back capital punishment'. To my pleasure, Cecil Parkinson was speaking. Clearly the Empress of Albion's favourite son, when he performed the audience was enthusiastic, swooning with forgiveness. As Parkinson spoke I parked myself quickly in a spare seat beneath him and started to read, in this choice position, Sara Keays's book concerning their . . . relationship. I almost wrote 'affair'; but it lasted twelve years, as she repeats and repeats. The Empress had wanted to appoint him Foreign Secretary before the story broke; maybe he would become Chancellor even now.

As – above me – Parkinson announced the privatisation of coal, I was reading of how he and his cronies, in the struggle to survive, had publicly smeared Keays. Jeffrey Archer (who once asked a friend of mine if he thought he, Archer, would win the Nobel Prize for Literature), was then Deputy Chairman of the party. He said of the anguished book, which Keays published herself: 'Not one of the twenty-seven major publishing houses in Britain wanted to touch it.'

In 1983 Norman Tebbit accused Keays of reneging on an undertaking that she wouldn't publicly talk about Parkinson. In 1988 Tebbit and his ghostwriter Michael Trend, busying themselves in the highest form of self-reflection, autobiography, and learning quite quickly, I am sure, that collectively they lacked the essential gift of reflection, repeated this claim (in my uninterfered-with version), about an undertaking which was never made.

I read of how in 1981 Parkinson failed to tell the police where his car was parked when it was broken into outside his lover's house. He also ensured that Keays, who'd been selected to stand as a candidate in Bermondsey, was stymied by him in her efforts to become an MP. Another time Parkinson rang Keays and accused her of trying to blackmail him into marrying her; he generally abused her. His wife was listening on the other line.

I wondered, as Parkinson pledged his commitment to nuclear energy, if any of this still mattered. Part of the failure of the Labour Party is its inability to mislead, to lie, practise treachery and be generally guileful. For a reason I cannot fathom, it appears to believe in honesty and plain speaking, democracy and fairness. But integral to the Tories' vision of Britain, articulated by Peregrine Worsthorne later in this revealing week, was that a future ruling élite would dutifully have to be an example to the lower orders. The price of omnipotence would be purity.

It was becoming apparent that the Conservatives resented what they saw as Labour's exclusive grip on the moral life. It wasn't enough to have seemed to have generated wealth, the Empress wanted to be seen to be good; she wanted to be liked now, loved even. I could see an ethical edifice being constructed, but it would be difficult for the Empress to pull it off: the only thing I never saw beneath the golden hair, as I sat looking at her blinking away hour after hour, was the slightest hint or possibility of that vagrant quality – love.

After Parkinson I left the hall and walked along the front. I would take in something less taxing this lunchtime, something that might turn out to be a little weird. I chose the Union of Muslim Organisations.

In the meeting room, which was virtually empty, I sat next to an Indian who once owned five restaurants in Brighton, though he only had one now. His complaint was that the immigration laws made it impossible for him to get staff. He wouldn't recruit British Asians, they were useless, the hours didn't suit them; grateful, freshly arrived Bangladeshis were just the job. He was very worried for the future of the corner shop, he whispered, as the meeting started.

Douglas Hurd had failed to turn up, but he'd sent two men from the Home Office to represent him. Like many other Tory men they had pink faces, white shirts with pink stripes, and fat bellies. Here amongst mostly Asians, they were on their best behaviour, especially as the Imam of the local mosque, in white cap and beard, started to recite from the Koran. Another Englishman was carrying a piece of quiche on a plate; as the Imam chanted the verses the Englishman stood stock still like a living sculpture in the centre of the room.

Then Dr Pasha, the chairman, told the room that he and other Muslims considered themselves proudly British, that this was the noble mother country they looked up to, that being a Muslim didn't conflict with being British. He set it up nicely; the men from the Home Office were listening happily. Then he came to the point. As Muslims were the second largest religious denomination in Britain the British government could surely give them more recognition. This applied especially to the law of blasphemy which should be invoked on their behalf. He'd written to the Home Secretary – at this Dr Pasha turned forcefully to the two Britishers – insisting that the film *The Blood of Hussein* be banned, and more importantly Salman Rushdie's novel *The Satanic Verses*, which was an attack on Islam, on the prophet himself! Why are those people fomenting hatred against us? cried Dr Pasha, his eyes burning into the pink faces of the men from the Home Office. Surely a religious attack on us is an attack on our beloved Home Secretary himself! Why are they not prosecuted for racism? The men from the Home Office lowered their eyes.

So the conference was warming up: certainly in the conference hall the speeches were emollient and predictable; the uninhibited face of Toryism was presented at the fringe meetings, I'd been told. But it had been restrained there too, so far. Until, after this hors d'oeuvre, I went to see Teresa Gorman speak.

The speakers at this meeting were in a fortunate position. After nine and a half years of Conservative rule there were few genuine enemies in power to rail against. The fortunate ones, those who could speak from experience, were those Conservatives actually in opposition – local politicians in Labour-controlled boroughs. There was, therefore, an excited sense of anticipation in this meeting: we would hear about life in the Red Republics, perhaps a microcosm of life under a Labour government.

It started off mildly enough, with a councillor speaking of young minds being inundated by left-wing propaganda. Gay literature was being smuggled into children's homes. There were gays-only swimming lessons, he said; there were creatures of indeterminate sex running the town halls. The room grumbled its disapproval. Not only that, there were illegal encampments of gypsies all over Haringey who were being given support by Catholic nuns. As a result, gangs of youths were defecating in pensioners' living rooms.

This talk of Red Faeces provoked howls and yelps of disgust; wild clapping followed. A man sitting in front of me, in a filthy suit which appeared to be entirely composed of stains, removed what seemed to be a snotty gumshield from his mouth and started to eat his tie. Two delicate Indian women came in and sat down next to me.

Soon there was talk of 'racist black shits who'd impregnated hundreds of white women'. Meanwhile garbage was piling up in the streets.

'No, no, no!' yelled the Worker's Party.

But the room soon hushed for Teresa Gorman. When she spoke she insisted that cuts in local services which led to garbage piling up in the streets were not to be worried about: 'We have a new way of looking at things. Until we get power we must try and enjoy the awfulness of socialism. We should encourage it! Wasn't there a Chinese philosopher who said that when being raped you should lie back and enjoy it?'

The racism of the meeting surprised me. After all, there were scores of Asian families who shared Conservative values. Surely the Tories didn't want to alienate blacks and Asians when potentially they could be a source of support? I'd thought that the hatred of homosexuals had, in general, supplanted blacks and Asians in Conservative demonology. Hadn't Nigel Lawson said that being gay was 'unfortunate'? I would find out. As I sat through this meeting I noticed that the next day there'd be a meeting of the Conservative Group for Homosexual Equality. I'd go to that.

This meeting, which was in a hotel, was hard to find and when I turned up, the name of the meeting wasn't printed on the notice board: coyly, there was only the initials CGHE. I went down some stairs, trudged through several corridors – under the whole damp hotel it seemed (perhaps this was the Channel Tunnel) – and emerged in a room full of chairs. The one man there, who wore glasses thick as welder's goggles and had a hare-lip, was hunched in a corner and jumped in surprise as I came in. He handed me a magazine called *Open Mind*. I wondered if this was perhaps the party's only out gay, which wouldn't have surprised me: Tory MP Geoffrey Dickens wanted to recriminalise sexual relations between adult men; and Rhodes Boyson has remarked that the promotion of positive images of gays could be 'the end of creation'.

In one article in the magazine, by 'Westminster Watcher', the writer commends the party: 'Although some queer-bashing Conservative journalists behaved very badly during the last election, the party at the national level appealed to prejudice with only one poster and a few remarks: at the constituency level the record was worse.' The paper's editorial also refers to this homophobic election poster and remarks wistfully that it was designed by the Jewish brothers Saatchi and Saatchi who should know better than to persecute people. Elsewhere in the paper, the writers urge heterosexuals not to be afraid of the end-of-creationists: 'Homosexuals are as much concerned as heterosexuals with maintaining institutions which contribute to the health and stability of society.'

Eventually a handful of men arrived; but they wouldn't sit down, and waited at the back. It was quiet in the room; no one looked at anyone else.

The speaker told us that the Labour Party tried to exploit gays, that all local government gay centres and organisations should be privatised and that Section 28 was unlikely to do any damage to sensible activities.

The Worker's Party was hugging its prejudices to itself; through them it defined itself; this was obviously not the time to expect it to relinquish them.

Later that night I was in a restaurant, at a table with various right-wing journalists and an MP. I started to talk to the MP about Enoch Powell, who I'd seen speak earlier in the day. Powell's was the most crowded and exuberant meeting I'd been to in Brighton, and Powell had been introduced, by a one-eyed speaker, as a man proved consistently right, a man who was not only a statesman but a Prophet. The straight-backed Prophet said, in his spine-chilling and monotonous voice, that he had never left the Conservative Party, it had left him. And now, he said, to cheers and whistles, it appeared to be approaching him again.

Now, at dinner, the MP told me that the Prophet was his hero. Since the late 1950s the Prophet had supported the free market in all things (except immigration) and had even been denounced by

Mosley's Union Movement in 1968 for stealing its ideas. The MP was proud to be a racist. The woman sitting opposite the MP intervened. 'By the way, I'm Jewish,' she said. 'Ah,' he said. 'Well, then, as a Jewess you should acknowledge that there are many races and your race is different to mine. The English are a provincial people uninterested in culture. And you Jews are a metropolitan people obsessed with it.'

Speaking of his admiration for the Prophet, the MP said that Powell was the living originator of Thatcherism, pre-dating Keith Joseph in his ideas and unlike Joseph able to bypass Parliament and communicate directly with the working class. The Prophet's time had come, but through Thatcher, who was a better politician.

This was interesting because the Prophet had this reconnection in common with another man frequently considered to have slipped beyond the boundaries of sanity: Peregrine Worsthorne, who would be speaking the next evening. However, for the remainder of this evening there would be the *Spectator* party. Perhaps it would be less ideologically taxing; perhaps there would be some ordinary people there.

But I didn't locate them. As soon as I arrived a young Tory, looking like an estate agent, hurried over to me, adrenalin high, and said: 'You don't look like a typical mindless right-wing idiot. What are you doing here?'

'Snooping around.'

'What for?'

I searched for a reply.

I said: 'I want to know what is going to energise this party. What it is they're going to offer the electorate at the next couple of elections.'

'Oh that's easy. We're going to privatise everything. That's obvious. The Health Service will go eventually. That'll take a long time.'

'What else?'

'There's the environment. But Tories don't really give a shit about that. The important thing is the moral mission. Authority, deference, respect, that's what we want.'

What I saw in his face, and in the faces of his young friends who had also gathered around me to help explain the future, was power, arrogance, supreme confidence. None of them doubted for a moment that their party would win the next election. They could do whatever they wanted, and with the compliant media they now had, nothing could frustrate them. Why should the slightest scepticism, doubt, or lack of nerve affect them? Labour might huff and puff over the intricacies of its defence policy but it was all irrelevant; the Left handed Britain over to Thatcher long ago and, that night, it seemed unlikely they would win it back for a long time.

I left the drinks party thinking I'd never see that particular Tory ever again. But the next day, before I was to go and hear Peregrine Worsthorne perform at a fringe meeting and talk about authority, discipline and its relation to the servant problem, I did see the Tory again, much to my surprise.

There was a demonstration across the road from the conference centre, a place now referred to as the Island, or the Island of the Mighty. About a thousand people, most of them young, had gathered; in their tight jeans and knitted sweaters and DMs, most of them, boys and girls alike, with long hair, they chanted and waved a variety of banners for 'Troops Out' and 'Stop Animal Experiments'. In the crowd I noticed an older man with a hand-painted sign, carefully done: on it he'd painted two words, one beneath the other: She Lies. As I was looking at the demonstration I glanced across the road and there he was, the Tory with the soul and suit of an estate agent.

He was leaning as far as he could over the crash barrier outside the hall, looking towards the demonstration. And he had extracted his wallet from his inside pocket; he was waving it at the kids, who were virtually his contemporaries, waving and screaming. Around him, other Tories, bored with the conference, too, or emerging from a debate, quickly returned to the hall to collect Union Jacks which, in a mass, they fluttered and poked at the kids.

As the demonstration dispersed, I noticed an old couple with a banner saying 'Justice for Pensioners'. As a group of Tories walked past them, one of the group, no spring chicken himself, chucked a handful of change at the pensioner's feet.

For Worsthorne the hall was full. Tonight it was an upmarket crowd, with Lord Weidenfeld, Paul Johnson and the editor of the *Spectator* in the audience. The tone of the evening was exultancy in the fact that Worsthorne, unlike most of the cabinet, had the guts to articulate those things which others would only admit in whispers. Earlier there had been, for example, Lawson's 'I am in favour of wealth being passed from generation to generation,' and Baker's talk of the 'civilising mission' and 'discipline'. But nothing like this, nothing so plain, so gloriously reactionary.

Worsthorne's argument was that England's egalitarian age had now, thank God, finally passed. The moment of its passing was the crushing of the miners' strike – a historic victory for the Tories. Britain would be, once more, a country in which wealth – property – would be inherited. This passing of new wealth to children would no longer be a privilege entirely of the very rich. Many of those who passed on this wealth would be yuppies; they would be vulgar, which was not surprising in the age of the common man where there were no established criteria for behaviour. In a few generations these people would gain noble values. But with the restoration of strict hierarchy the ruling class would once more exercise a civilising influence on the lower orders. Others would want to imitate them in manners, speech, education. The freshly re-established and confident ruling class would be the custodians of values and institutions.

The woman in front of me was trembling with excitement at this. 'He's right, he's right!' she repeated. 'Bring back snobbery!'

After he finished his lecture and responded to questions, Worsthorne talked of the importance of the middle class having servants. Not 'helps' which were usually other middle-class people – the middle class merely educating each other – but lower-class people who would be cooks, gardeners, butlers, and would find working in great houses a civilising influence.

That night, as I strolled through Brighton and saw the kids skateboarding in the deserted shopping centre – most of Brighton seemed deserted for the conference, as people had gone away to avoid it – I thought of them polishing pepperpots in the houses of the cabinet, some of whose children were heroin addicts. But I didn't want to think about any of this. Drinking now, I collapsed in one of the older hotels and watched Tories meeting in the bar before they went off to Thatcher's birthday party.

One woman wore a light blue sparkling mohair jumper; a man in evening dress wore trousers far too short and scruffy day shoes; another woman wore a turquoise sequined dress with a great Marks and Spencer overcoat on top. The young people wore cheap clothes and had cheap haircuts; they were brittle and gauche. I could see that for people like Worsthorne a Tory meritocracy wasn't enough. You didn't want the overthrow of egalitarianism, a new economic dynamic, the primacy of the market, the entire Thatcher miracle itself merely giving birth to a reinvigorated ruling class composed of Norman Tebbits, the kind of people who took out their wallets in public and thought Burke was a term of abuse. No; the Tory Party had barely started on its road to reestablishing former inequalities. Money wasn't enough; next would come a confident, rich establishment with power and influence and even better – authority, served by a respectful working class. At least in the hysterical, forced, undiluted atmosphere at the party conference that was the idea.

Tonight, how would I celebrate Thatcher's birthday? I hadn't been invited to the ball; I'd go to the Zap Club instead, which promised Frenzee and pure wild Acid House.

I walked past the crowds of police towards the beach. At random, cars were being stopped and searched. Brighton's Zap Club was apparently well known in London. The kids would go to Brighton on the last train and return home early in the morning on the milk train. The club was on the edge of the beach, in two tunnels bored under the road, neither of them much bigger than railway carriages. In the entrance was a small shop selling badges, T-shirts, paper fans. Further in, under fluorescent lighting, the people dancing wore white, some of the men with red scarves over their heads. Other men had long curly hair, which looked permed, and they wore vividly patterned shorts like American tourists. (In fact the whole style originated in Ibiza and other Spanish holiday resorts where you dress lightly and brightly.)

The long passages inside the tunnels were painted like terracotta Egyptian friezes, on the floor were stencilled emblems from the 1960s – the word 'love' was prominent.

The dancers were young, around sixteen or seventeen, and not one of them would have seen the Pink Fairies at the Roundhouse in 1968 from where their light-show had been lifted. As I leaned against a wall drinking, it seemed that this was more of a parody of the 1960s than a real impulse connected with rebellion. The 1960s and its liberations were blown to bits but its fripperies had re-emerged as style, as mere dressing-up. Nonetheless, few of the kids looked as if they'd willingly endure a spell in Peregrine Worsthorne's house listening to him discuss the hideous spectacle of people sprawling on the Northern Line with their legs apart.

The next day Thatcher's fans took their seats early for the Empress's big speech. They had their Thatcher mugs, spoons, thimbles, tea cosies and photographs in their laps. I'd been in and out of the hall all week but most of the audience had been there all along, listening to speeches for about thirty hours. Now the front bank of seats was occupied ninety minutes before Thatcher was due to start. The blue flags, the Union Jacks were unfurled; some people held up Thatcher/Bush posters. There was jigging and dancing in the aisles. 'Jerusalem' was sung. I must have heard the phrase 'England's green and pleasant land' at least three times a day in the past week.

The cabinet marched on to the platform. Thatcher was introduced. A curtain moved; she and Denis came on; the crystal voice of the Empress began. She recited her speechwriter's jokes without smiling, as if she were reading from the *Critique of Pure Reason*. There was some Dickens, everyone belonged to them now: 'Fog, fog everywhere.' I'd heard that America's finest speechwriter had been flown in to assist. The Empress's speeches were cobbled together like American films, by four or five people. There was much baby-language. 'All elections matter. But some matter more than others.' 'We are all too young to put our feet up.' 'Yes, our children can travel to see the treasures and wonders of the world.'

None of it mattered to the fans. It was the old familiar songs they liked best. They chanted: 'Ten more years.'

On the way out I heard one woman lamenting to another: 'I wish there'd been balloons. Next year they'll have balloons because I'm going to write to them about it. Thousands of balloons, falling all over us.'

Eight Arms to Hold You

First published in *Dreaming and Scheming*, 2002

One day at school – an all-boys comprehensive on the border between London and Kent – our music teacher told us that John Lennon and Paul McCartney didn't actually write those famous Beatles songs we loved so much.

It was 1968 and I was thirteen. For the first time in music appreciation class we were to listen to the Beatles – 'She's Leaving Home', with the bass turned off. The previous week, after some Brahms, we'd been allowed to hear a Frank Zappa record, again bassless. For Mr Hogg, our music and religious instruction teacher, the bass guitar 'obscured' the music. But hearing anything by the Beatles at school was uplifting, an act so unusually liberal it was confusing.

Mr Hogg prised open the lid of the school 'stereophonic equipment', which was kept in a big, dark wooden box and wheeled around the premises by the much-abused war-wounded caretaker. Hogg put on 'She's Leaving Home' without introduction, but as soon as it began he started his Beatles analysis.

What he said was devastating, though it was put simply, as if he were stating the obvious. These were the facts: Lennon and McCartney could not possibly have written the songs ascribed to them; it was a con – we should not be taken in by the 'Beatles', they were only front-men.

Those of us who weren't irritated by his prattling through the tune were giggling. Certainly, for a change, most of us were listening to teacher. I was perplexed. Why would anyone want to think anything so ludicrous? What was really behind this idea?

'Who did write the Beatles' songs, then, sir?' someone asked bravely. And Paul McCartney sang:

We struggled hard all our lives to get by,
She's leaving home after living alone,
For so many years.

Mr Hogg told us that Brian Epstein and George Martin wrote the Lennon/McCartney songs. The Fabs only played on the records – if they did anything at all. (Hogg doubted whether their hands had actually touched the instruments.) 'Real musicians were playing on those records,' he said. Then he put the record back in its famous sleeve and changed the subject.

But I worried about Hogg's theory for days; on several occasions I was tempted to buttonhole him in the corridor and discuss it further. The more I dwelt on it alone, the more it revealed. The Mopheads couldn't even read music – how could they be geniuses?

It was unbearable to Mr Hogg that four young men without significant education could be the bearers of such talent and critical acclaim. But then Hogg had a somewhat holy attitude to culture. 'He's cultured,' he'd say of someone, the antonym of 'He's common.' Culture, even popular culture – folk-singing, for instance – was something you put on a special face for, after years of wearisome study. Culture involved a particular twitching of the nose, a faraway look (into the sublime), and a fruity pursing of the lips. Hogg knew. There was, too, a sartorial vocabulary of knowingness, with leather patches sewn on to the elbows of shiny, rancid jackets.

Obviously this was not something the Beatles had been born into. Nor had they acquired it in any recognised academy or university. No, in their early twenties, the Fabs made culture again and again, seemingly without effort, even as they mugged and winked at the cameras like schoolboys.

Sitting in my bedroom listening to the Beatles on a Grundig reel-to-reel tape-recorder, I began to see that to admit to the Beatles' genius would devastate Hogg. It would take too much else away with it. The songs that were so perfect and about recognisable common feelings – 'She Loves You', 'Please, Please Me', 'I

Wanna Hold Your Hand' – were all written by Brian Epstein and George Martin because the Beatles were only boys like us: ignorant, bad-mannered and rude; boys who'd never, in a just world, do anything interesting with their lives. This implicit belief, or form of contempt, was not abstract. We felt and sometimes recognised – and Hogg's attitude towards the Beatles exemplified this – that our teachers had no respect for us as people capable of learning, of finding the world compelling and wanting to know it.

The Beatles would also be difficult for Hogg to swallow because for him there was a hierarchy among the arts. At the top were stationed classical music and poetry, beside the literary novel and great painting. In the middle would be not-so-good examples of these forms. At the bottom of the list, and scarcely considered art forms at all, were films ('the pictures'), television and, finally, the most derided – pop music.

But in that post-modern dawn – the late 1960s – I like to think that Hogg was starting to experience cultural vertigo – which was why he worried about the Beatles in the first place. He thought he knew what culture was, what counted in history, what had weight, and what you needed to know to be educated. These things were not relative, not a question of taste or decision. Notions of objectivity did exist; there were criteria and Hogg knew what the criteria were. Or at least he thought he did. But that particular form of certainty, of intellectual authority, along with many other forms of authority, was shifting. People didn't know where they were any more.

Not that you could ignore the Beatles even if you wanted to. Those rockers in suits were unique in English popular music, bigger than anyone had been before. What a pleasure it was to swing past Buckingham Palace in the bus knowing the Queen was indoors, in her slippers, watching her favourite film, *Yellow Submarine*, and humming along to 'Eleanor Rigby'. ('All the lonely people . . .')

The Beatles couldn't be as easily dismissed as the Rolling Stones, who often seemed like an ersatz American group, especially when

Mick Jagger started to sing with an American accent. But the Beatles' music was supernaturally beautiful and it was English music. In it you could hear cheeky music-hall songs and send-ups, pub ballads and, more importantly, hymns. The Fabs had the voices and looks of choirboys, and their talent was so broad they could do anything – love songs, comic songs, kids' songs and sing-alongs for football crowds (at White Hart Lane, Tottenham Hotspur's ground, we sang: 'Here, there and every-fucking-where, Jimmy Greaves, Jimmy Greaves'). They could do rock 'n' roll too, though they tended to parody it, having mastered it early on.

One lunchtime in the school library, not long after the incident with Hogg, I came across a copy of *Life* magazine which included hefty extracts from Hunter Davies's biography of the Beatles, the first major book about them and their childhood. It was soon stolen from the library and passed around the school, a contemporary 'Lives of the Saints'. (On the curriculum we were required to read Gerald Durrell and C. S. Forester, but we had our own books, which we discussed, just as we exchanged and discussed records. We liked *Candy*, *Lord of the Flies*, James Bond, Mervyn Peake, and *Sex Manners for Men*, among other things.)

Finally my parents bought the biography for my birthday. It was the first hardback I possessed and, pretending to be sick, I took the day off school to read it, with long breaks between chapters to prolong the pleasure. But *The Beatles* didn't satisfy me as I'd imagined it would. It wasn't like listening to *Revolver*, for instance, after which you felt satisfied and uplifted. The book disturbed and intoxicated me; it made me feel restless and dissatisfied with my life. After reading about the Beatles' achievements I began to think I didn't expect enough of myself, that none of us at school did really. In two years we'd start work; soon after that we'd get married and buy a small house nearby. The form of life was decided before it was properly begun.

To my surprise it turned out that the Fabs were lower-middle-class provincial boys; neither rich nor poor, their music didn't come out of hardship and nor were they culturally privileged. Lennon was rough, but it wasn't poverty that made him hard-edged. The Liverpool Institute, attended by Paul and George, was a good grammar school. McCartney's father had been well enough off for Paul and his brother Michael to have piano lessons. Later, his father bought him a guitar.

We had no life guides or role models among politicians, military types or religious figures, or even film stars for that matter, as our parents did. Footballers and pop stars were the revered figures of my generation and the Beatles, more than anyone, were exemplary for countless young people. If coming from the wrong class restricts your sense of what you can be, then none of us thought we'd become doctors, lawyers, scientists, politicians. We were scheduled to be clerks, civil servants, insurance managers and travel agents.

Not that leading some kind of creative life was entirely impossible. In the mid-1960s the media was starting to grow. There was a demand for designers, graphic artists and the like. In our art lessons we designed toothpaste boxes and record sleeves to prepare for the possibility of going to art school. Now, these were very highly regarded among the kids; they were known to be anarchic places, the sources of British pop art, numerous pop groups and the generators of such luminaries as Pete Townshend, Keith Richards, Ray Davies and John Lennon. Along with the Royal Court and the drama corridor of the BBC, the art schools were the most important post-war British cultural institution, and some lucky kids escaped into them. Once, I ran away from school to spend the day at the local art college. In the corridors where they sat cross-legged on the floor, the kids had dishevelled hair and paint-splattered clothes. A band was rehearsing in the dining hall. They liked being there so much they stayed till midnight. Round the back entrance there were condoms in the grass.

But these kids were destined to be commercial artists, which was, at least, 'proper work'. Commercial art was OK but anything that veered too closely towards pure art caused embarrassment; it was pretentious. Even education fell into this trap. When, later, I went to college, our neighbours would turn in their furry slippers and housecoats to stare and tut-tut to each other as I walked down the street in my Army Surplus greatcoat, carrying a pile of library books. I like to think it was the books rather than the coat they were objecting to – the idea that they were financing my uselessness through their taxes. Surely nurturing my brain could be of no possible benefit to the world; it would only render me more argumentative – create an intelligentsia and you're only producing criticism for the future.

(For some reason I've been long under the impression that this hatred for education is a specifically English tendency. I've never imagined the Scots, Irish or Welsh, and certainly no immigrant group, hating the idea of elevation through the mind in quite the same way. Anyhow, it would be a couple of decades before the combined neighbours of south-east England could take their revenge on education via their collective embodiment – Thatcher.)

I could, then, at least have been training to be an apprentice. But, unfortunately for the neighbours, we had seen *A Hard Day's Night* at Bromley Odeon. Along with our mothers, we screamed all through it, fingers stuck in our ears. And afterwards we didn't know what to do with ourselves, where to go, how to exorcise this passion the Beatles had stoked up. The ordinary wasn't enough; we couldn't accept only the everyday now! We desired ecstasy, the extraordinary, magnificence – today!

For most, this pleasure lasted only a few hours and then faded. But for others it opened a door to the sort of life that might, one day, be lived. And so the Beatles came to represent opportunity and possibility. They were careers officers, a myth for us to live by, a light for us to follow.

How could this be? How was it that of all the groups to emerge from that great pop period the Beatles were the most dangerous, the most threatening, the most subversive? Until they met Dylan and, later, dropped acid, the Beatles wore matching suits and wrote harmless love songs offering little ambiguity and no call to rebellion. They lacked Elvis's sexuality, Dylan's introspection and Jagger's surly danger. And yet . . . and yet – this is the thing – everything about the Beatles represented pleasure, and for the provincial and suburban young pleasure was only the outcome and justification of work. Pleasure was work's reward and it occurred only at weekends and after work.

But when you looked at *A Hard Day's Night* or *Help!*, it was clear that those four boys were having the time of their life: the films radiated freedom and good times. In them there was no sign of the long, slow accumulation of security and status, the year-after-year movement towards satisfaction, that we were expected to ask of life. Without conscience, duty or concern for the future, every- thing about the Beatles spoke of enjoyment, abandon and atten- tion to the needs of the self. The Beatles became heroes to the young because they were not deferential: no authority had broken their spirit; they were confident and funny; they answered back; no one put them down. It was this independence, creativity and earning-power that worried Hogg about the Beatles. Their naive hedonism and dazzling accomplishments were too paradoxical. For Hogg to wholeheartedly approve of them was like saying crime paid. But to dismiss the new world of the 1960s was to admit to being old and out of touch.

There was one final strategy that the defenders of the straight world developed at this time. It was a common standby of the neighbours. They argued that the talent of such groups was shallow. The easy money would soon be spent, squandered on objects the groups would be too jejune to appreciate. These musi- cians couldn't think about the future. What fools they were to forfeit the possibility of a secure job for the pleasure of having teenagers worship them for six months.

This sneering 'anyone-can-do-it' attitude to the Beatles wasn't necessarily a bad thing. Anyone could have a group – and they did. But it was obvious from early on that the Beatles were not a two- hit group like the Merseybeats or Freddie and the Dreamers. And around the time that Hogg was worrying about the authorship of

'I Saw Her Standing There' and turning down the bass on 'She's Leaving Home', just as he was getting himself used to them, the Beatles were doing something that had never been done before. They were writing songs about drugs, songs that could be fully comprehended only by people who took drugs, songs designed to be enjoyed all the more if you were stoned when you listened to them.

And Paul McCartney had admitted to using drugs, specifically LSD. This news was very shocking then. For me, the only association that drugs conjured up was of skinny Chinese junkies in squalid opium dens and morphine addicts in B movies; there had also been the wife in *Long Day's Journey into Night*. What were the Mopheads doing to themselves? Where were they taking us?

On Peter Blake's cover for *Sgt Pepper*, between Sir Robert Peel and Terry Southern, is an ex-Etonian novelist mentioned in *Remembrance of Things Past* and considered by Proust to be a genius – Aldous Huxley. Huxley first took mescalin in 1953, twelve years before the Beatles used LSD. He took psychedelic drugs eleven times, including on his deathbed, when his wife injected him with LSD. During his first trip Huxley felt himself turning into four bamboo chair legs. As the folds of his grey flannel trousers became 'charged with is-ness' the world became a compelling, unpredictable, living and breathing organism. In this transfigured universe Huxley realised both his fear of and need for the 'marvellous'; one of the soul's principal appetites was for 'transcendence'. In an alienated, routine world ruled by habit, the urge for escape, for euphoria, for heightened sensation, could not be denied.

Despite his enthusiasm for LSD, when Huxley took psilocybin with Timothy Leary at Harvard he was alarmed by Leary's ideas about the wider use of psychedelic drugs. He thought Leary was an 'ass' and felt that LSD, if it were to be widely tried at all, should be given to the cultural élite – to artists, psychologists, philosophers and writers. It was important that psychedelic drugs be used seriously, primarily as aids to contemplation. Certainly they changed nothing in the world, being 'incompatible with action and even with the will to action'. Huxley was especially nervous about the aphrodisiac qualities of LSD and wrote to Leary: 'I strongly urge you not to let the sexual cat out of the bag. We've stirred up enough trouble suggesting that drugs can stimulate aesthetic and religious experience.'

But there was nothing Huxley could do to keep the 'cat' in the bag. In 1961 Leary gave LSD to Allen Ginsberg, who became convinced the drug contained the possibilities for political change. Four years later the Beatles met Ginsberg through Bob Dylan. At his own birthday party Ginsberg was naked apart from a pair of underpants on his head and a 'do not disturb' sign tied to his penis. Later, Lennon was to learn a lot from Ginsberg's style of self-exhibition as protest, but on this occasion he shrank from Ginsberg, saying: 'You don't do that in front of the birds!'

Throughout the second half of the 1960s the Beatles functioned as that rare but necessary and important channel, popularisers of esoteric ideas – about mysticism, about different forms of political involvement and about drugs. Many of these ideas originated with Huxley. The Beatles could seduce the world partly because of their innocence. They were, basically, good boys who became bad boys. And when they became bad boys, they took a lot of people with them.

Lennon claimed to have 'tripped' hundreds of times, and he was just the sort to become interested in unusual states of mind. LSD creates euphoria and suspends inhibition; it may make us aware of life's intense flavour. In the tripper's escalation of awareness, the memory is stimulated too. Lennon knew the source of his art was the past, and his acid songs were full of melancholy, self-examination and regret. It's no surprise that Sgt Pepper, which at one time was to include 'Strawberry Fields' and 'Penny Lane', was originally intended to be an album of songs about Lennon and McCartney's Liverpool childhood.

Soon the Beatles started to wear clothes designed to be read by people who were stoned. God knows how much 'is-ness' Huxley would have felt had he seen John Lennon in 1967, when he was reportedly wearing a green flower-patterned shirt, red cord trousers, yellow socks and a sporran in which he carried his loose change and keys. These weren't the cheap but hip adaptations of work clothes that young males had worn since the late 1940s – Levi jackets and jeans, sneakers, work boots or DMs, baseball caps, leather jackets – democratic styles practical for work. The Beatles had rejected this conception of work. Like Baudelairean dandies they could afford to dress ironically and effeminately, for each other, for fun, beyond the constraints of the ordinary. Stepping out into that struggling post-war world steeped in memories of recent devastation and fear – the war was closer to them than *Sgt Pepper* is to me today – wearing shimmering bandsman's outfits, crushed velvet, peach-coloured silk and long hair, their clothes were gloriously non-functional, identifying their creativity and the pleasures of drug-taking.

By 1966 the Beatles behaved as if they spoke directly to the whole world. This was not a mistake: they were at the centre of life for millions of young people in the West. And certainly they're the only mere pop group you could remove from history and suggest that culturally, without them, things would have been significantly different. All this meant that what they did was influential and important. At this time, before people were aware of the power of the media, the social changes the Beatles sanctioned had happened practically before anyone noticed. Musicians have always been involved with drugs, but the Beatles were the first to parade their particular drug-use – marijuana and LSD – publicly and without shame. They never claimed, as musicians do now – when found out – that drugs were a 'problem' for them. And unlike the Rolling Stones, they were never humiliated for drug-taking or turned into outlaws. There's a story that at a bust at Keith Richards' house in 1967, before the police went in they waited for George Harrison to leave. The Beatles made taking drugs seem an enjoyable, fashionable and liberating experience: like them, you would see and feel in ways you hadn't imagined possible. Their endorsement, far more than that of any other group or individual, removed drugs from their sub-cultural, avant-garde and generally squalid associations, making them part of mainstream youth activity. Since then, illegal drugs have accompanied music, fashion and dance as part of what it is to be young in the West.

Allen Ginsberg called the Beatles 'the paradigm of the age', and they were indeed condemned to live out their period in all its foolishness, extremity and commendable idealism. Countless preoccupations of the time were expressed through the Fabs. Even Apple Corps was a characteristic 1960s notion: an attempt to run a business venture in an informal, creative and non-materialistic way.

Whatever they did and however it went wrong, the Beatles were always on top of things musically, and perhaps it is this, paradoxically, that made their end inevitable. The loss of control that psychedelic drugs can involve, the political anger of the 1960s and its anti-authoritarian violence, the foolishness and inauthenticity of being pop stars at all, rarely violates the highly finished surface of their music. Songs like 'Revolution' and 'Helter Skelter' attempt to express unstructured or deeply felt passions, but the Beatles are too controlled to let their music fray. It never felt as though the band was going to disintegrate through sheer force of feeling, as with Hendrix, The Who or the Velvet Underground. Their ability was so extensive that all madness could be contained within a song. Even 'Strawberry Fields' and 'I Am the Walrus' are finally engineered and controlled. The exception is 'Revolution No. 9', which Lennon had to fight to keep on the *White Album*; he wanted to smash through the organisation and accomplished form of his pop music. But Lennon had to leave the Beatles to continue in that direction and it wasn't until his first solo album that he was able to strip away the Beatle frippery for the raw feeling he was after.

At least, Lennon wanted to do this. In the 1970s, the liberation tendencies of the 1960s bifurcated into two streams – hedonism, self-aggrandisement and decay, represented by the Stones; and serious politics and self-exploration, represented by Lennon. He continued to be actively involved in the obsessions of the time, both as initiate and leader, which is what makes him the central cultural figure of the age, as Brecht was, for instance, in the 1930s and 1940s.

But to continue to develop Lennon had to leave the containment of the Beatles and move to America. He had to break up the Beatles to lead an interesting life.

I heard a tape the other day of a John Lennon interview. What struck me, what took me back irresistibly, was realising how much I loved his voice and how inextricably bound up it was with my own growing up. It was a voice I must have heard almost every day for years, on television, radio or record. It was more exceptional then than it is now, not being the voice of the BBC or of southern England, or of a politician; it was neither emollient nor instructing, it was direct and very hip. It pleased without trying to. Lennon's voice continues to intrigue me, and not just for nostalgic reasons, perhaps because of the range of what it says. It's a strong but cruel and harsh voice; not one you'd want to hear putting you down. It's naughty, vastly melancholic and knowing too, full of self-doubt, self-confidence and humour. It's expressive, charming and sensual; there's little concealment in it, as there is in George Harrison's voice, for example. It is aggressive and combative but the violence in it is attractive since it seems to emerge out of a passionate involvement with the world. It's the voice of someone who is alive in both feeling and mind; it comes from someone who has understood their own experience and knows their value.

The only other public voice I know that represents so much, that seems to have spoken relentlessly to me for years, bringing with it a whole view of life – though from the dark side – is that of Margaret Thatcher. When she made her 'St Francis of Assisi' speech outside 10 Downing Street after winning the 1979 General Election, I laughed aloud at the voice alone. It was impenetrable to me that anyone could have voted for a sound that was so cold, so pompous, so clearly insincere, ridiculous and generally absurd.

In this same voice, and speaking of her childhood, Thatcher once said that she felt that 'To pursue pleasure for its own sake was wrong'.

In retrospect it isn't surprising that the 1980s mélange of liberal economics and Thatcher's pre-war Methodist priggishness would embody a reaction to the pleasure-seeking of the 1960s and 1970s, as if people felt ashamed, guilty and angry about having gone too far, as if they'd enjoyed themselves too much. The greatest surprise was had by the Left – the ideological left rather than the pragmatic Labour Party – which believed it had, during the 1970s, made immeasurable progress since *Sgt Pepper*, penetrating the media and the Labour Party, the universities and the law, fanning out and reinforcing itself in various organisations like the gay, black and women's movements. The 1960s was a romantic period and Lennon a great romantic hero, both as poet and political icon. Few thought that what he represented would all end so quickly and easily, that the Left would simply hand over the moral advantage and their established positions in the country as if they hadn't fought for them initially.

Thatcher's trope against feeling was a resurrection of control, a repudiation of the sensual, of self-indulgence in any form, self-exploration and the messiness of non-productive creativity, often specifically targeted against the 'permissive' 1960s. Thatcher's colleague Norman Tebbit characterised this suburban view of the Beatle period with excellent vehemence, calling it: 'The insufferable, smug, sanctimonious, naive, guilt-ridden, wet, pink orthodoxy of that sunset home of that third-rate decade, the 60s.'

The amusing thing is that Thatcher's attempt to convert Britain to an American-style business-based society has failed. It is not something that could possibly have taken in such a complacent and divided land, especially one lacking a self-help culture. Only the immigrants in Britain have it: they have much to fight for and much to gain through being entrepreneurial. But it's as if no one else can be bothered – they're too mature to fall for such ideas.

Ironically, the glory, or, let us say, the substantial achievement of Britain in its ungracious decline, has been its art. There is here a tradition of cultural dissent (or argument or cussedness) caused by the disaffections and resentments endemic in a class-bound society, which fed the best fiction of the 1960s, the theatre of the 1960s and 1970s, and the cinema of the early 1980s. But principally and more prolifically, reaching a worldwide audience and being innovative and challenging, there is the production of pop music – the richest cultural form of post-war Britain. Ryszard Kapuscinski in *Shah of Shahs* quotes a Tehran carpet salesman: 'What have we given the world? We have given poetry, the miniature, and carpets. As you can see, these are all useless things from the productive viewpoint. But it is through such things that we have expressed our true selves.'

The Beatles are the godhead of British pop, the hallmark of excellence in song-writing and, as importantly, in the interweaving of music and life. They set the agenda for what was possible in pop music after them. And Lennon, especially, in refusing to be a career pop star and dissociating himself from the politics of his time, saw, in the 1970s, pop becoming explicitly involved in social issues. In 1976 Eric Clapton interrupted a concert he was giving in Birmingham to make a speech in support of Enoch Powell. The incident led to the setting up of Rock Against Racism. Using pop music as an instrument of solidarity, as resistance and propaganda, it was an effective movement against the National Front at a time when official politics – the Labour Party – were incapable of taking direct action around immediate street issues. And punk too, of course, emerged partly out of the unemployment, enervation and directionlessness of the mid-1970s.

During the 1980s, Thatcherism discredited such disinterested and unprofitable professions as teaching, and yet failed, as I've said, to implant a forging culture of self-help. Today, as then, few British people believe that nothing will be denied them if only they work hard enough, as many Americans, for instance, appear to believe. Most British know for a fact that, whatever they do, they can't crash through the constraints of the class system and all the prejudices and instincts for exclusion that it contains. But pop music is the one area in which this belief in mobility, reward and opportunity does exist.

Fortunately the British school system can be incompetent, liberal and so lacking in self-belief that it lacks the conviction to crush the creativity of young people, which does, therefore, continue to flourish in the interstices of authority, in the school corridor and after four o'clock, as it were. The crucial thing is to have education that doesn't stamp out the desire to learn, that attempts to educate while the instincts of young people – which desire to be stimulated but in very particular things, like sport, pop music and television – flower in spite of the teacher's requirement to educate. The sort of education that Thatcherism needed as a base – hard-line, conformist, medicinal, providing soldiers for the trenches of business wars and not education for its own sake – is actually against the tone or feeling of an England that is not naturally competitive, not being desperate enough, though desperate conditions were beginning to be created.

Since Hogg first played 'She's Leaving Home', the media has expanded unimaginably, but pop music remains one area accessible to all, both for spectators and, especially, for participants. The cinema is too expensive, the novel too refined and exclusive, the theatre too poor and middle-class, and television too complicated and rigid. Music is simpler to get into. And pop musicians never have to ask themselves – in the way that writers, for instance, constantly have to – who is my audience, who am I writing for and what am I trying to say? It is art for their own sakes, and art which connects with a substantial audience hungry for a new product, an audience which is, by now, soaked in the history of pop music and is sophisticated, responsive and knowledgeable.

And so there has been in Britain since the mid-1960s a stream of fantastically accomplished music, encompassing punk and New Wave, northern soul, reggae, hip-hop, rap, acid jazz and house. The Left, in its puritanical way, has frequently dismissed pop as capitalist pap, preferring folk and other 'traditional' music. But it is pop that has spoken of ordinary experience with far more precision, real knowledge and wit than, say, British fiction of the equivalent period. And you can't dance to fiction.

In the 1980s, during Thatcher's 'permanent revolution', there was much talk of identity, race, nationality, history and, naturally, culture. But pop music, which has bound young people together more than anything else, was usually left out. But this tradition of joyous and lively music created by young people from state schools, kids from whom little was expected, has made a form of self-awareness, entertainment and effective criticism that deserves to be acknowledged and applauded but never institutionalised. But then that is up to the bands and doesn't look like happening, pop music being a rebellious form in itself if it is to be any good. And the Beatles, the most likely candidates ever for institutionalisation, finally repudiated that particular death through the good sense of John Lennon, who gave back his MBE, climbed inside a white bag and wrote 'Cold Turkey'.

The Word and the Bomb

First published in *The Word and the Bomb*, 2005

Most of the English writers I grew up reading were fascinated by the British Empire and the colonial idea, and they didn't hesitate to take it as their subject. E. M. Forster, Graham Greene, Evelyn Waugh, J. R. Ackerley, George Orwell and Anthony Burgess all tackled this area and its numerous implications in one way or another, for most of their writing lives.

As a young man, living in the London suburbs with an Indian father and English mother, I wanted to read works set in England, works that might help make sense of my own situation. Racism was real to me; the Empire was not. I liked Colin MacInnes and E. R. Braithwaite, whose *To Sir with Love* so moved me when I read it under the desk at school. But where were the British equivalents of the black American writers: James Baldwin, Richard Wright and Ralph Ellison? Who was noting the profound and permanent alterations to British life which had begun with the Empire and had now, as it were, come home?

Oddly, most modern British writers have been reluctant to similarly engage with such subjects at home. Questions of race, immigration, identity, Islam – the whole range of issues which so preoccupy us these days – have been absent from the work of my white contemporaries, even as a new generation of British writers has developed, following the lead of V. S. Naipaul and Salman Rushdie.

Most writers would say, quite rightly, that their subjects choose them; that they are interested in whatever they are interested in for reasons they cannot explain, and that writing is an experiment which takes you where it has to. The vocation of each writer is to describe the world as he or she sees it; anything more than that is advertising. Jo Shapcott puts it nicely in her poem 'The Mad Cow Talks Back': 'My brain's like the hive: constant little murmurs from its cells/saying this is the way, this is the way to go.'

In the post-war period, race – and now religion – have become subjects around which we discuss what is most important to us as individuals and as a society, and what scares us about others. Race is a reason to think about free speech and 'hate' speech; about integration, or what we have to be in order for society to work, and about the notion of the 'stranger'. We use the idea of race to think about education, and what we assume our children should know; about national identity: whether we need an identity at all, and what such an idea means; about sexuality, and the sexual attitudes and powers we ascribe to others, as well as our place in the world as a nation, and what our values are. We think, too, through the often mystifying topic of multiculturalism, about how mixed and mixed-up we are, so much so that we find it disconcerting for others to be multiple, and even worse, for us to be so, too. And because our politicians are so limited in what they can say and think, we need artists, intellectuals and academics to keep our cultural conversation going, to help us orient ourselves.

Yet a curious sort of literary apartheid has developed, with the latest 'post-colonial' generation exploring the racial and religious transformation of post-war Britain, while the rest leave the subject alone. When British television, cinema and theatre saw it as their duty to explore these issues – and the strangeness of the silence which often surrounded them – British writers of the generation following Graham Greene seemed scared of getting it wrong, of not understanding, even as they complained of having nothing 'important' to write about, envying American writers for having more compelling subjects.

Not that this apartheid was entirely innocent. Salman Rushdie, in a 1983 essay entitled 'Commonwealth Literature Does Not Exist', describes the attempt of the literature business to exclude certain writers, shoving them to the periphery under the patronising term 'Commonwealth writers'. The idea here is to keep writing in English pure, to change the terms of English literature 'into something far narrower, something topographical, nationalistic, possibly even racially segregationist'.

It isn't as though race is a new subject in Britain. Sukhdev Sandhu, in his comprehensive study *London Calling: How Black and Asian Writers Imagined a City*, quotes a correspondent for *The Times* in 1867: 'There is hardly such a thing as a pure Englishman in this island. In place of the rather vulgarised and very inaccurate phrase, "Anglo-Saxon", our national denomination, to be strictly correct, would be a composite of a dozen national titles.'

If, for E. M. Forster, the Empire was about power rather than mixing, its effect was permanently to alienate and separate people from one another. At the end of *A Passage to India*, the Englishman Fielding and his Muslim friend Aziz are out riding. Forster writes: 'Socially they had no meeting place. Would he today defy all his own people for the sake of a stray Indian? Aziz was a memento, a trophy, they were proud of each other, yet they must inevitably part.' Aziz himself cries, 'Clear out, all you Turtons and Burtons.' And, 'We shall drive every blasted Englishman into the sea!'

George Orwell takes a scalpel to this subject, telling us that political domination can only lead to humiliation, on both sides. In his essay 'Shooting an Elephant', the opening line of which is, 'In Moulmein, in Lower Burma, I was hated by large numbers of people – the only time in my life that I have been important enough for this to happen to me,' Orwell draws an uncompromising picture of how this humiliation works. Sent to kill a rogue elephant, a crowd of 'two thousand' begins to follows him, fascinated by how the Englishman will act. He feels himself to be 'an absurd puppet'; all that the natives want to do – 'the sneering yellow faces' – is laugh at him. But how could they respond otherwise? Later, writing about Kipling, he says, 'He does not see that the map is painted red chiefly in order that the coolie may be exploited.'

It is clear, in both Forster and Orwell, that the 'coloured' man is always inferior to the Englishman. He is not worth as much; he never will be. When it comes to character as well as colour, the white man is the gold standard. However, Orwell also saw that the Empire – and I guess he'd have applied this to immigration – was primarily economic. This was how countries enriched themselves. If the Empire wasn't supposed to be a moral crusade with the aim of making everyone alike, the only way to do it was to be ruthless – not half-hearted, as he was when called upon to dispose of the elephant. If the elephant is the Empire and Orwell the representative Englishman, he has to remove something that cannot easily be got rid of. And the elephant is with us still.

During my childhood and youth, differences in British society were always based around class and the conflicts they gave rise to. The Labour Party grew out of such clashes; its existence was based on them. But technology and consumerism became our gods. Now people are not even divided over politics, as there is only one party, and the opposition is fragmented, disorganised and without passion or direction. The real differences in Britain today are not political, or even based on class, but are arranged around race and religion, with their history of exploitation, humiliation and political helplessness.

Forster's Aziz got his wish: the British left the subcontinent. But in the vacuum following this hurried departure, there was political failure and dictatorship. Who, there, was seriously addressing the needs of the poor? For me, visiting Pakistan in the early 1980s, it was bewildering to hear older people wishing that Britain still ruled. Pakistan was becoming a theocracy and no one knew how to stop it. The Americans had been afraid of the Left, and hadn't noticed the significance of the mosques.

One of the most significant reasons for the rise of Islamic extremism in the Third World is the presence of financial and political corruption, along with the lack of free speech, and the failure to make a space for even the mildest political dissent. Pakistan, for instance, was a country constantly on the verge of collapse. My family in Karachi, along with most of the other middle-class families, hoarded their money in the West 'just in case', and educated their children in Britain and the US.

If the political class and the wealthy stole money, promoted their relatives – my Uncle Omar, a journalist in Pakistan, called it 'the son-in-law also rises' culture – and ensured that they had a route out, political dissent for those who did not have such privileges became organised around the mosque and the outspoken clerics there. As with many revolutions, the route to freedom from oppression also became the route to more oppression, to a familiar tyranny – that of the 'just' as opposed to that of the 'unjust'.

Young British Asians, the committed Muslims of *My Son the Fanatic* and *The Black Album*, were aware of this corruption at home and often felt guilty that they were in a better situation in the West. Corruption in their parents' land was also an injustice they wanted to repair.

The downfall of the Shah and the Iranian revolution of 1979, followed by a religious dictatorship, showed, at least, the effectiveness of Islam in fomenting political change. However, most people in the West became aware of the force and determination of radical Islam during the period of the fatwa against Rushdie, in 1989. Young Muslims told me that although they didn't succeed in either suppressing *The Satanic Verses* or eliminating its author, they were aware of how powerful their disapproval could be, and what energy they could create when organised. The Muslim writer Shabbir Akhtar admitted in *Be Careful with Muhammad* that, 'The Rushdie affair is, in the last analysis, admittedly about fanaticism on behalf of God.'

These young men were highly politicised and passionate. Believing they had unique access to virtue – and virtue was to be had only through submission to God – they were prepared to give up their lives for a cause. Forgetting how zealous we had once been about our own description of equality – socialism – we could only be shocked by their commitment and solidarity, and by their hatred of injustice, as well as their determination to bring about social change. We had not seen religious revolutionaries for a long time. Apart from liberation theology in South America – the church being used as an outlet for Left opposition – the only significant religion we saw for a long time was the soft New Age, as well as other right-wing cults, like the Moonies. Even Martin Luther King was considered by us to be a black leader rather than a religious one.

For us, religious commitment, particularly if it was political too, entailed not emancipation but a rejection of the Enlightenment and of modernity. How could we begin to deal with it? You respect people who are different, but how do you live with people who are so different that – among other things – they lock up their wives?

For young religious radicals, extreme Islam worked in many ways. It kept them out of trouble, for a start, and provided some pride. They weren't drinking, taking drugs, or getting into trouble like some of their white contemporaries. At the same time, they were able to be rebels. Being more fervent Muslims than their parents – and even condemning their parents – kept them within the Muslim fold, but enabled them to be transgressive at the same time. It's a difficult trick, to be simultaneously disobedient and conformist, but joining a cult or political organisation can fit both needs. The puritanical young can defy their fathers, but keep to the law of the ultimate Father. They are good, virtuous children, while rebelling.

Not that these young people are either representative or anything like the majority of Muslims in Britain. Earlier this year, making a short television documentary, I took a camera around the country and interviewed numerous Indian waiters. Having eaten in Indian restaurants all my life, I was fascinated by what these normally silent and unnoticed figures might say. To me, Indian restaurants with their sitar music, flocked wallpaper and pictures of the Taj Mahal on the wall, reproduced the colonial experience in this country for the ordinary person; the experience, of course, was 'Disneyfied', made bland and acceptable for the British, while retaining some of its charm.

Most of these waiters were keen on their work; feeding others was important for them. They had worked hard, and either they, or their families, had endured a traumatic transplantation to find a place in this country. They were Muslims; they prayed; they went to the mosque. But, as Shabbir Akhtar says, 'For most Muslims, Islam is a "Friday religion".' The Islam they wanted was not incompatible with the West. The waiters wanted their children – boys and girls alike – to be well educated; they required a health service, housing and a democratic political structure. They were not segregated; they were important, well known and respected in their town. They had multiple identities: being British, Bengali, and Welsh too. They were truly multicultural.

However, one of the waiters said to me recently, indicating his arm, his skin, his colour, 'Now they are blaming us all.' He wanted me to know he saw the present danger as a resurgence of racism, this time aimed specifically at Muslims. The idea might be to root out extremists, but a whole community may end up becoming stigmatised. One of the waiters mentioned his fear that rather than embodying the 'immigrant dream' of wealth, individuality and respect, they would become the permanent scapegoats of British society, as the blacks have become in the US. I have heard calls among the British for the re-installation of Englishness, as though there has been too much multiculturalism, rather than not enough. This wish for rigid, exclusive identities mirrors extreme Islam itself; it is an attempt to counter fundamentalism with more fundamentalism. This is a form of shame, when it is our excesses we should celebrate. We have been beset by bogeys before – Papists, communists, pornography – without losing our minds.

Not that monoculturalism can work now: the world is too mixed. But there is the possibility of many new conflicts. After everything immigrants and their families have contributed to this country, the years of work and the racism faced, the war in Iraq, which Blair thought he could prosecute without cost or social division here, has brought more fragmentation. If Blair's 'third way' implies consensus and the end of antagonism, our literature will sharpen and map differences. 'Over-integration', the erasing of racial and religious differences, can become coercive or even fascistic. It can give rise to more racism, anger and resentment.

Edward Said wrote of the way Western writers constructed the East: the Orient as a convenient and simplistic fabrication, often as an obscene fantasy. Not that this is a fair picture of the work of writers like Forster or Orwell, who, from the inside, offered devastating critiques of their own class. Not that fantasies don't go both ways. Among Muslims, there has been a reverse Orientalism, or 'Occidentalism', at work. Many of the fundamentalists I met, indeed many Muslims, were keen to see the West as corrupt and over-sexualised; there was 'too much freedom'. The West could seem chaotic, over-individualistic; the family was less important, or constantly mutating. These Muslims refused to look at Western culture and science, or the institutions which can only flourish in a relatively free atmosphere, preferring to see the inevitable underside: addiction, divorce, social breakdown.

In the light of such deliberate mutual incomprehension, we might ask ourselves what the use of writing is. However, you might as well ask what the use of speaking or telling stories is. Edward Said identified useful writing as 'speaking the truth to power'. The attacks on Rushdie show us, at least, that the Word is dangerous, and that independent and critical thought is more important than ever. In an age of propaganda, political simplicities and violence, our stories are crucial. Apart from the fact that the political has to be constantly interrogated, it is in such stories – which are conversations with ourselves – that we can speak of, include and generate more complex and difficult selves. It is when the talking and writing stops, when the attempt is to suppress human inconsistency by virtue, that evil takes place in the silence. The antidote to puritanism isn't licentiousness, but recognition of what goes on inside human beings. Fundamentalism is dictatorship of the mind, but a live culture is an exploration, and represents our endless curiosity about our own strangeness and impossible sexuality: wisdom is more important than doctrine; doubt more important than certainty. Fundamentalism implies the failure of our most significant attribute, our imagination. In the fundamentalist scheme there is only one imaginer – God. The rest of us are his servants.

The freedom to speak is not only our privilege, but is essential to the oppressed, unheard and marginalised of the Third World, as they struggle to keep their humanity alive in conditions far worse than here. To retreat into a citadel of 'Englishness', to refuse to link up or identify with them, is to deliver them over to superstition and poverty of the imagination.

The Rushdie case remains instructive. In the end it is Islam itself which suffers from the repudiation of more sensual and dissident ideas of itself. Shabbir Akhtar – and his like – cannot understand that by leaving out, or attempting to suppress, so much of themselves, by parting company from an essential component of their own heritage, they are losing access to a source of enjoyment, energy and understanding. Radical Islam, then, far from looking like a new revolutionary movement, has come to rather resemble other totalitarian systems like Catholicism and communism, neither of which – under the rule of dull old men – could see the value of obscenity.

Immorality and blasphemy require protection. The roll-call of the censored is an account of our civilisation. If Islam is incapable of making any significant contribution to culture and knowledge, it is because extreme puritanism and censoriousness can only lead to a paranoia which will cause it to become more violent and unable to speak for those it is intended to serve. That which we seek to exclude returns to haunt us.

Fear Eats the Soul

An extract from this essay was broadcast on
BBC Radio 4's *The Verb*, March 2011

In 1974 the renowned and often notorious young German director Rainer Fassbinder made a simple and relatively small film set mostly in a Munich bar and an apartment. This modest but resonant piece concerns the relationship between a late-middle-aged cleaning woman, Emmi, and Ali, a Moroccan immigrant she meets and dances with in a bar near her flat after a thunderstorm.

I can't have seen *Fear Eats the Soul* until the early 1980s, when I suspect that though it might be quite different in its details, it reminded me of the relationship between my parents. (The film could easily have been set in any British town.) Although Britain and other European countries were changing rapidly in terms of their racial identity, I wasn't aware of any other films about European racism or 'integration', and this film seemed to be saying something important and necessary.

Fassbinder was an extremely imaginative artist with his own somewhat peculiar preoccupations; however, there are few directors as aware of their time and place as him. He was born at the end of the war and became obsessed with its consequences, making films with women at the centre of them. (He had many relationships with actresses, as well as with men.) Fassbinder resembles Brecht in his ability to combine political analysis with a passion for understanding women. Like Brecht he wanted to see the centre from the position of the outsider; that way he could speak the forbidden. The dignified presence of El Hedi ben Salem as Ali – a lover of Fassbinder, who hanged himself in a French prison just before the director's last film, *Querelle*, was released – can only remind us of how few black and Asian actors appeared in the great European cinema of the 60s and 70s.

Fear Eats the Soul is not over-aestheticised; the camera barely moves and the actors are often impassive. Nor is Fassbinder much interested in the psychology of the characters. It is their social situation which compels him. Haunted by the recent past, the 1970s were certainly violent and disruptive in Germany. Early on in the film Emmi admits that she and her mother were both in the Nazi party. Nonetheless, she likes Ali instantly and he spends the night in her flat. (Usually he shares a room with six other 'guest-workers'.) 'Come on,' Emmi says to Ali on the stairs. 'We're all forever saying "but". And everything stays the same.'

'Arabs with Germans not good,' Ali warns her. 'Arabs not human in Germany.' What Fassbinder then explores is the traumatic impact of this disconcerting love on those around the couple, including her children. Emmi's neighbours and friends even begin to suspect her of not being one of them; they point out that her name – Kurowski – sounds foreign. Her workmates say of the '*Gastarbeiters*', 'dirty pigs the lot of them. The way they live. Whole families in a single room. All they're after is money. The women who go with them are whores.'

Ali is dignified, impeccably polite and good-looking, though he is no saint. He also appears somewhat isolated, if not lonely. As as a 'guestworker' he is not a German citizen and seems stranded far from home. We never see he and Emmi making love, but they like to talk. Fassbinder might have been known for his exploration of sexuality and its instability, but this is a love story. These two people really like one another.

When Emmi and Ali marry and move in together Emmi is isolated by her colleagues and neighbours. The local grocer won't serve Ali because, he claims, he doesn't speak German. The neighbours call the police when Ali plays cards with some friends. Someone says, 'Four Arabs in her apartment. You know what they're like. Bombs and all that.'

At their wedding lunch the couple are alone while being stared at by strangers, eating in the Munich restaurant Hitler used to frequent.

At this point Fassbinder moves the story on. When Ali and Emmi return from their honeymoon attitudes moderate. Her children can use Emmi as their babysitter; the grocer welcomes Ali: he has been made aware of their mutual dependence now he is afraid of losing customers to the expanding supermarkets. 'In business,' he says, 'you have to hide your aversions.' Emmi's colleagues take up with her again when they find another victim to bully, this time a Yugoslav woman. Not only that, her female friends begin to find Ali attractive, even feeling his muscles.

Towards the end of the film, after a confused and persecuted Ali sleeps with a girl from the bar, Emmi goes to some trouble to win him back, insisting their love is more important than any minor transgression. Then, when Ali falls ill with a perforated stomach ulcer, she takes him to hospital where he is left in the care of a doctor – Fassbinder's father was a doctor – who informs her that Ali will have to return because his ulcer won't get better. The doctor has seen this before with other immigrants: their lives are so difficult they fall ill repeatedly.

The notion of integration is one that is discussed constantly in Europe today, and the character of Ali perfectly illustrates the difficulties and double-binds it involves. The language used against him is the familiar vocabulary of the racist, whether the victim is a Jew, Negro or Muslim, and it involves the most important things: money, sexuality, disease and social status. Considering their envy of this Arab man is, at least, a way for those around him to be reminded of what matters most to them – if only in inverted fantasy.

The immigrant should work but not belong; he mustn't forget his place as an outsider. If he 'integrates' too much he is accused of taking over, or of fracturing the organic unity of the existing society. If he keeps his distance he is living in a ghetto, thus creating social disintegration. In the end he is indigestible, and Ali represents in his sick body the contradictions of the society he now inhabits.

There are no Black Shirts, political parties, marches, or any mention of the Holocaust in *Fear Eats the Soul*. The hatred is deliberately low-level; it is simple everyday bourgeois racism. Fassbinder is showing us that fascism starts at the bottom, rather than being imposed from above. It is not the authorities who harass Ali, it is his neighbours. And although Fassbinder is too pure an artist to become didactic, he is reminding us that Europe has been through this before and that this is how it might start again.

The society which Ali has moved into is shown by Fassbinder to be stagnant, if not decadent. Emmi's children are cruel towards her, indolent and envious, and without motivation or desire. Seemingly traumatised by the past, they are numb and uninterested in their mother's passion for Ali. Their souls have been devoured by hatred, and Fassbinder cannot find much about their way of life which is valuable or alive.

Ali as the alien, scapegoat or awful Thing – he is both a question and a provocation – appears to occupy an empty place, a position that almost any outsider could be put in. (Jews were often referred to as 'the Negroes of Europe'.) Ali is not hated because he is in reality dirty, over-sexualised and ambitious etc. He is considered to have these qualities because he is an immigrant. That is what the immigrant has been made into.

Perhaps if the host community can focus their hate on Ali, he at least absolves those around him from hating one another. His presence seems to create some kind of unity. This is not unlike the son Gregor Samsa in Kafka's great story *Metamorphosis*. The gain of Gregor becoming an insect is that his horrible transformation creates accord and, eventually, happiness and freedom in the family. The last line of *Metamorphosis* runs, 'And it was like a confirmation of their new dreams and excellent intentions that at the end of their journey their daughter sprang to her feet and stretched her young body.'

But Ali also reminds those around him that although they don't want anything to change, they might require a catalyst. In this regard Ali represents the future; there will be more like him, and deeper difficulties. How will these Others be absorbed, and how will everyone have to change in order to make a productive life possible? What sort of society can be made from these elements?

In 1989, fifteen years after *Fear Eats the Soul*, when the Berlin Wall came down and communism collapsed in Eastern Europe, a fatwa was placed on the life of Salman Rushdie.

There is no Muslim community in *Fear Eats the Soul*, only a group of Moroccan buddies in inhospitable territory. But by 1989 in Britain the Muslim community was becoming a force; they were no longer innocent like Ali, but active and persecutory themselves. Quickly they were able to pass around information about *The Satanic Verses*, organise for the book to be burned in Bolton and Bradford, and put pressure on both the publishers Penguin and the British government to have it banned.

There's no reason to think the Muslim community would be any more cohesive than any other. However, there was one issue which briefly brought these believers together. It wasn't inequality, discrimination or hatred which created this organisation, but an insult. And it wasn't the host community they were attacking, but another Muslim, a highly regarded writer. The community was a community because of its underlying religion. Being an immigrant wasn't an identity, or enough of one, except for others. The 'deviant' Rushdie created a brief unity.

The Satanic Verses begins with a terrorist attack on an aeroplane, and this explosion presages the explosion of identities Rushdie explores in the book. As Rushdie himself put it, 'How does newness come into the world? How is it born? Of what fusions, translations, conjoinings is it made?'

The super-acceleration of the world in the 80s; migration and metamorphosis: if you can't go home again because both you and home have already changed, you can at least remake yourself in the new place although it rejects you. But you'll be different to your parents, and most likely far from what they wanted you to be. You might feel you have betrayed them, but that the way to return is via religion.

Amongst other things, *The Satanic Verses* is a celebration of fragmentation, hybridity and breakdown, psychosis by another name. This is a painful mad state which might require the reintroduction of limits. The authorites are called in when there is too much enjoyment; they re-establish order and renunciation over the vortex of obscene enjoyment. One cure they might offer could be the safety of certainty, knowledge of the absolute truth; the certainty of the very religion Rushdie, as an artist, can't help being sceptical about.

If novelists and the religious are envious and fascinated by one another it is because religions and literature approach the same subject, knowledge of the world and how to live in it as sexual and dying beings. Like literature, religions are a form of myth, a creative function of the human imagination; Mohammed, Jesus and the Virgin Mary can resemble characters in a drama, and we can argue about their virtues and failings as we would with anyone else.

Religions are, among other things, a form of explanation, of storytelling and order-making. As with literature, these stories are, then, useful delusions. But where religions seek to eradicate conflicts, installing some notion of ultimate harmony, literature sustains conflicts as arguments worth having. *The Satanic Verses* is concerned with the necessity of doubt in this process, returning religious myths and narratives to man as objects of creativity and of enquiry. All texts, like all lives, are endlessly open to interpretation, satire, slander, idealisation. Religions, like the novel, are mankind's dream and a high form of useful play. God is man's greatest creation, as well as his worst. Man is more creative than God.

But if forms of worship are man-made, they can be modified by man; they can be reinvented, according to need. But where literature is critical – Baal in *The Satanic Verses* states, 'a poet's work is to name the unnamable, to point out frauds, take sides, start arguments' – religions, called 'sacred', require obedience and often silence. If religion is man at his most creative, it is also him at his most authoritarian. Not that you can underestimate the pleasures of obedience.

Nietzsche writes, 'What we do in dreams we also do when we are awake; we invent and fabricate the person with whom we associate – and immediately forget we have done so.' As Fassbinder points out, we fictionalise the immigrant, turning him into the monster of our imagining. At times he is an oppressed or greedy immigrant, and at others a revolutionary fascist, a proto-bomber hating the West, wanting to change it into his own idealised image.

We can frighten ourselves, taking these stories literally. But myths are imperative: nothing is still, migration and metamorphosis are our destiny, a passage to death. We live in fantasy, hallucination and imagination. The self cannot be mastered or contained; parts of it are always liable to sheer off and fly about, looking for a character to inhabit.

Newness in the World:
An Introduction to *The Black Album*

First published in the *Guardian*, June 2009

It was in the summer of 2008 that I suggested to Jatinder Verma that we attempt a theatrical dramatisation of my second novel *The Black Album*.

The Black Album was a novel I had begun to think about in 1991, not long after the publication of my first book, *The Buddha of Suburbia*. Unlike that story, which I'd been trying to tell in numerous versions since I first decided to become a writer, aged fourteen, *The Black Album* was more or less contemporary, a 'state of Britain' narrative not unlike the ones I'd grown up watching, in the theatre and on TV.

Around the time of its original publication in 1993, and after the BBC film of *The Buddha of Suburbia*, there had been talk of filming *The Black Album*. But instead of returning to something I'd just written and was relieved to have done with, it seemed easier to write a new piece, with similar themes. This was a film, *My Son the Fanatic*, starring Rachel Griffiths and Om Puri.

However, as the twentieth anniversary of the fatwa was approaching, and with *The Black Album* set in 1988/9 and concentrating on a small group of fundamentalists, both Jatinder and I thought that my pre-7/7 novel might shed some light on some of the things which had happened since.

Not that I had read the novel since writing it; and if I felt hesitant – as I did – to see it revived in another form, it was because I was anxious that in the present mood, after the bombings and atrocities, it might, at times, seem a little frivolous. But the young radical Muslims I came to know at the time did appear to me to be both serious and intelligent, as well as naive, impressionable and half-mad, and my account of their activities and language reflected what I learned in mosques and colleges. The novel records the kind of debates they had. And it wasn't as though the subject of liberalism and its relation to extreme religion had gone away.

It was debate and ideological confrontation that Jatinder and I had in mind when we sat down to work on the translation from prose to play. The novel, which has a thriller-like structure, is a sprawl of many scenes in numerous locations: pubs, a further education college, a mosque, clubs, parties, a boarding house, cafes, Deedee's house and the street. As it was impossible in the theatre to retain this particular sense of late 80s London, we had to create longer scenes and concentrate on the important and even dangerous arguments between the characters as they interrogated Islam, liberalism, consumer capitalism, as well as the place and meaning of literature and the way in which it might be critical of religion.

The first draft was too much like a film and would have been unwieldly to stage. Jatinder reminded me that we had to be ruthless. He also reminded me, with his persistence and imagination, how much I've learned about editing from the film and theatre directors I've worked with. If we were to create big parts for actors in scenes set in small rooms, we needed to turn prose into fervent talk, having the conversation carry the piece. We had to ensure the actors had sufficient material to see their parts clearly. Each scene had to be shaped. The piece had to work for those who hadn't read the book.

It was this we worked on over a number of drafts, and it was the usual business of writing: cutting, condensing, expanding, developing, and trying material in different places until the story moved forward naturally. I was particularly keen to keep the humour and banter of students and their often adolescent attitudes, particularly towards sexuality. This was, after all, one of their most significant terrors: that the excitement the West offered would not only be too much for them, but for everyone.

Nevertheless, the matter was deadly serious. The fatwa against Salman Rushdie in February 1989 had re-ignited my concern about the rise of Islamic radicalism, something I'd first become aware of while in Pakistan in 1982, where I was writing *My Beautiful Laundrette*. But for me that wasn't the whole story. Much else of interest was happening around the end of the 80s: the music of Prince; the collapse of communism and the 'velvet revolution'; the rise of the new dance music along with the use of a revelatory new drug, Ecstasy; Tiananmen Square; Madonna using Catholic imagery in *Like a Prayer*; and post-modernism, 'mash-ups' and the celebration of hybridity – of exchange and creative contamination – which is partly the subject of *The Satanic Verses*.

This was also the period, or so I like to think, when Britain became aware that it was changing, or, in effect, had already changed from a monocultural to a multi-racial society, and had realised, at last, that there was no going back. This wasn't a mere confrontation with simple racism, the kind of thing I'd grown up with, which was usually referred to as 'the colour problem'. (When I was a young man it was taken for granted that to be black or Asian was to be inferior to the white man. And not for any particular reason. It was just the case: a fact.)

No, it was much more. Almost blindly, in the post-war period, a huge, unprecedented social experiment had been taking place in Britain. The project was to turn – out of the end of the Empire and on the basis of mass immigration – a predominantly white society into a racially mixed one, thus forming a new notion of what Britain was.

And now was the time for this to be evaluated. The fatwa in 1989, and the debate and arguments it stimulated, seemed to make this clear. Was it not significant that many of these discussions were about language? The Iranian condemnation of a writer had, after all, been aimed at his words. What, then, was the relation between free speech and respect? What could and could not be said in a liberal society? How would different groups in this new society relate – or rather, speak – to one another?

The coercive force of language was something I had long been aware of. As a mixed-race child growing up in a white suburb, the debased language used about immigrants and their families had helped fix and limit my identity. My early attempts to write now seem like an attempt to undo this stasis, to create a more fluid and complicated self through storytelling. One of the uses of literature is that it will enable individuals to enlarge their sense of self – their vocabulary, the store of ideas they use to think about themselves.

In the 1970s, many of us became aware, via the scrutiny of the gay, feminist and Black movements, of the power that language exerted. If the country was to change – excluding fewer people – so did the discourse, and why not? Language, which implicitly carried numerous meanings, developed all the time; if it was never still it could be revised, coaxed in other directions. There were terms applied to certain groups which were reductive, stupid, humiliating, oppressive. (Children, of course, are described constantly by their parents in ways which are both narrowing and liberating – and they have a good idea of what it is to live in an authoritarian world. It wasn't for nothing that I had been fascinated in my late teens by Wittgenstein's apophthegm, 'The meaning of a word is its use.')

If there were to be better words the language had to be policed in some way, the bad words being replaced by the good. This, of course, became known as Political Correctness, where language was forced to follow the – usually Leftist – political line. Inevitably there was a backlash, as this form of political control seemed not only harsh and censorious but sometimes ludicrous and irrelevant.

Liberals were in a tricky position, having to argue both for linguistic protectionism in some areas and for freedom in others. So that when some Muslims began to speak of 'respect' for their religion and the 'insult' of *The Satanic Verses* the idea of free speech and its necessity and extension was always presented as the conclusive argument. Criticism was essential in any society. This could be said, but not *that*. But how would this be decided, and by whom?

The Marxists, too, were finding the issue of the fatwa difficult. It was only partly a coincidence that Islamic fundamentalism came to the West in the year that that other great cause,

Marxist-communism, disappeared. The character of the stuttering socialist teacher in *The Black Album* – Deedee Osgood's husband Brownlow – was partly inspired by some of the strange convolutions of the disintegrating Left at the time.

At a conference in Amsterdam in 1989 I remember arguing with John Berger, who was insisting that complaints about *The Satanic Verses* were justified, as they came from the downtrodden proletariat. Why, he said, would he want to support a privileged middle-class artist who was – supposedly – attacking the deepest beliefs of an otherwise exploited and humiliated Muslim working class? This seemed to me to be an eccentric and perverse point of view, particularly from a writer who had previously valued freedom, and when it was obvious that the opportunity to dissent, to be critical of leaders and authorities – and to be free of censorship – was necessary for anyone to live a good life, as the many writers, critics and journalists in prison in Muslim countries would no doubt attest.

To struggle my way through this thicket of fine distinctions, difficult debates and violent outcomes, I invented the story of Shahid, a somewhat lost and uncertain Asian kid from Kent – whose father has recently died – and who joins up, at college, with a band of similar-minded anti-racists. The story develops with Shahid discovering that the group are going further than anti-racist activism. They are beginning to organise themselves not only around the attack on Rushdie, but as Islamo-fascists who believe themselves to be in possession of the truth.

This is a big intellectual leap. As puritanical truth-possessors, Riaz's group and those they identify with have powerful, imperialistic ideas of how the world should be and what it should be purged of. Soon, believing the West has sunk into a stew of decadence, consumerism and celebrity obsession – a not untypical fantasy about the West, corresponding to a not-unsimilar fantasy of the West about the sensual East, as Edward Said has argued – they believe it is their duty to bring about a new, pure world. They want to awaken benighted people to the reality of their situation.

To do this they insist on a complete dominance of people's private lives, and of female sexuality in particular.

Some of these attitudes were familiar to me, as I grew up in the 60s and 70s, when the desire for revolution, for violent change, for the cleansing of exploitative capitalists and a more moral world, was part of our style. Almost everyone I knew had wanted, and worked in some way to bring about, not only the modification of capitalism, but its overthrow. For us, from D. H. Lawrence to William Burroughs and The Sex Pistols, blasphemy and dissent was a blessed thing, kicking open the door to the future, bringing new knowledge, freedom and ways of living. The credo was: be proud of your blasphemy, these vile idols have been worshipped for too long! The point was to be disrespectful, to piss on the sacred. As Guy Debord wrote, 'Where there was fire, we carried petrol.'

But there was, mixed in with this liberation rhetoric, as in all revolutions – either of the left or right – a strong element of puritanism and self-hatred. There was a desire for the masochism of obedience and self-punishment, something not only illustrated by the Taliban, but by all revolutionary movements which are inevitably bloated with the egotism of self-righteousness and in love with self-sacrifice. This concerns not only the erotics of the 'revolutionary moment', the ecstasy of a break with the past and the fantasy of renewal, but also the human penchant for living in authoritarian societies and intransigent systems, where safety and the firm constraint of the leader is preferable to liberal doubt, uncertainty and change. As Georges Bataille reminds us in an essay written in 1957, 'Man goes constantly in fear of himself. His erotic urges terrify him.'

Riaz, the solemn, earnest and clever leader of the small group which Shahid joins, understands that hatred of the Other is an effective way of keeping his group not only together but moving forward. To do this, he has to create an effective paranoia. He must ensure that the image and idea of the Other is sufficiently horrible and dangerous to make it worth being afraid of. The former colonialistic Western Other, having helped rush the East into premature modernity, must have no virtues. Just as the West has generated fantasies and misapprehensions of the East for its own purposes, the East – this time stationed in the West – will do the same, ensuring not only a comprehensive misunderstanding between the two sides, but a complete disjunction which occludes complexity.

Of course, for some Muslims this disjunction is there from the start. To be bereft of religion is to be bereft of human value. Almost unknowingly, Muslims who believe this are making a significant sacrifice by forfeiting the importance of seeing others, and of course themselves, as being completely human. In Karachi, I recall, people were both curious and amazed when I said I was an atheist. 'So when you die,' said one of my cousins, 'you'll be all dressed up with nowhere to go?' At the same time Islamic societies, far from being 'spiritual', are – because of years of deprivation – among the most materialistic on earth. Shopping and the mosque have no trouble in getting along together.

Some of the attitudes among the kids I talked to for *The Black Album* reminded me of Nietzsche's analysis of the origins of religion, in particular his idea that religion – and Nietzsche was referring to Christianity – was the aggression of the weak, of the victim or oppressed. These attacks on the West, and the religion they were supposed to protect, were in fact a form of highly organised resentment or bitterness, developed out of colonialism, racism and envy. The violent criticism of Rushdie, an exceptionally gifted artist of whom the community should have been proud, was in fact a hatred of talent and of the exceptional, a kind of forced equalisation from a religion which had not only become culturally and intellectually mediocre, but which was looking to the far past for a solution to contemporary difficulties.

Towards the end of *The Black Album*, with the help of his lecturer and soon-to-be girlfriend Deedee Osgood, Shahid understands that he has to withdraw from this group in order to establish himself on his own terms at last. This isn't easy, as the group has provided him with support, friendship and direction. It also doesn't want to let him go.

He gets out, in part, by beginning to discover the exuberance of his own sexuality and creativity. 'How does newness come into the world? How is it born? Of what fusions, translations, conjoinings is it made?' asks Salman Rushdie, relevantly, at the beginning of *The Satanic Verses*.

It is also no accident that British and American pop, as exemplified for Shahid by Prince's intelligent, sensual and prolific creativity, is in a particularly lively phase. The clubs and parties Deedee takes Shahid to represent a continuing form of the youthful celebration that Britain has enjoyed since the 60s. If religions are among man's most important and finest creation – with God perhaps being his greatest idea of all – Shahid also learns how corrupt and stultifying these concepts can become if they fetishise obedience, if they are not renewed and re-thought. Like language itself, they can become decadent, and newness and vigour doesn't have an easy time. If blasphemy is as old as God, it is as necessary, because religion and blasphemy are made for one another. Without blasphemy religion has no potency or meaning. If there's nothing like a useful provocation to start a good conversation, this can only be to the advantage of religion.

It turns out that Shahid is one of the lucky ones, strong enough to find out – after flirting with extreme religion – that he'd rather affect the world as an artist than as an activist. The others in his group are not so intelligent or objective; or perhaps they are just more passionate for political change. Whatever the reasons – and it is probably too late for psychological explanations – something had begun to stir in the late 80s, which has had a profound effect on our world, and which we are still trying to come to terms with.

Back to the *Borderline*

First published in the *Guardian*, 2006

It was with some trepidation that I looked again at *Borderline*, a play I wrote in 1981. The Royal Court Theatre – where it was originally presented – wanted to mount a reading of it, as part of the celebrations to mark fifty years of that theatre. My father was alive in 1981, and sat enthusiastically through many performances, laughing at everything, particularly at the character of the father, who rather resembled him. Now, twenty years later, two of my sons, aged twelve, were present. I couldn't help wondering what it would mean to them – or indeed to anyone, now.

The original director Max Stafford-Clark, whose idea the play was, had worked often with Joint Stock, a touring company started by David Hare and Bill Gaskill with the intention of getting political theatre out of London. The company played in schools, community centres and gyms around the country. We would cast the play, do the research in Southall – an immigrant area of west London – and then I would write it. It would then tour, playing finally at the Royal Court. This was political theatre, emerging from the turbulent radical intensities of the 1970s. The idea was to show the community through its differences: different ages, political outlooks, and different hopes for the future, interweaving numerous characters and points of view.

At that time, getting a writing gig with Joint Stock was, as Max would say, 'very high status'. I was in my mid-twenties, living with my social worker girlfriend in a low-rent council flat next to a railway line in Barons Court, west London. I can't have been making a living as a writer; I must have been on the dole. So far I had written only two full-length plays, and many unpublished novels.

There were very few Asian or Afro-Caribbean writers, actors or directors who made a living from their work. Why did I think I'd be any different?

I was extremely nervous about the whole thing, and with good reason. It was, as far as I knew, the first play by an Asian to be produced on the main stage at the Royal Court, a theatre known for its innovation and daring. The only other black playwright I knew was Mustapha Matura, whose work I'd admired. But his work was poetic; he was no social documentarian.

For me the Joint Stock process had been frantic, if not hair-raising. The actors and theatres had been hired; everything was in place, but the play had not been written, not a word of it, and we were to start rehearsing in six weeks. I was just beginning to find out whether I could be a writer or not, trying to find a subject, characters, and words for them to say. I was already learning a lot from the directors I worked with, and from the actors: as they began to speak, the clumsiness of the lines was obvious. Fortunately, I was hard-working then, with a fierce ambition.

The play did get written. It also got re-written. This, I saw, was when the real work began. If I'd had too 'pure' a view of the artist, I was soon to learn that aesthetic fastidiousness wasn't a helpful attitude. Max was severe and precise, sending me into a dressing room with instructions to write a scene about so-and-so, with certain characters in it. I re-wrote as we rehearsed; I re-wrote as we played it around the country; I re-wrote it when we opened at the Royal Court, and even after that. This was the first time I'd worked in such a way and it was an important proficiency to develop; it came in handy two years later when I worked with Stephen Frears on *My Beautiful Laundrette*, and was required to re-write on set.

I was also ambivalent about the journalistic process. I was full of material already; I had hardly touched on my own experience as a British Asian kid. Why were we interviewing strangers in order to generate material? Yet as we began to talk with people I found these conversations were not chatter; they were serious – some taking place over a number of days – and always moving. I was fascinated to hear strangers talk. It was something like a crude psychoanalysis, as one only had to ask a simple question to be drawn into a whirlpool of memories, impressions, fears, terrors. (Max's father, David Stafford-Clark, had written several interesting books about Freud.) I was shocked by how much people revealed of themselves, and how much they wanted to be known, to be understood. The community was close and supportive, but the cost of this was inhibition and constraint.

Most of the actors who took part in this year's rehearsed reading of *Borderline* were younger than ten when the Southall riots took place. One of them, who had appeared in Michael Winterbottom's 'Guantanamo Bay' film, had been arrested and held under the Anti-terrorism Act at Heathrow a few days before, on his way back from the Berlin Film Festival, where the movie won the Silver Bear.

The actors required a quick history lesson. We played The Specials' 'Ghost Town' and The Jam's 'That's Entertainment'. We mentioned monetarism, Norman Tebbit, the Falklands, the miners' strike, and rioting in Brixton, Bristol, Liverpool – and Southall, a suburban Asian area in west London, not far from Heathrow airport, where many Asians worked.

When I was approached by Max with the subject for *Borderline*, Southall had recently become the focus of discontent and violence. Racism was a daily occurrence for most Asians in Britain. But the characters in the play refer often to the possibility of an 'invasion', something they were afraid of and disturbed by, as it had already happened. In April 1979 the police allowed the fascist National Front to hold a meeting in Asian Southall. Two weeks earlier the residents met with the Labour Home Secretary Merlyn Rees to ask him to ban the Front's meeting. On the day before the march, five thousand people went to Ealing Town Hall in support of banning the National Front's meeting, handing in a petition signed by ten thousand residents. Local factories also agreed to strike in protest. Rees refused to give way. It was a question of free speech, even for fascists.

During the protest which followed the fascist meeting, organised by the Asians themselves along with the Anti-Nazi League – a front for the Trotskyite Socialist Workers Party – the police on horses attacked the crowds; vans were driven at them. Blair Peach, a young left-wing teacher, was struck and killed by the notorious SPG (The Special Patrol Group), a shadowy police/army group whose job, it was commonly said, was to beat people up. Many older Asian people, who still respected the police and the British legal system, were shocked and disillusioned by the number of injuries and the unrestrained violence of the police. Meanwhile the media represented the riots as an 'attack on the police'.

In June 1979, when the lockers of the SPG were searched, one officer was found to be in possession of Nazi regalia, bayonets and leather-covered sticks. But no officer was prosecuted.

This, then, partly explains the atmosphere of paranoia and fear in which the play's events take place. This is why the arguments the characters have, about how to proceed socially and politically, are so important to them. They are thinking all the time about the kind of Britain in which they are living, and the kind of country the young will inherit and seek to re-make.

To my surprise, looking at the play again after twenty years, I was not startled either by the naivety of the piece, or by the nature of my personal preoccupations then. Obviously it had dated, but in noteworthy ways. What did strike me was how little talk of religion there was among the characters. The unifying ideology of that time and place was socialism, with feminist groups like the Southall Black Sisters, as well as some anarchist and separatist groups, also contributing to the debate. The play itself was written out of the 1970s and at each stage the question would have to be asked: how does this scene, or these lines, further the cause, not only of the play, but of the social movement we are pursuing? What are we saying, about Asians, women, the working class: how do we push the argument along?

By the 1990s political theatre was dead. It had come to seem crude as a device for explaining the world, or for bringing news from unexplored parts of the country. But in this age of mendacity, deception and violence, there is the need, once again, for public debate about contemporary issues. Political theatre can be quick, immediate and adapted to changing circumstances, unlike most films.

Ten years after the Southall riots, in 1989 – the year communism died in Europe – there was another significant demonstration by Asians, this time in Hyde Park, central London. It was not about racial attacks, unemployment or indeed any of the concerns shown in *Borderline*. It was a demonstration against the publication of Salman Rushdie's *The Satanic Verses*, and Muslims had travelled from all over the country to protest.

In *Borderline* Amina's young lover Haroon wants to leave the area to become a lawyer. But why would he want to join the white world which so clearly hates them? He also intends to write a novel. This ambition is met with much scorn. Not only is it considered self-indulgent, there are other concerns. Will he be critical of them? Will it separate him from the community? Will he not only leave his own community – and his childhood – but what will they look like through his eyes? How will they appear? For his part, Haroon criticises the community for its narrowness. Unsurprisingly, the 'attacks' and 'invasions' have contributed to making them inward-looking and over-insular. He accuses them of having a village mentality while they consider him a sell-out.

But why would any novel be considered dangerous? Why would a community, still embattled and with much to fight for – yet making progress in Britain – turn on one of their own, a writer they could be proud of? What ideology entailed such a hatred of artists? What had changed in those ten years?

In *Borderline* the father Amjad refuses to let his wife Banoo speak. This is not only because he, as a patriarch, is in charge of speaking in the family, but because he is afraid of what she will say, and what it will do to him. Speaking is dangerous; it changes things. To hear her would be an acknowledgement of others' freedom. It might entail having to hear Amina, his daughter, too. This form of control is recognised by some of the other characters.

Susan, the white journalist in the play, befriends the young girl Amina and gives her books to read, encouraging her to hear other voices, consider other positions and points of view. If the community is cut off by racism, it is also beginning to isolate itself from important ideas. Later, when we attempted to take the piece to Southall, the Youth Movement portrayed in the play refused to allow it: they threatened to burn down the hall in which we wanted to perform the piece.

In 1978, Michel Foucault, sponsored by the Italian daily newspaper *Corriere della Sera*, visited Iran for the first time. For him capitalism had failed; totalitarian communism didn't appeal either. However, the events in Iran 'offered a new hope'; he began to speak of 'political spirituality' as an antidote not only to corruption in most Muslim countries, but to increasing materialism everywhere. Banoo, the isolated and distressed mother in the play, referring to her husband's efforts – thirty years of work in a bakery – speaks of the 'emptiness' of washing machines, televisions, vacuum cleaners. For her something nourishing is missing, though she doesn't know what it is. At the end of the play, when her husband has died, she returns to Pakistan.

At the anti-Rushdie demonstration in Hyde Park in 1989, a group of Asian female demonstrators – perhaps from a group not unlike the Southall Black Sisters – who were carrying placards saying 'Women Against Fundamentalism', were attacked by Muslim men. As these dissident voices were suppressed, as secular and socialist Asian voices were discouraged across the community, a range of new issues emerged, many to do with the idea of speaking, books, writing, words, and the place of the artist and intellectual as critic.

During the ten years between the Southall riot and the demonstration against *The Satanic Verses*, Islam imposed an identity and solidarity on a besieged community. Radical Islam came to mean rebellion, purity, integrity. But it was also a trap. Once this ideology had been adopted – and political conversations could only take place within its terms – it entailed numerous constraints, locking the community in, as well as divorcing it from possible sources of creativity: dissidence, criticism, sexuality. Its authoritarianism, stifling to those within, and appearing fascistic to those without, rejected the very liberalism the community required in order to flourish in the modern world. It was tragic: what protected the community came to tyrannise it.

The Arduous Conversation Will Continue

First published in the *Guardian*, July 2005

We no longer know what it is to be religious, and haven't for a while. During the past two hundred years sensible people in the West have contested our religions until they lack significant content and force. These religions now ask little of anyone and, quite rightly, play little part in our politics.

The truly religious, following the logic of submission to political and moral ideals, and to the arbitrary will of God, are terrifying to us and almost incomprehensible. To us 'belief' is dangerous and we don't like to think we have much of it.

Confronted by this, it takes a while for our 'liberalism' to organise itself into opposition and for us to consider the price we might have to pay for it. We also have little idea of what it is to burn with a sense of injustice and oppression, and what it is to give our lives for a cause, to be so desperate or earnest. We think of these acts as mad, random and criminal, rather than as part of a recognisable exchange of violences.

The burning sense of injustice that many young people feel as they enter the adult world of double standards and dishonesty shocks those of us who are more knowing and cynical. We find this commendable in young people but also embarrassing. Consumer society has already traded its moral ideals for other satisfactions, and one of the things we wish to export, masquerading as 'freedom and democracy', is that very consumerism, though we keep silent about its consequences: addiction, alienation, fragmentation.

We like to believe we are free to speak about everything, but we are reluctant to consider our own deaths, as well as the meaning of murder. Terrible acts of violence in our own neighbourhood – not unlike terrible acts of violence which are 'outsourced', usually taking place in the poorest parts of the Third World – disrupt the smooth idea of 'virtual' war that we have adopted to conquer the consideration of death.

'Virtual' wars are conflicts in which one can kill others without either witnessing their deaths or having to take moral responsibility for them. The Iraq war, we were told, would be quick and few people would die. It is as though we believed that by pressing a button and eliminating others far away we would not experience any guilt or suffering – on our side.

By bullying and cajoling the media, governments can conceal this part of any war, but only for a while. If we think of children being corrupted by video games – imitation violence making them immune to actual violence – this is something that has happened to our politicians. Modern Western politicians believe we can murder real others in faraway places without the same thing happening to us, and without any physical or moral suffering on our part.

This is a dangerous idea. The only way out is to condemn all violence or to recognise that violence is a useful and important moral option in the world. Despite our self-deception, we are quite aware of how necessary it is, at times, to kill others to achieve our own ends and to protect ourselves. If we take this position we cannot pretend it is morally easy and seek to evade the consequences.

We were dragged into this illegal and depressing war by many lies and much dissembling. A substantial proportion of us were opposed to it. During wars ordinary citizens feel they lack information and moral orientation while governments act decisively and with brutality.

Governments may be representative but they and the people are not the same. In our disillusionment, it is crucial that we remind ourselves of this. States behave in ways that would shame an individual. Governments persuade individuals to behave in ways that individuals know are morally wrong. Therefore governments do not speak for us; we have our own voices, however muffled they may seem. If communities are not to be corrupted by the government, the only patriotism possible is one that refuses the banality of taking either side, and continues the arduous conversation. That is why we have literature, the theatre, newspapers – a culture, in other words.

War debases our intelligence and derides what we have called 'civilisation' and 'culture' and 'freedom'. If it is true that we have entered a spiral of violence, repression and despair that will take years to unravel, our only hope is moral honesty about what we have brought about.

And not only us. If we need to ensure that what we call 'civilisation' retains its own critical position towards violence, religious groups have to purge themselves of their own intolerant and deeply authoritarian aspects.

The body-hatred and terror of sexuality that characterise most religions can lead people not only to cover their bodies in shame but to think of themselves as human bombs. This criticism on both sides is the only way to temper an inevitable legacy of bitterness, hatred and conflict.

The Carnival of Culture

First published in the *Guardian*, July 2005

Recently a friend sent me an article which he thought I'd find interesting, as it was an attempt to sustain a non-violent version of Islam, one in which meddling and manipulative clerics had no authority. Without the requirement of intermediaries, no one could come between you and God. The clerics were seen here as political figures, rather than the best interpreters of Islam. If these fanatics and fundamentalists had twisted the word of God for their own political ends, why shouldn't the Koran be reclaimed and reinterpreted by the better intentioned? This, the writer stated, was the only way for Islam to go.

In the early 1990s, after my first visit to Pakistan, where I'd had a taste of what it was like to live in a (more or less) theocratic state; after the fatwa against Salman Rushdie and, finally, the death of my father, I began to visit various London mosques. Perhaps I was trying to find something of my father there, but I was also beginning to research what became *The Black Album*, a novel which concerned a group of students, young radical Muslims in west London, who burn *The Satanic Verses* and, later, attack a bookshop. A film I wrote for the BBC, *My Son the Fanatic*, about a young man who becomes a fundamentalist while his father falls in love with a prostitute, also emerged from this material.

I believed that questions of race, identity and culture were the major issues post-colonial Europe had to face, and that intergenerational conflict was where these conflicts were being played out. The British-born children of immigrants were not only more religious and politically radical than their parents – whose priority had been to establish themselves in the new country – but they despised their parents' moderation and desire to 'compromise' with Britain. To them this seemed weak.

My father was an Indian Muslim who didn't care for Islam; his childhood hadn't been much improved by a strict schooling, and teachers with sticks. Towards the end of his life he preferred Buddhism to Islam, as there was less aggression and punishment in it. ('And altogether less religion,' as he put it.) He had also become disillusioned with the political version of Islam, which my father's school friend, Zulfi Bhutto – who the liberal classes thought would become a democratic and secular leader in the new Pakistan – was introducing to Pakistan.

The mosques I visited, in Whitechapel and Shepherd's Bush, were nothing like any church I'd attended. The scenes, to me, were extraordinary, and I was eager to capture them in my novel. There would be passionate orators haranguing a group of people sitting on the floor. One demagogue would replace another, of course, but the 'preaching' went on continuously, as listeners of all races came and went. I doubt whether you'd see anything like this now, but there would be diatribes against the West, Jews, and – their favourite subject – homosexuals. In my naivety I wondered whether, at the end of his speech, the speaker might take questions or engage in some sort of dialogue with his audience. But there was nothing like this. Most of the audience for this sort of thing were, I noticed, under thirty years old.

I had the good sense to see what good material this was, and took notes, until, one afternoon, I was recognised, and four strong men picked me up and carried me out on to the street, telling me never to return.

Sometimes I would be invited to the homes of these young 'fundamentalists'. One of them had a similar background to my own: his mother was English, his father a Muslim, and he'd been brought up in a quiet suburb. Now he was married to a woman from the Yemen who spoke no English. Bringing us tea, she came into the room backwards, and bent over too, out of respect for the men. The men would talk to me of 'going to train' in various places, but they seemed so weedy and polite I couldn't believe they'd want to kill anyone.

What did disturb me was this. These men believed they had access to the Truth, as stated in the Koran. There could be no doubt – or even much dispute about moral, social and political problems – because God had the answers. Therefore, for them, to argue with the Truth was like trying to disagree with the facts of geometry. For them the source of all virtue and vice was the pleasure and displeasure of Allah. To be a responsible human being was to submit to this. As the Muslim writer Shabbir Akhtar put it in his book *A Faith for All Seasons*, 'Allah is the subject of faith and loving obedience, not of rational inquiry or purely discursive thought. Unaided human reason is inferior in status to the gift of faith. Indeed, reason is useful only in so far as it finds a use in the larger service of faith.'

I found these sessions so intellectually stultifying and claustrophobic that at the end I'd rush into the nearest pub and drink rapidly, wanting to reassure myself I was still in England.

It is not only in the mosques but also in so-called 'faith schools' that such ideas are propagated. The Blair government, while attempting to rid us of radical clerics, has pledged to set up more of these schools, as though a 'moderate' closed system is completely different to an 'extreme' one. This might suit Blair and Bush. A benighted, ignorant enemy, riddled with superstition, incapable of independent thought, and terrified of criticism, is easily patronised.

Wittgenstein compared ideas to tools, which you can use for different ends. Some open the world up. The idea that you can do everything with one tool is ridiculous. Without adequate intellectual tools and the ability to think freely, too many Muslims are incapable of establishing a critical culture which goes beyond a stifling Islamic paradigm. As the Muslim academic Tariq Ramadan states, 'Muslims now need, more than ever, to be self-critical. That means educating young Muslims in more than religious formalism.'

If the idea of multiculturalism makes some people vertiginous, monoculturalism – of whatever sort – is much worse. Political and social systems have to define themselves in terms of what they exclude, and conservative Islam is leaving out a lot. In New York recently, a Turkish woman told me that Islam was denying its own erotic heritage, as shown in the *Arabian Nights*, *The Perfumed Garden*, and the tales of Hamza. Indeed, the Arabic scholar Robert Irwin states, of the *Arabian Nights*, 'In the modern Middle East, with certain exceptions, the *Nights* is not regarded by Arab intellectuals as literature at all.'

It is not only sexuality which is being excluded here, but the whole carnival of culture which comes from human desire. Our stories, dreams, poems, drawings, enable us to experience ourselves as strange to ourselves. It is also where we think of how we should live.

You can't ask people to give up their religion; that would be absurd. Religions may be illusions, and they may betray infantile wishes in their desire for certainty, but these are important and profound illusions. But they will modify as they come into contact with other ideas. This is what an effective multiculturalism is: not a superficial exchange of festivals and food, but a robust and committed exchange of ideas – a conflict which is worth enduring, rather than a war.

When it comes to teaching the young, we have the human duty to inform them that there is more than one book in the world, and more than one voice, and that if they wish to have their voices heard by others, everyone else is entitled to the same thing. These children deserve better than an education which comes from liberal guilt.

Humouring the State:
The PEN/Pinter Prize Lecture, 2010

Delivered at the British Library, 20 October 2010

I would like to thank PEN and the judges, and say what a huge pleasure and honour it is for me to receive this prize.

Harold Pinter is a writer I have enjoyed and loved since I was a teenager, coming up from Bromley on the train to queue for tickets to see, several times, Gielgud and Richardson in *No Man's Land*. And I'd read, while waiting on the station, the famous 1966 Pinter interview in the *Paris Review*, where he states clearly the writer's task, 'One tries to get the thing . . . true.'

Before this I had seen *The Caretaker* somewhere, and, to my surprise – having heard that Pinter was a difficult, if not opaque writer – laughed as much as if I'd been at a farce.

Harold Pinter is well known for his mastery at representing the unfortunate preoccupations of the twentieth century – terror, paranoia, persecution – both domestically and, later in his career, in larger politics. But it shouldn't be forgotten that Pinter is a comic writer, and a devil with the mad insult. This is from *The Homecoming*: 'He brings a filthy scrubber off the street . . . I've never had a whore under this roof before. Ever since your mother died.'

Pinter brilliantly understands how wit and humour can be used as a medium of humiliation and degradation, to destroy the victim's defences and turn the individual into nothing. But he is also aware of how language as wit can be used to attack authority, to undermine power and pomposity, to subvert.

In Milan Kundera's 1967 masterpiece, *The Joke*, set in the 1950s, the young Czech protagonist is arrested and imprisoned for sending a postcard to his girlfriend. 'Optimism is the opium of the people!' it says – a relatively mild joke but one that becomes a suicide note, and a kind of self-sacrifice. 'A healthy atmosphere stinks of stupidity! Long live Trotsky!'

In 1980, Milan Kundera told Philip Roth, 'I learned the value of humour during the time of Stalinist terror. I could always recognise a person who was not a Stalinist, a person whom I needn't fear, by the way he smiled. A sense of humour was a trustworthy sign of recognition. Ever since, I have been terrified by a world that is losing its sense of humour.'

It is a stretch to think of a great writer who isn't also comic: Gogol, Dostoevsky, Proust, Kafka, Beckett and so on are, at times, what Roth calls sit-down comedians. Jokes undo knots and undermine dictators. The powerful may have many attributes, but a sense of humour is never one of them.

Writing, then, is playful, a form of loose collaborative excitement, creating, with the reader, a shared experience of pleasure. Writers are, from one point of view, as I like to explain to my writing students, in show business. They must entertain, and give good value, otherwise there is nothing going on between reader and writer. From another point of view writers are scrupulous critics. Comedy and wit, which combine both, are ways of seeing into, and seeing through.

It's a serious and necessary business, amusement, and you can tell how serious it is by the number of journalists and writers who are in prison around the world, as well as by the attempts there are, as PEN would confirm, to shut writers up, to censor and impede them, always a sure sign that a writer, somewhere, is doing her job and that she has some authority in a cynical world.

Let's remind ourselves: words are very dangerous, they are dynamite. Jokes can't start a revolution, but they can loosen the bricks in the wall. A joke introduces a little anarchy into the world, a bit of disruption. It tests the limits; it pushes them.

In Pakistan, when Zulfikar Bhutto first began to compromise with the Islamists, my father, his brothers and other liberal friends referred to this as 'the great leap backwards'. They liked to say the country was being 'sodomised' by religion, a line I later used in *My Beautiful Laundrette*. Their political impotence and sense of helplessness led them to make jokes continuously, even as the situation worsened. At least humour represents love, a promiscuous combining of elements, which will help form solidarity among dissenters.

Behind this idea is partly the modernist notion of the writer as devil, as dangerous, as a rebel. But I have come to think that it is insufficient; more is required. It is almost adolescent as a view: humour as the revenge and refuge of the powerless, the last stand of the already defeated, giggling as they go down.

My father was born and brought up in India under British rule. There was some equality there, he liked to say. As a child he was beaten by Catholic nuns as well as by the Maulvis who instructed children on the Koran.

The racial ideas my father faced, in India, under colonialism, and in Britain, when he first came here in the early 50s, were of a kind which have mostly been driven out now, as Britain's aggressively self-important sense of itself has declined. However, it might be useful to remind ourselves of these notions.

As an Indian my father was always uncomfortably aware that he was considered inferior; that he was less of a man than the other men who ruled. It was part of the general attitude of the time, and not only in Britain. Whites were superior as human beings to what were known as 'the coloured races'. My father and his family despised and mocked their British masters, while wanting to be like them. The English gentleman was their ideal. This class of Indian also wanted to be recognised as an equal by the master who despised them. It was an impossibly ambivalent position to be in, and no one was satisfied.

As the son of an Indian father and English mother, I didn't want to be like the English, I was already English, almost. But I became aware that I represented some sort of problem for the English, because they kept asking me who I was, where I fitted in, where I belonged and how long I'd be staying, not difficulties which my father, an Indian, had had. I was asked these questions so often I began to lose my bearings. What was I doing to the neighbours to make them so philosophical?

And so, as a teenager, I began to write. I wrote for my life. The idea of having an identity by calling myself 'a writer' suddenly seemed both consolidating and liberating, like a Cartesian assertion of existence. Critics sometimes like to characterise me as an autobiographical writer, and I like to reply that all writing is as autobiographical as a dream, in which every element both does and doesn't belong to the dreamer, and is somehow beyond them. 'Who's there?', the first line of *Hamlet*, is the question writers ask themselves when they sit down to write, perhaps in the hope, one day, of finding out. But there are multitudes there.

I was aware that I did want to speak of the experience of my family and myself. This seemed necessary and important for my survival. It was something of an epiphany as I sat at my typewriter every day, after school, and found I had my own words, however clumsy and derivative. Those of us like me were not, then, merely subject to the denigrations and descriptions of others. We could talk back. Writing would be a message to the world outside my family, and outside the suburbs. I would inform people what was going on, what life in the new Britain – a Britain unknowingly transforming itself for ever – was like for us. This was not writing as a form of defence, but, for me, as a way of situating myself fully in the alien world, an attempt to work out a place in it – writing as an attempted solution to various internal and external conflicts.

Through my Indian family, I became aware, as a young man, of this very full form of speaking, the novel. The British writers I admired, Forster, Orwell, Greene, Waugh, had all put colonialism, and what dominion does to people, at the centre of their work. Indeed, Forster regrets, at the end of *A Passage to India*, that certain kinds of free and equal relationships will not be possible while one consciousness dominates another. And J. G. Farrell wrote, 'The loss of the British Empire is the only interesting thing that happened in my adult life.'

Not that some of these attitudes don't remain. A friend said to me recently, 'Surely you have to acknowledge that people like your father only wanted to come here because of the peace, prosperity and high level of civilisation we have made.' It should go without saying, of course, that the economic prosperity and creativity of the West has always been partly based on colonialism and immigration. If there has been a failure to acknowledge this – and even a tendency to despise and attack those whose labour made, and continues to make, this prosperity and freedom possible – it is the hatred of the Master for those he depends on; hatred for the necessary subaltern without whom nothing good happens. This is partly because the subaltern is hardly noticed; he is only a quarter present, almost invisible, glimpsed from the corner of the eye.

But how then might he or she be seen? First there would have to be a political presence, of course. Margaret Thatcher, as we know, revived nationalist sentiment by attempting to resuscitate wartime versions of English patriotism. She was an exclusionist who didn't want too much 'difference' or 'otherness'. The early-to-mid-1980s in Britain, when I was working in the theatre and had begun to write films, were a rough time for minorities. The defining struggle of the less deferential Second Generation, against prejudice and police discrimination and brutality, was at its height. Out of this came civil unrest, and riots in Brixton, Bristol and Birmingham.

It had begun to occur to people that immigrants and their children were here for good, and Britain had changed for ever. There was a reluctance to accept this, and, at the same time, a demand, from people who felt disenfranchised and ghettoised, for recognition, as well as for just and equal treatment. Multiculturalism and identity politics were a good idea, a form of self-protection, when social cohesion, under Thatcher, was breaking up, and racism was unchecked. It seemed, for a time, that not only the idea of Britishness, but Britain itself would disintegrate under these pressures.

Multiculturalism reminded us that there are certain attributes which can't be subtracted from people without asking them to forfeit their links to the past, and to others in the future. Numerous groups had begun to explore their own history – often a history of persecution – and tried to determine how they were made in relation to it. Where once there had been silence, and the pressure of a majority culture, multiculturalism (or a counter-history), celebrated difference, multiplicity and pluralism within the same place. After all, the wish to wipe out another's history and culture is a form of genocide, and what is repressed is always more compelling than the sanctioned story.

When culture is only an extension of power, if it is an official culture, if you like, one can see how a joke can expose suppression. It shouldn't be forgotten that along with the superiority of the white man went the superiority of his culture, which was, for a long time, monolithic. If we can recall how difficult it was for the cinema to be taken seriously as an art form, and then pop, we ought to have an idea of how much that cultural dominance can exclude in other areas, of how people can be dispossessed of knowledge, a particularly cruel form of authority. As Kundera also reminded us, 'the struggle of man against power is the struggle of memory against forgetting.'

But I can also recall, in the mid-1980s, being told by an Afro-Caribbean acquaintance that ideas like socialism, feminism and liberalism were no good for blacks and Asians. They were white people's ideas, and since the whites hated us and it would be rational for us to hate them back, we had to repudiate all their ideas. According to him, the only way forward was for us to re-connect with our history, as if what was called 'our history' had nothing to do with anyone else's. This is similar to something a cousin of mine – but not an uncle – once said to me: 'Since we are Muslims, we have to create here in Pakistan, only a Muslim not a

Western society,' with the Koran, of all things, providing the blueprint for the future.

It's not difficult to see here that once attributes and differences become fetishised – if the subject becomes a series of idiosyncrasies or typical marks, and even begins to believe that this is what he really is – then the possibility of creative collaboration and renewal is cancelled. Marginalisation and alienation become permanent. Among the many good reasons for immigration, at least one is to ensure the free circulation of people, ideas and culture, for that is how, as Rushdie puts it in *The Satanic Verses,* 'newness is brought into the world'.

But if multiculturalism becomes the gated community of the minority, if it becomes another monoculturalism, that which was once protective becomes a prison. Identities become traps, rather than temporary accommodations between selves and the outside world. When it comes to a description of what a human being is, and what she might need to lead a fulfilling life, multiculturalism, while it once opened the door to other narratives, has come to seem inadequate and reductive, and, for its supposed beneficiaries, has closed off the rest of the world.

The finest poetry, novels and plays might be a good place to look when we require new paradigms for both criticising and understanding the world. Works of art, which describe and re-describe experience until we grasp its complexity, can liberate us from the static points of view that multiculturalism seems to generate. Great works of art are different to one another, but they are almost always concerned with the individual and her struggle with the majority view.

Universal values, particularly those of freedom and equality, are the basis of any minority community having a presence at all. If diversity and pluralism are to mean anything, they have to apply to a knowledge of a range of religions as solutions to human helplessness, as well as knowledge of ideas of atheism, secularism and doubt, and their place in a liberal, developing society. For instance, a universal value would be the use of education as a force for emancipation, for critical and objective evaluation, rather than for religious indoctrination.

As we all know, there's been some hard thinking on these difficult issues, particularly in the period since the fatwa on Salman Rushdie in 1989, which was a turning point for both literature and liberalism. This attack on a book, an author, freedom of expression and a literary culture, has left nothing the same.

But what of the desire to censor and control? What does it really mean? Sigmund Freud insists that although we have a fantasy of maintaining a reign of authority over ourselves, the truth is that each day, and, in particular, each night, our real life passes in a chaos of fumblings, bumblings, bingeings, forgettings, fantastic uprisings, wild dreams and delinquent fantasies, a comedy of errors and idiocies. Our lives are more like a Laurel and Hardy film than they are like a Stalinist state.

A mere joke can remind us, therefore, that the authoritarian regime can never succeed. As with the mischievous postcard in Kundera's novel, the imp of truth escapes. Kundera's novel will last longer than the regime it attacked. The forced empire of the self – the imperious ego – is always in danger of being undermined; the creative is never far away, since the disowned and the repressed inevitably return. The system creates dissidents, and the dissident speaks suppressed parts of the authority, parts which eventually have to be returned to him – as a reminder of the human.

Sometimes this is the writer's work, even if he or she would repudiate the political labelling. Rushdie, Pamuk, Mahfouz, Kundera and Pinter himself have all, at times, represented something honest in the State, and have been attacked, on occasions violently, for telling the truth.

A comedian can only make people laugh, whereas a good writer should have a wide palette and be able to intrigue, upset, shock and excite – transporting us from mood to mood in the same piece. Nevertheless, a joke is a marvellous moment of liberation, while being a reminder of constraint. Laughter is a recognition that something has to be freer.

Free speaking and writing are always difficult because they are always under threat. This guarantees their authenticity. In his *Paris Review* interview, Pinter notes the following, 'The speech only seems funny. The man in question is actually fighting for his life.' And if we are not fighting for our own lives, and by extension, others' lives, what are we doing?

FILMS

Introduction to *My Beautiful Laundrette*

First published with the screenplay, 1985

I wrote the script of *My Beautiful Laundrette* in my uncle's house in Karachi, Pakistan, in February 1984, during the night. As I wrote, cocks crowed and the call to prayer reverberated through crackly speakers from a nearby mosque. It was impossible to sleep. One morning as I sat on the verandah having breakfast, I had a phone call from Howard Davies, a director with the Royal Shakespeare Company, with whom I'd worked twice before. He wanted to direct Brecht's *Mother Courage*, with Judi Dench in the lead role. He wanted me to adapt it.

That summer, back in England and at Howard's place in Stratford-upon-Avon, I sat in the orchard with two pads of paper in front of me: on one I rewrote *My Beautiful Laundrette* and on the other I adapted Brecht from a literal translation into language that could be spoken by the RSC actors.

As *Laundrette* was the first film I'd written, and I was primarily a playwright, I wrote each scene of the film like a little scene for a play, with the action written like stage directions and with lots of dialogue. Then I'd cut most of the dialogue and add more stage directions, often set in cars, or with people running about, to keep the thing moving, since films required action.

I'd had a couple of lunches with Karin Bamborough of Channel 4. She wanted me to write something for *Film on Four*. I was extremely keen. For me *Film on Four* had taken over from the BBC's *Play for Today* in presenting serious contemporary drama on TV to a wide audience. The work of TV writers like Alan Bennett (much of it directed by Stephen Frears), Dennis Potter, Harold Pinter, Alan Plater and David Mercer influenced me greatly when I was young and living at home in the suburbs. On my way up to London the morning after a *Play for Today* I'd sit in the train listening to people discussing the previous night's drama and interrupt them with my own opinions.

The great advantage of TV drama was the people who watched it; difficult, challenging things could be said about contemporary life. The theatre, despite the efforts of touring companies and so on, has failed to get its ideas beyond a small enthusiastic audience.

When I finished a draft of *My Beautiful Laundrette*, and *Mother Courage* had gone into rehearsal, Karin Bamborough, David Rose and I discussed directors for the film.

A couple of days later I went to see a friend, David Gothard, who was then running Riverside Studios. I often went for a walk by the river in the early evening, and then I'd sit in David's office. He always had the new books and the latest magazines; and whoever was appearing at Riverside would be around. Riverside stood for tolerance, scepticism and intelligence. The feeling there was that works of art, plays, books and so on, were important. This is a rare thing in England. For many writers, actors, dancers and artists, Riverside was what a university should be: a place to learn and talk and work and meet your contemporaries. There was no other place like it in London and David Gothard was the great encourager, getting work on and introducing people to one another.

He suggested I ask Stephen Frears to direct the film. I thought this an excellent idea, except that I admired Frears too much to have the nerve to ring him. David Gothard did this and I cycled to Stephen's house in Notting Hill, where he lived in a street known as 'directors' row' because of the number of film directors living there.

He said he wanted to shoot my film in February. As it was November already I pointed out that February might be a little soon. Would there be time to prepare, to rewrite? But he had a theory: when you have a problem, he said, bring things forward; do them sooner rather than later. And anyway, February was a good month for him; he made his best films then; England looked especially unpleasant; and people worked faster in the cold.

The producers, Tim Bevan and Sarah Radclyffe, Stephen had worked with before, on promos for rock bands. So the film was set up and I started to rewrite. Stephen and I had long talks, each of us pacing up and down the same piece of carpet, in different directions.

The film started off as an epic. It was to be like *The Godfather*, opening in the past with the arrival of an immigrant family in England and showing their progress to the present. There were to be many scenes set in the 1950s; people would eat bread and dripping and get off boats a lot; there would be scenes of Johnny and Omar as children and large-scale set pieces of racist marches with scenes of mass violence.

We soon decided it was impossible to make a film of such scale. That film is still to be made. Instead I set the film in the present, though references to the past remain.

It was shot in six weeks in February and March 1985 on a low budget and 16mm film. For this I was glad. There were no commercial pressures on us, no one had a lot of money invested in the film who would tell us what to do. And I was tired of seeing lavish films set in exotic locations; it seemed to me that anyone could make such films, providing they had an old book, a hot country, new technology and were capable of aiming the camera at an attractive landscape in the hot country in front of which stood a star in a perfectly clean costume delivering lines from the old book.

We decided the film was to have gangster and thriller elements, since the gangster film is the form that corresponds most closely to the city, with its gangs and violence. And the film was to be an amusement, despite its references to racism, unemployment and Thatcherism. Irony is the modern mode, a way of commenting on bleakness and cruelty without falling into dourness and didacticism. And ever since the first time I heard people in a theatre laugh during a play of mine, I've wanted it to happen again and again.

We found actors – Saeed Jaffrey, for whom I'd written the part; and Roshan Seth I'd seen in David Hare's play *Map of the World*, commanding that huge stage at the National with complete authority. I skidded through the snow to see Shirley Anne Field and on arriving at her flat was so delighted by her charm and enthusiasm, and so ashamed of the smallness of her part, that there and then I added the material about the magic potions, the moving furniture and the walking trousers. It must have seemed that the rest of the film was quite peripheral and she would be playing the lead in a kind of 'Exorcist' movie with a gay Pakistani, a drug-dealer and a fluff-drying spin-drier in the background.

Soon we stood under railway bridges in Vauxhall at two in the morning in March; we knocked the back wall out of someone's flat and erected a platform outside to serve as the balcony of Papa's flat, which had so many railway lines dipping and criss-crossing beside and above it that inside it you shook like peas in maracas; in an old shop we built a laundrette of such authenticity that people came in off the street with their washing; and I stood on the set making up dialogue before the actors did it themselves, and added one or two new scenes.

When shooting was finished and we had about two-and-a-quarter hours of material strung together, we decided to have a showing for a group of 'wise ones'. They would be film directors, novelists and film writers who'd give us their opinions and thereby aid in editing the film. So I sat at the back of the small viewing cinema as they watched the film. We then cut forty-five minutes out.

The film played at the Edinburgh Film Festival and then went into the cinema.

Some Time with Stephen: A Diary

First published in *Dreaming and Scheming*, 2002

2 JUNE 1986

I shove the first draft of *Sammy and Rosie Get Laid* through Stephen Frears's letterbox and run, not wanting him to see me. A few hours later he rings and says: 'This isn't an innocent act!' and refuses to read it. He says he's going to Seattle with Daniel Day Lewis for the weekend to attend a film festival and he'll read it on the plane.

I have many doubts about the script and in lots of ways it's rough, but I can't get any further with it at the moment. In fact, I can't even bear to look at it.

9 JUNE 1986

Scared of ringing Frears and asking his opinion on the script, I ring Dan and ask about the Seattle trip. I also ask – and I am shaky here – if he managed to glance at the script himself, if he perhaps had a few moments in which to pass his eyes over it. He says firmly that he did read it. I ask if Frears liked it. He says Frears did like it. Finally I ring Frears and after much small talk about cricket he says: 'I know why you've rung and it's very good!' It begins then.

10 JUNE 1986

I see the great Indian actor Shashi Kapoor on TV, on the balcony of the Indian dressing-room at the Test match. I'd like him to play the lead in the film, the politician. I've had him in mind since Frears met him in India and said how interesting he was. We try to track him down, but by the time we get to him he's left the country.

12 JUNE 1986

Frears rings me to talk about his availability. He's not going to be around for a while, being preoccupied with *Prick Up Your Ears* and then a film he's shooting in India. I wonder if this is a subtle way of his saying he doesn't want to direct the film.

Meanwhile I send the script to Karin Bamborough at Channel 4. She and David Rose commissioned and paid for all of *My Beautiful Laundrette*. Then I ring Tim Bevan and tell him what's going on.

Bevan is a tall, hard-working man in his mid-twenties, in love with making films and doing deals. He and his partner Sarah Radclyffe are relative newcomers in films, but between them they've been involved in several recent British films: *My Beautiful Laundrette, Caravaggio, Personal Services, Elphida, Wish You Were Here* and *A World Apart*, with many more in the pipeline. Bevan has learned and developed very quickly. He's had to, moving rapidly from making pop promos to major features. His strength as a producer is his knowledge of all aspects of film-making and his ability to protect writers and directors from financial and technical problems. He's not a frustrated writer or director either. While he makes suggestions all along about the script, the direction, the actors, he ensures that everyone is working freely in their own area; his views are valuable and informed, but he never attempts to impose them.

He's keen to read the script and thinks that after the success of the *Laundrette* in the US it shouldn't be a problem raising some of the money there. But Frears won't give Bevan a script to read because Bevan's going to LA and Frears doesn't want him to try and raise money for it. Frears is still working out how best to get the film made. He doesn't want to be pushed into doing it any particular way.

It's a relief to me that other people are involved. Getting a film going is like pushing a huge rock up the side of a mountain and until now, writing the script, I've been doing this alone. Now other people can take the weight.

13 JUNE 1986

I've known Stephen Frears since October 1984 when I sent him the first draft of *My Beautiful Laundrette*. It was made in February and March 1985 and released later that year. After its success in Britain and the US it is slowly opening around the world and Frears, Bevan, the actors and I are still promoting it in various places.

Frears is in his mid-forties and has made four feature films: *Gumshoe*, *The Hit*, *My Beautiful Laundrette* and *Prick Up Your Ears*. He's also produced and directed many films for television, where he served his apprenticeship and worked with many of the best British dramatic writers: Alan Bennett, David Hare, Stephen Poliakoff, Peter Prince, Christopher Hampton. Frears was part of the *Monty Python* generation at Cambridge, where he studied law; many of his contemporaries went into film, TV, theatre and journalism. Later he worked at the Royal Court Theatre as an assistant to Lindsay Anderson.

Whatever Frears wears, he always looks as if he's slept in his clothes and his hair just stands straight up on the top and shoots out at the sides as if he's been electrocuted. His idea of dressing up is to put on a clean pair of plimsolls. The sartorial message is: I can't think about all that stuff, it means nothing to me, I'm a bohemian not a fashion slave. When we were shooting the *Laundrette* Daniel Day Lewis would go up to Stephen as if Stephen were a tramp, and press 20p in his hand, saying: 'Please accept this on behalf of the Salvation Army and buy yourself a cup of tea!'

I was drawn to him from the start because of his irreverence and seriousness, his directness and kindness. While he hates words like 'artist' and 'integrity', since they smack of self-regard, he is immensely skilled and talented; and though he talks a lot about how much money certain directors make, he never makes a film entirely for the money. He has great interest and respect for the young, for their music and films and political interests. As his own generation settles down into comfort and respectability, he is becoming more adventurous and disrespectful of British society, seeing it as part of his work to be sceptical, questioning, doubting and polemical.

Frears's nonconformity and singularity, his penchant for disruption and anarchy, suit and inform the area of film we inhabit, an area which has been especially exciting recently, that of low-budget films made quickly and sometimes quite roughly; films made, to a certain extent, outside the system of studios and big film companies, films that the people involved in can control themselves.

The freshness of these films has been due partly to the subject matter, the exploration of areas of British life not touched on before. Just as one of the excitements of British culture in the 1960s was the discovery of the lower middle class and working class as a subject, one plus of the repressive 1980s has been cultural interest in marginalised and excluded groups.

So I ring Frears and give him an earful about why I think he should direct *Sammy and Rosie Get Laid*. I lay off the flattery for fear of making him extra suspicious, and get technical. I emphasise that it'll be a continuation of the work we've started with *Laundrette* – the mixture of realism and surrealism, seriousness and comedy, art and gratuitous sex.

Frears listens to all this patiently. Then he suddenly says we should make the film for television, on 16mm. I quickly say that I'm not convinced by that. He argues that the equipment is much lighter; you can make films faster. So he suggests we give it to the BBC. If they like it, he says they'll pay for it and our problems will be over. I counter by saying they've become too reactionary, terrified of ripe language and screwing, cowed by censors. If you want to show an arse on the BBC, they behave as if their entire licence fee were at stake.

All the same, he says finally, he sees it as a TV thing, done in the spirit of *Laundrette*.

I watch scenes on TV of South African police beating up protesters and wonder what the minds of the cops must be like. That's partly what I want to get at with *Sammy and Rosie* – it's my puzzling about the mind of a torturer, the character of a man capable of extreme violence and cruelty while he continues to live a life with others. Does he speak of love in the evenings?

Receive a letter from an aunt who lives in the north of England. After seeing *Laundrette* she frequently rings my father to abuse him. 'Your son is a complete bastard!' she screeches down the phone, as if it's my father's fault I write such things. 'Can't you control the little bastard!' she yells. 'Humiliating us in public! Suppose people find out I'm related to him!'

In her letter she says: 'I tried to phone you, but I believe you were in the USA boring the pants off the Americans with your pornography . . . Worst of all, the film was offensive to your father's distinguished family. Uncle was portrayed in a very bad light, drunk in bed with his brand of vodka, and uncut toenails . . . this was totally uncalled for and mischievous. It only brings to light your complete lack of loyalty, integrity and compassion . . . We didn't know you were a "poofter". We do hope you're aware of AIDS and its dangers, if not, then a medical leaflet can be sent to you. Why oh why do you have to promote the widely held view of the British that all evil stems from Pakistani immigrants? Thank goodness for top quality films like *Gandhi*.'

I think of something Thackeray wrote in *Vanity Fair:* 'If a man has committed wrong in life, I don't know any moralist more anxious to point his errors out to the world than his own relations.'

I decide to name the Asian lesbian in *Sammy and Rosie* after her.

Earlier this year I ran into Philip Roth at a party and told him about the hostility I'd received from this aunt and other Pakistanis complaining about their portrayal in *Laundrette* and other things I'd written. Roth said the same thing happened to him after *Portnoy's Complaint*. Indeed he writes about this in *The Ghost Writer*.

In that novel, Nathan, a young Jewish novelist 'looking for admiration and praise', writes a story about an old family feud. He shows it to his father. The father is shattered by the public betrayal. 'You didn't leave anything out,' he moans. Except the achievements, the hard work, the decency. He adds sadly: 'I wonder if you fully understand just how little love there is in this world for Jewish people.'

When Nathan protests that they are in Newark, not Germany, the father seeks a second opinion, that of Judge Leopold Wapter. Wapter immediately applies the literary acid test which he believes every Jewish book must endure: will the story warm the heart of Joseph Goebbels? The result is . . . positive. So why, why, screams Wapter, in a story with a Jewish background, must there be adultery, incessant fighting within a family over money and warped human behaviour in general?

What Wapter's Complaint demands is 'positive images'. It requires useful lies and cheering fictions: the writer as public relations officer, as hired liar.

Like *Laundrette*, *Sammy and Rosie* is quite a personal story, autobiographical, not in its facts, but emotionally. The woman involved (I'll call her Sarah) asked to read the script. I said no, because the character will change as the film goes through several drafts; the actress playing the part will also change it, as will Frears when he starts to work on it. It's also difficult to write accurately about real people in fiction – however much you might want to – because the demands of the idea are usually such that you have to transform the original person to fit the constraints of the story. All the same, I'm nervous about what Sarah will think of it. I know that in certain passages I've been spiteful.

On the phone Frears talks about Art Malik for the part of Sammy. He's an attractive actor, but we both wonder if he's fly enough for the role.

20 JUNE 1986
Meeting at Channel 4 with Karin Bamborough and David Rose to discuss the film. Together they've been the architects of a remarkable number of low-budget independent films which are mostly (or partly) funded by TV money for theatrical release. This series of films has ensured a revival in British film-making (they're almost the only people making films in Britain today) and has

given encouragement to women and black film-makers, first-time directors and writers, working on material that wouldn't be acceptable to the mainstream commercial world.

Their success has partly been due to their initiative in approaching writers from other forms – novelists, playwrights, short-story writers and journalists – to write films. They know that usually the best screenplays are not written by people who call themselves screenwriters, but by good writers, writers who excel in other forms. After all, the 'rules' of screenwriting can be learned in an hour. But the substance of a decent screenplay, character, story, mood, pace, can only come from a cultivated imagination. Although it's virtually impossible to make a good film without a good screenplay, screenwriting itself is such a bastardised, ignoble profession (director Joseph Mankiewicz said 'the screenwriter is the highest-paid secretary in the world') that writers who wish to survive have to avoid it, turning only to the movies as a well-paid sideline, regrettably not regarding it as a serious medium.

Karin tells me that the characters in the first draft aren't strong enough yet. I'll have to do two or three more drafts. David Rose says he regrets it all being set in London since he feels too many C4 films have been set there. Can't I set it in Birmingham, he says.

21 JUNE 1986
The contract arrives from C4 offering a commission for *Sammy and Rosie*. They're offering a pathetic amount of money.

6 JULY 1986
My agent rings me in New York to say the idea now is to form a three-way company to make the film: Frears, Bevan and Sarah Radclyffe, and I. This way we'll be able to control everything about the film.

9 JULY 1986
I speak to Frears who is about to start filming *Prick Up Your Ears*. He says he wants to prepare *Sammy and Rosie* after he's finished his Indian film. This means we'll shoot it in the autumn of 1987.

It's a long time to wait: I feel let down, life goes slack once more. But it'll force me to write something else in the mean time.

9 AUGUST 1986

Lunch at '192' in Notting Hill with Bevan and Radclyffe, and Frears. Shashi arrives with his secretary after everyone else. He has on a loose brown costume, with a dark red and chocolate scarf flung over his shoulder. He is so regal and dignified, stylish and exotic, that a shiver goes through the restaurant.

I mention that though this is the first time we've met, I saw him on the balcony at the Lord's Test. He says he wore the same clothes then and had trouble getting into the pavilion, so conventional and uptight are the MCC. So he told them he'd just had lunch with Mrs Thatcher and if his national dress was good enough for the Prime Minister surely it would be acceptable to the MCC.

In the charm department he has real class and yet he is genuinely modest. I feel a little embarrassed at asking him to be in this film, small and fairly sordid as it is. But Shashi says he thinks the script is better than that for *Laundrette*. He adds that he's available at our convenience.

It's a sunny day and when Shashi leaves we stroll back to Frears's house, pleased with Shashi's enthusiasm. We talk a bit about the other parts: Claire Bloom as Alice, with Miranda Richardson or Judy Davis as Rosie perhaps.

Frears talks about the part of Anna, the American photographer, saying she isn't sympathetic enough: I've parodied her. He's right about this and I lack grip on the character. The process of writing is so much one of seeking ideas in one's unconscious, whatever they are, and then later justifying them, filling them out and finding what the hell they mean, if anything. The entire script will have to be subject to this scrutiny.

14 AUGUST 1986

At last I give the script to Sarah to read. Sarah and I met at university and lived together for six years. Since she moved out, we've continued to see a lot of each other.

When Sarah reads it she is angry and upset at the same time. I've said things that she feels are true, but which I've never said to her. The worry is, she adds, that people will think she is Rosie and she'll be petrified like that for ever, with her freedom possessed by the camera. She'll no longer be in reasonable control of the way people think of her. Won't they have this crude cinema idea?

All this makes me feel guilty and sneaky; it makes me think that writers are like spies, poking into failures and weaknesses for good stories. Necessarily, because that's how they see the world, writers constantly investigate the lives of the people they are involved with. They keep private records of these private relationships. And on the surface they appear to be participating normally in life. But a few years later, it's all written down, embellished, transformed, distorted, but still a recognisable bit of someone's lived life.

Bevan has sent the script to Art Malik and Miranda Richardson, who I ran into the other day at the Royal Court. I told her about the film and she seemed interested, but it seems she'll be doing the Spielberg film *Empire of the Sun* at the same time.

1 SEPTEMBER 1986

To Paris with Frears, Bevan and Daniel Day Lewis. Everywhere you go here British films are showing: *Clockwise, Mona Lisa, Room with a View, Laundrette.* There seem to be more cinemas per square kilometre here than anywhere else I've been. I do interviews all day through an interpreter who is the daughter-in-law of Raymond Queneau.

Dan is something of a star now, and as an actor has moved on to another plane. He's here rehearsing for the movie of *The Unbearable Lightness of Being.* Dan dresses in black and doesn't shave. He carries a black bag hooped across his body and looks like an artist, a painter, as he strides across bridges and down boulevards.

We meet to chat in the bar of the George V Hotel where Frears is being interviewed. The journalist says admiringly to Frears: 'I've met a lot of men like you, only they're all Italian.'

Frears has thought a great deal about how to do *Sammy and Rosie* and has now decided that the best thing is to make it on 35mm for theatrical release, keeping the budget as low as possible. Bevan thinks we can raise most of the money for the film in America. Frears thinks this is a good idea since it'll save Channel 4 money: they'll be able to give the money to film-makers who can't get money elsewhere.

18 DECEMBER 1986

Suddenly we're going into production at the beginning of January, shooting early in March, as Frears's Indian project has been delayed. So the script has to start looking ready. Try to get the story going earlier, Frears says. And the riots: we're too familiar with them from television. Something more has to be going on than people throwing bottles at policemen. I interpret this to mean that what happens between the characters during these scenes is of primary interest.

I meet Frances Barber in the production office. She's a very experienced theatre actor and I've known her work for years, as she's risen up through the fringe to join the RSC. She's done some film work (she was in *Prick Up Your Ears*), but not yet played a major role. The feeling is that she's ready, that she's at the stage Daniel was at just before *Laundrette*. She talks well about the script and can see the problems of playing against characters with the charm I've tried to give Rafi, and the bright childishness of Sammy. Rosie mustn't seem moralistic or self-righteous.

Later Frears rings me, delighted to be in the middle of an interview with a young Pakistani actor, Ayub Khan Din, who is upstairs having a pee and is being considered for the part of Sammy. Art Malik, who we discussed first but were sceptical of, has anyway complained about the scenes in bed with Anna and about the scene where Sammy wanks, snorts coke and sucks on a milkshake at the same time. In the end he says the script isn't good enough. I think he prefers easier and more glamorous kinds of roles.

Ayub had a small part in *Laundrette* which was later cut from the film. I remember him coming to the cast screening, eager to see himself in his first film, and Frears having to take him to one side to explain that, well, unfortunately, he'd had to cut his big scene. Since then Ayub has grown and developed, though he's only twenty-five and the part was written for someone older.

Now the film is going ahead and other people are starting to get involved, I can feel my responsibility for it diminishing. This is a relief to me. I've done most of the hard work I have to do. Now I can enjoy the process of the film being shot and released. Any rewriting I do from now on will be nothing compared with the isolated and unhelped strain of working out the idea in the first place.

I remember sitting in a hotel room in Washington, overlooking the Dupont Circle, drinking beer after beer and trying to jump over the high wall which was the halfway point of the script. I got stuck for months with the film after the 'fuck' night – the climax, the section at the centre where the three couples copulate simultaneously. (Originally I wanted to call the film *The Fuck*.) What would be the consequences of these three acts? What would they mean to all the characters and how would these acts change them? It wasn't until I decided to extend the waste ground material and the consequent eviction, until I introduced this new element, that I was able to continue. The problem was whether this material would be convincing. It wasn't based on anything I'd known, though for a long time I've been interested in anarchist ideas – a respectable English political tradition, from Winstanley, through William Godwin and onwards. If anything, it was based on some of the young people who'd attended theatre workshops I'd given. They had terrific energy, intelligence and inventiveness. But because of poverty, homelessness, unemployment and bad schooling, they were living in the interstices of the society: staying in squats, dealing drugs, and generally scavenging around. It seemed to me that this society had little to offer them, no idea how to use them or what to do with their potential.

Because of this block I frequently thought of abandoning the film. I wrote the same scene twenty-five or thirty times in the hope of a breakthrough. I'd set up this complicated story; I'd invented the characters and let things happen between them, but then it all stopped. This is where real life or direct autobiography fails you: the story has to be completed on its own terms.

Sarah Radclyffe has some reservations about the script. She doubts whether Sammy and Rosie would be ignorant of Rafi's involvement in the torture of his political enemies, especially if they'd been to visit him in his own country. Karin Bamborough said something similar and suggested I change it so the film opened with them all meeting for the first time. That would be a considerable rewrite. Also, there's no reason why they should have found out about the details of Rafi's crimes since he would have worked through hired hit-men and through people who wouldn't necessarily have been immediately identified with him. It would have taken years for this information to be discovered and collated.

This morning in our office it was like the Royal Court in exile. Frears, myself, and Debbie McWilliams (the casting director) all worked at the Court. Tunde Ikoli, a young writer and director who worked as Lindsay Anderson's assistant at the Court, was in the office. We see a number of interesting and experienced black actors. Things have certainly changed in that respect from four or five years ago. Many of these actors who have either worked at the National Theatre's Studio with Peter Gill (ex-Royal Court) or at the Court serve to remind us of the importance of the theatre, not only in itself, but as a seedbed for film and TV.

We talk about the audience there is for our kind of films. Aged between eighteen and forty, mostly middle-class and well educated, film- and theatre-literate, liberal progressive or leftish, this massive and sophisticated audience doesn't want to be patronised by teen films: they'll support a poor and rough cinema rich in ideas and imagination.

21 DECEMBER 1986

Michael Barker from Orion Classics rings to say Orion are going to push for an Oscar nomination for me. He doesn't think I'll win – Woody Allen will win for *Hannah and Her Sisters* – but he thinks he can swing the nomination.

23 DECEMBER 1986

Hugo, the film's designer, rings to say they've found an excellent location for the caravan site. This is in Notting Hill. The flat concrete curve of the motorway hangs above a dusty stretch of waste ground which itself is skirted by a mainline railway line and a tube track. I know the area he means and it's excellent.

They're also looking for a house in the area to serve as Sammy's and Rosie's flat. There's been talk of building it in a studio which would be easier, but Frears feels at the moment it should be done on location.

Bevan is trying to find an area where we can stage the riots. There are obviously problems with the police over this, and I'll have to prepare a doctored script to show them. When he goes to see them he refers to the riots as 'scuffles'!

I run into Claire Bloom in the street nearby and yesterday I met her husband, Philip Roth, in a health-food shop in Notting Hill. He asks how the film is going and tells me he prefers to keep away from films, not having liked any of the films made from his books. It reminds me of the second time I met Philip and Claire. Frears and I were outside the American Embassy walking through the crowd protesting against the bombing of Libya. Mostly the occasion was like a Methodist church fête. Then, there at the barrier nearest to the Embassy were Philip and Claire, very angry.

24 DECEMBER 1986

Frears and I talk about *Sammy and Rosie* in its style and rhythm, being far more leisurely than *Laundrette*. The relationships are more developed; it needs more room to breathe. It's less of a shocker; more of a grown-up film.

29 DECEMBER 1986

Frears slightly miffed by the realisation of how much Thatcher would approve of us: we're a thrifty, enterprising, money-making small business. I say: But part of our purpose is to make popular films which are critical of British society. He says: Thatcher wouldn't care about that, she'd just praise our initiative for doing something decent despite the odds; the real difficulty of making films in Britain today made more difficult by this government.

4 JANUARY 1987

Long meeting with Frears last night at his house. The first time, really, we've sat down and discussed the script. His ideas are exactly the stimulation I've been waiting for to enable me to find a resolution to the film. After the 'fuck' night the film fragments, the intercutting is too quick, the scenes are too short. This is because I haven't worked out exactly what is going on, what I want to say. What Frears and I do, as we talk, as he puts his children to bed, is invent new elements to bind the story together: Rani and Vivia putting pressure on Rafi; Rani and Vivia putting pressure on Rosie with regard to Rafi living in her flat; some of the other women pursuing Rafi through the city, perhaps harrying him to his death; all the characters (and not just some of them, as it is now) meeting at the eviction scene and their relationships being resolved there.

Now I have to sit down and look at the whole thing again. It's not as if I can rewrite bits and pieces. It'll be an entirely new draft. I suppose if you want to be a decent writer you have to have the ability to rip up what you've done and go back and start again, tear up your best lines and ideas and replace them with better lines and ideas, however hard this is and however long it takes.

5 JANUARY 1987

I get up at six in the morning unable to sleep, so paranoid am I about this thing ever getting rewritten. In this frozen deserted city I start to fiddle with the script, contra what I said yesterday. When I realise the futility of this fiddling I put a fresh sheet in the typewriter and start at page 1. I do no planning, give it no thought and just go at it, walking out on the tightrope. The idea is not to inhibit myself, not be over-critical or self-conscious or self-censoring, otherwise I'll get blocked and the act of writing will be like trying to drive a car with the brakes on.

Today is the first day of pre-production and everyone officially starts work: the director, the casting director, the production manager, designer and so on. The young lighting cameraman, Oliver Stapleton, is going to shoot this film, as he did *Laundrette*. That film was his first feature, though since then he's done *Absolute Beginners* and *Prick Up Your Ears*. So it's all terrifically exciting. What a shame that it feels as if the script is disintegrating in my hands. The new ideas touch every other element in the film, altering them, giving them different significance. Little of what I've written seems secure now, except the characters; certainly not the story. As the whole thing goes into the mixer my fear is that it'll all fall apart.

7 JANUARY 1987

I write a scene this morning between Rani, Vivia and Rosie at the end of the party, which is crucial to the film. Rani and Vivia accuse Rosie of lacking political integrity. It's a dramatic scene and will wind the film up just when it needs it. I'm surprised that it's taken me so long to see how useful this kind of pressure on Rosie could be. It's partly because it's only since that conversation with Frears that I've seen the point of Rani and Vivia in the film. They were in the first draft – I dropped them in because unconsciously I knew they'd be of use. It's taken me till the fourth draft to find out for what exactly.

8 JANUARY 1987

I spend most of the day trying to write a final scene for the film, which at the moment is Rafi staggering around on the waste ground during the eviction, and Sammy standing on the motorway shouting down at Rosie without being heard. This isn't satisfactory. So I try going back to a previous ending, which has Rosie and Margy and Eva, her women friends, deciding to move into the flat with Rosie while Sammy goes off on his own to a house he's bought. But I don't believe in this ending.

Usually when I have a block I put the film or story in a drawer for thirty days, like putting a pie in the oven, and when I take it out it's cooked. But there isn't time for that now.

So I put the last few pages in the typewriter and rewrite them, trying to quieten my mind and allow fresh ideas to pop in as they will. So it occurs to me, or rather it writes itself, that Rafi should hang himself. As the words go down I know I'm on to something dramatic and powerful. I'm also doing something which will be depressing. I've no idea how this suicide will affect the rest of the film and no idea what it means or says. I can work that out later. It's a relief to have had a new idea, and a creative pleasure to solve a problem not by refining what one has already done, but by slamming down a bizarre and striking fresh image!

10 JANUARY 1987

Bevan, Rebecca (the location manager), Jane (production manager) and I go to North Kensington to look at locations for the scenes at the beginning of the film with Rosie visiting the old man and finding him dead in the bath, waiting for the ambulance, and watching the boys' bonfire in the centre of the estate. To the thirtieth floor of a tower block (which won design awards in the 1960s), with several young kids in the lift. The lift is an odd shape: very deep, with a low roof. Jane says this is so they can get bodies in coffins down from the thirtieth floor. We walk around other blocks in the area. They are filthy, derelict places, falling down, graffiti-sprayed, wind-blown, grim and humming with the smell of shit, implacable in the hatred of humanity they embody. The surrounding shops are barricaded with bars and wire mesh. I was brought up in London. It's my city. I'm no Britisher, but a Londoner. And it's filthier and more run-down now than it's ever been.

I get home and speak to Frears on the phone. The double imperative: that the rewritten script be handed in on Monday and yet, as he says, be more intricate. 'Deeper' is the word he uses. Christ. Have told no one yet about the new ending.

I have the sense today of the film starting to move away from me, of this little thing which I wrote in my bedroom in Fulham now becoming public property. On the crew list there are now already fifty names, at least a quarter of them from *Laundrette*.

12 JANUARY 1987

Frears comes over. I sit opposite him as he turns over the pages of the script. We talk about each page. Because the film is about the relations between men and women in contemporary Britain and has political content, we're beginning to realise how important it is that it says what we want it to say. That means working out what it is we believe!

As Frears gets nearer the end I get more nervous. I've typed up the scene where Rafi hangs himself and it's quite different from the innocuous and rather dissipated finales so far.

After reading it Frears says nothing for a while. He jumps up and walks round and round the flat. It's started to snow outside; it's very cold. Is he just trying to keep warm?

We talk until one-thirty about this end and worry whether it's too brutal both on the audience and as an act of aggression by Rafi against the rest of the characters he's become involved with. We talk about the possibility of Rafi dying of a heart attack! But this is too contingent. It's the power of the deliberate act that we like.

We discuss Chekhov's *Seagull*. I say Rafi's suicide could be like Trepliov's at the end of that play: understated, with the action off-stage, one person discovering it and then returning to the room to tell everyone else. In this room there'd be: Rani, Vivia, Alice, Anna, Eva, Bridget, Rosie.

We decide to leave it for the moment. More importantly, we're going to New York soon to cast Anna the photographer. I'm still not clear what she's doing in the film. I've deliberately avoided rewriting her bits.

Seven in the morning and freezing cold. Streets covered in snow. Behind me I can hear the tubes rattling along at the back of the house. Outside the careful traffic and people starting to go to work. I'm not in the mood for rewriting this thing. Still a few scenes to be revised, but I'm sick of it. It says on the piece of paper in front of me: fifth draft, but in reality it must be the eighth or ninth. If each draft is about 100 pages, that's 900 pages of writing!

When I first moved into this part of west London, in 1978, I felt vulnerable. It was like living on the street. People walked by on their way to work just yards from my head. In time I relaxed and would lie in bed and hear and feel London around me, stretching out for miles.

These west London streets by the railway line have gone wrong. In 1978 most of the five-storey houses with their crumbling pillars, peeling façades and busted windows were derelict, inhabited by itinerants, immigrants, drug-heads and people not ashamed of being seen drunk on the street. On the balcony opposite a man regularly practised the bagpipes at midnight. Now the street is crammed with people who work for a living. Young men wear striped shirts and striped ties; the women wear blue jumpers with white shirts, turned-up collars and noses, and pearls. They drive Renault 5s and late at night as you walk along the street, you can see them in their clean shameless basements having dinner parties and playing Trivial Pursuit on white tablecloths. Now the centre of the city is inhabited by the young rich and serviced by everyone else: now there is the re-establishment of firm class divisions; now the 1960s and the ideals of that time seem like an impossible dream or naivety.

Though I was at school and not politically active in 1968, I was obsessively aware of the excitement and originality of those years. I had the records, the books, the clothes; I saw the 1960s on TV and was formed by what I missed out on. I wasn't involved enough to become disillusioned. The attitudes that formed me are, briefly: that openness and choice in sexual behaviour is liberating and that numerous accretions of sexual guilt and inhibition are psychologically damaging; that the young are innately original and vigorous, though this special quality is to do with not being burdened with responsibility and the determinations of self-interest; that there should be a fluid, non-hierarchical society with free movement across classes and that these classes will eventually be dissolved; that ambition and competitiveness are stifling narrowers of personality; and that all authority should be viewed with suspicion and constantly questioned.

The past ten years of repression have been a continuous surprise to me. Somehow I haven't been able to take them seriously, since I imagine the desire for more freedom, more pleasure, more self-expression to be fundamental to life. So I continue to think, in that now old way, in terms of the 'straight' world and the rest, the more innocent and lively ones standing against the corrupt and stuffy. I still think of businessmen as semi-criminals; I'm suspicious of anyone in a suit; I like drugs, especially hash, and I can't understand why people bother to get married. Ha!

14 JANUARY 1987

Frears rings and says the scene where Alice tells Rafi to go, at the end of the film after he's been chased out of Sammy's and Rosie's flat by Vivia and Rani, is boring, boring, boring. There has to be a dramatic action rather than extended verbals as it is now. I say: well what fucking dramatic action? He says: no idea – you do the paperwork, I just do the pictures!

16 JANUARY 1987

Frances Barber seems enthusiastic about the rewrites but says she'd been disturbed by the new end. It reverses the film, she thinks, in that Rafi now seems to accept his guilt for torturing people. Frances says this seems inconsistent with his having argued so strongly for political expediency in the restaurant scene. I say I don't want him committing suicide out of guilt. It's that he's come to the end. No one wants him. There's nowhere for him to go, neither at home nor in Britain.

Frears has a session with Frances and Ayub, which he video-tapes. Ayub is very nervous, not surprisingly. We've cast Frances and probably Ayub will be offered the part tomorrow.

17 JANUARY 1987

We look at the tape of Frances and Ayub together. They look good together. Ayub waits downstairs in his agent's office, refusing to go home until we make our decision. He comes into the room looking dazed with tension. We offer him the job. He thanks us all and shakes hands with us.

Frears has decided that the film should be much more about young people than I'd imagined. Because of Ayub being five years younger than Frances we could as easily cast the people around them down in age as up. Frears says casting it young will make it more cheerful. I'm all for cheerfulness, though worried that Rosie will seem oddly older than everyone else.

18 JANUARY 1987

Frears talks about the problems of shooting the riots, especially after a friend said: Oh no, not a lot of black people rioting. So we talk about avoiding the TV news-footage approach: screaming mobs, bleeding policemen. What you don't get in news footage is detail. In *The Battle of Algiers*, for example, the director humanises the violence. You see the faces of those to whom violence is being done. In the torture scene, you don't see the act, but only the faces of those around it, streaming tears.

In *Sammy and Rosie* you do see the circumstances from which the riot comes – the shooting of a black woman by the police. And we see, in the circumstances, how justifiable the riot is. The difficulty arises from the fact that black people are so rarely represented on TV; if when they are shown, they're only throwing rocks at the police, you're in danger of reinforcing considerable prejudice. I suppose this depends partly on how you see the riot, or revolt. I know I supported it, but as Orwell says about Auden, it's easy to say that if you're elsewhere when the violence takes place.

After Frears said the Alice–Rafi parting scene at the end of the film isn't dramatic enough I shake my brains and come up with a Miss Havisham scene set in the cellar of the house. I have Alice furiously throwing open a suitcase in which she's packed the clothes she'd intended to take on her planned elopement with Rafi in the mid-1950s. I also have her showing Rafi the diaries she kept then, in which she poured out her heart to him – the physical and visual representation of what was formerly just dialogue.

To the opera on Friday with a vegetarian friend. A woman in a long sable coat sits next to us. My friend says: I wish I carried a can of spray paint in my bag and could shoot it over her coat. Thought it might be an idea to stick in the film. But where?

20 JANUARY 1987

Debbie McWilliams saw a pop group, the Fine Young Cannibals, on TV and asks the singer, Roland Gift, to come into the office. He shows up looking splendid, proud and vulnerable, with his manager. I ask the women in the office to get a look at him through the office window and let us know if they want to rip his clothes off with their teeth. As most of them seem to want this, Roland inches closer to the part of Danny.

On the way home from the movies the other night, at Piccadilly tube station a group of young Jewish kids gathers at the top of the escalator. Suddenly, around them, are a bunch of Arsenal football supporters who stand and chant 'Yiddo, yiddo!' at these kids. The kids look embarrassed rather than frightened, but they do move closer together, standing in a little huddle. It's a difficult moment. What do you do when it comes to it? Walk on, watch, or pile in? What are you made of? What would you give up? I can see a lot of other dithering people in the vicinity have this dilemma. But no one does anything. The chanting goes on. Then the youths disappear down the escalator, their voices echoing around the building. It's the first time I've seen this kind of anti-Semitism in London. Decide to put it in the film somewhere. The structure is secure enough now for anything odd or interesting that happens to have a place. All the bits and pieces will just have to get along with each other, like people at a party.

23 JANUARY 1987

Problems with Meera Syal, the actress we want to play Rani. Max Stafford-Clark, artistic director of the Royal Court, rings to say Meera has already committed herself to Caryl Churchill's play *Serious Money*. She also wants to play Rani in our film. At the moment the schedule can't be arranged so she can do both. We don't want to press her to choose, for fear she'll choose the Court. It's painful to her, especially as Asian actors get offered so little work.

Anyway, we'll deal with it later. In the mean time we're going to my favourite city, New York!

25 JANUARY 1987

New York. This city is snowbound and every time you look round, someone has skidded on to their back in the street. New York is cold in a way London never is: here your face freezes, here the fluid in your eyes seems to ice over.

The entrance of our hotel, on Central Park West, has a silver-lined overhang in which bright lights are embedded. This ensures that the hotel shines like a battery of torches in a blackout for hundreds of yards around; indeed, if you're driving through the park you can see it glowing through the trees. In this overhang there are heaters which warm the street and melt insubordinate snowflakes which may drift on to the hotel's red carpet or float on to the hat of the doorman. Everywhere you go in this city there are notices urging you to save energy while outside this hotel they are heating the street!

Frears is a prisoner in his hotel room, doing publicity for *Prick Up Your Ears*. Food and drink is brought up to him. Between interviews he looks out of the window at Central Park. His talk schedule is exhausting. There was a time when I thought that talking about yourself to someone who said little, listened intently and made notes or recorded what you said was the ideal relationship. But after the first three hours your tongue is dry, your mouth will not work, your jaws ache, as after six hours of fellatio. The only respite is to question the journalists and hope they'll revive you by telling you about themselves.

A journalist asks me how I came upon the central idea of *Sammy and Rosie*. I start to think about it, but it is complicated; an idea usually has many sources.

One source was the great Japanese film *Tokyo Story* in which an old couple who live in the country go to visit their children in the city and are treated shabbily by them. I started off thinking of *Sammy and Rosie* as a contemporary remake of this desperately moving and truthful film. Sometimes I wish my own script had the simplicity, luminosity and straightforward humanity of Ozu's masterpiece, that I hadn't added so many characters, themes and gewgaws.

Another source was a play I once wrote and abandoned about an Asian politician living in London in the 1960s and having an affair with a young woman. I retained the politician and dropped everything else.

There was also a story I was told about a member of my family who loved an Englishwoman, left her after promising to return to England to marry her, and never came back, though the word is she loves him still and continues to wait.

When Frears has finished his interviews for the day he says a journalist told him, when they were discussing British films, that he didn't think anything dramatic ever happened in Britain now. This journalist's view of Britain sounds like Orson Welles in *The Third Man* talking about Switzerland, only capable of producing the cuckoo clock!

The journalist's remark hits a nerve. It relates to the British sense of inferiority about its film industry: not only the feeling that the British can't really make good films, but that contemporary British subjects and themes are really too small, too insignificant. So British films are often aimed at American audiences and attempt to deal with 'universal' or 'epic' themes as in *Gandhi*, *The Mission*, *The Killing Fields*, *Cry Freedom*.

The journalist's view isn't entirely surprising since a lot of English 'art' also dwells, gloats on and relives nostalgic scenarios of wealth and superiority. It's easy therefore for Americans to see Britain as just an old country, as a kind of museum, as a factory for producing versions of lost greatness. After all, many British films do reflect this: *Chariots of Fire*, *A Room with a View*, the Raj epics, and the serials *Brideshead Revisited* and *The Jewel in the Crown*. Even the recent past, the Beatles, punks, the numerous Royal Weddings, are converted into quaintness, into tourist mugs and postcards, into saleable myths. If imperialism is the highest form of capitalism, then tourism is its ghostly afterlife in this form of commercial nostalgia which is sold as 'art' or 'culture'.

But some British dignity remains, unlike in New York where a friend of mine rings a fashionable restaurant on a Saturday night and they tell him they don't have a table. My friend, who in the American manner is very persistent, says he is bringing a screenwriter with him – me. The person in the restaurant asks: We may be able to squeeze your party in, sir, but please tell me: what are the screenwriter's credits?!

26 JANUARY 1987

We troop off to the famous theatrical restaurant Sardi's for an award dinner. Like executioners, photographers in black balaclavas crowd the entrance. Going in, I realise we've arrived too early. We sit down and they bring us our food while others are still arriving. The salmon tastes like wallpaper. Around the walls there are hideous caricatures of film stars and famous writers. Thankfully the ceremony is not televised or competitive: you know if you've won; they don't torment you with any opening of envelopes. Sissy Spacek and Lynn Redgrave, obviously experienced at the awards game, time it just right, so that when they arrive the whole room is in place and is forced to turn and look at them. Photographers shove through the crowd and climb across tables to get to them.

I see Norman Mailer come in. He is stocky like a boxer and healthy of face, though he looks frail when he walks. It will be a thrilling moment for me to have the great man rest his eyes on me when I receive my award for the *Laundrette* screenplay. When the playwright Beth Henley announces my name I eagerly look out for Mailer from the podium. I start into my speech but almost stop talking when I see Mailer's place is now vacant and across the restaurant he is rapidly mounting the stairs to watch the final of the Super Bowl on TV.

27 JANUARY 1987
Spend two mornings in the hotel room interviewing actresses for the part of Anna. About twenty come in and we have longish conversations with all of them: they're frank and lively and seem healthier and more confident than their British counterparts, somehow less beaten down by things. They are less educated too. The American film world isn't adjacent to the theatre or literary world as it can be in London. It's closer to rock 'n' roll, if anything.

An actress called Wendy Gazelle seems untypical of the group we see. She is less forthright, more sensitive and attractive in a less orthodox way. When Wendy reads, in that room overlooking the park through which people are skiing, it is heartbreaking. I'm so pleased she can invest the somewhat duff dialogue with feeling and meaning that I urge the others to choose her.

In the evening to the Café Luxembourg with Leon from Cinecom, the company that, along with Channel 4, is financing our film. Frears and I refer to Leon as 'the man that owns us', which he doesn't seem to mind. He's thirty-four, friendly and intelligent, with long hair in a pigtail. Bevan, Frears and I are apprehensive about the pressure his company might put on us to massage or roll our film in a certain direction. We'll just have to wait and see.

28 JANUARY 1987
To a smart party on the Upper West Side, given by a New York agent for the German director Doris Dorrie. It's a large apartment in front of which is a courtyard and behind it a view of the river.

Marcie, the publicist for *Laundrette* in New York says: I wouldn't object to being the accountant of the people in this room! She points out: Isabella Rossellini, Alan Pakula, Matthew Modine, Michael Douglas and various others. Michael Douglas, polite and friendly, praises the British Royal Family to Frears and me for a considerable time, obviously thinking this'll please us. On the way back we pass a laundromat called *My Beautiful Laundrette* done up in neon: it offers Reverse Cycle Washing, Fluff Drying and Expert Folding. Two days later I go back and this laundrette has closed for good.

We wonder why the film has done well in the US. It's partly, I think, because of its theme of success at any price; and partly because the puritan and prurient theme of two outcast boys (outcast from society and having escaped the world of women) clinging together in passionate blood-brotherhood is a dream of American literature and film from *Huckleberry Finn* to the work of Walt Whitman and on to *Butch Cassidy and the Sundance Kid*.

29 JANUARY 1987

I ride the subway across New York to have lunch with Leon at the Russian Tea Room. In the subway car a couple with a kid kiss shamelessly. A legless black man in a wheelchair propels himself through the car, carrying a paper cup. Everyone gives him something. The streets here are full of beggars now; every block someone asks you for money. Before going out I ensure I have a selection of loose change to give away, just as I would in Pakistan.

The young people in NY that you see on the street or subway are far less eccentric, original and fashionable than kids are in Britain. The kids in London, despite unemployment and poverty, have taste; they're adventurous and self-conscious. They're walking exhibitions: billboards of style, wearing jumble-sale and designer clothes together. In Britain fashion starts on the street. Here the kids are sartorial corpses. They all wear sports clothes. *There are even women wearing business suits and running shoes.*

Some time with Stephen: A Diary

The Russian Tea Room is a fashionable restaurant for movie people. It's plusher than Sardi's, apparently more 'cultured', and patronised by people who have money. It has semi-circular booths in red and gold: booths for two in the entrance, convenient for both seeing and being seen, and larger ones inside. It has a festive atmosphere. There are shining samovars, red and gold pompoms on the lamp-shades and the staff wear red tunics. It's like a kind of Santa's grotto with waitresses. Powerful New York agents do business here, reserving several booths for their clients and associates and moving from booth to booth like door-to-door salesmen, dealing and negotiating.

Leon has this time brought with him some serious reinforcements to deal with the script 'difficulties', a beautiful and smart woman called Shelby who works with him.

Oh, how we eat! Oh, how I like life now! I have dark brown pancakes on which the waitress spreads sour cream. She forks a heap of orange caviar on to this and pours liquid butter over the lot. This is then folded. This is then placed in the mouth.

Shelby leans forward. As each caviar egg explodes on my tongue like a little sugar bomb, Shelby tells me she has just read all five drafts of the script. I am flattered. But more, she has compared and contrasted them all. More wine? She talks knowledgeably about them. She seems to know them better than I do. Scene 81 in draft 2, she says, is sharper than scene 79 in draft 4. Perhaps I could go back to that? Well. I look at her. She is telling me all this in a kindly tone. In the end, she implies, it is up to me, but ... She expresses her reservations, which are quite substantial, at argued length.

I nod to everything, not wanting to induce indigestion. I am also experimenting with the Zen method of bending with the wind, so that when the cleansing storm stops, the tree of my spirit will gaily snap back to its usual upright position. But will this helpful puffing ever stop?

We talk about the end of the film and the hanging of Rafi. They suggest Rafi be murdered by the Ghost. I manage to say (though I object on principle to discussing such things at all) that this would be predictable. Leon says: How can a Ghost murdering a politician in an anarchist commune be predictable?

By now I am sucking and licking on light ice-cream with whipped cream and grenadine. Shelby is into her stride. Perhaps my lack of response means I am thinking about what she is saying? The script hasn't necessarily improved at all, it's become cruder, more obvious. Why have you developed the black women, Vivia and Rani? Well . . . I almost begin to fight back when she starts to fumble in her bag. She brings out a letter. There, read this please, she says. It's from someone who cares.

The letter, from a reader in the company, is addressed to me. Its tone implores me to see sense. 'The version I read in October was just about perfect and the fifth draft has been tinkered with entirely too much . . . The fifth draft seems a little preachy and one-dimensional. It's lost so much for the sake of clarity and it's not nearly as successful as a film . . . I hope you'll consider going back to the terrific screenplay you wrote in October.'

I leave the restaurant burping on caviar and heavy with ice-cream. All afternoon I wander the city. Two dozen wasps are free within my cranium. Perhaps all those people are right. I don't know. Can't tell. God knows. My judgement has gone, swept away by the wind of all this advice. Eventually I settle down in an Irish bar – a grimy piece of Dublin – and have a few beers. I toast myself. The toast: long may you remain waterproof and never respect anyone who gives you money!

30 JANUARY 1987
Motivated entirely by greed I stay in the hotel room all day writing a 1,000-word piece about Frears for an American film magazine. They promise me $1,000. On finishing it, sending it round and listening to their reservations, I realise how rarely any kind of writing is simple and how few easy bucks there are to be made. Whatever you write you always have to go back and rethink and rewrite. And you have to be prepared to do that. You never get away with anything.

5 FEBRUARY 1987

London. Good to talk to Frears again. We both say that some of the people around us have made us gloomy by expressing doubts, by emphasising the difficulty of what we want to do. We want to work confidently, with certainty, and with pleasure. Frears is an extraordinarily cheerful man who takes great pleasure in his work and in the company of others. There's no poisonous negativity in him. It's as if he knows how close dejection and discouragement always are, that they are the converse of everything you do, and how comforting it is to let them put their arms around you.

He says this is the hardest film he's made. He said the same about *Laundrette*, and I remember feeling glad that we were doing something risky and dangerous.

10 FEBRUARY 1987

Meeting at Channel 4 with David Rose and Karin Bamborough. Karin says I'll have to give Sammy more substance as he's such a jerk and constantly making glib, flip remarks. Stephen and Tim Bevan sit chuckling at me, knowing there's some autobiography in the character. We tell Karin that Ayub is such a delightfully complicated person and so intent on playing the Oedipal relationship that he'll give the character depth. I also explain that the end will be rewritten. At the moment Rafi just hangs himself. It seems an ignoble act whereas Frears and I want it to be a justified thing, chosen, dignified, something of a Roman act.

Shashi sends his measurements in and hasn't lost any weight. We feel he's too big for the part and should look fitter and trimmer. The plan has been for Shashi to arrive a few weeks before shooting and then Bevan will shunt him off to a health farm. But so far, no sign of Shashi. Some of us are wondering whether he'll turn up at all.

As we've been concentrating on casting the other parts it now seems that Claire Bloom may not be available. A real nuisance. Fortunately the problems with Meera have been worked out and she's going to be in the film.

I go into the production offices off Ladbroke Grove to talk about casting. There is a row of offices with glass partitions. About twenty yards away I can see Bevan waving his arms. He dashes up the corridor to tell me there's been a call from the States to say I've been nominated for an Oscar. I call my agent and she says: Goody, that'll put a couple of noughts on your fee.

I think of a letter Scott Fitzgerald wrote from Hollywood in 1935 where he was working on the script of *Gone with the Wind*: 'It's nice work if you can get it and you can get it if you try about three years. The point is once you've got in – Screen Credit 1st, a Hit 2nd, and the Academy Award 3rd – you can count on it for ever . . . and know there's one place you'll be fed without being asked to even wash the dishes.'

Later in the day Frears and I drive to west London to check out an actress for the part of Alice. Frears says what a strange cast it is: a mixture of inexperienced young people, a rock singer, a famous and glamorous movie star who's never worked in Britain, and a theatre actress without a great deal of film experience.

The irascible actress we've come to see, in her genteel west London sitting room, starts off by flapping the letter we've written her and saying how flattered she is to be offered the part of Anna. Surely though, at her age, early fifties, she shouldn't be expected to have two Ws tattooed on her buttocks.

I look at Frears. As he sits there in her high-backed leather chair with his ripped green-striped plimsolls resting on her cream carpet, I can't help thinking of him as a punk at heart. He is a little distracted, though perfectly polite. I know what he doesn't like to do is explain things. Art Malik has complained to me that Frears wouldn't explain Sammy's role in the movie to him. Frears said he didn't know that much about Sammy's role in the movie: it's all so much in Hanif's head, he says; let's hope we can pull it out some time near the day. Malik was horrified by Frears's flipness. But Frears wants people to work intuitively and spontaneously. He wants them to work things out for themselves and not be lazy;

what they've worked out they'll bring to the film. He also expects other people to be as intelligent as he is.

Frears pulls himself together and hastily explains that the actress is being considered for the part of Alice, not Anna. She then looks at me as if I'm a very small boy and asks, severely, what the film is about. I explain that it concerns a number of relationships unfolding against a background of uprising and social deterioration. 'That's easy to say,' she says. 'Very easy. Now can you tell me what it's about?' I tell her I'm not one of those people who think plays or films ought to be 'about' anything. 'What are you trying to say then?' she asks, putting her head in her hands and making a frightening gurgling noise. At first I think she's choking; I consider hammering her on the back. But surely she's crying? When she looks up I can see she's laughing hysterically. 'Oh, poor England's changed,' she says. 'And I don't know where it's gone. A black boy attacked me in the street the other day. Before, you'd never even lock the door to your house.'

Frears is knocking back a fat slug of whisky and looking in the other direction. The actress starts up on a rambling monologue about her career. She keeps you alert because you have no idea what she's going to say next. In some ways she is rather like Alice, delicate, decent and unable to understand why her world has changed.

16 FEBRUARY 1987

Roland Gift who is playing Danny comes over. He admits being nervous of Frears's method of working, of not rehearsing. I tell him of the dangers of over-preparation which kill spontaneity and creativity; also that he's in the film partly because of what he'll bring of himself to the part, not because of his technical abilities as an actor. The idea is to avoid performances. British actors, because of their training, tend to be theatrical on film.

Roland talks about being brought up in Birmingham and being in a class at school in which there were only five white kids. And then moving to Hull and being the only black kid in the class. The racism was constant and casual. One day he was walking along and heard someone calling out, 'Nigger, nigger, nigger.' When he turned round he saw it was a woman calling her dog.

Later he worked as a nude model for architects. Architects? In a life-drawing class, he says, so the barbarians of the future would get a sense of beauty.

We talk about the character of Danny being underwritten. Roland might fill it out by having a strong sense of what the character is. He thinks there's much of himself he can bring to the part.

Bevan has managed to get permission from the police to block off some streets in North Kensington to stage the riot scenes, or the 'scuffles' as he describes them. They don't even ask to see a script.

17 FEBRUARY 1987

To see Claire Bloom, Stephen and I. Chat for a while to Philip Roth. Roth fizzes and whirls with mischief and vibrant interest in the world. He is a wicked teller of tales! I tell him that on taking his advice and writing some fiction, a story I've written for the *London Review of Books* may not be accepted in the US because of the sex and four-letter words in it. He says he's had similar trouble: imagine the nuisance, he tells me, of having to find a suitable synonym for the perfectly adequate 'dogshit' just so your story can be published in the prissy *New Yorker*. He also tells us with great glee that he'd written a story called 'The Tormented Cunt', but had to change the title.

Claire looks younger than her fifty-six years and I did want Alice older than that, partly so that the scene I lifted from *A Sentimental Education* – the woman lets down her hair and it has gone white – is effective. Claire hunts through the script for a line she doesn't understand. It is: 'The proletarian and theocratic ideas you theoretically admire grind civilisation into dust.' It seems to me that no clearer line has ever been written. Frears explains the line and adds that the line 'that country has been sodomised by religion' in *Laundrette* mystified him long after the film had been finished. Claire looks sceptical and says she doesn't think she can say something she doesn't understand.

On the way home Frears says Shashi has rung to ask if he can leave early on the first day of shooting to go to a cocktail party. Frears says if this is how stars behave, it might all be difficult to deal with.

23 FEBRUARY 1987

I run into Roland. He says: Why does Danny have to have a girl-friend and a kid? I say because it makes the character seem more complex. I can see Roland wants Danny to be more romantic. I tell him the character's unreal enough and idealised as it is.

Talk to Karin Bamborough about the end of the movie. The idea of it ending with the hanging is still not necessarily the best. It'll send people away in a gloomy mood. Karin thinks there should be some image of reconciliation. I say, well, if one occurs to me I'll put it in. I'm not sure Sammy and Rosie should be reconciled at the end of the film, not sure they'd want that.

Stephen and I talk about the music we'll use in the film. Some kind of street music, plus some American soul, perhaps Otis Redding or Sam Cooke, music from the 1960s which seems to me to have really lasted, something that everyone recognises.

24 FEBRUARY 1987

Roland, Ayub and Wendy Gazelle (who has just flown in from New York) are in the production office today and on the walls are photographs of Meera and Suzette Llewellyn, who are playing Rani and Vivia respectively. Ayub and Wendy together look like Romeo and Juliet! Their all being so young will mean there's little bitterness in the film, so a story that involves the shooting of a black woman by the police, an exiled torturer and the eviction of dozens of people from their homes, while ending with a hanging, won't be as grim as this description sounds.

The actors are pretty nervous and complain to me that Frears and I haven't spent much time talking about the backgrounds to their characters. I urge them to work it out for themselves, maybe writing out a few pages of background detail. Despite their worries, when I sit down with them and they discuss various scenes with each other, they seem to know what they're about. The important thing is that they like each other and can relax. I know they've started to hang out together.

Stephen and I talk about the end of the film once more. It's still not worked out properly. Maybe there should be another scene, after the hanging, maybe with Sammy and Rosie in each other's arms, a scene that was cut from earlier in the script. I'm not against the idea; but maybe there's something more interesting I could write.

25 FEBRUARY 1987

To Milan for the opening of *Laundrette* in Italy. I do an interview through an interpreter and go to the bar with the publicist, the distributor and the journalist. They talk politics. The journalist, a fashionably dressed woman in her thirties, turns to me and says: Isn't it funny, all the Italians round the table are communists? It's a disconcerting remark, since I haven't heard anyone describe themselves as a communist for at least ten years, since I was a student. Indeed, I reflect, it's only with embarrassment and in low voices that the people I know in London will admit to being socialists. Generally we don't admit to believing in anything at all, though we sometimes disapprove of the worst abuses. It's as if in London it's considered vulgar or exhibitionist to hold too strongly to anything, hence the London contempt for Mrs Thatcher along with the failure to do anything about her. In some ways this British insouciance is a manifestation of British scepticism and dislike of extremes; in another way it's just feebleness.

To a massive Gothic church in Milan. The stained-glass windows tell, in sequence, like bright cartoons, biblical stories. And with strong sunlight behind each of them, they resemble the frames of a film.

26 FEBRUARY 1987

To Florence by train. The fast and comfortable Italian trains and the businessmen around me in their sharp clothes. The care they take: everything matches; not a garment is worn or shapeless. What surprises me is the affluence and attractiveness of northern Italy and that despite Thatcher's talk about the boom in British industry, compared with this place it's in desperate straits.

In Florence I do more interviews. This publicising of films is an odd business. I have no Italian money and little grasp of what is going on. Norboto, the publicist, takes me from city to city. When I am thirsty he buys me a Coke; when I am hungry he fetches me a sandwich. He takes me to the hotel and in the morning he wakes me up. It reminds me of being a kid and being out with my father. You veer in these publicity tours between feeling you are important, a minor celebrity, someone to be listened to, and the predominant feeling that you're a kind of large parcel, a property at the disposal of a nervous distributor with which things can be done, films sold and money made. You hope in return that you'll get a decent view of the Grand Canal from the window of your Venice hotel.

27 FEBRUARY 1987

To Venice for the Carnival. I stand in the railway station and read the board: there are trains to Vienna, Trieste, Munich, Paris, Rome. That these places are merely a train ride away gives one a sense of being a part of Europe that isn't available in Britain. When I'm in the US and people talk of making a trip to Europe it still takes me a beat to realise they're also referring to Britain. I think of the legendary sign at Dover: Fog over Channel, Continent cut off.

Then out into the crumbling, drowning city of tourists which is packed with people in medieval costumes and gold masks. They dance all night in St Mark's Square and fall to the ground where they sleep beneath people's feet until morning. Looking at the bridges I wonder how they don't collapse under the weight of people. I walk with the distributor through this wild celebration to a cinema where *Laundrette* is opening. The cinema is virtually empty. A man is asleep and snoring loudly, the sound filling the place. To my horror the film is dubbed: strange Italian voices are coming from the mouths of Saeed Jaffrey and Roshan Seth. The Italian hairdresser on *Sammy and Rosie* said he grew up hearing Cary Grant, Frank Sinatra and Marlon Brando all with the same voice, dubbed by the same Italian actor.

I watch the audience watching the film. At the points where the audience usually laugh there is complete silence. The film is no longer a comedy.

I get up to speak. The snoring man opens his eyes briefly, looks at me and goes back to sleep. The audience puts questions to me through the interpreter. But though she has a good accent, what the interpreter says to me makes no sense. So I describe how the film came to be made and talk a little about the gay theme. She blushes when I say this. Then she stumbles and backs away from me and the microphone. I glare at her. She recovers and talks to the audience for a long time. But I know she isn't repeating what I said. So I turn to her and say the aim of the film is to induce world-wide sexual excitement. Now she won't go to the microphone at all. She is backing away, wide-eyed. The audience whistles and shouts and claps. I get out as soon as I can.

3 MARCH 1987

First day of shooting. I go to pick up Shashi who turned up late last night. 'I nearly didn't come at all,' he says. 'I've got big tax problems. Rajiv Gandhi himself had to sort them out.' Shashi has three Indian writers staying with him in his flat. They're working on a script Shashi will direct at the end of the year. He tells me that Indian film-writers often write ten films a year and earn £250,000. Some writers only work out the story and are no good at dialogue, while others just come in for the verbals.

Shashi looks splendid, if a little plump. He's less familiar with the script than I'd hoped – and in the car he asks me to remind him of the story – but he's serious and keen. Soon everyone is in love with him.

We shoot the scene of Rosie finding the old man dead in the bath. I turn up and find Frances in a long green coat with a furry black collar. On her head she has a black pillbox hat. Instead of a social worker she looks like an extra from *Doctor Zhivago*. I take it as a direct blow to the heart, as if it's a complete misunderstanding of everything I've been trying to do. Frances is very nervous and apprehensive, as it's the first day, and she clings to the coat as if it's a part of Rosie's soul. But Frears is enjoying himself. He can get along with actors. Where I'd have them by the throat with my foot in the back of their neck, he sits down and talks gently with them. Frances changes the coat. But it's not the last we'll see of that coat.

When Shashi comes on set – we're shooting the scene outside and inside the off-licence – the local Asians come out of their shops in amazement. One immediately gives him three boxes of crisps. Another gives him perfume and aftershave. For them Shashi is a massive star, like Robert Redford, and he has been around for considerably longer, making over 200 films since he first started, aged eight. When they believe it is him, the kids dress up in their best clothes – the Asian girls in smart *salwar kamiz* and jewellery – to be photographed with him. Others ring their relatives who come in cars across London and wait patiently in the freezing cold for a break in filming so they can stand next to their idol.

Seeing the off-licence with wire-mesh across the counter, the dogs, the siege-like atmosphere – it is based on places I know in Brixton, where buying a bottle of wine can be like entering a battle zone – Shashi is taken aback, as Rafi would be. Shashi asks: Are there really places like this in London?

Shashi decides to wear a moustache for the part. It makes him look older and less handsome, less of a matinée idol; but also formidable, imposing and sort of British in the right military, authoritarian sort of way.

4 MARCH 1987
Sarah comes to the set where we're shooting a scene between Sammy and Rosie set in a looted Asian grocer's shop. Frances is still tense and unsure and she complains to Frears about Sarah being there watching her as she is trying to create the character of Rosie. Sarah

leaves. She is amused by the clothes Frances is wearing, as if a social worker would wear a mini-skirt and three-inch-high heels to work. Before that, of course, the hours in make-up, the hairdresser constantly standing by to adjust any hair that might fall out of place. All seemingly absurd when the attempt is to do something that is, in some ways, realistic. But then the cinema has never stopped being a palace of dreams. Even in the serious cinema there is some emphasis on the ideal. Imagine casting a film with only ugly or even just ordinary-looking actors. The cinema cannot replace the novel or autobiography as the precise and serious medium of the age while it is still too intent on charming its audience!

5 MARCH 1987

Much falsity in what I wrote in anger yesterday, partly to do with my failure to let go of the script and let Frears make the film he has to make. I think that despite the clothes and the paraphernalia of glamour, the voice of the film collaborators can transcend the trivial messages of escape that the cinema must transmit if it is to reach a large audience.

Also, and today I have to repeat this to myself, the film-writer always has to give way to the director, who is the controlling intelligence of the film, the invisible tyrant behind everything. The only way for a writer to influence a film is through his relationship with the director. If this is good then the film will be a successful collaboration; if not, the writer has had it. And most writers are lucky if directors even allow them on the set.

Presumably, it is because of this contingency that serious writers don't venture into the cinema. You don't find many American writers – in a country with a film industry – thinking of film as a serious possibility.

Also contra what I said yesterday: I do think the constraints of playing to a wide audience can be useful. You have to ensure that your work is accessible. You can't indulge yourself; you have to be self-critical; you have to say: is this available? So, to take a literary analogy, you have popular Thackeray and Dickens, say, as opposed to some recent American writing, loaded with experiment, innovation and pretty sentences which is published by minor magazines for an audience of acolytes, friends and university libraries.

I wake up, pull the curtains and it is snowing! The snow is settling too. This morning we're shooting the aftermath of the riots, when Rafi decides to go out for a walk. He meets Danny and they go to visit Alice.

When I get to the set the snow doesn't seem to matter. Burnt-out cars are scattered about; there are mobs throwing rubber bricks and police with batons charging them. Padded stuntmen dive over cars and policemen kick them. Among it all, in the awful cold, wanders Shashi, bearing a bunch of flowers. The kids in the mob are locals, not extras. These kids refuse to sit in the caravan with the actors in police uniform in case their friends think they're fraternising with the police.

The charges and fighting look terrifying and we haven't shot the main riot yet. That's tonight. Frears says: If we can get through that we'll be OK, we'll survive!

6 MARCH 1987

Night shoot. A row of derelict houses and shops with asbestos over their windows with gas-fired jets in little window boxes in front of them to give the impression of the neighbourhood in flames. In front of this are exploding cars, fire-engines, ambulances and a divided mob of 200 extras plus police with riot shields. There are four cameras. It's massive, for a British film, and brilliantly organised. I think of the script: it just says something like: in the background the riot continues!

The rioting itself is frightening, thrilling and cathartic. It's not difficult to see how compelling and exciting taking part in a riot can be and how far out of yourself such compulsion can take you. On some takes the kids playing rioters continue to attack the extras in uniform after we've cut. Some of the extras playing police threaten to go home if this doesn't stop!

Late at night from the mob emerges a strange sight. Nearby is a hostel for the blind and about fifteen bewildered blind people with dogs emerge from the mob and walk across the riot area as cars explode around them and Molotov cocktails are flung into shops. At the far end of the set they release their dogs into a park.

I see rushes of yesterday's material. It looks pretty effective. I can see how thrilling it must be to film large-scale set-pieces. It's far easier and often more effective than the hard stuff: subtle acting and the delineation of complicated relationships.

Each day Frears asks me to give him a detailed report of the rushes: what was that scene like? he asks. And the other one? He refuses to watch rushes. The discovery that he can avoid this has liberated him from the inevitable discouragement of staring daily at his own work and its limitations.

10 MARCH 1987

More rushes and some of the riot material cut together. At last it comes alive! I talk to Oliver (the lighting cameraman) about the way he's shot it. He's eschewed the pinks and blues of *Laundrette*, going for a more monochrome look, though at times the screen positively glows! Originally I was sceptical of this, liking the heightened and cheap quality of *Laundrette*. But Oliver felt that the more real *Sammy and Rosie* looks the better as the oddness of the story and strangeness of the juxtapositions are sufficient unreality. He has given the film a European quality, sensuous and warm. I haven't seen a film like it made in Britain.

It's a hard film to make and much to do in six weeks. Everyone looks exhausted already, not surprisingly. They start work at eight in the morning and usually knock off around eleven at night. With night shoots we've been starting at six in the evening and finishing at seven in the morning, though people aren't getting to bed till nine.

The worries about Ayub: he's stiff at the moment and the humour of the part is beyond him. He's better in close-up, being handsome. In mid-shot he wilts and looks as if he doesn't quite know what to do with his body. His pleasantness of character comes through, playing against the unpleasantness of Sammy. But it's going to be difficult for him in the first big part he's played. Wendy looks effective in the rushes, powerful and vulnerable. American actors are trained for the screen. Where you sometimes feel Ayub is delivering his performance to the back of the stalls, Wendy understands the intimacy of the cinema.

On the way to today's shoot, in an East End loft, a battleship passes along the river. The taxi I'm in stops. 'Why have you stopped?' I ask. 'I can't go on,' the driver says, gazing at the ship. 'My eyes have misted over. Doesn't it do you in?' I refrain from telling him the battleship is French. When I turn up I find they've managed to work the battleship into the scene. Let's hope people think it's a symbol.

In the script most of the scenes between Anna and Sammy take place in Anna's bed. But Frears opens them up, using the whole space, even creating a new scene by moving into the loft's tiny bathroom which has a spectacular view over London. Because of these scenes I write new dialogue for Anna about an exhibition she's having, called 'Images of a Decaying Europe'.

13 MARCH 1987

Today Frears rails at the actors for lacking flair, for thinking too much about their costumes, for being too passive and not helping him enough. He's been cheerful all through it, but now the strain is starting to tell. It's partly because the scene we're shooting – outside Sammy's and Rosie's flat, with Rosie returning with Danny on a motorbike, the Ghost walking past, Vivia watching Rafi from the window and Rosie's two friends also watching Rafi – is very complicated. The cold – working fifteen hours a day in snow flurries – is getting people down. Frears also blames me for this scene going badly: 'You should never set a scene as complicated as this outside,' he says. 'Haven't you learned that yet? I can't control it out here!' In fact, this is the only scene in the film we will have to reshoot.

16 MARCH 1987

To Frears's last night to discuss the waste ground eviction scene at the end of the film. It has to be choreographed precisely and it hasn't been yet. What I've written isn't clear. So we work out, almost shot by shot, the final relationships between the characters. The problem with the end of the film, with the eviction as opposed to the already shot riot scene, is the danger of it being sentimental. Ambiguities and ironies have to be excavated just as Rafi and Sammy and Anna bumbling around during the riots made all the difference to a scene which could easily be one-dimensional.

Have the idea that in order to reflect on what has gone on in the film it might be a good notion to have, during the closing credits, some of Anna's photographs shown to us.

17 MARCH 1987

Shooting the waste ground material on the large piece of unused ground under the motorway. Bit of a shock to turn up at the location and find Frances Barber in a black and white corset. I look at her wondering if she has forgotten to put the rest of her clothes on. Her breasts, well, they are jammed into an odd shape: it looks as though she has two Cornish pasties attached to her chest. I tell Stephen she looks like a gangster's moll from a western. He takes it as a compliment. 'That's exactly what I intended,' he says. 'John Ford would be proud of me.'

Between takes, the corset debate continues between us, as in a snowstorm Shashi sits in a filthy flea-ridden armchair in front of a smoking fire, surrounded by young people in grey costumes banging tins. Frears argues that the corset is an inspired idea; it liberates Rosie from do-goodery; she looks bizarre, anarchistic and interesting, not earnest or condescending. What he then describes as the 'simplistic politics of the film' he says are transcended by imaginativeness. At the end of the argument he calls me a prude and for the rest of the afternoon he refers to me as Mrs Grundy.

The corset depresses me because after everyone's work on the film it is still easy to hit a wrong note. I feel uneasy in complaining because I think Frears's judgement is less conservative than my own; I could be wrong. Maybe, too, I'm being sentimental about the woman the character is based on, a more dignified and sensitive person than the one signified by the corset.

19 MARCH 1987
We shoot the eviction and exodus from the waste ground. With the trailers and caravans whirling in the mud and dust, the bulldozers crashing through shops, lifting cars and tossing them about, the straggly kids waving flags and playing music as the police and heavies invade and evict them, it is like a western! Frears runs among it all, yelling instructions through a megaphone.

It is tough on Shashi. India's premier actor, a god to millions, is impersonating a torturer having a nightmare while bouncing on a bed in the back of a caravan which is being wildly driven around a stony waste ground in a snowstorm. Books scatter over his head. When he emerges, shaken and stirred, dizzy and fed up, he threatens to go back to Bombay. The next morning, when we tell him as a joke that we have to reshoot his scene in the back of the caravan, he goes white.

It is obvious that he has a difficult part. The character of Rafi is complex and contradictory and he has to play against many different kinds of character. Shashi is not used to making films in English and the part is physically demanding. But with his modesty, generosity and un-English liking for women, he is the most adored person on the film.

So a glorious day – mostly to do with the pleasure of working with other people, especially the 'straggly kids' who jam all day and some of the night by the fire. Most of them are alternative comedians and buskers from the London Underground. Few of them have a regular place to live, and when Debbie wants to inform them of a day's shooting, she has to send her assistants round the tube stations of central London to find them.

Coming out of my hutch for this film has made me realise how hard it is sometimes to bear the isolation that all writers have to put up with.

20 MARCH 1987

To Kew where we're shooting the suburban material – in Alice's house and the street she lives in. We film the scene where Alice comes to the door and sees Rafi for the first time for thirty years. We do several takes and find it works best when Claire and Shashi do least, when they contain their reaction and we have to strain to imagine their feelings.

Here, where it is quiet and sedate, leafy and affluent, we have more complaints from residents than at any other location, though there are no charging bulldozers and we burn nothing down, though severely tempted.

Being brought up in the suburbs myself, this location reminds me of slow childhood Sundays on which you weren't allowed to yell in the street and your friends were kept in for the holy day. Sundays in the suburbs were a funeral and it's still beyond me why the celebration of God's love for the world has to be such a miserable business.

I know now that England is primarily a suburban country and English values are suburban values. The best of that is kindness and mild-temperedness, politeness and privacy, and some rather resentful tolerance. The suburbs are also a mix of people. In my small street lived a civil servant, an interior decorator, secretaries, a local journalist, an architect, a van driver, a milkman, and so on, all living together in comfortable houses with gardens, in relative harmony.

At worst there is narrowness of outlook and fear of the different. There is cruelty by privacy and indifference. There is great lower-middle-class snobbery, contempt for the working class and envy of the middle class. And there is a refusal to admit to humanity beyond the family, beyond the household walls and garden fence. Each family as an autonomous, self-sufficient unit faces a hostile world of other self-contained families. This neurotic and materialistic privacy, the keystone of British suburban life, ensures that the 'collective' or even the 'public' will means little to these people. It's interesting that the Labour leader, Neil Kinnock, has repudiated the now discredited notion of the collective in favour of left-wing individualism. He has said: 'They have got to be told that socialism is the answer for them because socialism looks after the individual.'

My love and fascination for inner London endures. Here there is fluidity and possibilities are unlimited. Here it is possible to avoid your enemies; here everything is available. In the suburbs everything changes slowly. Heraclitus said: 'You can't step in the same river twice.' In the inner city you can barely step in the same street twice, so rapid is human and environmental change.

I sit in the first sunshine of the year in this English garden in Kew reading the papers. There is much written today about the verdict in the Blakelock case, where a policeman was hacked to death during an uprising on the Broadwater Farm Estate in north London. A man was sentenced to life imprisonment for the killing. The uprising followed the death of a much respected middle-aged black woman, Cynthia Jarrett, who died of a heart attack during a police raid on her home on the estate. The Police Commissioner, Sir Kenneth Newman, claimed that 'anarchists and Trotskyists' planned the uprising in advance, though there is no evidence for this. There is confusion and inconsistency in the police account of the incident, to say the least. The police also broke numerous rules and acted illegally in their treatment of two young 'suspects'. A fifteen-year-old boy was held three days without access to his parents or a solicitor. A sixteen-year-old, with a mental age of seven, was interrogated without his mother or solicitor.

It's all depressing, as was the incident around which I based the opening of the film: the shooting of a black woman, Cherry Groce, who was permanently paralysed after being shot during a police raid in which her son was being sought.

But what are we doing using this material in the film? Today, when confronted once more by the racism, violence, alienation and waste of the Broadwater Farm Estate uprising, our little film has to be justified over again. After all, real life has become part of a film, reduced perhaps, maybe trivialised. We will make money from it; careers will be furthered; film festivals attended. But aren't we stealing other people's lives, their hard experience, for our own purposes? The relation we bear to those people's lives is tangential, to say the least. Perhaps because of that we seriously misunderstand their lives.

I can't work out today if the question about the relation between the real people, the real events, and the portrayal is an aesthetic or moral one. In other words, if the acting is good, if the film is well made, if it seems authentic, does that make it all right, is the stealing justified? Will the issue be settled if experience is successfully distilled into art?

Or is the quality of the work irrelevant to the social issue, which is that of middle-class people (albeit dissenting middle-class people) who own and control and have access to the media and to money, using minority and working-class material to entertain other middle-class people? Frequently during the making of the film I feel that this is the case, that what we're doing is a kind of social voyeurism.

At the same time I can justify our work by saying it is the duty of contemporary films to show contemporary life. This portrayal of our world as it is is valuable in itself, and part of the climate of opposition and dissent.

In one part of me I do believe there is some anger in the film; and it does deal with things not often touched on in British films. In another part of me, when I look at the film world, run by the usual white middle-class public-school types, with a few parvenu thugs thrown in, I can see that the film is just a commercial product.

Frears and I talk this over. He says the film is optimistic about the young people portrayed in it: their vivacity, lack of conformity and rebelliousness are celebrated in it.

In the evening to rushes – uncut takes of the waste ground material. It looks good and people are pleased with their work.

Leon from Cinecom is there, as is his boss. Leon sleeps through the rushes and his boss says: For rushes they're not bad, but it's not family entertainment.

After, we drive through London and go to a pub. It's a shock that London and other people's lives are continuing while we're making a film. Film-making is an absorbing and complete world; the relationships are so intense and generous, the collaboration so total, that the rest of the world is blanked out.

24 MARCH 1987

In the studio at Twickenham at last and off the street. Here we're shooting all the material in Sammy's and Rosie's flat. It is easier to watch the performances in this calmer and more controlled place, even if the atmosphere is slightly flat.

It seems to me that Shashi is going to turn out to be very good, portraying a complex and dangerous character, a murderer and a man eager to be loved, a populist and an élitist. Frears is carefully and patiently teasing out the power and subtlety in Shashi by getting him to act simply and underplay everything. You can see the performance developing take by take. After eight or nine takes Shashi is settled, a little tired and bored, more casual and relaxed. Now he is able to throw the scene away. And this is when he is at his best, though he himself prefers the first few takes when he considers himself to be really 'acting'. Sometimes he can't see why Frears wants to do so many retakes.

Ayub improving too. He is inexperienced as an actor (it is of course difficult for Asian actors to gain experience), but Oliver is doing a wonderful job in making him look like a matinée idol. The balance of the script has gone against Sammy. It is Rafi and Rosie that I've developed as there is more scope for conflict with them. Sammy doesn't believe in a great deal, so it's hard to have him disagree much with anyone. His confusion isn't particularly interesting. Rosie is a more complex character and harder to write, especially as she isn't a character I've written before.

25 MARCH 1987

I turn up on the set and find that Frears has Rosie going out to meet her lover not only in that ridiculous coat, but wearing only her underwear. He seems to think that someone would go to see their lover, via a riot, wearing only a thermal vest and a pair of tights. I certainly wouldn't. I hope I'll be able to watch the film in the future without suffering at this moment.

Thank God I'm leaving London in a couple of days for the Oscar ceremonies. I've been on the set every day, though I'm not sure it's been as essential as it was on *Laundrette*. There hasn't been much rewriting this time.

28 MARCH 1987

Los Angeles. I wind down the window of the cab as we hit the freeway and accelerate. Air rushes in, gloriously warm to me after an English winter of freezing balls. I pull three layers of clothes over my head. LA is blazingly green and bright: how easy it is to forget (one's senses accustomed to dullness) that this industry town is also subtropical; its serious and conservative business takes place among palm trees, exotic birds and preternaturally singing flowers. Everything is as resplendent as if I'd taken LSD. Walking into the hotel, the Château Marmont, a small, friendly European place on a hill, the grass appears to have been sprayed with gloss and the air pumped full of perfume. It is eucalyptus.

The phone calls begin as soon as I open the windows of my room: from agents, press people, producers, recommending the numerous totally beautiful human beings I should impress in the next few days. I say to my agent: But most of these people do not interest me. She says: Dear, all that is important is that you interest them – whatever you do, don't discourage them. As long as they're saying your name as they eat all round this city you've got nothing to worry about.

As we talk I eat some fruit. Swollen nature in my hands: strawberries long as courgettes, thick as cucumbers. Here the most natural things look unnatural, which is fitting in a mythical city in a hotel in which Bogart proposed to Bacall, where John Belushi died, where Dorothy Parker had an apartment and Lillian Hellman and Norman Mailer would come to tea and no one wanted to be the first to leave, and in which, when I get into bed to read – Robert Stone's *Children of Light* – I find myself staring into a novel about a burned-out screenwriter living at the Château Marmont drinking and drugging himself while a screenplay he wrote is being shot in another country.

29 MARCH 1987

At breakfast the waiters are discussing films they've seen recently. Then they start to worry about the Oscars. They can't believe that *Betty Blue* is the French entry in the Best Foreign Picture Category. What about *Vagabonde*? At another table a young man is hungrily explaining the plot of a film he's written to an older man. 'This film could change lives,' he says, not eating. The other man eats croissants as big as boomerangs. 'It's about an alien disguised as a policeman. But it's a good alien, right? It's about the renewal of the human spirit.'

Later, with some friends, I drive through this baking city to Venice Beach. I'm being shown the city. How attractive it is too, and not vulgar. I notice how few black people there are. What little poverty. I'd have thought this city was bereft of unhappiness if I hadn't stayed downtown on my last visit here. That time the manager of the hotel said, when I checked in: Whatever you do, sir, don't go out after dark.

Venice Beach – so called because of the rotting bits of Venetian architecture still left over from a time when a minor Venice was being contemplated here. It is in its wild spirit something like the Venice, Italy, I saw a few weeks ago, though less stylish and more eccentric, which you'd expect in a country without an aristocratic culture. Herds of people cruise the boardwalk. A man is juggling a chainsaw and a ball, hurling the humming saw into the air and catching it. A dog in sunglasses watches. A man with pierced nipples, with rings hanging from them, also watches. All along the beach there are masseurs, rolfers, shiatsu experts, astrologers, yoga masters and tattoo freaks. Further along, at Muscle Beach, in an enclosed area, men and women work out, twitching, shaking, vibrating, tensing and generally exhibiting their bodies to the crowds.

Back at the hotel the phone rings constantly. People tell me: The greatest day of your life is approaching. I try to think of the one day in my life in which I had more happiness than any other.

Later, to a cocktail party given by Orion, the distributors of *Laundrette* in the US. It is as interesting as a convention of carpet salesmen. I sit next to a woman whose husband is an executive in the company. In her early twenties, she tells me how she hates it all, how you just have to keep smiling if you want your husband to be promoted and how desperate she is to go home and get some drugs up her nose. Everyone leaves early. Drive the LA streets at eleven and they're deserted. It's like Canterbury. Everyone goes to bed early because they work so hard.

30 MARCH 1987

After lunch in Santa Monica near the beach, to the Bel-Air hotel with its lush gardens, its white Moorish architecture and its private suites and cottages in the grounds with their own patios. Here, you go somewhere, get out of your car and someone parks it. When you leave the restaurant, bar or hotel, the car is waiting outside. If you've got the dough, there's always someone around to save you doing something yourself. I'm beginning to see how addictive such a luxurious place as this could become. Once you'd really got the taste for it, how could you be detoxicated? To which clinic could you go to dry out from the juices of wealth and pleasure that had saturated you in this city?

It's interesting how few notable American film directors actually live in Los Angeles: Coppola, Pakula, Pollack, Scorsese, Demme, all live in other cities. The directors and writers who do live here are British, often successful in British television, now flailing around in the vacuum of Los Angeles, rich but rootless and confused, attempting the impossible task of finding decent work, exiled from a country that doesn't have a film industry.

31 MARCH 1987

The day of the Oscars. People leave work after lunch in order to get home and watch it on TV at five o'clock. All over the city Oscar parties are beginning in lounges and beside pools. For weeks since the nominations, there has been speculation about possible winners. Turn on the TV and grave pundits are weighing the merits of Bob Hoskins and Paul Newman; open a paper and predictions are being made. Here the Oscars are unavoidable, as competitive and popular as a Cup Final, as dignified and socially important as a Royal Wedding.

A last swim on my back in the hotel pool, watching the sky through the trees before the extensive pleasures of the bathroom where I sip champagne and receive phone calls and gifts. Slipping on my elastic bow-tie I suspect this will be the best time of the day. Outside in the lane the limo is already waiting. By now I have definitely had enough of people saying: It's enough to be nominated, it's an honour in itself. By now that isn't enough: by now I want to win; by now, I know I will win!

When your four-seater black stretch limo pulls up outside the venue all you see on either side of you are other limos, a shimmering sea of shining black metal. When you slide out, you see the high grandstands lining the long walk to the entrance. In these packed grandstands screaming people wave placards with the names of their favourite films written on them. '*Platoon, Platoon, Platoon!*' someone is yelling. Another person bellows: '*Room with a View, Room with a View!*' One man holds a placard which says: 'Read the Bible.'

Inside there are scores of young people, the women in long dresses, the men in tuxedos, who have small signs around their neck saying: 'The 59th Academy Awards'. They are the seat-fillers.

Their role is essential, so that when the cameras sweep across the auditorium there isn't an empty seat in the place, whereas in fact the sensible people are in the bar watching it all, like everyone else, on TV, only going in to sit down for their bit. In the bar with friends we look out for stars and discuss them: doesn't Elizabeth Taylor look tiny and doesn't her head look big – perhaps she's had all the fat in her body sucked out by the modish vacuum method; doesn't Bette Davis look shrivelled and fragile; doesn't Sigourney Weaver look terrific and what was wrong with Jane Fonda and doesn't Dustin Hoffman always look the same?

When it comes to your section and Shirley MacLaine starts to read out the names of the nominees, you silently run over your speech, remove a speck of dried semen from your collar and squeeze the arms of your seat, ready to propel yourself into the sight of a billion people. You wonder where in the sitting room you'll put your Oscar, or maybe you should hide it somewhere in case it's stolen? What does it weigh anyway? You'll soon find out.

When they make a mistake and don't read out your name you vow never to attend any such ridiculous ceremony of self-congratulation, exhibitionism and vulgarity again.

1 APRIL 1987

The next day by the pool drinking iced tea, several young producers come by. My impression is that they come to have a look at you, to check you out, to see if there's anything in you for them. One drives me around the city in his Jag. He asks me if I want to fly to San Francisco for lunch. I ask if there isn't anywhere a little nearer we can go. He swears eternal love and a contract.

An idea for a story: of someone who inadvertently writes a successful film and lives off its reputation for years, so afraid of ending the shower of financial seductions and blandishments that he never writes anything again.

2 APRIL 1987

I return to find Frears in heaven on the set, sitting with his plimsolls up and gossiping, waiting for a shot to be set up. To ruin his day I tell him about the directors I've met in Hollywood and how much they earn and the kind of luxury in which they live. Frears goes into agonies of frustration and jealousy, especially when I mention money. He keeps saying: 'What am I doing here, fuck all this art, just give me the money!' This makes Shashi laugh and laugh. But there is another element of neurosis in all this American craziness which is more serious, especially for a film-maker. Since the 1950s the United States is the place where the action is, where things happen, and because the US has the central role in the world which England had in the nineteenth century, America is always present for players in the culture game. Like a mountain that you have to climb or turn away from in disgust, it is an existential challenge involving complicated choices and threats and fear. Do you make an attempt on this height or do you withdraw into your corner? How much of yourself are you prepared to put into this enterprise? Unfortunately for British film-makers, America has been something of a Bermuda Triangle into which many careers have crashed without trace.

They are shooting the party scenes and some kissing between Rani and Vivia; also between Rani and another woman, Margy. I remember Meera (who plays Rani) as a student coming to see me in 1981 at Riverside Studios where we were rehearsing a play for the Royal Court. She asked me if I thought she would ever become an actress. She desperately wanted to go into the theatre, and she wanted to write too. There was some resistance from her parents who, like the parents of many Asian girls, were mostly concerned with her having an arranged marriage. But her enthusiasm and ambition were so obvious, I just told her to stick at it. I wonder what her parents would say if they could see her having a grape removed from between her teeth by the tongue of another actress!

Perhaps these kisses, like the ones between Johnny and Omar in *Laundrette* –

Each kiss a heart-quake, – for a kiss's strength
I think it must be reckon'd by its length.

– are subversive in some way. It's as if they poke social convention and say: There are these other ways to live; there are people who are different, but aren't guilt-ridden. When I went to see *She's Gotta Have It* recently, and it was mostly a young black audience, when the two women kissed the audience screamed with disapproval and repulsion.

We also shoot the scene where Rafi arrives at Sammy's and Rosie's flat and finds Rosie's friends putting a condom on a carrot. Later in the scene Rani and Vivia stand in the centre of the room and kiss, rather ostentatiously. Shashi is agitated by all this and yells for his agent, a taxi, and a first-class flight to Bombay.

God knows what this film will look like when it's all stuck together. I suppose it's a film of juxtapositions and contrasts, of different scenes banging hard together. One danger is that the film lacks narrative force and focus; it may be too diffuse.

3 APRIL 1987

Frears and I rejig the scene where Rafi comes home from the party and finds Vivia and Rani in bed. Originally they chase him around the room with lumps of wood and attempt to beat him to a pulp. He barricades himself in the study and climbs out of the window and down the drainpipe. When it comes to shooting it, it doesn't seem as believable or funny as when I wrote it.

So at lunchtime we rework it. Rafi comes in, finds Vivia and Rani in bed, and is outraged. Abusing them in Punjabi, a row breaks out. So Shashi and Meera work out a couple of pages of abuse to scream at each other. Meera will also throw things at him. It's terrifying when we come to shoot it, with Meera hammering a piece of wood with nails in it into the door behind which Shashi is cowering! As the scene is all Punjabi abuse we talk about putting subtitles on it.

7 APRIL 1987

We shoot Sammy and Rosie crying and rocking together on the floor at the end of the film, with the women slowly leaving the flat behind them. I get to the studio at eight in the morning and leave at nine in the evening. This seems to me to be an ideal solution to living: erect this saving girder of necessity around you: you don't have to think or decide how to live!

Frears saw a good deal of the film on Saturday, as it's being edited as we shoot it. He says: Christ, it's a weepie, a complete heartbreaker! We'll have to put hundreds of violins on the soundtrack!

8 APRIL 1987

I look at a good chunk of the film on the tiny screen of an editing machine at Twickenham Studios. It makes me laugh, partly, I think, with relief that it isn't completely terrible. It's less rough than *Laundrette*, more glamorous, more conventional, with Hollywood colours. I look at the scene where Rafi catches Rani and Vivia in bed; they attack him and he climbs out of the window and down the drainpipe. We were thinking of cutting him climbing out of the window, it seemed unconvincing. Yet looking at it in context, I think it'll work.

Frears comes into the cutting room while I'm watching and talks to Mick, the editor. It's very impressive the way Frears can hold every shot of the film in his head at once, even though he's barely seen any of it. He can remember every take of every shot. So when he's talking to Mick about scenes he shot weeks ago, he'll say: Wasn't take 5 better than take 3? Or: Didn't the actress have her hand over her face on take 11 on the mid-shot and not on take 2?

We talk about the kind of harmless threat of disorder that films like *Laundrette* or *Prick Up Your Ears* represent, which partly explains their success. The pattern is one of there being a fairly rigid social order which is set up in detail in the film. Set against this order there is an individual or two, preferably in love, who violate this conventional structure. Their rebellion, their form of transgressional sex, is liberating, exciting. Audiences identify with it. Films as diverse as, say, *Billy Liar, Room with a View, Midnight Cowboy, Guess Who's*

Coming to Dinner, have this pattern, following an alienated individual or couple, unable to find a place for themselves in the society as it is. Usually there's some kind of individual reconciliation at the end of the film; or the individual is destroyed. But there is rarely any sense that the society could or should be changed. The pattern is, of course, a seductive one because we can see ourselves in the alienated, but authentic, individual standing up against stuffiness, ignorance and hatred of love. In all this we are not helped to think in any wider sense of the way societies repress legitimate ideals, groups of people, and possible forms of life.

In some films of the middle and late 1960s, when the rigid social order was eschewed entirely as no longer relevant, and only 'liberated' individuals were portrayed, the films have little power or interest, lacking the kind of conflict and tension that the classic pattern necessarily produces.

9 APRIL 1987

Filming in the cellar of a pub in Kew. Cramped and dusty; the lights keep going out. Claire, whose performance until now has been, rightly, contained, starts to reveal her power in this cellar scene with Shashi. Furiously jerking things out of the suitcase she packed thirty years ago, and shoving the whole lot on the floor, she reveals such a combination of wild anger, vulnerability and pain, that when the camera cut, there was complete silence. Even Shashi looked shaken. It was especially difficult for her as the Ghost was in the scene as well, standing at her elbow.

10 APRIL 1987

We spend the day in a South Kensington restaurant filming the confrontation scene between Rosie, Rafi and Sammy when they go out to dinner. This is the pivotal scene of the movie. It starts off simply. The three of them are at the table; the violinists play a little Mozart in the background, the drag queen sits behind them. But the violinists have extraordinary faces: English features, pale shoulders (ready to be painted by Ingres), Pre-Raphaelite hair, and after twelve solid hours of fiddling, very worn fingers.

As the day progresses Shashi and Frances become more heated in their argument. The playing of the violinists becomes more frenzied. The drag queen does a very exasperated flounce. Shashi eats a finger made from sausage meat and spits out the nail, putting it politely on the side of the plate.

I can see Frears's imagination racing as he uses these few elements to their fullest and most absurd effect. He becomes increasingly inventive, his control and experience allowing him to play. I am a little afraid the scene will be drowned in effects, but I did write the scene in a similar spirit – putting the people in the restaurant and experimenting until something came of it.

Of course, the conditions of Frears's creativity are different from mine. Alone in a room I can take my time and rewrite as often as I like. I can leave the scene and rewrite it in two weeks' time. For Frears in that small restaurant crowded with seventy people there is no way of going back on the scene. It has to be done there and then and it has to work. It takes a lot of nerve to play with a scene under those conditions, especially as the medium is so ridiculously expensive.

I notice how comfortable Frances is in her part now. She has discovered who she is playing; and that is something you find out only in the course of filming. But unlike the theatre, there's never another opportunity to integrate later discoveries into earlier scenes.

If the conditions in which film directors usually work make it difficult for them to be original, a film actor's life is certainly no bed of roses. You are picked up at seven or earlier in the morning; you may shoot your first scene at ten or eleven, if you're lucky. Or you may be hanging around until three or four before you begin work. Wendy came in early for several days, thinking they were going to shoot her 'fuck night' scene with Ayub that day, then nothing was done, though she didn't know that until early evening. But if your scene is going to be shot, however bored and cold and confused by the entire thing you are, you have to drag your concentration to the sticking place, you have to pull out your performance immediately. You may have to play a very emotional scene and you have to play it now! But whatever you're doing, it's very expensive, so the faster you do it the more you will be appreciated. As there's little time for exploration and experiment you will probably have to give a performance much like one you've given before because at least you can be sure it will work.

When that acting job's finished there might possibly be another one. Should you turn it down and hope something better will turn up? Perhaps it won't; but perhaps it will. If it does, the director may be duff or the script no good or the part too small. Whatever happens, most of the work actors get doesn't stretch them and 80 per cent of the directors they work with will have little talent. Of the good 20 per cent, 5 per cent will be tyrants who think of actors as puppets.

Despite these difficulties, all the British actors I know have one thing in common: they are well-trained, skilled and dedicated people who want to do good work and give of their best within a profession that only rarely gives them the opportunity to reach their potential. No wonder so many actors become neurotic or dull through lack of interest in anything but their careers.

11 APRIL 1987

In a tiny studio off the Harrow Road we film the interior scenes set in Danny's caravan. Outside the caravan, a row of gas jets reproduce the waste ground fires. The props man and the assistant art director wearily dance behind the gas jets to reproduce the celebration of the 'fuck' night as Frances and Roland roll around naked. Frears sinks down in a chair next to me. 'I've become completely paranoid,' he says. 'I've had it. Is this any good or not?' 'I don't know,' I say. 'What's it about anyway?' he says. 'Fuck knows,' I reply. He needs support and for no one to speak in too loud a voice. Anything above a whisper is interpreted as hatred. 'We should have had more time,' he says, after a while. 'About two more weeks would have done it. But it would have cost £300,000 and we didn't have it.'

I leave early and go to a book publishing party. On the way I see the police have stopped a black man and woman and are questioning them. It's odd going to the party: the world going on as normal. Later, I see someone I recognise coming towards me, black hair sticking up, face white, a week's growth on his face. I try and work out who it is. At last I know: Stephen Frears.

Later, I run into a friend who drags me away from the restaurant and tells me to sit in her car. She says there's something I have to see that I've never seen before. Well, she drives me to an arts centre in west London. I take one look at the scene and try to leave. It looks as if she's brought me to an Asian wedding. Women and kids of all ages are sitting on rows of chairs around the walls, not talking. The men, mostly Sikhs, stand together at the bar, talking. The women have gone to a lot of trouble tonight, really dressing up for this one in much jewellery, in *salwar kamiz* threaded with silver and gold. By ten o'clock the hall is packed with Asian families, with babies and children and old men and women. I've no idea what to expect. The stage is full of rock 'n' roll gear.

The band comes on: eight men in red and white costumes. They look like assistants in a fast-food joint. One of them announces the singers: 'Welcome the greatest Bhangra singers in the world!' Two men bounce on stage in spangled T-shirts and tight white pants.

The music starts. The music is extraordinary. After years of colonialism and immigration and Asian life in Britain; after years of black American and reggae music in Britain comes this weird fusion. A cocktail of blues and r 'n' b shaken with Indian film songs in Hindi, cut with heavy guitar solos and electric violin runs and African drumming, a result of all the music in the world being available in an affluent Asian area, Southall, near Heathrow Airport – it is Bhangra music! Detroit and Delhi, in London!

For a few seconds no one moves. The dance floor is a forbidden zone with everyone perched like tense runners around it. Then no one can hold themselves back. Men fly on to the floor. They dance together, thrusting their arms into the air and jerking their hips and thighs, tight-buttocked. Sometimes the men climb on each other's shoulders or wrap their legs around others' waists to be swept in dizzy circles inches from the floor. Women and girls dance with each other; women dance with tiny babies. An old Indian colonel with a fine moustache and military importance weaves amongst it all, taking photographs.

And they all know each other, these people. They were at school together and now they live in the same streets and do business with each other and marry amongst themselves. This gig, such a celebration, is unlike any other I've been to for years: it's not to do with boys and girls trying to pick each other up; it's not aggressive. Makes you aware of the violence and hostility you expect of public occasions in Britain.

12 APRIL 1987

Now we've almost finished filming, in the morning I sit down and try to write something new.

I've enjoyed being out of the house every day and the intense involvement of film-making. The cliché of film-making which talks of the set as being a family is inaccurate, though the set is hierarchical and strictly stratified in the family way. But unlike with a family the relationships are finite, everyone knows what they're doing and there's a strong sense of purpose. The particular pleasure of a film set is in being with a group of people who work well and happily together.

Now, back at the desk, I immediately feel that writing is something of a dingy business. Why this unhealthy attempt to catch life, to trap it, rearrange it, pass it on, when it should be lived and forgotten? Why this recreation in isolation of something that had blood and real life in it? The writer's pretence and self-flattery that what is written is even realer than the real when it's nothing of the kind.

16 APRIL 1987

To Frears's house. He's being photographed with his kids to coincide with the opening of *Prick Up Your Ears*. David Byrne comes by in a green and black tartan jacket, jeans, with a little pigtail. He has a luminous round face, and bright clear skin. It's the first time I've met him, though his band, the Talking Heads, are heroes of mine. We walk round the corner to the Gate Diner where the waiter inadvertently sits us under a poster for *Stop Making Sense*. Various people in the street recognise him and a woman comes over to our table and gives him a note with her phone number on it, thanking him for his contribution to music and films.

Byrne is shy and clever and unpretentious. The disconcerting thing about him is that he listens to what you say and thinks it over before replying seriously. The only other person I've met who has done this is Peter Brook. A most unusual experience.

Byrne was given the script of *Sammy and Rosie* in New York by the great fixer David Gothard, and wants to do some music for it. Byrne has picked up some African music in Paris, composed by street musicians, which Frears thinks is superb. Byrne talks about using similar rhythms in the music he might do for *Sammy and Rosie*. We'll show Byrne a cut of the movie as soon as possible and he can put music over the parts that interest him. The problem is time, as Byrne is composing the music for the new Bertolucci film, *The Last Emperor*, as well as writing the songs for the new Talking Heads record.

In the street waiting for a cab with Byrne I see the cops have stopped another car with black people in it. The black people are being very patient. What the hell is going on in this city?

18 APRIL 1987

Big day. First rough assembly of the film. I meet the editor, Mick Audsley, who is pulling the film on a trolley in its numerous silver cans through the streets. It's 110 minutes long, he says. As it's a rough-cut the film is a little like a home movie, with the sound coming and going; and of course there's no music.

We watch it in a small viewing theatre off Tottenham Court Road. The first forty minutes are encouraging and absorbing and we laugh a lot. Shashi is excellent: both menacing and comic, though his performance seems to lack subtlety. I am elated all the same. Then it begins to fall apart. My mind wanders. I can't follow the story. Entire scenes, which seemed good in themselves at the time of shooting, pass without registering. They bear no relation to each other. It is the centre of the film I'm referring to: the party, the 'fuck' night, the morning after, the breakfasts. Towards the end the film picks up again and is rather moving.

Each of us, cameraman, editor, director, me, can see the faults of the thing from our own point of view. I can see the character of Danny fading out; can see that the character of Anna is not sufficiently rounded; that the riots are not developed in any significant way.

But there are pluses: Shashi of course. And Frances, who portrays a strong, complex person very clearly. Roland too, especially as I'd worried that he might have been a little wooden.

What I don't get is any sense of the freshness of the thing, of how surprising and interesting it may be to others.

After, I stagger from the viewing theatre, pleased on the one hand that it's up on the screen at last. On the other, I feel disappointed that after all the work, the effort, the thought, it's all over so quickly and just a movie.

Frears is pleased. These things are usually hell, he says, but this wasn't, entirely. Some of it, he says, is the best work he's done; it's a subtle and demanding film. Part of the problem with it, he thinks, is that maybe it's too funny at the beginning and not serious enough. He suggests it could be slowed down a bit. I say I don't want to lose any of the humour, especially as the end of the film is so miserable. It's a question, over the next few weeks, of reconciling the two things.

30 APRIL 1987

Mick Audsley has been furiously cutting the film for the last two weeks. When we all walk into the preview theatre – including Karin Bamborough and David Rose from Channel 4 – to see how the film's progressed, Mick's as nervous as a playwright on a first night. I reassure him. But it's his film now; this is his draft; it's his work we're judging. 'I've taken some stuff out,' he says nervously. 'And moved other things around.'

There are about twelve people in the room. Frears's film *Prick Up Your Ears* is successful in the States and Bevan's *Personal Services* is number three in the British film charts, so they're both pretty cheerful.

For the first forty minutes I can't understand what's happened to the film. It's more shaped now, but less bizarre somehow, less unpredictable. I suppress my own laughter in order to register every gurgle and snort of pleasure around me. But there is nothing: complete silence.

The film begins to improve around the 'fuck' night and takes off when the Ghetto-lites dance and mime to Otis Redding's 'My Girl' and we cut between the avid fuckers. It's unashamedly erotic, a turn-on, running right up against the mean monogamous spirit of our age. There must be more jiggling tongues in this film than in any other ever made.

I cringe throughout at the ridiculousness of the dialogue, which seems nothing like the way people actually talk. A lot of this will go, I expect, or we can play some very loud David Byrne music over it, though I am attached to some of the ideas contained in the more strident speeches.

At the end I feel drained and disappointed. I look around for a chair in the corner into which I can quietly disappear. I feel like putting a jacket over my head.

Then you have to ask people what they think. David Rose is a little enigmatic. He says the film is like a dream, so heightened and unreal it is. It bears no relation to the real world. I say: We want to create a self-sustaining, internally coherent world. He says, yes, you've done that, but you can't be surprised when what you've done seems like an intrusion to those it is about.

Frears says it's a different film from the one we watched two weeks ago. Now we have to fuse the seriousness of this version with the frivolity of the first version.

A journalist who came to see me the other day asked why I always write about such low types, about people without values or morality, as it seems all the characters are, except for Alice. It's a shock when he says this. I write about the world around me, the people I know, and myself. Perhaps I've been hanging out with the wrong crowd. Reminds me of a story about Proust, who when correcting the proofs of *Remembrance of Things Past*, was suddenly disgusted by the horrible people he'd brought to life, corrupt and unpleasant and lustful all of them and not a figure of integrity anywhere in it.

4 MAY 1987

A very confused time for us in trying to work out what kind of film we want to release. We talk frequently about the shape of it, of pressing it experimentally all over to locate the bones beneath the rolling fat. But you have to press in far to touch hardness. There's barely any story to the thing. If there is a story, it belongs to Shashi. Frears is talking of 'taking things out'; he says, 'Less means better,' and adds ominously, 'There's far too much in it.' It's painful, this necessary process of cutting. I think, for consolation, of Jessica Mitford's: 'In writing you must always kill your dearest darlings!'

7 MAY 1987

Frears on good form in the cutting room. He hasn't been so cheerful for days. He's cutting swathes out of the movie. It's funnier and more delicate, he says. He adds: Your talent will seem considerably greater after I've done with it!

He's put his finger on something which will inevitably bother film-writers. If the movie is successful you can never be sure to what extent this is due to you, or whether the acting, editing and direction have concealed weaknesses and otherwise lifted an ordinary script which, if it were to be shown in its entirety or as written, wouldn't work at all.

11 MAY 1987

Frears rings and says it's vital I come in later today and see the film. You'll have to brace yourself, he adds, ringing off.

The first shock is in the first minute: the shooting. Mick has obviously worried a great deal about this. He has removed the moment when the black woman gets shot, when you see her covered in blood and falling to the ground. Even Frears is surprised that this has come out, but he's pleased with it. What such a powerful and upsetting moment does, they both argue, is overwhelm the opening. Frears also says that its removal improves the subtlety of the storytelling – we find out later what has happened. I do like the shooting, not for aesthetic reasons, but for didactic ones: it says, this is what happens to some black people in Britain – they get shot up by the police.

Halfway through this cut I can see it's going to work. The shape is better, it's quicker, less portentous. Danny's long speech has gone, as have various other bits of dialogue. A scene between Anna and Sammy has gone, which means that Anna's part in the film is diminished. Alice's speech on going down the stairs, before the cellar scene, has gone, which I missed. I'll try and get them to put it back.

I argue to Frears that in some ways the film has been depoliticised, or that private emotions now have primacy over public acts or moral positions. In one sense, with a film this is inevitable: it is the characters and their lives one is interested in. Frears argues that, on the contrary, the film is more political. Ideas are being banged together harder now: the audience is being provoked. But I can see that my remark has bothered him.

I can't deny it's a better film: less grim, less confused and lumpy, funnier and maybe tear-jerking at the end. Frears has put the music from *Jules et Jim* over the scene where Sammy tells us what he likes about London, which brings that section to life, thank God, especially as three or four people have moaned about it being redundant. Next week Frears will shoot a couple more sections for that particular homage to Woody Allen and maybe reprise the music at the end.

After the viewing we talk about there being another scene at the very end of the film, a scene between Sammy and Rosie under a tree, maybe at Hammersmith, by the river. Of course, there's the danger of sentimentalizing this, of saying that despite everything – the shooting, the revolts, the politics of Rafi – this odd couple end up being happy together, the implication being that this is all that matters. This is, of course, the pattern of classical narration: an original set-up is disrupted but is restored at the end. Thus the audience doesn't leave the cinema thinking that life is completely hopeless. I say to Frears that at least at the end of *Jules et Jim* Jeanne Moreau drives herself and her lover off a bridge. He says, sensibly: Well, let's shoot the scene and if it doesn't work we can dump it.

17 MAY 1987

Frears and I talk about the odd way in which *Sammy and Rosie* has developed. The oddness is in not being able to say in advance what kind of film it is since the process seems to have been to shoot a lot of material and then decide later, after chucking bits of it away, what the film will be like. It's like a structured improvisation. Frears says: Shouldn't we be more in control at the beginning? Surely, if we had more idea of what we're doing we could spend more time on the bits we're going to use? But, with some exceptions, it's difficult to tell what's going to be in the final film, partly because I'm no good at plots, at working out precisely what the story is.

21 MAY 1987

Frears and I were both moaning to each other about the Tory election broadcast that went out yesterday. Its hideous nationalism and neo-fascism, its talk of 'imported foreign ideologies like socialism' and its base appeals to xenophobia. Seeing the film once again Frears has taken the socialist Holst's theme from 'Jupiter' in *The Planets*, later used for the patriotic hymn 'I Vow to Thee My Country' (which was, incidentally, played at the Royal Wedding) from the Tory broadcast, and played it over the eviction scene, giving it a ritualistic quality.

Later there is intense discussion of the film between David and Karin, Mick, Bevan, Frears and me. I find these discussions quite painful. But Frears invites them. He listens carefully to everything people have to say and then he goes back to the film. So secure is he in what he is doing that he isn't threatened by criticism; he can absorb it and use it to improve his work.

An election has been called. I do some leafleting for the Labour Party. I cover estates which I walk past every day, but haven't been inside since the last election. In the mean time, the buildings have been 'refurbished'. From the outside the blocks and low-rise houses look modern: rainproof, wind-resistant, nature-blocking. I wonder if they have really changed since the last time around. My trips to New York and Los Angeles now seem utterly unimportant when there are parts of my own city, my own streets, for Chrissakes, five minutes' walk from me, that are unknown to me!

I walk off the main road and across the grass to the entrance of the first block. The door is open; the glass in the door is smashed. A woman in filthy clothes, in rags I suppose, stands in the entrance waving her arms around. She is in another place: stoned. I go on through and into the silver steel cage of the lift. Inside I hold my nose. At the top of the block the windows are smashed and the wind blows sharply across the landing. Broken bottles, cans and general detritus are whisked about.

Someone has a sign on their door: 'Don't burgle me I have nothin''. Many of the doors have been smashed in and are held together with old bits of wood. The stench of piss and shit fills the place.

An old distressed woman in a nightdress comes out of her flat and complains that a party has been going on downstairs for two days. One man comes to the door with a barely controlled Alsatian. Come and take back this fucking leaflet, he screams at me; come and get it, mate!

There are at least two dogs on each floor, and you can hear their barking echo through the building.

It is difficult to explain to the people who live here why they should vote Labour; it is difficult to explain to them why they should vote for anyone at all.

23 MAY 1987

Last day of shooting. Bits and pieces. Colin McCabe at the ICA, Sammy and Rosie by the river (for the last shot of the film) and Aloo Baloo at the Finborough pub in Earls Court for the 'Sammy and Rosie in London' part of the film. It is a strange day because these are all things Sarah and I have done together; they are places we go. So you live them and then go back a few weeks later with some mates, a camera, and some actors, and put it all in a film. Sarah has yet to see the film and that's good, I think, as it is improving all the time. But she rang me last night, angry at being excluded, thinking this was deliberate, or just more evidence of my general indifference. Whatever it is, she has started to call the film 'Hanif Gets Paid, Sarah Gets Exploited'.

5 JUNE 1987

Frears and Stanley Myers are working away on the music. Charlie Gillett, the great rock DJ and music expert, is suggesting various bands and styles of music to go over different parts of the film. David Byrne, from whom we've heard not a word for ages, has finally said he's too busy to do anything.

Sarah finally comes to see the film. She sits in front of Frances Barber. After, she tells me she likes it. She confidently says she can see it as an entire object, just a good film, something quite apart from herself.

10 JUNE 1987

My agent Sheila goes to see the uncompleted *Sammy and Rosie* and rings this morning. Some of it's wonderful, she says. But it's heartless and anti-women. Why anti-women? I ask. Because all the women in the film are shown as manipulative. And Rosie doesn't care for Sammy at all. When he sleeps with someone else it doesn't appear to bother her. I thought, she says, that this was because you were going to show Rosie as a lesbian. I ask her why she should think this. Because most of her friends are lesbian. Plus, she adds, you make Sammy into such a weak, physically unattractive and horrible character it's difficult to see how she could take much interest in him. Is he what you and Stephen think women like?

Sheila doesn't like the end of the film, with Sammy and Rosie sitting crying on the floor. It makes them seem callous, especially with all the women trailing out of the flat and not doing or saying anything. In addition she dislikes the 'Sammy and Rosie in London' sequence, one of my favourites in the film, which she compares to a cheap advertisement. That just has to go, she says, it's so ridiculous. Anyway, couldn't at least fifteen minutes of the film be cut? Like what? Well, Alice's speech to Rafi on walking down the stairs, just before the cellar scene. One doesn't listen to all this, she says. Well, I feel like saying, we could chop fifteen minutes out. But that would make the film just over an hour long. We'd have to release it as a short.

For a while after this conversation I am perforated by doubt and think Sheila might be right; our judgement has gone and the entire thing is some terrible, arrogant mistake.

There's going to be at least another eighteen months of this, of exposure, of being judged. This is a 'profession of opinion' as Valéry calls it, where to make a film or write a book is to stand up so that people can fire bullets at you.

I go off to the dubbing theatre where the actor playing the property developer is yelling into the mike about communist, lesbian moaning minnies. This will be put through a megaphone and added to the eviction scene. Frears is in good cheer as ever. When I tell him about Sheila's attack on the film he says we will get attacked this time around. People will want to engage with the issues the film raises; they'll want to argue with the movie and they'll get angry. It won't be an easy ride as with *Laundrette* or *Prick*, with people just being grateful these kinds of films are being made at all.

As we walk through Soho, Frears and Mick are talking once more about the shooting of the black woman at the beginning of the film. They're now thinking of putting it back. It's a hard decision to make: do you forfeit an important and powerful scene because it throws out the balance of the film?

I spend the evening leafleting the estates again, as it's the day before the election. The feeling in the committee room, where people are squatting on the floor addressing envelopes, is that it'll be close. No one actually thinks we'll put an end to Thatcherism this time, but at least Thatcher won't have put an end to socialism.

I'd seen Kinnock at a Labour rally held in a sports hall in Leicester on Friday. There are at least 2,000 people there and it is strictly an all-ticket affair: they are very nervous of hecklers, as the meeting is being televised. There is a squad of large women bouncers who, when a heckler starts up, grab the dissident by the hair and shove her or him out of the hall at high speed. They are also nervous of anything too radical: I've been instructed not to use the word 'comrade' in my speech, though it is Kinnock's first word.

The Labour organisation has wound up the crowd expertly and they are delirious, kicking out a tremendous din with their heels against the back of the wooden benches. When I introduce Kinnock, he and Glenys come through the hall surrounded by a brass band, pushing through photographers and fans like a couple of movie stars.

Kinnock speaks brilliantly, contrasting levity and passion, blasting off with a string of anti-Tory jokes. I know that various sympathetic writers and comedians have been sending lines and gags round to his house and he's been working them into the speeches he always insists on writing himself. The impression is of someone who is half stand-up comic and half revivalist preacher. What is also clear is his humanity and goodness, his real concern for the many inequalities of our society. At the end of the meeting the crowd sings 'We Shall Overcome' and 'The Red Flag' and we cheer and cheer. For these two hours I can't see how we can fail to win the election.

15 JUNE 1987
Everyone still reeling from the shock of the election defeat and from the knowledge that we were completely wrong about the extent of the Labour failure. We lost in Fulham by 6,000 votes,

though we'd won the seat at a recent by-election. Someone tells me that the people on the estate I leafleted voted 3 to 1 for the Tories. What this Tory victory means is the death of the dream of the 1960s, which was that our society would become more adjusted to the needs of all the people who live in it; that it would become more compassionate, more liberal, more tolerant, less intent on excluding various groups from the domain of the human; that the Health Service, education, and the spectrum of social services would be more valued and that through them our society would become fairer, less unequal, less harshly competitive; and that the lives of the marginalised and excluded would not continue to be wasted. But for the third time running, the British people have shown that this is precisely what they don't want.

We invite a bunch of friends to a showing of *Sammy and Rosie*, mainly to look at two significant changes: one is the putting back of the shooting of the black woman; the other the inclusion of Roland's long speech about domestic colonialism.

Well, as we stand around in the preview theatre, some people argue that we don't need the shooting as it's too obvious. Others say you need its power and clarity. I can see that Frears has made up his mind in favour of it at last. I can also see that he is glad to have put back Roland's speech as it anchors the first half of the film and gives Danny's character more substance. The hardest scene to decide about is the very end, with Sammy and Rosie walking by the river. Frears says he hates unhappy endings, so he'd added it to lighten the tone. But someone else says it gives the movie two endings; and, worse than that, it's an attempt to have it both ways – to cheer up what is a sad and rather despairing film.

Despite these bits and pieces, I feel it now has shape and thrust and pace, due to the incredible amount of work Frears and Mick Audsley have done in the editing.

Sarah also comes to this screening, and we leave together, walking down Charing Cross Road. She has said little so far and when I ask about the film this time around, her reaction is more ambiguous. She says: 'Yes, this time it wasn't so easy. Rosie seemed too hard and uncaring; surely I am not hard and uncaring? Perhaps I am like that and haven't been able to see that side of myself? Perhaps that is your objective view of me. Oh, it's difficult for me because I have had the sensation recently, when I'm at work or with a friend – it just comes over me – that I'm turning into the character you've written and Stephen has directed and the actress has portrayed. What have you done?'

19 JUNE 1987

Frears exceedingly cheerful and enjoying finishing the film, putting the frills on, playing around with it. He never stops working on it or worrying about it. He talks about using some of Thatcher's speeches: over the beginning, he says, just after the credits, the St Francis speech would do nicely. And somewhere else. Where? I ask. You'll have to wait and see, he replies.

Stanley Myers, who is in charge of the music, gives me a tape of music which has been put together by Charlie Gillett. It's terrific stuff: bits of African rhythms, reggae, and some salsa and rap stuff.

8 JULY 1987

To see the almost finished *Sammy and Rosie*. It's been dubbed now; the sound is good and the music is on. Frears has put back the scene between Anna and Sammy where she pushes him half out of her studio and interrogates him about his other girlfriends. I thought this scene had gone for good, but Frears continues to experiment. He'd said it would be a surprise where he'd use the Thatcher material. It is. It's right at the front, before the credits, over a shot of the waste ground after the eviction. It works as a kind of prologue and hums with threat and anticipation, though with its mention of the 'inner city' it also seems to be presenting an issue film. But anger and despair following the election have gone straight into the film, giving it a hard political edge. Frears's struggle over the last few weeks has been to reconcile those two difficult things: the love of Sammy and Rosie for each other, and the numerous issues that surround them. At last he's given the story a clarity and definition I couldn't find for it in the script.

I sit through the film in a kind of haze, unable to enjoy or understand it. I can see how complete it is now, but I have no idea of what it will mean for other people, what an audience seeing it freshly will make of it. Only then will the circle be complete. We'll just have to wait and see.

After the screening someone says how surprised they are that such a film got made at all, that somehow the police didn't come round to your house and say: This kind of thing isn't allowed! Of course it won't be when the new Obscenity Bill goes through.

Later that night I go out for a drink with a friend in Notting Hill. We go to a pub. It's a dingy place, with a dwarf barmaid. It's mostly black men there, playing pool. And some white girls, not talking much, looking tired and unhealthy. On the walls are warnings against the selling of drugs on the premises. Loud music, a DJ, a little dancing. A fight breaks out in the next bar. Immediately the pub is invaded by police. They drag the fighters outside and throw them into a van. People gather round. It's a hot night. And soon the air is full of police sirens. Six police vans show up. The cops jump out and grab anyone standing nearby. They are very truculent and jumpy, though no one is especially aggressive towards them. We leave and drive along the All Saints Road, an area known for its drug dealers. Twice we're stopped and questioned: Where are we going, why are we in the area, what are our names? Black people in cars are pulled out and searched. Eventually we park the car and walk around. The area is swamped with police. They're in couples, stationed every twenty-five yards from each other. There's barely anyone else in the street.

14 JULY 1987

A showing of *Sammy and Rosie* at nine in the morning. Frears and Audsley have been working all weekend, juggling with bits and pieces. It seems complete, except for some music which has been put on over the cellar scene and seems to dissipate the power of Claire's performance at that point. Otherwise the film works powerfully, with a lot of soul and kick. We talk about how much has gone back in and Frears says how foolish it seems in retrospect to have taken out so much and then put it back. But of course that process of testing was essential, a way of finding out what was necessary to the film and what not.

We stand outside the cutting room in Wardour Street and Frears says: Well, that's it then, that's finished, we've made the best film we can. I won't see it again, he adds, or maybe I'll run it again in five years or something. Let's just hope people like it.

Introduction to *London Kills Me*

First published with the screenplay, 1991

One day in the summer of 1989 I was followed along the Portobello Road by a boy of about twenty-one. He was selling drugs, as were many people around there, but this kid was an unusual salesman. For a start, he didn't mumble fearfully or try to intimidate. And he didn't look strong enough to shove a person in an alley and rob them. He was open-faced, young and direct; and he explained unasked the virtues of the drugs he was selling – hash, acid, Ecstasy – holding them up as illustration. As I vacillated, he explained lyrically about the different moods, settings and amounts appropriate for each drug.

We started to meet regularly. He liked to stand outside pubs, discussing people in the street. He'd think about which drug they'd prefer and wonder whether they'd purchase it from him, perhaps right now. Then he'd follow them.

He relished the game or challenge of selling, the particular use of words and the pleasures of conscious manipulation. He liked to con people too, selling them fake drugs, or promising to deliver the deal to them later. On the whole he was proud of his craft. He reminded me of the salesmen in Barry Levinson's *The Tin Men*. He was in a good position, that particular summer of love. He had a regular supply of drugs and there were plenty of customers. The kid knew there was a limitless market for what he had to sell. After all, drug-taking was no longer the sub-cultural preserve of those who knew its arcane language. Thirty years of a worldwide, sophisticated and mass culture, introduced by the Beatles, the Doors, Hendrix, Dylan and others, had spread the drug word, making certain drugs both acceptable and accessible. There was no combating it.

223

Now, new drugs like Ecstasy were especially in demand. Unlike LSD, for example, these were party drugs, weekend drugs, without noticeable after-effects. More usefully for the end of the 1980s, they were compatible with both holding down a full-time job and dancing in a field at four in the morning.

So most of the time the kid didn't much care if he made a sale or not. He wasn't desperate – yet. He moved from squat to squat and wasn't yet weary of being ejected, often violently, in the middle of the night. Anyhow, if things didn't go well he'd leave for Ibiza, Ecstasy Island, where many other young people were headed.

He loved to talk about himself, dwelling in vivid and creative detail on the fantastic adventures and tragedies of his life. Along with his drug dealing, these horrific and charming stories were his currency, his means of survival, enabling him to borrow money, ask a favour or stack up an ally for the future. So he told them to anyone who'd listen and to plenty of people who wouldn't. Again, it was a while before these stories became repetitive and self-pitying.

This kid's subject, his speciality let us say, or his vocation, was illegal drugs. He'd discuss enthusiastically the marvels and possibilities of Ecstasy, the different varieties of the drug and the shades of feeling each could induce. He looked forward to the new drugs he believed were being produced by hip chemists in San Francisco. This evangelical tone reminded me of the way LSD was talked about in the 1960s. I kept thinking that had the kid known about, say, the Victorian novel in the same detail, he'd have been set up for life by some university.

But a penchant for getting high and dealing to strangers was getting him banned from local pubs. He'd been stabbed, beaten up and slashed across the face. Sometimes he was picked up by the police, who 'disappeared' him into a police cell for two or three days, without charging him or informing anyone he was there. He'd been comforted and warned by social workers, probation officers and drug counsellors. Despite his glorious stories, he led a hard and painful life, not helped by the fact he was foolish as well as smart, indiscreet too, and without much foresight.

The intensity of this kid's life as he ran around the rich city, stealing, begging, hustling, was the starting point for *London Kills Me*. But his activities were bound up with the new music – hip-hop, house, acid jazz – and the entrepreneurial bustle surrounding it; the bands, record labels, shops, raves and warehouse parties organised in the squats, pubs and flats of Notting Hill. This reliable generational cycle of new music, fashion and attitude amounted to a creative resurgence reminiscent of the mid-1960s, and, of course, of the mid-1970s punk and New Wave, which was DIY music of another kind.

Notting Hill seemed an appropriate setting for the London branch of what had been a mostly provincial and northern music movement. The North Kensington area had always had a large immigrant community: Afro-Caribbean, Portuguese, Irish, Moroccan. Many Spanish people, escaping fascism, had settled there. Its mixture of colours and classes was unique in London and it had a lively focal point, the Portobello Road and its market. Of the other previously 'happening' places in London, Chelsea had become a tourists' bazaar; and Soho had been overrun by the advertising industry. But like both these places, Notting Hill had cultural history. George Orwell was living in the Portobello Road in 1928 when he started to write the first pages of a play (one character of which was called Stone). Colin McInnes was part of the area's 1950s bohemia. In the late 1960s the seminal *Performance* was set and filmed there. Not long afterwards Hockney took a studio in Powis Terrace. And in the 1970s the Clash's first album featured a montage of the 1976 carnival riot on its cover.

In 1959, after seeing Shelagh Delaney's *A Taste of Honey*, Colin McInnes wrote: 'As one skips through contemporary novels, or scans the acreage of fish-and-chip dailies and the very square footage of the very predictable weeklies, as one blinks unbelievingly at "British" films, it is amazing – it really is – how very little one can learn about life in England here and now.'

A few years later his wish began to be granted. There developed a tradition, coming out of Brecht and stemming from the Royal Court and the drama corridor of the BBC, of plays, series and films which addressed themselves to particular issues – unemployment, or racism, or housing – usually seen through the inescapable British framework of class. This work was stimulated by the idea of drama having a use or purpose, to facilitate society's examination of itself and its values, creating argument and debate about the nature of life here and now. Many actors, writers, directors and designers were trained to see their work in this way.

Out of this came the brief resurgence of low-budget British films in the mid-1980s. The myriad tensions of life under Thatcher were irresistible to writers and film-makers. Here was the challenge of a Conservatism that had, at last, admitted to being an ideology. Here were ideas – at a time when the Left had none. The cultural reply was not presented in the language of social realism; both victims and heroes of the class struggle were eschewed. These were popular films wishing to reach a large audience hungry for debate about the new age of money and what it meant.

One issue rarely discussed in this way has been drug use. It's an odd omission as, since the mid-1960s, in most towns and cities of a good deal of the world, young people have been using illegal drugs of various kinds. There hasn't been much fiction about this subject and the life that goes with it; and remarkably little hard information about drugs is provided to people, though cautionary and scary stories are propagated in the vain hope of frightening them.

Although drugs are fundamental to the story, *London Kills Me* was never primarily 'about' drug use. The film is concerned mainly with the lives of the characters. It was always, for me, a story about a boy searching for a pair of shoes in order to get a job as a waiter in a diner. Even so, when we were seeking out money for the movie – and it was not expensive – there was criticism from potential backers about the drug use in the film. They were worried that they might be accused of 'recommending' drugs.

Many films and more television plays are planned meticulously before they start shooting. There are shot-lists and storyboards for every second of the film. The director, cameraman, producer, art director and assistants work out the camera- and actor-moves on scale plans before shooting begins. Making the film itself is then a process of reproduction. It isn't the necessary requirements of planning that make this way of working seem objectionable. It is the expectation or hope of safety and security that is deadening, the desire to work without that moment of fear – when you really don't know how to go on – and therefore to create without utilising the unexpected.

I've never written in a planned way and I tried, even as a first-time director, not to work like this. It would bore me to know in the morning what exactly I'd be doing in the afternoon. And Stephen Frears, whose advice I sought, said it was 'fatal' to work to a strict plan. Having worked with him twice as a writer, I didn't want to have any less enjoyment than he clearly had when shooting a film.

Much to my surprise, having written the film and then being in the powerful position of being able to direct it too, I felt less possessive about my dialogue and the shape of the script than I had when someone else was in charge. In the end, all I clung to was the story, to getting that, at least, in front of the camera.

The script of *London Kills Me* was only ninety pages long: a tight little film without much wastage. I couldn't see there'd be much to lose in the editing. I thought every scene was essential and in the best place. We wouldn't waste a lot of time shooting material we'd never use. Editing would be relatively simple. So I was pretty surprised when the first rough assembly of the film was over two and a half hours long. I found myself in the odd position of having written a film and then shot it – and still I didn't know what sort of movie I was supposed to be making, what the tone was to be. The editing, like writing, I realised, would also become a form of exploration and testing of the material. It was all, even this, an attempt to tell a story by other means.

The Boy in the Bedroom

First published in *Dreaming and Scheming*, 2002

I hadn't intended to write the scripts for the BBC's version of *The Buddha of Suburbia*. My wish was to hand the book over to someone else, forget about it, and watch the series when it appeared on TV. After all, I'd written and rewritten the book, and promoted it in several countries. It was time to move on. Sometimes I wish I were better at doing things I don't really want to do, but it can also be a strength.

The first writer hired to make the adaptation took my text and presented it as Karim's voice-over, with accompanying pictures. I could see the point of the narration, and later, when Roger Michell and I were writing the script, we discussed it constantly and experimented with it. (There are, after all, scores of good films which use a first-person voice-over.) In the end, however, it seemed lazy and had a deadening effect, as if the events were not happening in the present. If the serial wasn't to be like watching an illustrated talk, the first-person point of view had to be abandoned. The challenge was to dramatise everything.

The second writer was, apparently, instructed to 'capture the spirit' of the novel. Consequently, opening the script at random, I saw a scene set in a chip shop, featuring characters whose names I didn't recognise, as if this 'spirit' was not necessarily present in the scenes I'd created, of which only a minimum remained.

Directors came and went, having refused to shoot the scripts. Finally, having been informed that at this rate the project would never get made, and being made to feel that my misgivings were obstructing it, I agreed to write it. An office would be provided at the BBC. The latest director, Roger Michell, and I would collaborate.

I enjoyed packing my briefcase in the morning, buying my newspaper at the tube station on the corner, getting on the bus and going to the office, like other people. It made me feel normal, in what was, for me, a far from normal period.

Only a few months before, my father had died; my father, who'd always encouraged me to take up this precarious craft and living, and never suggested I become a doctor, accountant or bus driver, had made me see that someone like me could do something like this, although the odds were not in one's favour. And, once I'd started seriously to do it, he kept me going. Strangely, now I think about it, I never rebelled against this conviction and it remained implacably within me. You would have thought, with such a parent, who burned to be a novelist, and insisted I live the life he craved for himself, the sensible son would, without hesitation, sign up for the Navy. It's possible, however, that my resistance consisted of my including him, parodically, in *The Buddha*; I know he was shocked, but he never complained.

Also during the same period, a film, *London Kills Me*, which somewhat innocently I'd directed, wanting to see if this was something I might like to learn about, had been roundly abused. Finally, I was sick, waiting to go into hospital for a back operation. I couldn't stand or even shuffle without thinking a dagger was being turned in my lower back, and electric shocks administered to my legs, all day, perhaps by critics. How much pleasure pain sucks from life, making one weary and dispirited! I was swallowing pills by the handful, imagining that if I took enough the pain would stop for good. However, I had at least made a decision.

For over a year I'd been rolled and thumped and examined naked and robbed blind by numerous osteopaths, physiotherapists, chiropractors, aromatherapists and acupuncturists. (Everyone I knew swore by their own genius who had brought them back from imminent invalidity; for all of them in London, and further afield, I dutifully removed my trousers and bent over.) I had had more hands on me than Linda Lovelace, and on a few occasions went to bed with packets of frozen Brussels sprouts strapped to my lower back by pyjama cords. But one day, on a routine visit to an acupuncturist who favoured 'the natural way', I was lying on the table with pins in me, imagining I'd been reincarnated, in this life, as a cactus, when I heard odd noises. I twisted my stiff neck to look at him behind me, and opened my eyes wide. My physician was dancing barefoot at the end of the table, with his eyes closed. Not only that, he was waving a joss stick and murmuring an incantation. It was at that moment I decided to go under the knife. But this being on the National Health Service, I was waiting, waiting, for the releasing incision.

And so, when Roger and I got started, I was bad-tempered and more impatient than usual. It is difficult for an adapter, working on another person's characters and ideas. But if that person is lying on his stomach at your feet, his mind jumbled and wheeling madly, while a secretary treads his aching back, it must be particularly trying. Fortunately Roger Michel was well organised. He worked out the order of the scenes and the entire structure. As we had decided the serial should last four hours, in hour-long episodes, the most important thing, at that length, was that everything held together. Each episode had to have a shape, as did the whole story. Most of the characters had to be kept going and developed, but new ones had to be introduced too. It was a challenging technical exercise.

Steadfastly, Roger struggled to maintain the novel as it was. I wanted to try adding new material, ideas that had occurred to me since publication. For instance I wanted to develop the relationship between Changez and Jamila, so that he became a sort of Scheherazade. The disciple of Conan Doyle and Harold Robbins would tell stories to maintain his reluctant but beloved wife's attention, enabling him to gaze on her for as long as he could make her listen, hoping that as the tales unfolded, one within another, she would fall in love with him. And perhaps she would. I wanted to see if she could be seduced by his stories of India, a place she'd never been but which determined the nature of her life. After all, some scholars believe that all great stories originate in India, as did the original tales of the Arabian Nights. The framing device, of stories within stories, is considered to be of Indian origin. Already in the novel I had hinted at this development of the Changez/ Jamila relationship, but I'd left it at that, in order not to move too far away from Karim. But since I'd finished the book, the characters remained in my mind, they were people I knew well. It would be enjoyable to give them more life.

But we discovered that there wasn't sufficient room for new tangents. Already it was proving difficult enough to get the story as it existed told in four hours. So most of our work was organisational, plus essential cutting and fiddling around. We had numerous disputes and arguments, but the bulk of the work had already been done, in the novel. We completed the scripts in six weeks.

The most difficult part of casting *The Buddha* was finding someone to play Changez. The dialogue I'd written for him was in strange Anglo-Indian grammar; the sentences ran like mazes. Roger found Harish Patel in Bombay; he was the last actor they saw on that casting trip. I met Harish a few days after he'd set foot for the first time in London. He'd been thinking hard about how Changez talked, walked and used his crippled hand, determined to include his own amazement and confusion at this country in the part.

The shoot itself was interminable, during a wet and cold winter; the light went early, sometimes at two-thirty. We filmed *The Buddha* in the streets where I'd grown up, on the roads where I'd cycled every day. Naveen Andrews, playing Karim, wore a copy of my school uniform, and sat miserably in a bedroom not unlike the one in which I listened to the John Peel Show on the radio, to drown out the sound of my parents arguing. (Its introduction was a brilliant Jimmy Page guitar break from Led Zeppelin's 'Heartbreaker'.) This was the room in which, after school, I'd written novels instead of doing my homework. Then I'd pack them up in brown paper and string and carry them to the Post Office where my grandmother worked behind the counter, and send them to publishers in London. (It was never long before they came back, the first chapter a little rumpled, with a printed rejection slip pinned to the front. The pain of that final, impersonal rejection, not of a book, but of one's whole self! Goodbye hope!)

It was the room to which I'd brought my first girlfriends back, after parties, having walked miles home at four in the morning from Peckham or Crystal Palace, shouting out lines from Ginsberg, ('angelheaded hipsters burning for the ancient heavenly connection to the starry dynamo in the machinery of night . . .') after my father brought home the Penguin American Poets collection which also included Corso and Ferlinghetti. Parties: there were plenty. I hung out with a large group of boys who knew one another from school and spent the weekends together, playing records, slitting their wrists, jamming, tripping, having sex, often in the houses of absent parents. Later, the more adventurous remnants of this group, called 'the Bromley contingent' by Johnny Rotten, formed Siouxsie and the Banshees and Generation X. At school they were a group I'd longed to join, just as Karim desperately wants Charlie Hero to be his friend. But they didn't admit just anyone who'd frayed their jeans and dumped their grandfather's tied-up vest in the sink, along with a tin of orange dye. Their sartorial and tonsorial snobbery, along with a freezing coolness, could only have been a version of their parents' resistance to the vulgar – in the suburbs the working class were never far away, on the heels of the lower middle class. I was finally deemed fit to join after I ran away to the Isle of Wight pop festival.

In February 1993 I was, fortuitously, invited by an American magazine to interview David Bowie. He'd attended, ten years previously, the school I'd gone to, though he had got out long before us, leading the way so that others, like Charlie Hero, could follow. 'I knew at thirteen,' he said to me, 'that I wanted to be the English Elvis.' Throughout the 1970s he'd extended English pop music: he'd established 'glam rock', worn dresses and make-up, claimed to be gay, and written clever, knowing songs. He'd introduced people like Lou Reed and Iggy Pop to British audiences and written songs about Andy Warhol and Dylan. His influence on punk was crucial. And he'd made, with Brian Eno, experimental music – *Low, Heroes, Lodger* – which had lasted, which you could listen to today.

He wasn't merely rich or successful either. I could see he had movie-star glamour, that unbuyable, untouchable sheen which fame, style and a certain self-consciousness bestow on few people. He was, as well, extremely lively and curious, very enthusiastic about movies and books, and in particular, painting and drawing. (At school we'd had the same art teacher, Peter Frampton's father.) Bowie was a man constantly bursting with ideas for musicals, movies, records; he appeared creative all day, drawing, writing on cards, playing music, ringing to ask what you thought of this or that, travelling, meeting people.

I had agreed with Roger that I would ask Bowie to give permission for various old tracks, like 'Changes' and 'Fill Your Heart', to be used on the film. He agreed; emboldened, as we left the restaurant and his black chauffeur-driven car sat there, engine running, I asked if he might fancy writing some original material too. He said yes and asked for the tapes to be sent to him.

A couple of months later Roger and I went to Switzerland to hear what Bowie had done. How could we not feel intimidated? What could schoolboys like us say to the greatest and most famous, who had written over three hundred songs, including 'Rebel Rebel'? (In the pub in Bromley High Street we played his records on the jukebox constantly, kids at different tables suddenly yelling, as one, during conversation 'Suffragette City, oh yeah!') Now we were sitting a few paces from Lake Geneva; yards away, in the other direction, was the house in which Stravinsky composed *The Rite of Spring*. And in the studio the familiar pictures of *The Buddha* ran on the monitor suspended over the mixing desk, which was dotted with dozens of buttons, levers and swinging gauges, alongside which were banked computers. All this, not to launch space-ships, but to make sweet music!

At the end we sighed. Relief was palpable. Bowie saw, though, that some of the music altered the mood of the scene. Repeatedly he rewrote, adjusted cues and thought about how composing music for films is different to writing songs. Later he produced an excellent album called *The Buddha of Suburbia*, developing ideas he'd begun on the film.

They were heady, enjoyable days. The series was, in the end, broadcast as we'd made it. Typically, the BBC did, the day before transmission – although they'd had the tapes for months – attempt to censor it a little, but their nerve held.

The Road Exactly

First published as the introduction to the screenplay of
My Son the Fanatic, 1998

The idea for *My Son the Fanatic*, as for *The Black Album*, was provided by my thinking about the fatwa against Salman Rushdie, announced in February 1989. At that time various politicians, thinkers and artists spoke out in the media about this extraordinary intellectual terror. A surprising number of statements were fatuous and an excuse for abuse and prejudice; some expressed genuine outrage, and most were confused but comfortingly liberal. The attack on Rushdie certainly made people think afresh about the point and place of literature, about what stories were for, and about their relation to dissent.

But few commentators noticed that the objections to *The Satanic Verses* represented another kind of protest. In Britain many young Asians were turning to Islam, and some to a particularly extreme form, often called Fundamentalism. Most of these young people were from Muslim families, of course, but usually families in which the practice of religion, in a country to which their families had come to make a new life, had fallen into disuse.

It perplexed me that young people, brought up in secular Britain, would turn to a form of belief that denied them the pleasures of the society in which they lived. Islam was a particularly firm way of saying 'no' to all sorts of things. Young people's lives are, for a lot of the time, devoted to pleasure: the pleasure of sex and music, of clubbing, friendship, and the important pleasure of moving away from one's parents to develop one's own ideas. Why was it important that this group kept pleasure at a distance? Why did they wish to maintain such a tantalising relation to their own enjoyment, keeping it so fervently in mind, only to deny it? Or was this puritanism a kind of rebellion, a brave refusal of the order of the age – an over-sexualised but sterile society? Were these young Muslims people who dared to try nothing? Whatever the reason, there was, clearly, a future in illusion; not only that, illusions were once more becoming a sound investment. But what sort of future did they require?

To the surprise of most of us, it sometimes seems that we are living in a new theocratic age. I imagined that the 1960s, with its penchant for seeing through things, and pulling them apart with laughter and questions, had cleared that old church stuff away. But the 1960s, in the West, with its whimsy and drugged credulity, also helped finish off the Enlightenment. It was during the 1960s that weird cults, superstitious groups, New Agers, strange therapists, seers, gurus and leaders of all kinds came to prominence. This need for belief and the establishment of new idols was often innocuous – a mixture of the American idea of self-fulfilment and the Greek notion of fully extended man, vitiated by a good dose of ordinary repression.

But the kind of religion favoured by the young Muslims was particularly strict and frequently authoritarian. An old religion was being put to a new use, and it was that use which interested me. I wondered constantly why people would wish to give so much of their own autonomy, the precious freedom of their own minds, to others – to Maulvis, and to the Koran. After all, the young people I met were not stupid; many were very intelligent. But they put a lot of effort into the fashioning of a retributive God to which to submit.

Clearly, where there is a 'crisis of authority', when, it seems, people aren't certain of anything because ancient hierarchies have been brought down, the answer is to create a particularly strict authority, where troubling questions cannot be admitted. 'There's too much freedom,' one of the young men, Ali, kept saying to me, someone who'd always thought that freedom was something you couldn't get enough of. This intrigued me.

Ali worked for a well-known supermarket chain, stacking shelves, though he had a degree. It was boring work; to get anywhere you had to grovel, or go to the bar and drink and exchange unpleasant banter. Sometimes you had to shake hands with women. Anyhow, the Asians didn't get promoted. A reason for this, he liked to muse, was that the major businesses were run by Jews. He applied for jobs all the time, but never got them. I couldn't see why this was so. He was certainly courteous. He brought me presents: a tie, mangos, the Koran. He was intellectually curious too, and liked showing me the new books he bought constantly. He knew a great deal about the history and politics of the Middle East, about which, he claimed, the average Westerner knew little. Ali knew the West, but the West didn't know him except through tendentious media images. The West, therefore, had no idea of its own arrogance, and was certainly not concerned about the extent to which it had no interest in anything outside itself.

Just when I thought there wasn't much Ali and I could argue about, he would say he didn't disapprove of the killings of journalists – and others – in Algeria. They were 'enemies'; he took it for granted that they were guilty. Perhaps, for him, the fact they were murdered made them guilty. During such conversations he liked to quote Malcolm X's phrase at me: 'By any means necessary', a modern motto of liberation thus becoming a tool of tyranny. I couldn't recall the context in which Malcolm X's phrase was first used, but it was clear that it could be applied to anything; its meaning had become unstable. These days not even language would hold still. Indeed, Ali himself could be called a 'fundamentalist', a word newly minted to mean a fanatical Muslim. It was a word he even applied to himself. At the same time he complained about Muslims being portrayed in the press as 'terrorists' and 'fanatics'. This argument, which had begun because of a book, continued to be about language and about what words mean, as much as anything.

The 'West' was a word, like liberalism, for anything bad. The West's freedom made him feel unsafe. If there was too much freedom you had to make less of it. I asked him about the difficulty of giving up things. He had been keen on clubs; he'd had an affair with a married woman. Renunciation made him feel strong, he said, while giving in made him feel weak. Wasn't the West full of addicts?

The West, therefore, was a place full of things he disliked – or where he liked to put them; and where people gave in to things he disapproved of. He gave me a flyer for a Muslim rally in Trafalgar Square that stated, 'Endemic crime, homosexuality, poverty, family breakdown, drug and alcohol abuse shows Western freedom and democracy just aren't working.' Because of this, Ali and his friends would never bring up their children here. But it also meant that he hated his own background, the forces that influenced him and the place he lived in.

His attitude kept reminding me of something I had heard before. Finally I realised it took me back to a paragraph in Czeslaw Milosz's *The Captive Mind* (Milosz is here referring to Eastern European communist intellectuals): 'The official order is to evince the greatest horror of the West. Everything is evil there: trains are late, stores are empty, no one has money, people are poorly dressed, the highly praised technology is worthless. If you hear the name of a Western writer, painter or composer, you must scoff sarcastically, for to fight against "cosmopolitanism" is one of the basic duties of a citizen.'

Constraint could be a bulwark against a self that was always in danger of dissolving in the face of too much choice, opportunity and desire. By opposing that which continually changes around us, by denying those things we might want, we keep ourselves together. In the face of such decadent possibilities and corrupt pleasures – or where there is the fear of what free or disobedient people might do – Islam would provide the necessary deprivation and could attenuate the repertoire of possible selves.

Open the Koran on almost any page and there is a threat. 'We have adorned the lowest heaven with lamps, missiles for pelting devils. We have prepared a scourge of flames for these, and the scourge of Hell for unbelievers: an evil fate!'

There is, then, sufficient regulation and punishment available. Without harsh constraint things might get out of hand, particularly in the post-modern world, where no one knows anything for sure. And so, against the 'corruption' of the West to which so many had innocently travelled, a new authority could be posited – that of Islam and, in particular, those who spoke for it. Without the revolutionary or opposing idea of Purity there wouldn't be those who knew what it was and could tell us when it had been violated. These men – and they were always men – became very powerful. The young invested a lot of authority in them.

Edward Said wrote: 'There are now immigrant communities in Europe from the former colonial territories to whom the ideas of "France" and "Britain" and "Germany" as constituted during the period between 1800 and 1950 simply excludes them.'

It must not be forgotten, therefore, that the background to the lives of these young people includes colonialism – being made to feel inferior in your own country. And then, in Britain, racism; again, being made to feel inferior in your own country. My father's generation came to Britain full of hope and expectation. It would be an adventure, it would be difficult, but it would be worth it.

However, the settling in, with all the compromises and losses that that implies, has been more complicated and taken longer than anyone could imagine. Yet all along it was taken for granted that 'belonging', which means, in a sense, not having to notice where you are, and, more importantly, not being seen as different, would happen eventually. Where it hasn't there is, in the children and grandchildren of the great post-war wave of immigrants, considerable anger and disillusionment. With some exceptions, Asians are still at the bottom of the pile; more likely to suffer from unemployment, poor housing, discrimination and ill-health. In a sense it hasn't worked out. The 'West' was a dream that didn't come true. But one cannot go home again. One is stuck.

Clearly this affects people in different ways. But without a doubt it is constraining, limiting, degrading, to be a victim in your own country. If you feel excluded it might be tempting to exclude others. The fundamentalists liked to reject the usual liberal pieties, sometimes for histrionic reasons. But their enemies – gays, Jews, the media, unsubmissive women, writers – were important to them. Their idea of themselves was based, like the MCC, or like any provincial snob, on who they excluded. Not only that, the central tenets of the West – democracy, pluralism, tolerance, which many people in Islamic countries, Muslim and non-Muslim alike, are struggling for – could be treated as a joke. For those whose lives had been negated by colonialism and racism such notions could only seem a luxury and of no benefit to them; they were a kind of hypocrisy.

Therefore, during our conversations Ali continuously argued that there are no such things as freedom or democracy, or that those abstractions were only real for a small group. For him, if they didn't exist in the purest possible form, they didn't exist at all. Milosz might call Ali's attitude, with some sadness, 'disappointed love', and it was a disappointment that seemed to attach itself to everything. Which isn't to say there wasn't hope too. For instance, he believed that when the existing corrupt rulers of Muslim countries were swept away, they would be replaced by 'true' Muslims, benign in every way, who would work for the benefit of the people, according to the word of God. If the present was unsatisfactory and impossible to live in, as it always would be for him, there was the perfect future, which would, probably, safely remain the future – the best place for it, for his purposes.

Fundamentalism provides security. For the fundamentalist, as for all reactionaries, everything has been decided. Truth has been agreed and nothing must change. For serene liberals on the other hand, the consolations of knowing seem less satisfying than the pleasures of puzzlement, and of wanting to discover for oneself. But the feeling that one cannot know everything, that there will always be maddening and live questions about who one is and how it is possible to make a life with other people who don't accept one, can be devastating. Perhaps it is only for so long that one can live with that kind of puzzlement. Rationalists have always underestimated the need people have for belief. Enlightenment values – rationalism, tolerance, scepticism – don't get you through a dreadful night; they don't provide spiritual comfort or community or solidarity. Fundamentalist Islam could do this in a country that was supposed to be home but which could, from day to day, seem alien.

Muslim fundamentalism has always seemed to me to be profoundly wrong, unnecessarily restrictive and frequently cruel. But there are reasons for its revival that are comprehensible. It is this that has made me want to look at it not only in terms of ideas, but in stories, in character, in terms of what people do. For a writer there cannot be just one story, a story to end all stories in which everything is said, but as many stories as one wants, serving all sorts of purposes and sometimes none at all. The primary object, though, is to provide pleasure of different kinds. And one must remember that perhaps the greatest book of all, and certainly one of the most pleasurable, *The One Thousand and One Nights*, is, like the Koran, written in Arabic. This creativity, the making of something that didn't exist before, the vigour and stretch of a living imagination, is a human affirmation of another kind, and a necessary and important form of self-examination. Without it our humanity is diminished.

Sex and Secularity

First published as the introduction to
Collected Screenplays One, 2002

To me writing for film is no different to writing for any other form. It is the telling of stories, only on celluloid. However, you are writing for a director and then for actors. Economy is usually the point; one objective of film writing is to make it as quick and light as possible. You can't put in whatever you fancy in the hope that a leisured reader might follow you for a while, as you might in a novel. In that sense films are more like short stories. The restrictions of the form are almost poetic, though most poems are not read aloud in cineplexes. Film is a broad art, which is its virtue.

Nevertheless, it didn't occur to any of us involved in *My Son the Fanatic*, for instance, that it would be either lucrative or of much interest to the general public. The film was almost a legacy of the 1960s and 70s, when one of the purposes of the BBC was to make cussed and usually provincial dramas about contemporary issues like homelessness, class and the Labour Party.

I had been aware since the early 1980s, when I visited Pakistan for the first time, that extreme Islam, or 'fundamentalism' – Islam as a political ideology – was filling a space where Marxism and capitalism had failed to take hold. To me this kind of Islam resembled neo-fascism or even Nazism: an equality of oppression for the masses with a necessary enemy – in this case 'the West' – helping to keep everything in place. When I was researching *The Black Album* and *My Son the Fanatic*, a young fundamentalist I met did compare his 'movement' to the IRA, to Hitler and to the Bolsheviks. I guess he had in mind the idea that small groups of highly motivated people could make a powerful political impact.

This pre-Freudian puritanical ideology certainly provided meaning and authority for the helpless and dispossessed. As importantly, it worked too, for those in the West who identified with them; for those who felt guilty at having left their 'brothers' behind in the Third World. How many immigrant families are there who haven't done that? Most of my family, for instance, have long since fled to Canada, Germany, the US and Britain; but some members refused to go. There can't have been a single middle-class family in Pakistan who didn't always have a bank account in the First World, 'just in case'. Those left behind are usually the poor, uneducated, weak, old and furious.

Fundamentalist Islam is an ideology that began to flourish in a conspicuous age of plenty in the West, and in a time of media expansion. Everyone could see via satellite and video not only how wealthy the West was, but how sexualised it had become. (All 'sex and secularity over there, yaar,' as I heard it put.) This was particularly shocking for countries that were still feudal. If you were in any sense a Third Worlder, you could either envy Western ideals and aspire to them, or you could envy and reject them. Either way, you could only make a life in relation to them. The new Islam is as recent as post-modernism.

Until recently I had forgotten Saeed Jaffrey's fruity line in *My Beautiful Laundrette*, 'Our country has been sodomised by religion, it is beginning to interfere with the making of money.' Jaffrey's lordly laundrette owner was contrasted with the desiccated character played by Roshan Seth, for whom fraternity is represented by rational socialism rather than Islam, the sort of hopeful socialism he might have learned at the LSE in London in the 1940s. It is a socialism that would have no hope of finding a base in either 1980s Britain, or in Pakistan.

What Hussein, Omar and even his lover Johnny have in common is the desire to be rich. Not only that: what they also want, which is one of the West's other projects, is to flaunt and demonstrate to others their wealth and prosperity. They want to show off. This will, of course, induce violent envy in some of the poor and dispossessed, and may even encourage their desire to kill the rich.

One of my favourite uncles, a disillusioned Marxist, and a template for the character played by Shashi Kapoor in *Sammy and Rosie Get Laid*, had, by the mid-1980s, become a supporter of Reagan and Thatcher. Every morning we'd knock around Karachi, going from office to office, where he had friends, to be given tea. No one ever seemed too busy to talk. My uncle claimed that economic freedom was Pakistan's only hope. If this surprised me, it was because I didn't grasp what intellectuals and liberals in the Third World were up against. There was a mass of people for whom alternative political ideologies either had no meaning or were tainted with colonialism, particularly when Islamic grass-roots organisation was made so simple through the mosques. For my uncle the only possible contrast to revolutionary puritanism had to be acquisition; liberalism smuggled in via materialism. So if Islam represented a new puritanism, progress would be corruption, through the encouragement of desire. But it was probably too late for this already; American materialism, and the dependence and quasi-imperialism that accompanied it, was resented and despised.

In Karachi there were few books written, films made or theatre productions mounted. If it seemed dull to me, still I had never lived in a country where social collapse and murder were everyday possibilities. At least there was serious talk. My uncle's house, a version of which appears in *My Beautiful Laundrette*, was a good place to discuss politics and books, and read the papers and watch films. In the 1980s American businessmen used to come by. My uncle claimed they all said they were in 'tractors'. They worked for the CIA; they were tolerated if not patronised, not unlike the old-style British colonialists the Pakistani men still remembered. No one thought the 'tractor men' had any idea what was really going on, because they didn't understand the force of Islam.

But the Karachi middle class had some idea, and they were worried. They were obsessed with their 'status' or their position.

Were they wealthy, powerful leaders of the country, or were they a complacent parasitic class – oddballs, Western but not, Pakistani but not – about to become irrelevant in the coming chaos of disintegration?

A few years later, in 1989, the fatwa against Rushdie was announced and, although I saw my family in London, I didn't return to Karachi. I was told by the Embassy that my safety 'could not be guaranteed'. Not long after, when I was writing *The Black Album*, a fundamentalist acquaintance told me that killing Rushdie had become irrelevant. The point was that this was 'the first time the community has worked together. It won't be the last. We know our strength now.'

I have often been asked how it's possible for someone like me to carry two quite different world-views within, of Islam and the West: not, of course, that I do. Once my uncle said to me with some suspicion, 'You're not a Christian, are you?' 'No,' I said. 'I'm an atheist.' 'So am I,' he replied. 'But I am still Muslim.' 'A Muslim atheist?' I said, 'it sounds odd.' He said, 'Not as odd as being nothing, an unbeliever.'

Like a lot of queries put to writers, this question about how to put different things together is a representative one. We all have built-in and contrasting attitudes, represented by the different sexes of our parents, each of whom would have a different background and psychic history. Parents always disagree about which ideals they believe their children should pursue. A child is a cocktail of its parents' desires. Being a child at all involves resolving, or synthesising, at least two different worlds, outlooks and positions.

If it becomes too difficult to hold disparate material within, if this feels too 'mad' or becomes a 'clash', one way of coping would be to reject one part entirely, perhaps by forgetting it. Another way is to be at war with it internally, trying to evacuate it, but never succeeding, an attempt Farid makes in *My Son the Fanatic*. All he does is constantly reinstate an electric tension between differences – differences that his father can bear and even enjoy, as he listens to Louis Armstrong and speaks Urdu. My father, who had similar tastes to the character played by Om Puri, never lived in Pakistan. But, like a lot of middle-class Indians, he was educated by both mullahs and nuns, and developed an aversion to both. He came to love Nat King Cole and Louis Armstrong, the music of black American former slaves. It is this kind of complexity that the fundamentalist has to reject.

Like the racist, the fundamentalist works only with fantasy. For instance, there are those who like to consider the West to be only materialistic and the East only religious. The fundamentalist's idea of the West, like the racist's idea of his victim, is immune to argument or contact with reality. (Every self-confessed fundamentalist I have met was anti-Semitic.) This fantasy of the Other is always sexual, too. The West is recreated as a godless orgiastic stew of immoral copulation. If the black person has been demonised by the white, in turn the white is now being demonised by the militant Muslim. These fighting couples can't leave one another alone.

These disassociations are eternal human strategies and they are banal. What a fiction writer can do is show the historical forms they take at different times: how they are lived out day by day by particular individuals. And if we cannot prevent individuals believing whatever they like about others – putting their fantasies into them – we can at least prevent these prejudices becoming institutionalised or an acceptable part of the culture.

A few days after the September 11 attack on the World Trade Center, a film director friend said to me, 'What do we do now? There's no point to us. It's all politics and survival. How do the artists go on?'

I didn't know what to say; it had to be thought about.

Islamic fundamentalism is a mixture of slogans and resentment; it works well as a system of authority that constrains desire, but it strangles this source of human life too. But of course in the Islamic states, as in the West, there are plenty of dissenters and quibblers, and those hungry for mental and political freedom. These essential debates can only take place within a culture; they are what a culture is, and they demonstrate how culture opposes the domination of either materialism or puritanism. If both racism and fundamentalism are diminishers of life – reducing others to abstractions – the effort of culture must be to keep others alive by describing and celebrating their intricacy, by seeing that this is not only of value but a necessity.

Filming *Intimacy*

First published in *Dreaming and Scheming*, 2002

I am in a screening room somewhere in the suburbs of Paris, waiting for the film of my novel *Intimacy* to begin. A few months ago, during the shooting, I saw some of the rushes, but I have seen no cut material. Now the film is almost finished, with most of the scenes in their definitive order and a good deal of the music in place. The only missing scene is the final one, where the characters played by Kerry Fox and Mark Rylance meet for the last time.

The French director Patrice Chéreau sits somewhere behind me. There is a handful of people present, the editor and others connected with the film. But the room is big; people seem to disappear into the plush velvet of the deep seats. I forget they are there.

Although Patrice and I worked closely together at times, and the film was shot in English, the script was written by his own writer, a woman, in French. I had decided I'd spent long enough with the material and lacked the heart to look at it again. Nevertheless, the film will be something that a number of us – director, writers, actors, editor, cameraman – have made together. And after all the talk, I have little idea what it will be like; evaluating a film from the rushes is like taking a few sentences from a novel and trying to work out the plot. So it is my film but not mine. I made the characters and most of the story, but Patrice transformed, cast and cut it; and, of course, his style and voice as a director are his own.

Patrice arranged to come and see me in London a couple of years ago. He was shy, he said, and didn't speak good English. My French is hopeless, but it seemed better to meet without an interpreter. Whether or not you want to spend a lot of time and energy working with someone you barely know is something, I guess, you can realise only intuitively.

Patrice explained that he wanted to make a film of *Intimacy*, which he had read in French. Also, he said he liked my stories, particularly 'Nightlight', collected in *Love in a Blue Time*. In this story a couple who run into each other by chance begin to meet once a week, on Wednesday afternoons, to make love. Somehow, they never speak; after a while they are unable to.

At that time I did not know Patrice's work in the theatre, opera and cinema as a director and occasional actor. I had seen neither of the films for which he is best known internationally, *La Reine Margot* and *Those Who Love Me Can Take the Train*, and had no idea of his impressive reputation in France. This made it easier for me to see him without enthusiasm or dismay. After we'd looked at one another for a bit – not unlike the couple at the beginning of the film, about to embark on something big, neither one knowing the 'little things' about the other – I said he should take what he wanted from my work and make the film he wanted to make.

It was easy to say. I didn't quite mean it. Nonetheless, it seemed like a good way to start, and I knew, at least, that I did want to start. Later I thought, what can these two strangers, a gay Frenchman and a straight British-Indian make together, if anything? What is possible between us and what impossible? How far can we go? What will this do to me? It would be the first time I'd worked with a non-British director. Would there be anything particularly 'French' about Patrice, or, for that matter, 'English' about me? My instinct was that the French have a better visual sense than the English, though less narrative grasp. But this was really only a prejudice.

Patrice is, I suppose, ten years older than me and about the same size, with similar back problems. He is gentle, unpretentious and willing to be amused. He is modest but not unaware of his own ability. He is certainly less impatient and bad-tempered than me. He goes out more than I do. He is more decisive. I noticed that we tended to dislike the same things, which is always a comforting complicity.

In the end, I am not sure what it is that my imagination likes to do with him, but just looking at Patrice, or hearing his voice on the phone, cheers me up; he makes me want to try to be a better artist. He respects me, and I him, but not too much.

When I first started to write, as a teenager in the suburbs, I wanted to be a novelist. I thought that writing books in a room on my own was all I would do. The work was self-sufficient. For me, as a young man, that was the point. There were no intermediaries or inter-preters – the reader just read what you wrote. Some people, I guess, become writers because they're afraid of others or addicted to solitude. Perhaps they read a lot, or drew or watched television alone as children. Being with others might be the problem that isolation can solve.

However, when you are writing at last, the same questions appear repeatedly. Why am I doing this? Who is this for? Why write this rather than that? I'm sure people in other professions don't have an existential crisis every morning. It's as if you are seeking any excuse to stop. You can, of course, grow out of these questions, or tire of yourself and your own preoccupations. Or you can hope that collaboration will push you past them. A director will have different doubts and fears. You want to see how others work, and – why not? – be changed by them.

My first professional project was a play called *The King and Me*, produced at the Soho Poly theatre in 1980. It was about a woman's infatuation with Elvis Presley, and was directed by Antonia Bird, who I knew from the Royal Court. Her enthusiasm, and the final production, made me feel that what I'd written had some objective merit. A couple of years later, working with the theatre company Joint Stock, I collaborated with the director Max Stafford-Clark and the actors we selected, to 'make' a play for the Royal Court – *Borderline*. I discovered how enjoyable it could be to write for specific actors. Writing new scenes and lines in the rehearsal room, it was possible, almost straight away, to see whether they worked. After, I found it difficult, and depressing, to return to my room and, alone, begin to generate material from scratch.

Since then I have collaborated with more than a dozen directors. Most of my work, including the prose, has passed through others' hands before it reaches an audience. If being imaginative alone can be difficult enough, I am both scared and intrigued by what others will do with what I have started.

What will you think or say if you free-associate, if you let your mind run without inhibition? There are plenty of anxieties there. What, then, will it be like making mistakes, saying daft things, having strange ideas, in front of someone else? Will you be overwhelmed or forced into compromise by the other; or vice versa? Will you feel liberated by them, or will new fears be aroused? Which fears might they be?

The challenge of collaboration is to find a process where both of you can be fearlessly foolish; to see whether your union will be a dilution or expansion of your combined abilities. You want to be surprised by the other, not limited by them. Neither of you wants to waste time pursuing an idea that is uninteresting.

However, collaboration is like friendship or like writing; you can only start off with a vague idea of where you are going. After a bit, if you're lucky, you begin to see whether or not there is a worthwhile destination ahead.

Most artists with a distinct voice soon develop their area of interest – the characters, scenes, moods – which they will work on for most of their lives; and most artists, like most lives, are repetitious. A collaboration is an attempt, then, to enlarge or multiply selves, to extend range and possibility. You might make something with another person that you couldn't make alone. Whether the purpose of this is the final product – the film – or the intimacy of partnership, the pleasure of meeting someone regularly, to talk about something that excites you both, I'm not sure. Probably it is all of these things.

Each of the many directors I have worked with in the theatre, television and cinema has been interested in sponsoring a different aspect of my work. There was a particular thing the piece said to them, that they wanted to emphasise, or to say through me. Then, once the work commenced, I began to write for them, for their idea of the project, and to their doubts and strengths. This process makes you become a different kind of writer – a different person, to a certain extent – with each director.

I can think of scores of good collaborations. The ones that come to mind are from dance, or theatre, or music. I think of Miles and Coltrane; Miles and anyone; and of Zakir Hussain, John McLaughlin and Jan Garbarek; of Brian Eno and David Byrne. The list could be endless.

It would be a mistake to put the purity of isolated creativity on one side, and collaboration on the other. In a sense all creativity will be collaborative: the artist works with his material, with his subject and with the history of his chosen form.

As well as this, most artists, I assume, relish a certain amount of the unexpected, of chance and contingency, of something odd but useful that might just turn up. What did you see, hear, say, yesterday? How might it be incorporated into the present work? Something going wrong in the right way can be fruitful. Another person could be the 'contingency' that helps this to happen. Maybe all artistic activity is a kind of collage, then, the putting together of various bits and pieces gathered from here and there, and integrated into some kind of whole. How are the elements selected or chosen? I don't know. It has to be an experiment.

Which isn't to say that all attempts at collaboration always work. A couple of years before I met Patrice, I was asked by a director to come up with an idea we would then develop into a script.

Together, he and I sat in an expensive rented room every weekday afternoon, for a month. Most of the time he seemed to have his head in his hands, while I made notes on various stories I was writing, and then put my head in my hands. What we could never do was put our heads in each other's hands. We would go round and round, and back and forth, but rarely forwards. Occasionally we'd have an idea we liked, or break into laughter, but we remained mysterious to one another, too guarded and too respectful. I expected him to take the lead, to tell me what he wanted. Or maybe he expected me to take the lead and tell him what I wanted. The project disappeared into a miasma of misplaced politeness. After these sessions, on the tube going home, I would become claustrophobic, thinking I would go mad or start screaming. The work became like being at school, or in a hated job. I suspect the problem was that we were both trying to do the same thing, write, and were inhibiting one another.

There was little hesitation in Patrice; he didn't lack tenacity or appear to doubt that this was a film he wanted to make. A film never leaves you alone, even when you're not with it, and there is always more you could be doing. A film, a project beginning in a room with a couple of people saying 'why don't we try so-and-so', ultimately involves scores of people, a huge amount of money and, more importantly, an enormous store of hope and belief.

Patrice and I started to meet regularly in London. We decided early on that *Intimacy* was too internal, and, probably, too dark, to make a film – a conventional film, that people might watch – on its own. It could, though, function as the background to, or beginning of, another film. We needed something else 'on top'; more stories, characters, action.

I showed him a collection of my stories in manuscript, *Midnight All Day*, to see whether there was anything in them he fancied. Some of the material from the story 'Strangers When We Meet' went into the film; parts of 'In a Blue Time' were utilised, and, possibly, ideas from other stories; I forget which.

During our meetings we improvised stories; we gossiped; we talked about the theatre, literature, our lives, our relationships with parents. If our age seems 'unideological' compared to the period between the mid-1960s and mid-1980s; if Britain seems pleasantly hedonistic and politically torpid, it might be because politics has moved inside, into the body. The politics of personal relationships, of private need, of gender, marriage, sexuality, the place of children, have replaced that of society, which seems uncontrollable.

So we talked about bodies, about death and decay; about Lucian Freud and Bacon, and the hyper-realism of some recent photography and how close you could get to the face without losing the image altogether. We talked about how many contemporary visual artists are interested in the body and its needs: the body rather than the mind or ideas; and the body on its own, in relative isolation. The history of photography and painting is, among other things, the history of how the body has been regarded.

We talked about what bodies do and what they tell us. After the twentieth century it is, it seems, a culture of disgust and of shock that we inhabit, in which humans are reduced to zero, the achievements of culture rendered meaningless – a stance often called the human condition. Yet this kind of fastidious despair can become an aesthetic pose, creating its own cultural privileges and becoming a kind of vanity.

We talked about my character Jay, about London and the speed with which it is changing into an international city, about the couple who meet without speaking. Why don't they talk rather than touch? What is the terror of communication? If you speak to someone, what might happen? If you don't, what other possibilities are there? To what extent are people disposable? What do we owe them or they us?

Patrice seemed interested in the power of impersonal sexuality, in passion without relationship, in the way people can be narcissistically fascinated by one another's bodies and their own sexual pleasure, while keeping away strong feeling and emotional complexity. We talked about what sex enables people to do together, and what it can stop them doing. Impersonality frees the imagination, of course; but, in the end, the imagination isn't sufficient when it comes to other people. What we usually need is more of them and less of us. We have to let a certain amount of them in. But that can seem like the hardest, most frightening thing, particularly as you get older, particularly when you feel you have failed before.

What Patrice wanted was to capture the desperation of Jay and Claire's lovemaking. These intense sessions were called 'the Wednesdays' and would punctuate the film, being different each time.

We are, of course, fascinated by what goes on in other couples' privacy. Their bodies, thoughts and conversation are compelling. They were for us as children and continue to be so. However, I can't help wondering whether sexuality is better written than filmed. Looking may be more erotic than reading; it is more immediate. But looking may also fail to capture the intricacies of feeling; it won't necessarily increase our understanding. In fact all it might do is make us embarrassed or conscious that we are watching a choreographed sexual act; it might merely make us feel left out.

Perhaps this is because of the way sexuality is usually portrayed on film. Patrice and I talked about keeping the camera close to the bodies; not over-lighting them, or making them look pornographically enticing or idealised. It will be a sexuality that isn't sanitised, symbolised or bland, that isn't selling anything. The point is to look at how difficult sex is, how terrifying, and what a darkness and obscenity our pleasures can be. Patrice will, therefore, have to make a sexually explicit film. To a certain extent the actors will have to go through what the characters experience, which will be difficult for everyone.

This will, initially, I guess, seem shocking in the cinema. Not that it won't take long for the shock to wear off, and for the act to seem common. The kiss between the boys in *My Beautiful Laundrette* seemed outrageous and even liberating, to some people, in the mid-1980s; now you can hardly turn on the television without seeing boys snogging, particularly on the sports channels.

Interest in sexuality takes different forms at different times: it might be paedophilia, perhaps, or miscegenation, gerontophilia, lesbianism or fetishism. But there always seems to be some aspect of desire that is of concern. It's the one thing that never goes away, or leaves people's minds. Perhaps desire never stops feeling like madness.

Shocking people, however, can be a mixed blessing. It can be amusing to disturb but there can be no guarantee that you won't be resented for the annoyance you have caused. Recently someone gave me what they considered an 'important' novel to read, warning me that it was 'shocking'. The novel was as they described – it did offend and displease me – mostly because it was violent. The violence kept my attention even as it horrified me. Not that it was a good novel. I was no better off after reading it than I was before. I felt, in fact, that the violence was partly directed at the reader. I had been shaken awake by someone who had nothing to tell me.

The conversations between Patrice and me would fertilise the film rather than determine it. I generated ideas for him to use, alter or throw away, as he liked – trying not to become too possessive of them. Certainly, Patrice had his own interests and preoccupations which intersected in some places with mine. He is not the sort merely to find a style to fit the writer. What we tried to do was find a starting point in order to help one another.

Not long after a series of these talks, the French scriptwriter began work. Scripts started to arrive regularly at my house. They got longer and longer. It is always like this and it always seems endless, the continuous sifting of material. Patrice moved to London, looked for locations and began to see actors for the main parts. Almost all the male actors we met were terrified of having others see their bodies: there was no way they would strip for the camera. The women seemed to expect that this would be required.

As the film went into production I was less involved. Some directors, like Stephen Frears, enjoy the writer being around – it is, after all, something of the writer's world that has to be captured. Therefore the creative work continues on the set, and during the editing. Other directors can become quite paranoid about writers, feeling them to be critical, cramping presences. After the initial meeting, the next time they want to see the writer is at the wrap party, or the première. The writers can seem to have too much authority over the material. On the other hand, it can also be traumatic for the writer to acknowledge that the director will need to change the script in order to possess it, to feel it's his. Writer and director can become jealous of one another. Not that Patrice is like this. He has worked with many writers.

For me, the writer can have one crucial function. Directors, particularly after they have made a number of films, can become over-involved in the technique of film-making. Writers, too, of course, can become over-interested in language, say, or in certain technical problems only of interest to them. Perhaps decadence in art is like narcissism in a person – there's no one else in mind.

But audiences, I like to believe, look 'through' the film-making and even the performances, to the story, to the characters' lives and dilemmas. They require a human truth, in order to examine the violence of their own feelings. If they cannot see something of themselves in the story, they are unlikely to see anything else. It should be part of the writer's job to remind the director of this. The writer's detachment from the film-making can be an advantage: like the director, he will have a sense of the whole film, but can also function, at times, as a stand-in for the needs and desire of the audience.

During the filming Patrice sometimes dropped by in the evening for a drink. I could see on his face how stressful and difficult making a movie is. On top of everything else, Patrice was making a film in a foreign language, with a mostly English crew, in a city he didn't know well.

Unsurprisingly, most film directors I know are a walking bag of maladies. They want you to know how tough their jobs are. What exactly is tough about it? I suppose it is hard wanting something to be so good; it is hard to care so much about something which could so easily be dismissed, a mere film when there are so many films. Fortunately, Patrice mostly shot what he needed and was pleased with the actors' performances.

Now the almost completed film rushes at me. The camera moves quickly; the cutting is fast and the music loud, in the modern manner, but not only for effect, as in videos, but to show us the force, speed and impersonality of London today. Perhaps it takes a foreign director to make London look the way it feels. This seems like the city I live in. The method of filming represents, too, the wild fury of Jay's mind.

At the end of the screening my mind and my feelings seem to be going in all directions at once. I try to clear my head. What do I feel? Relief, confusion, excitement, dismay, delight! Bits of criticism surface. I have to try and say something coherent. My mind feels crowded with important and irrelevant remarks.

As always Patrice is patient; he listens; we talk and argue. I am laudatory, critical and apologetic at the same time. I have ideas for cuts, changes, rearrangements. There are several things I don't understand, that don't seem clear. I keep saying that I have only seen the film once. He tells me that that is the number of times, if we are lucky, that the audience will see the film. More screenings, he says, and you'll be too sympathetic; you'll understand too much.

He is right; my compliance will do him no good. Most directors have plenty of that as it is. If we argue, both of us, along with our friendship, will survive.

In the end, when finishing the film, I know he will go his own way, which is all he can do. That is what I would recommend; it is what I would do. For me, it is enough that what has been accomplished was worth the effort and a pleasure. Whether anyone else will agree is another matter and up to them.

Mad Old Men:
The Writing of *Venus*

First published with screenplay of *Venus*, 2006

Sometimes, if I am writing, and things are not going well, or if I am just bored, I will stop to read, until I want to write again. It is rare that I will read much fiction; the last thing a writer needs is another insistent writer's voice in his head. So these days I read only on trains or planes, where I can get dreamy with a book away from others, and with nothing else to do, and no other obligations. Also, it is an increasingly rare pleasure to discover a writer one has hardly heard of before, a writer one instantly likes and wants to read more of, a writer who speaks to you.

It was on a long train journey that I first read Tanizaki's novel *Diary of a Mad Old Man*. It had been sent to me by an American friend who knew I'd just read Tanizaki's *The Key*. I had been told it was his best book, but I was keen to read other works. Tanizaki's name might not mean a lot even to well-informed readers – he was a huge influence on Mishima – but his books have remained in print in most European languages.

Diary of a Mad Old Man, a novella, is the story of a dying man and his son's wife, with whom he becomes infatuated, even as she treats him cruelly – and violently – at times. Other parts of the novel concern the kabuki theatre and the actors who work in it. It is not only a good novel: had it just been that, I could have read it and put it down. But as I began to read, there was a surge of recognition: I had been seeking this for a while. In the three years since the last film Roger Michell directed from my work, *The Mother*, I had been considering a similar idea to Tanizaki's, one I hadn't been ready to write, not knowing how to approach it. The difficulty of beginning a new piece of work is

259

often the difficulty of finding a point a view, a way into the story, a place to start.

I read *Diary of a Mad Old Man* quickly and didn't read it again. It was not my intention to adapt the novel for film. This had already been done, and it seemed pointless to try to squash a work successful in one form into another. I would have to start again. But there was a lot in the story which appealed to me. Unlike Tanizaki, though, I was interested in another subject I believed I could use too: friendship between older men. One way to engage with another writer, to get closer to him than by mere reading, is to 'write around' his ideas, to develop them in your own register until the original becomes almost unrecognisable.

On most Fridays for years I have been having breakfast with a group of friends in Notting Hill. Occasionally, we would persuade a couple of younger women to join us. Mostly, nevertheless, it was only older men – actors, writers, theatre and film directors – people I'd known since I first began to work in London, in the mid-70s. One morning we were talking about sleep and how to induce it, a popular and important subject amongst the over-forties. We discussed sleeping pills and sleeping draughts, and then about how to overcome the inevitable addiction. One of my friends and I would then shuffle off to the chemist, where he would get his pills. This friend said he found our Friday mornings to be particularly relaxing, compared to the difficulty of the rest of his life. He suggested he'd be happy sitting in a coffee shop, like old men he'd seen in Cairo, discussing world affairs while drinking tea and smoking a hookah.

It seems like a good idea; but how satisfying would it really be? In his long autobiographical essay 'In Praise of Shadows', Tanizaki movingly tells us how he built his house. He speaks of a kind of Zen attentiveness; he wants to praise age, slowness, wandering, curiosity, and the infinite pleasures of aesthetic appreciation. As in his fiction, baths and toilets are never far from his thoughts. Tanizaki tells us he likes to listen to the 'softly falling rain' while sitting on the toilet.

It is an admirable essay in many ways, reminding us of the virtues of silence and of listening; of space, emptiness and patience. Interestingly, Tanizaki's attitude towards the West at that time is not unlike that of some of the Muslim world today. The West represents the dangerous new: tradition and stability is being destroyed by an inferno of consumerism and post-modern sexuality. Tanizaki speaks of suffering 'a severe nervous disorder'.

The attitudes expressed in the essay sit uneasily with the rest of his work; indeed, they seem to be at odds with it. To a certain extent this illustrates the falsity, or impossibility perhaps, of an autobiography, of the belief that one can say, 'I am speaking the truth,' and be sure that that is what one is doing. This assumes that 'the truth' resides in what one knows, rather than in that which one doesn't. It might have to be admitted, then, that the 'truth' of an artist is more likely to be discovered in their fiction than in direct witness. In his 'lies', and in the relation between the characters, Tanizaki seems to get closer to the way things seem. Not only do his people not know anything about themselves for certain, they certainly don't know who they will become; the more they try to control themselves, the more out of hand everything becomes. It is not insignificant that, after writing screenplays and directing a movie, Tanizaki translated into Japanese Wilde's *The Picture of Dorian Gray* – the story of a sexually obsessed man who is unable to remain true to the image he has of himself.

By the time he wrote *The Key*, Tanizaki's work had been stripped down to the essentials of human interaction. He wrote: 'Western writers are over-rich in their production. The offerings of writers like Zola and Balzac are like a feast within a feast. Just looking at the menu is enough to make us melancholy and get our laxatives ready.'

The Key concerns a middle-aged, ordinary couple with an adult daughter who still lives with them. From the ruins of what appears to be a long dead marriage, something starts to stir. We like to believe – it is a common misconception – that erotic relationships only deteriorate, that there is nothing new that can happen between a long-established couple. This is something we are so certain of that it must be incorrect. A deep involvement may become so distressingly pleasurable that we might feel danger-ously addicted. As such a relationship develops, distance might be required, as the relationship begins to feel dangerous, even incestuous.

The novel opens with a middle-aged man drugging his sexually cold wife in order to spend more time with her feet. The sexuality of both of them is in the process of being re-aroused by the constant presence in their house of their daughter's fiancé. Here jealousy makes passion possible. As Lacan puts it, 'The other holds the key to the object desired.' Tanizaki doesn't bother with social detail but provides only the most necessary information about the city and the characters' social circumstances. And despite the fact that his characters are always medicating themselves – they are often sick, or imagine they are; no one is ever allowed to forget their body – his novels are frantic. In *The Key*, and in *Diary of a Mad Old Man*, the male and female characters, of whatever age, are too pas-sionately involved with one another's desire – and the satisfaction, humiliation and family complications which follow from it – to settle for the seemingly nirvanic existence their circumstances might allow.

The couple begin drinking heavily; she becomes more Western-ised. A formerly modest woman, she repeats, with her husband, the ways of lovemaking she has just practised with her lover, whom she meets in the afternoons. When she then calls out the name of this other man – the man who will, at the end of the book, marry her daughter – the husband writes in his diary, 'At last, as her voice was rising once again, I took her. At that moment I felt I had burst into another world. This was reality, the past was only an illusion. Perhaps it would kill me, but this moment would last for ever.' His wish is granted. In the end, he dies, or is killed, perhaps by the effort involved, while making love to his wife.

Desire is the devil in Tanizaki, a torment you can never escape or fulfil, except temporarily. Yet without it there is inertia, emptiness, routine. On top of this, particularly as people age and there is less novelty available to them, desire is only sustained by others; by jealousy, rivalry, secrecy and human obstacles. Relief is only ever a reprieve, and the characters are forced towards extinction by their never-ending desire. Tanizaki is not an experimental writer himself; he is a straightforward writer, not a modernist. But his characters' lives become experimental once they engage with what they really want, once they realise they cannot escape their sexuality. Self-knowledge is impossible, foolish even, and wisdom a waste of time. All you can do is try to follow your body.

Feet are important to Tanizaki but there is something else too. Perverse objects are invested with symbolic magic. The fetish, not unlike Winnicott's 'transitional object', enables the child to pass from the mother to the world, carrying a piece of her. It could be anything: shoes, an item of underwear, hair, leather, silk, depending on where in his life the subject became fascinated by something he desired but was unable to understand. Freud even quotes the example of a man who fetishises 'the shine on someone's nose'. Couldn't a fetish be a book? Presumably this wouldn't be unusual in a writer.

In the end, as it would have to be, we discover that the key to *The Key* is writing – the human desire to make an authentic mark. Whether it be a cave drawing, scratching one's name on a cell wall, writing a novel, or cutting one's arm, all are communications, addressed to someone else, whether or not they exist in reality. *The Key* is constructed from diaries; the entire adventure is sustained by the erotics of secret writing and the fact that none of the characters can be sure whether the other is reading their diary at all. They can only hope – and fear – that they are. It is only here, in the intimate confessional of their words, in the truth of their unconscious, as it were, that one may come to know the other.

What is amazing to me is how a writer like Tanizaki can still speak to us. Before, let's say, the mid-70s, when the Murdoch press began in earnest in Britain, it seemed there were areas of privacy into which no one but the novelist could venture. A novel didn't have to be sexually explicit to lay bare and obvious the intricacies of subjective private life. It did this fictionally and metaphorically. These were made-up stories, but we knew they represented real people in their deepest selves. But the 'real' itself was protected, it was behind the veil. Now, it seems, we know everything because nothing is hidden. I feel I would recognise Bill Clinton's penis in a crowd of other penises.

Yet a novel like *The Key* can still resonate and seem aggressively contemporary, making our desire seem as strange, and even alien – surely the point of literature – as it was before the age of explicitness. What is the truth about sexuality? Is sex pornography, prostitution or perversion? Is it being blown by a stranger in a toilet? Is it being tied up or is it fantasy? Or is it really full genital sex with one's spouse while thinking of no one else? Tanizaki shows us that sex is everywhere, and it involves not only transgression, but punishment, too, and suffering; it is a dirty business and probably has to be.

Tanizaki's work reminds me in some ways of the photographer Araki's work. (There is a photograph by Araki which leads me to Tanizaki. It is a nude in black gloves and stockings, with a key suspended from a band around her throat.) Araki has never taken an ugly picture; he is a photographer who, given time, would photograph the whole world. His pictures are a diary of his numerous interests. He is, obviously, more explicit in every way than Tanizaki, and perhaps more perverse. (In Tanizaki the women speak, act and deny; in Araki they are only ever objects.) But Araki is very good at picking up on the sexuality of the ordinary. He can photograph flowers, fruit, street scenes, and see the sexuality in them. Is this the extremity of perversion, or is it love for the world?

In Tanizaki's earlier novel *Naomi*, the male protagonist, much older than his lover, who becomes a convert to the pleasures of group sex, states, 'I started a diary in which I recorded everything about Naomi that caught my attention.' Naomi herself becomes almost a prostitute, except that, subversively, she refuses to be paid for the pleasure she receives and gives.

Written four years after *The Key*, *Diary of a Mad Old Man* is, of course, another diary. 'Even if you're impotent you have a kind of sex life,' writes the seventy-four-year-old protagonist, somewhat optimistically. Unfortunately, he has false teeth, and, looking at himself, states, 'Not even monkeys have such hideous faces. How could anyone with a face like this appeal to a woman?'

But he does appeal to her – in some way – though Tanizaki doesn't give us her point of view. And she appeals to him. This woman, his son's wife, Satsuko, is spiteful, sarcastic, a bit of a liar, a little power-crazed. Even so, he begins to love her, horribly so. With some encouragement from her, he tries to peep at her in the shower. When she slaps him, he buys her jewellery. In return she lets him kiss her feet and suck her toes. She forbids him to kiss her – making it clear she finds him disgusting – but at one point she lets drop a little saliva into his mouth.

His deterioration, the story of a man becoming aware of his imminent death, takes up as much space as this intriguing love-making. There is also more than enough about pills, painkillers and suppositories. (Physical illness and decline serves, perhaps, as a metaphor for sexual corruption.) Then, in a delirium, he recalls a recent dream about his mother, a beautiful woman who smokes a pipe and whose feet, like those of Satsuko, he admires. 'Mother's feet were fairly broad, like those of the Bodhisattva of Mercy.' His mother, he knows, would be appalled by him 'petting' with his son's wife, 'even sacrificing his wife and children to try to win her love,' as he puts it.

When, for a short time, the old man's health improves, he requests to be taken on a trip to Kyoto. He wants to see the city for the last time, and to find a burial place. He also wants to have his headstone carved. He will have the imprints of Satsuko's feet – which he will take himself – carved into his headstone, along with an image of the Bodhisattva of Mercy. The women he loves, mother and 'lover' combined, will be walking on him throughout eternity.

It seems scandalous, humorously dishonest even, for an old man to prefer a young woman's feet to his own wife, or to anyone in his family. Yet Tanizaki appears to be saying that even at the very end of a life the self doesn't only want to survive. The *Diary* shows, at least, the persistence of desire; it is, perhaps, a tribute to its strength. But there is no doubt that it is a fetishistic relationship, and could be described as infatuation, not as love. This might have been intriguing had Tanizaki provided more idea of what Satsuko wants from the old man, apart from his fascination. He seems to suggest that she is only materialistic, and manipulative; anyhow, the relationship doesn't alter much as it goes on.

Tanizaki's *Diary of a Mad Old Man* provokes more questions than it seems to answer, which is part of its intelligence. How little guilt the protagonist feels, and no embarrassment, over his attachment to Satsuko's feet! He seems so at ease with his fetish that we cannot forfeit the impression that he has pursued it before. But Tanizaki fails to tell us the place of such preoccupations in the old man's life, whether this is a late outbreak – a final burst, as it were – or whether his fetishism has been his life's work. If you were adapting the novel for film these are questions you'd not only have to ask, but to decide on.

In 1927, around the time he was thinking about religion and society, Freud wrote an essay, 'Fetishism', in which he mentions the Chinese custom of mutilating the female foot, and of worshipping it when it has been mutilated. He says, 'It seems as though the Chinese male wants to thank the woman for having submitted to being castrated.' Tanizaki became interested in Freud as a student and the Complete Works were translated and published in Japan between 1929 and 1933. Also in this paper, Freud tells us that the fetish is a substitute for the penis, being an 'approach to the genitals from below'. But not any penis. Here Freud makes a bold, new move: he tells us that the fetish stands for the missing penis of the woman; of, in fact, the mother. All fetishists, according to Freud, have an aversion to the actual genitals, for which the object is a substitute. Not that this is unusual. Freud makes a further startling statement here, 'Probably no male human being is spared the fright of castration at the sight of a female

266

genital.' (Freud suggests that it is enough to make anyone homosexual.)

If an old man sucks on a younger woman's toes, is he, at this moment, regressing also to childhood? Oddly, and perhaps wisely – showing his subtlety as a writer – Tanizaki doesn't comment on the old man's obsession: he merely shows it. Tanizaki is a psychologist in the sense that he is spellbound by his characters' internal lives, of that which is offered only symbolically to the world. But he'd never be so crude as to tie a whole aspect of experience to one cause. By not being over-insistent or too schematic, Tanizaki leaves us with more symbolic complexities. The work of an imaginative writer is to suggest, not to solve.

Yet without doubt there is something of an enigma in the book here. The old man himself, an intelligent, cultured man, has no curiosity about his own preferences. It seems unlikely, but he never questions this sudden enthralment. This is not so unusual: Freud asserts that few people seek analysis because of a fetish. Most go because they have difficulties at work; the fetish might not be mentioned for a long time, if at all. Not that fetishistic pleasure would be that unusual. For Freud, the child is the ultimate narcissist and pervert, concerned only with his own pleasure and, perhaps, how to stage and re-stage it. Others are merely actors in this scenario. Perhaps sexual feeling is so powerful it has to be modified, by an obstacle, in order to be bearable.

In his own way Tanizaki does take these ideas further, throwing open the whole question of love itself, of what it is we love about the other. The characters in his work are deeply involved with others. But in what way and what does it mean? How do perversion and love interact? Is fetish love real love? Is being excited by only a part of the other real sex? Is fetishism a version of love, or its obverse? Is it only, as Havelock Ellis designated it, 'auto-erotic'?

Much as they might like to be, Tanizaki's characters cannot be self-sufficient. They never stop needing one another, or trying to solidify that need. As both characters struggle for ultimate, complete control over the other, the engagement is almost comical.

Tanizaki is aware that in the end you are always dependent on the other; indeed, you are, partly, creating them, having them play a role with which you identify. This is not only the case in exhibitionism or voyeurism, but in sadism too. Yet the freedom of the other, which resides in their words – or perhaps a diary – will ultimately elude you; it has to. Total control would end in the death or murder of one of the subjects, at which point the game ends.

The novel left me with a strong after-impression, and the sense that the film I wanted to write would be concerned with some of these ideas. After I'd made some notes and sketched out several scenes, the director, Roger Michell, and I, began to assemble the elements of the film, which would concern two elderly actors and a girl who comes to stay with one of them.

It wasn't long before *Venus* began to move away from the Tanizaki set-up. The relationship had to be less claustrophobic and more complex, always dipping and turning. If the man wants something from the girl, she wants something else from him, so that their relationship becomes a series of successful misunderstandings. Failed exchanges are, at least, a kind of exchange. *Venus* also concerns a girl finding a father; at the end, briefly, she finds a mother too. Then she can leave home again.

It is the girl who makes the story work. Her entry on to the scene disturbs all their lives. But why a girl? Even political correctness always leaves someone – or a group – out; it needs to. A new scapegoat is created. I noticed that young working-class women – slags, mingers, munters, dogs, chavs – were easy targets, perfectly representing our greed, lasciviousness, immorality. Condemned for the pursuit of pleasure, and regarded only as consumers without inner texture, they are one of the few groups who can be satirised without complaint, damned for their stupidity and inarticulacy; a group with no lobbyists and little power. It is a new snobbery, and almost unnoticed. Why not develop such a character, and, combining them with the conventional idea of a stranger coming to stay, see where it goes?

I couldn't move forward with the film until I saw how it might end. I tried numerous exits. Perhaps I didn't want to accept it could only end one way. It was Roger who saw it had to finish with a journey and a death. As a child my family would go on holiday to the Kent resorts, and I'd started taking my children to Whitstable with its beach huts and stony beach. For a while I'd been thinking of setting a story there. Of course, both *The Key* and the *Diary* end with the death of the male protagonist; and it is, in fact, illness which precipitates them into late desire. How else, then, could the novel end? It is only death which gives life true intensity.

WRITING

Something Given: Reflections on Writing

First published as the introduction to
Dreaming and Scheming, 2002

'Now, whether it were by peculiar grace,
A leading from above, a something given . . .'
Wordsworth, 'Resolution and Independence'

My father wanted to be a writer. I can't remember a time when he didn't want this. There were few mornings when he didn't go to his desk – early, at about six o'clock – in one of his many suits and coloured shirts, the cuffs pinned by bejewelled links, before he left for work carrying his briefcase, alongside the other commuters. Writing was, I suppose, an obsession, and as with most obsessions, fulfilment remained out of reach. The obsession kept him incomplete but it kept him going. He had a dull, enervating civil service job, and writing provided him with something to look forward to. It gave him meaning and 'direction', as he liked to put it. It gave him direction home too, since he wrote often about India, the country he left in his early twenties and to which he never returned.

Many of my dad's friends considered his writing to be a risible pretension, though he had published two books for young people, on the history and geography of Pakistan. But even for my father, who loved seeing his name in print – I remember him labouring over the figures for average rainfalls, and on the textile industry – this was not authentic writing. He wanted to be a novelist.

He did write novels, one after another, on the desk he had had a neighbour build for him in the corner of the bedroom he shared with my mother. He wrote them, and he rewrote them, and he rewrote them. Then he typed them out, making copies with several sheets of carbon paper. Sometimes, when his back hurt, he sat on the floor and wrote, with his spine pressed against the wardrobe. But whatever his posture, every workday morning I would hear his alarm, and soon after he would be hammering at his big typewriter. The sound pounded into us like artillery fire, rocking the house. He wrote at the weekends too, on Sunday afternoons. He would have liked to write in the evenings but by nine o'clock he'd be asleep on the sofa. My mother would wake him, and he'd shuffle off to bed.

In one sense his persistence paid off. By the time he was sixty he must have completed five or six novels, several short stories and a few radio plays. For many writers this would be considered a lifetime's work. Often he became dejected – when he couldn't make a story live; or when he could, but had to break off and leave for the office; or when he was too tired to write; and in particular when his books were turned down by publishers, as all of them were, not one of them ever reaching the public. His despair was awful; we all despaired along with him. But any encouragement from a publisher – even a standard letter expressing interest – renewed his vigour. Whether this was folly or dedication depends on your point of view. In the end all he wanted was for someone to say: 'This is brilliant, it moved me. You are a wonderful writer.' He wanted to be respected as he respected certain writers.

Once, in Paris, where I was staying, I went to a restaurant with one of my father's elder brothers. He was one of my favourite uncles, famous for his carousing but also for his violent temper. After a few drinks I admitted to him that I'd come to Paris to write, to learn to be a writer. He subjected me to a tirade of abuse. Who do you think you are, he said, Balzac? You're a fool, he went on, and your father's a fool too, to encourage you in this. It is pretentious, idiotic. Fortunately, I was too young to be discouraged; I knew how to keep my illusions going. But I was shocked by what my father had had to endure from his family. You couldn't get above your station; you couldn't dream too wildly.

Perhaps my uncles and father's acquaintances found his passion eccentric because Asian people in Britain hadn't uprooted themselves to pursue the notoriously badly paid and indulgent profession of 'artist'. They had come to Britain to make lives for themselves that were impossible at home. At that time, in the mid-1960s, the images of India that we saw on television were of poverty, starvation and illness. In contrast, in the south of Britain people who had survived the war and the miserable 1950s were busily acquiring fridges, cars, televisions, washing-machines.

For immigrants and their families, disorder and strangeness is the condition of their existence. They want a new life and the material advancement that goes with it. But having been ripped from one world and flung into another, what they also require, to keep everything together, is tradition, habitual ideas, stasis. Life in the country you have left may move on, but life in the diaspora is often held in a strange suspension, as if the act of moving has provided too much disturbance as it is.

Culture and art was for other people, usually wealthy, self-sufficient people who were safe and established. It was naive to think you could be a writer; or it was a kind of showing-off. Few of Father's friends read; not all of them were literate. Many of them were recent arrivals, and they worked with him in the Pakistan Embassy. In the evening they worked in shops, or as waiters, or in petrol stations. They were sending money to their families. Father would tell me stories of omnivorous aunts and brothers and parents who thought their fortunate benefactor was living in plenty. They knew nothing of the cold and rain and abuse and homesickness. Sometimes they had clubbed together to send their relative to England who would then be obliged to remit money. One day the family would come over to join him. Until this happened the immigrant would try to buy a house; then another. Or a shop, or a factory.

For others, whose families were in Britain, the education of their children was crucial. And this, along with money, was the indicator par excellence of their progress in the new country. And so, bafflingly to me, they would interminably discuss their cars.

Even we had to get a car. Most of the time it sat rusting outside the house, and my sister and I would play in it, since it took Father six attempts to get through the driving test. He became convinced that he was failed because of racial prejudice. Eventually he complained to the Race Relations Board, and next time he passed. Not long after he crashed the car with all of us in it.

Writing was the only thing Father wanted to be interested in, or good at, though he could do other things: cook, be an attentive and entertaining friend, play sports. He liked being a father. His own father, a doctor, had had twelve children, of which ten were sons. My father had never received the attention he required. He felt his life had lost 'direction' due to lack of guidance. He knew, therefore, what a father should be. It wasn't a question for him. He and I would play cricket for hours in the garden and park; we went to the cinema – mostly to watch war films like *Where Eagles Dare*; we watched sport on television, and we talked.

Father went to the library every Saturday morning, usually with me in tow. He planted notebooks around the house – in the toilet, beside his bed, in the front room beside his television chair – in order to write wherever he was. These notebooks he made himself from a square of cardboard and a bulldog clip, attaching to them various odd-shaped sheets of paper – the backs of flyers which came through the letterbox, letters from the bank, paper he took from work, envelopes. He made little notes exhorting himself onwards: 'the whole secret of success is; the way to go is; one must begin by . . .; this is how to live, to think, to write . . .' He would clench his fist and slam it into the palm of his other hand, saying, 'one must fight'.

Father was seriously ill during much of my youth, with a number of painful and depressing ailments. But even in hospital he would have a notebook at hand. When dying he talked of his latest book with his usual, touching but often infuriating grandiosity. 'In my latest novel I am showing how a man feels when . . .'

My mother, quite sensibly, wondered whether he might not be better off doing something less frustrating than shutting himself away for most of his spare time. Life was slipping away; he wasn't getting anywhere. Did he have to prefer failure as a writer to success at anything else? Perhaps she and he could do things together. Nothing changed, that was the problem. The continuous disappointment that accompanied this private work was hard for everyone to bear, and it was the atmosphere in which we lived. Sometimes Mother suggested the illnesses were precipitated by his hopeless desire for the unattainable. But this was not something Father liked to hear.

He was convinced that she didn't understand what such a passion entailed. The fact was, she did. Yet he wanted to get to people. He had something to say and wanted response. He required attention. The publishers who rejected his work were standing between him and the audience he was convinced was waiting.

Father was good company – funny, talkative, curious, nosy and gossipy. He was always on the look-out for stories. We would work out the plots together. Recently I found one of his stories, which concerns the Indian servant of an English couple living in Madras before the Second World War. The story soon makes it clear that the servant is having an affair with his Mistress. Towards the end we learn that he is also having an affair with the Master. If I was surprised by this fertile story of bisexuality, I always knew he had an instinct for ironies, links, parallels, twists.

He liked other people and would talk with the neighbours as they dug their gardens and washed their cars, and while they stood together on the station in the morning. He would give them nicknames and speculate about their lives until I couldn't tell the difference between what he'd heard and what he'd imagined he'd heard. 'Suppose, one day,' he'd say, 'that man over there decided to . . .' And off he would go. As Maupassant wrote, 'You can never feel comfortable with a novelist, never be sure that he will not put you into bed one day, quite naked, between the pages of a book.'

It amused Father, and amazed me – it seemed like a kind of magic – to see how experience could be converted into stories, and how the monotony and dullness of an ordinary day could contain meaning, symbolism and even beauty. The invention and telling of stories – that most indispensable human transaction – brought us together. There was amusement, contact, entertainment. Whether this act of conversion engaged Father more closely with life, or whether it provided a necessary distance, or both, I don't know. Nevertheless, Father understood that in the suburbs, where concealment is often the only art, but where there is so much aspiration, dreaming and disappointment – as John Cheever illustrated – there is a lot for a writer.

Perhaps after a certain age Father couldn't progress. Yet he remained faithful to this idea of writing. It was his religion, his reason for living, the God he couldn't betray and the God who wouldn't let him down. Father's art involved a long fidelity and a great commitment. Like many lives in the suburbs, it was also a long deferral. One day in the future – when his work was published and he was recognised as a writer – good things would happen to him and everything would change. But for the time being everything remained the same. He was fixed, and, from a certain point of view, stuck.

Writers are often asked – and they certainly ask themselves – what they would do if they were not published. I suspect that most writers would like to think that they would continue as they do already, writing to the best of their ability without thought of an audience. Yet even if this is true – that most of the satisfactions are private – you might still need to feel that someone is responding, even if you have no idea who they are. Until you are published it might be difficult to move on; you could easily feel that nothing had been achieved, and that by failing to reach another person – the reader – the circle had not been completed, the letter posted but not received. Perhaps without such completion a writer is destined to repeat himself, as people do when having conversations with themselves, conversations never heard by anyone.

Yet Father would not stop writing. It was crucial to him that these stories be told. Like Scheherazade, he was writing for his life.

Where do stories come from? What is there to write about? Where do you get material? How do you start? And: why are writers asked these questions so often?

It isn't as if you can go shopping for experience. Or is it? Such an idea suggests that experience is somehow outside yourself, and must be gathered. But in fact, it is a question of seeing what is there. Experience is what has already happened. Experience, like love and hate, starts at home: in the bedroom, in the kitchen. It happens the moment people are together, or apart, when they want one another and when they realise they don't like their lover's ears.

Stories are everywhere, and they can be made from the simplest things. Preferably from the simplest things, as Father would have said, if they are the right, the precise, the correct things, and if the chosen material is profitable, useful and sufficiently malleable. I say chosen, but if the writer is attentive the stories she needs to shape her urgent concerns will occur unbidden. There are certain ideas, like certain people, that the writer will be drawn to. She only has to wait and look. She cannot expect to know why this idea has been preferred to that until the story has been written, if then.

There is a sense – there has to be a sense – in which most writers do not entirely understand what they are doing. You suspect there might be something you can use. But you don't know what it is. You have to find out by beginning. And what you discover probably will not be what you originally imagined or hoped for. Some surprises can be discomfiting. But this useful ignorance, or tension with the unknown, can be fruitful, if not a little unreliable at times.

The master Chekhov taught that it is in the ordinary, the everyday, the unremarkable – and in the usually unremarked – that the deepest, most extraordinary and affecting events occur. These observations of the ordinary are bound up with everyone else's experience – the universal – and with what it is to be a child, parent, husband, lover. Most of the significant moments of one's life are 'insignificant' to other people. It is showing how and why they are significant and also why they may seem absurd, that is art.

The aged Tolstoy thought he had to solve all the problems of life. Chekhov saw that these problems could only be put, not answered, at least by the part of yourself that was an artist. Perhaps as a man you could be effective in the world; and Chekhov was. As a writer, though, scepticism was preferable to a didacticism or advocacy that seemed to settle everything but which, in reality, closed everything off. Political or spiritual solutions rendered the world less interesting. Rather than reminding you of its baffling strangeness, they flattened it out.

In the end there is only one subject for an artist. What is the nature of human experience? What is it to be alive, suffer and feel? What is it to love or need another person? To what extent can we know anyone else? Or ourselves? In other words, what it is to be a human being. These are questions that can never be answered satisfactorily but they have to be put again and again by each generation and by each person. The writer trades in dissatisfaction.

How, then, can the novel, the subtlest and most flexible form of human expression, die? Literature is concerned with the self-conscious exploration of the lives of men, women and children in society. Even when it is comic, it sees life as something worth talking about. This is why airport fiction, or 'blockbusters', books which are all plot, can never be considered literature, and why, in the end, they are of little value. It is not only that the language in which they are written lacks bounce and poignancy, but that they don't return the reader to the multifariousness and complication of existence. This, too, is why journalism and literature are opposed to one another, rather than being allies. Most journalism is about erasing personality in favour of the facts, or the 'story'. The personality of the journalist is unimportant. In literature personality is all, and the exploration of character – or portraiture, the human subject – is central to it.

Writers are often asked if their work is autobiographical. If it seems to me to be an odd, somewhat redundant question – where else could the work come from, except from the self? – I wonder whether it is because there remains something mysterious about the conversion of experience into representation. Yet this is something we do all the time. We work over our lives continuously; our minds generate and invent in night-dreaming, daydreaming and in fantasy. In these modes we can see that the most fantastic and absurd ideas can contain human truth. Or perhaps we can see how it is that important truths require a strange shape in order to be made acceptable. Or perhaps it is simply true that the facts of life are just very strange.

Still, it is odd, the public's desire to see fiction as disguised, or treated, or embellished, autobiography. It is as if one requires a clear line between what has happened and what has been imagined later in the construction of a story. Perhaps there is something childish about the make-believe of fiction which is disconcerting, rather like taking dreams seriously. It is as if we live in too many disparate worlds at once – in the solid everyday world, and in the insubstantial, fantastic one at the same time. It is difficult to put them all together. But the imagination and one's wishes are real too. They are part of daily life, and the distinction between the softness of dreams and hard reality can never be made clear. You might as easily say, 'we live in dreams'.

Sometimes I wonder whether the question about autobiography is really a question about why some people can do certain things and not others. If everyone has experience then everyone could write it down and make a book of it. Perhaps writers are, in the end, only the people who bother. It may be that everyone is creative – after all, children start that way, imagining what is not there. They are always 'telling stories' and 'showing off'. But not everyone is talented. It is significant that none of the many biographies of Chekhov – some have more of the 'facts' than others – can supply us with an answer to the question 'why him?' That a man of his temperament, background and interests should have become one of the supreme writers, not only of his time but of all time, is inexplicable. How is it that he lived the life he did and wrote the stories and plays he did? Any answer to this can only be sought in the work, and it can only ever remain a mystery. After all, everyone has some kind of life, but how that might be made of interest to others, or significant or entertaining, is another matter. A mountain of facts don't make a molehill of art.

Writing seems to be a problem of some kind. It isn't as if most people can just sit down and start to write brilliantly, get up from the desk, do something else all day, and then, next morning start again without any conflict or anxiety. To begin to write – to attempt anything creative, for that matter – is to ask many other questions, not only about the craft itself, but of oneself, and of life. The blank empty page is a representation of this helplessness. Who am I? it asks. How should I live? Who do I want to be?

For a long time I went to my desk as if my life depended on it. And it did; I had made it so, as my father did. Therefore any dereliction seemed catastrophic. Of course, with any writer the desire to write will come and go. At times you will absolutely rebel against going to your desk. And if you are sensible, you will not go. There are more pressing needs.

There are many paradoxes here. Your work has to mean everything. But if it means too much, if it is not sufficiently careless, the imagination doesn't run. Young writers in particular will sometimes labour over the same piece of work for too long – they can't let it go, move on or start anything new. The particular piece of work carries too heavy a freight of hope, expectation and fear.

You fear finishing a piece of work because then, if you hand it over, judgement starts. There will be criticism and denigration. It will be like being young again, when you were subject to the criticism of others, and seemed unable to defend yourself, though most of the denigration people have to face has been internalised, and comes from within. Sometimes you feel like saying: Nobody dislikes my work quite as much as I do. Recently I was talking to a friend, a professional writer, who is conscious of not having done as well as she should have, and hasn't written anything for a while. She was complaining about her own work. 'It isn't any good, that's the problem,' she kept saying. But as good as what? As good as Shakespeare?

You don't want to make mistakes because you don't want a failure that will undermine you even more. But if you don't make mistakes nothing is achieved. Sometimes you have to feel free to write badly, but it takes confidence to see that somehow the bad writing can sponsor the good writing, that volume can lead to quality. Sometimes, too, even at the end of a piece of writing, you have to leave the flaws in; they are part of it. Or they can't be eliminated without something important being lost, some flavour or necessary energy. You can't make everything perfect but you have to try to.

At one time I imagined that if I wrote like other people, if I imitated writers I liked, I would only have to expose myself through a disguise. I did this for a time, but my own self kept coming through. It took me a while to see that it isn't a question of discovering your voice but of seeing that you have a voice already just as you have a personality, and that if you continue to write you have no choice but to speak, write, and live in it. What you have to do, in a sense, is take possession of yourself. The human being and the writer are the same.

Not long ago I was working with a director on a film. After I'd completed several drafts he came to me with pages of notes. I went through them and some of his ideas and questions seemed legitimate. But still I baulked, and wondered why. Was this only vanity? Surely it wasn't that I didn't want to improve my film? After thinking about it, I saw that the way I had originally written it was an expression of my voice, of my view of the world. If that was removed, not much remained apart from the obligatory but uninspiring technical accomplishment.

One of the problems of writing, and of using the self as material, is that this will recall powerful memories. To sit at a desk with a pen is to recall familiar fears and disappointments – and in particular, conflicts – which are the essence of drama. This is partly the difficulty of coming to terms with the attitude to learning that you have already picked up from your parents and teachers, from the experience of being at home and at school; and from the expectations of all of these. There is the inability to concentrate and the knowledge that you must do so for fear of punishment. There is boredom, and the anxiety that more exciting things are going on elsewhere.

How soon memories of this kind of learning bring back other discouraging ideas. The limitless power of parents and teachers – that they know everything and you know nothing, for instance; and that if you resist them you are either stupid or obstinate. You recall, too, somehow being taught that work is boring but that you must endure it; and that endurance – putting up with uninterest-ing things – is a necessary quality in the everyday world. You must be unquestioningly prepared for a good deal of tedium otherwise you are indolent or useless.

How soon, too, when you start to write, do several other things become clear. How much you want to succeed, for instance. Or how much you require the reassurance of some kind of success, or of some kind of enviable status that you believe that writing will bring. To begin to write is to recognise both how much you require such reassurance, and how far away it really is.

But you might also recall the concentration of childhood play – long periods of absorption and reverie as the unforced imagination runs. You concentrate then out of pleasure; there is no conflict. Often, the self seems to disappear. There is, however, a puzzle here. How is playing – playing with the language, playing with ideas – going to produce the necessary result? After all, children just play. They don't make complete objects. They don't revise; their games aren't for anyone else.

Perhaps writing requires the regularity of work and the inspira-tion and pleasure of play. But this inspiration and pleasure cannot just be conjured up on demand. Or can it? Children never think of such things. If a toy or game doesn't give them pleasure they throw it aside and seek something that does. But if you did that as a writer, just went off when you felt like it, nothing would get done. Or would it? A good deal of writing is finding a method that will make the writing happen. And how the writing happens depends on the ideas we already have about ourselves. We shouldn't forget that we create our creativity, and imagine our imagination.

You have to tackle all this while knowing that these are, really, questions about who you are, and who you will become.

I started to write seriously around the age of fourteen or fifteen. At school I felt that what I was expected to learn was irrelevant and tedious. The teachers didn't conceal their boredom. Like us, they couldn't wait to get out. I felt I was being stuffed with the unwanted by fools. I couldn't make the information part of myself; it had to be held at a distance, like unpleasant food. The alternative was compliance. Or there was rebellion.

Then there was writing, which was an active way of taking possession of the world. I could be omnipotent, rather than a victim. Writing became a way of processing, ordering, what seemed like chaos. If I wrote because my father did, I soon learned that writing was the one place where I had dominion, where I was in charge. At a desk in my study, enwombed, warm, concentrated, self-contained, with everything I needed to hand – music, pens, paper, typewriter – I could make a world in which disharmonies could be contained, and perhaps drained of their poison. I wrote to make myself feel better, because often I didn't feel too good. I wrote to become a writer and get away from the suburbs. But while I was there my father's storytelling enlivened the half-dead world for me. Stories were an excuse, a reason, a way of being interested in things. Looking for stories was a way of trying to see what was going on within and without. People write because it is crucial to them to put their side of the story without interruption. This is how they see it; this is how it was for them – their version. They need to get things clear in their own minds, and in everyone else's. To write is to be puzzled a second time by one's experience; it is also to savour it. In such reflection there is time to taste and engage with your own life in its complexity.

*

285

Experience keeps coming. If the self is partly formed from the blows, wounds and marks made by the world, then writing is a kind of self-healing. But creativity initiates disturbance too. It is a kind of scepticism which attacks that which is petrified. Perhaps this is a source of the dispute between Rushdie and the mullahs. Art represents freedom of thought – not merely in a political or moral sense – but the freedom of the mind to go where it wishes; to express dangerous wishes. This freedom, of course, is a kind of instability. Wishes conflict with the forbidden, the concealed, with that which cannot or should not be thought, and certainly not said. The creative imagination is usefully aggressive; it undermines authority; it can seem uncontrollable; it is erotic and breaks up that which has become solid. I remember some of my father's friends complaining to him about my work, particularly *My Beautiful Laundrette*. For Asians in the West, or for anyone in exile, intellectual and emotional disarray can seem unbearable. The artist may be a conduit for the forbidden, for that which is too dangerous to say, but he isn't always going to be thanked for his trouble.

I wrote, too, because it was absorbing. I was fascinated by how one thing led to another. Once I'd started banging on my typewriter, in my bedroom above Father's, I wanted to see what might be done, where such creative curiosity might lead me. You'd be in the middle of a story, in some unfamiliar imaginative place, but you'd only got there because you'd been brave enough to start off. I was impatient, which hindered me. As soon as I began something I wanted to get to the end of it. I want to succeed rather than search. I wanted to be the sort of person who had written books, rather than a person who was merely writing them. Probably I inherited Father's desperation as a kind of impatience. I am still impatient; it isn't much fun sitting at a desk with nothing happening. But at least I can see the necessity for impatience in writing – the desire to have something done, which must push against the necessity to wait, for the rumination that allows you to see how a piece of writing might develop or need to find its own way over time, without being hurried to a conclusion.

286

When, after my teenage interest in literature, I decided on graduating to do nothing but write, my enthusiasm and indeed my spirit fell away. I found that it is one thing to write for yourself in your bedroom after school, but that it is another to do it eight hours a day for a living. It was tough; the only response I met was silence and indifference. I starved myself of other people's attention and it is difficult to write in a vacuum, though this is what I did. From the window of my flat I would watch the people going to work in the morning, envying their hurry and purpose. They knew what they were doing; they weren't floundering.

I made myself sit for hours at the desk feeling nothing but a strong desire to be elsewhere. Eventually I would go elsewhere but would feel nothing but the desire to return to my desk. I'd stare at the paper, wanting it to come, wanting to force it, knowing it cannot be forced. But if you don't push a little, you feel helpless, as if nothing is being done. Learning to wait is a trial if you don't know what you're waiting for. Soon I found it difficult to go out; it was almost impossible for me to communicate; I couldn't see any reason to continue. Hatred of others and of myself was all I felt; and then despair. I made myself depressed.

I couldn't see the extent to which pleasure had to be part of the work. Perhaps I had picked this up from my father: writing is unrewarding in the long run. There is much rejection to bear. Mostly it is failure and defeat; a sort of prolonged martyrship. In fact, this wasn't my experience. As soon as I started to write plays they were produced. But I lived as if it were.

I knew I was a writer but no one else was aware of this important fact. I knew I was a writer but I hadn't written anything I was pleased with, anything that was any good or any use to anyone. In fact I didn't know what to write; I didn't know what my characters should say to one another. I'd write a line, scratch it out, write another, scratch it out, and despise myself for my failure. Writing was an excuse to attack myself. Father had both encouraged and discouraged my efforts. He could be caustic, dismissive, curt. His contempt for himself and his own failed efforts were visited on me.

I was afraid to write because I was ashamed of my feelings and beliefs. The practice of any art can be a good excuse for self-loathing. You require a certain shamelessness to be any kind of artist. But to be shameless you need not to mind who you are.

Sometimes writers like to imagine that the difficulty of becoming a writer resides in convincing others that that is what you are. But really the problem is in convincing yourself. You can become trapped within an odd, Beckettian paradox. There is the internal pressure of what must be said. At the same time you are possessed by the futility of all speaking. The image I have is of an open mouth, saying nothing. It is as if you have translated your words into the language of zero at the moment of their delivery, for fear of how powerful they might be.

If there isn't a commitment, if you keep yourself semi-serious and don't quite believe in the writing project yourself, you can back out without feeling that you have failed. You recruit others, then, to convince you of something you don't believe yourself. But they will sense your scepticism and return it to you. It is only when you give yourself to your work that you will get anywhere. But how to get to that point?

The people outside on the street walking to work had 'discipline'. Surely, if I were to get anywhere, I had to sit still for long periods. Discipline, then, is a kind of violence and involves the suppression of other wishes. It becomes necessary when really you'd much rather do something else. Sometimes it is important to believe that behind everything worthwhile there is difficulty. It is imagined that difficulty and moral strength – or virtue – go together. It is as if the harder something has been to write, the more painful the conception, the better it will be.

If artists suffer it is not only because their work involves sacrifice and dedication. It is because they are required to have close contact with the unconscious. And the unconscious – bursting with desire as it is – is unruly. That is often how creativity is represented, as being an unruly force, a kind of colonial mob or animal instinct that must be suppressed. Artists become representative of the unruly forces within everyone. They have to live these out, and live with them, all the time. It is the price they pay for 'talent'. If most people in the bourgeois world have to live constrained lives, artists do a certain kind of crazy living for those who can't.

One of the conditions of being a writer is the ability to bear and enjoy solitude. Sometimes you get up from your desk under the impression that your inner world has more meaning than the real one. Yet solitude – the condition of all important creative and intellectual work – isn't something we're taught, nor is it much attended to as a necessary human practice. People often avoid the solitude they need because they will feel guilty at leaving other people out. But communing with yourself, the putting aside of time for the calm exploration of inner states where experience can be processed, where dim intuitions, the unclear and inchoate can be examined, and where the undistracted mind drifts and considers what it requires, is essential. In this solitude there may be helplessness. You may be aware of too much experience, and an inability to see, for some time, what the creative possibilities are.

The solitude of writing is not the same as loneliness or isolation. When the words are flowing the self disappears and your anxieties, doubts and reservations are suspended. There isn't a self to be lonely. But such solitude can become mixed up with loneliness. You can delude yourself that everything you need can be obtained within, in the imagination; that the people you create and move around as characters can supply everything that real people can. In a sense you are asking too much of your art. You have to learn to separate these things out. In that sense writing, or becoming a writer, is, like sexuality, a paradigm for all one's learning, and for all one's relationships.

I conceived the idea of what became *The Buddha of Suburbia* on the balcony of a hotel room in Madras, my father's birthplace. Until then, as a professional writer, I had written plays and films, though I'd already published the first chapter of *The Buddha of Suburbia* as a short story. Ever since it had appeared in print the characters and situation remained with me. Normally you finish something with a sense of relief. It is over because you are bored with it and, for now – until the next time – you have said as much as you can. But I had hardly begun. I knew – my excitement told me – that I had material for a whole book: south London in the 1970s, growing up as a 'semi-Asian' kid; pop, fashion, drugs, sexuality. My task was to find a way to organise it.

Often, to begin writing all you need is an idea, a germ, a picture, a hint, a moment's recognition – an excuse for everything else you've been thinking to gather or organise around, so that everything falls into place. In the search for stories you look for something likely and malleable, which connects with the other things you are thinking at the time. I have to say that with *The Buddha of Suburbia* I was also excited by the idea of being occupied for two years, of having what was, for me, a big project.

Looking at the journal I kept at the time, I can see how much I knew of what I was doing; and, concurrently, how little. It had to be a discovery – of that which was already there. I am reminded of a phrase by Alfred de Musset: 'It is not work. It is merely listening. It is as if some unknown person were speaking in your ear.'

I spent ages trying to unblock myself, removing obstacles, and trying to create a clear channel between the past and my pen. Then, as now, I wrote pages and pages of rough notes; words, sentences, paragraphs, character biographies, all, at the time, disconnected. There was a lot of material but it was pretty chaotic. It needed order but too much order too soon was more dangerous than chaos. I didn't want to stifle my imagination just as it was exploding, even if it did make me feel unstable. An iron control stops anything interesting happening. Somehow you have to assemble all the pieces of your puzzle without knowing whether they will fit together. The pattern or total picture is something you have to discover later. You need to believe even when the only basis for belief is the vague intuition that a complete story will emerge.

The atmosphere I had already. But the characters and the detail – the world of the book – I had to create from scratch. Establishing the tone, the voice, the attitude, the way I wanted to see the material, and the way I wanted the central character, Karim, to express himself, was crucial. Once I found the tone, the work developed independent life; I could see what should be in or out. I could hear the wrong notes.

The Buddha of Suburbia was written close to myself, which can make the writing more difficult in some ways, if not easier in others. I knew the preparation – living – had already been done. But in writing so directly from the self there are more opportunities for shame and embarrassment. Also, these characters are so much part of oneself, that you can almost forget to transfer them to the page, imagining that somehow they are already there.

There are other dangers. You might want the control that writing provides, but it can be a heady and disturbing sort of omnipotence. In the imaginative world you can keep certain people alive and destroy or reduce others. People can be transformed into tragic, comic, or inconsequential figures. They are at the centre of their own lives, but you can make them extras. You can also make yourself a hero or fool, or both. Art can be revenge as well as reparation. This can be an immense source of energy. However, the desires and wishes conjured by the free imagination can make the writer both fearful and guilty. There are certain things you would rather not know that you think. At the same time you recognise that these thoughts are important, and that you can't move forward without having expressed them. Writing might, therefore, have the aspect of an infidelity or betrayal, as the pen reveals secrets it is dangerous to give away. The problem, then, with explorations, or experiments, is not that you will find nothing, but that you will find too much, and too much will change. In these circumstances it might be easier to write nothing, or to block yourself. If we are creatures that need and love to imagine, then the question to ask has to be how, why and when does this stop happening? Why is the imagination so terrifying that we have to censor it? What can we think that is, so to speak, unimaginable?

A block holds everything together; it keeps important things down, for a reason. A block might then work like depression, as a way of keeping the unacceptable at a distance, even as it continuously reminds you that it is there.

Once I'd embarked on *The Buddha of Suburbia* I found characters and situations I couldn't have planned for. Changez, in particular, was a character who sprang from an unknown source. I knew Jamila had to have a husband who'd never been to England before. In my journal of January 1988 I wrote 'Part of me wants him to read Conan Doyle. Another part wants him to be illiterate, from a village. Try both.' Originally I had imagined a cruel, tyrannical figure, who would clash violently with Jamila. But that kind of cruelty didn't fit with the tone of the novel. I found, as I experimented, that the naivety I gave Changez soon presented me with opportunities for irony. If arranged marriages are an affront to the romantic idea that love isn't something that can be arranged, what would happen if Changez did fall in love with his wife? What if she became a lesbian?

Many of the ideas I tried in the book seemed eccentric even as I conceived them. I taught myself not to be too dismissive of the strange. There was often something in peculiar ideas that might surprise and startle the reader just as I had been jolted myself.

When my films were made and books published Father was delighted, if not a little surprised. It was what he wanted, except that it happened to me rather than to him. Towards the end of his life, which coincided with my becoming a professional writer, he became more frantic. He left his job, wrote more, and sent his books around the publishing houses with increasing desperation. At times he blamed me for his failure to get published. Surely I could help him as he had helped me? Even as he took pride in what I was doing, my success was mocking him. For the first time he seemed to have become bitter. If I could do it, why couldn't he? Why can some people tell jokes, do imitations, juggle with knives and balance plates on their nose, while others can only make soufflés? How is it that people might persist in wanting to do something they will never excel at? Is writing difficult? Only if you can't do it.

I like to work every day, in the morning, like my father. That way I am faithful to him and to myself. I miss it badly if I don't do it. It has become a habit but it is not only that. It gives the day a necessary weight. I'm never bored by what I do. I go to it now with more rather than less enthusiasm. There is less time, of course, while there is more to say about the process of time itself. There are more characters, more experience and numerous ways of approaching it. If writing were not difficult it wouldn't be enjoyable. If it is too easy you can feel you haven't quite grasped the story, that you have omitted something essential. But the difficulty is more likely to be internal to the work itself – where it should be – rather than in some personal crisis. I'm not sure you become more fluent as you get older, but you become less fearful of imagined consequences. There has been a lot to clear away; then the work starts.

Dreaming and Scheming:
Reflections on Teaching and the Writing Life

First published in *Dreaming and Scheming*, 2002

Twenty young people drift into a room beside a theatre for the start of a new writing workshop. Nervous or uncertain, most have never met before and won't know what will be asked of them or what a writing workshop involves. All sorts of alliances, liaisons and friendships will develop over the months, but now I am as anxious as anyone: whether the fear is of what will happen, or of what might not happen, I don't know. But I am the teacher; like it or not, I have the authority. I am not entirely certain of what I will say or do – and I don't want to be – yet it's up to me to make these meetings worthwhile.

In the hope of dissipating some of the self-consciousness, I play a few standing-up 'name' games, where people introduce themselves. Then we run about a bit, before sitting down to play some word games. Whatever you do at the beginning, it will always take a few weeks for people to begin to feel at ease, for them to be able to speak to each other about their writing or read it aloud. All workshops generate some kind of work, but the most inspiring ones are often those which are concentrated over a weekend or week away; or, like this one, they will continue for months until the participants begin to see how they can use them – and the other people there – to benefit their writing. They might even get an idea of what 'their writing' is.

At last we sit in a circle where everyone can see everyone else. But the 'democratic' circle is too big and the chairs are crammed together. Around half of this size, about twelve or less, is the best number. Over the weeks, of course, some people will leave.

As far as I can tell, it seems to be a disparate group in terms of race and background. I would prefer more diversity of age and experience – most young people only have friends of the same age – but at the Royal Court the age limit is twenty-five.

One of the students is a journalist; another guy teaches English as a Foreign Language in the morning, and works as a cashier in a betting shop in the afternoon. Several are at university, or have just left, and almost all the others work in television or film, often as researchers, runners or receptionists. Few have children. As usual there are a couple of writers who seem to have trudged around most of the workshops in town, who have existed on the fringes of the writing world, about to 'make it', for years. A number will be dithering about whether to give up their jobs in order to concentrate on writing. Everyone seems serious about what they do; I guess they're aware that their decisions about jobs or professions will affect the rest of their lives. They're young but they know the possibilities are already closing down.

There will always be those who talk too much and tend to dominate, and there will be others who are shy. It is difficult to hide in the 'democratic' circle, but I did teach a hijab-wearing girl who said not one word to me or to anyone else. I wondered for ages whether I should prompt her, but decided that as the workshop was neither a school nor therapy, if she didn't want to speak, it was up to her. In the end she sent me her work with a letter saying she was grateful that, unlike other teachers, I hadn't pressed her to contribute. Each week, she posted me a chapter of the novel she was writing at night when her children were asleep, after having 'written it in her mind' during the day, holding the words inside her. In a few months she had completed a first draft.

Since the early 1980s, when I first became involved with the Royal Court Young People's Theatre, I have usually been running some kind of writing group somewhere. Why do I do it? When I think about this, which is often, I'm reminded of a remark Stephen Frears made when asked why he taught at film school.

'Because no one else ever asks me the questions my students do,' he replied.

As working writers get older it is easy for them to become cynical or lost in their own minds and projects, refusing contact with anyone unlike them, not wanting to be changed. A workshop is a good place to have conversations about writing, and to hear stories of various kinds. There is also the opportunity to discuss, by way of writing, whatever else the participants might be thinking about: politics, race, parents, love, childhood, creativity, failure, criticism, happiness. These can be serious talks, more concentrated than chats with friends, and less competitive and formal – more usefully rambling – than university seminars. There is also the pedagogical and parental pleasure of seeing someone develop, of watching them find something unexpected and witnessing their surprise or joy, and feeling that somehow you were present when this happened.

After a certain amount of talk about what we might do, I set a writing exercise and send people off on their own. This surprises and terrifies some students, who expected only to listen. There's a rush of anxiety in the room. Some people haven't brought pens or paper; one person leaves for good.

Soon there is silence; everyone is working. I try always to have the students write something, however rough, in the workshop. Plenty can be done in twenty minutes' concentrated writing. But sometimes the warm-up 'discussions' – of the relation between craft and talent, of movies, or of what it is like to be male or female – can go on for an hour or more. It is difficult to plan the work these groups will do as you never know what will stimulate people. Recently, we began talking about men as fathers and ended up talking about parents and children, particularly a parent's failure to see or understand the 'real' nature of the kid. After a while this seemed to reconnect with writing, with the urge, later in life, to put your side of the story; to speak in order to have others know you when once you were encouraged to remain silent. Schools, too, in my day, and for many of the people in the workshop, were basically authoritarian. You remained – mostly – silent, and information was put into you, which you retained until the exams. The pupil was of no interest in herself, except as a receptacle.

Some people turn to writing in order to locate an identity; they even feel that if they don't do something like this, they will disintegrate.

Can writing be taught? There is usually strong feeling about this question, with some derision on both sides, even as more writing courses are being developed. I guess people want to know where this particular talent, or any talent for that matter, originates; how it got to be a talent in the first place, who put it there or what can be done with it. I like to reply: 'I don't know, but we'll meet once a week anyway.'

Certainly there are discussions about writing, and about trying to make anything new, which are worth having, which can be constructive and even improving. This, it seems to me, is plenty. The problem with the writing schools, or with over-academic writing courses, is that they have too narrow a notion of competence and tend only to choose the best students. What would happen if such an idea was abandoned altogether? I wouldn't even say that talent is important. The less accomplished writers and the novices are no less interesting than the brilliant ones. It is moving to see someone speak when they hardly dared before. Who can say what anyone will produce in the future? Who doesn't have something to say? Why fetishise talent or approve most of those who please their teacher?

The idea, really, is to be inspiring; to make others see, through one's enthusiasm, that this is worth doing. Of course people have to understand this themselves; if they don't, there's nothing there and the teacher only demonstrates his intelligence while the learning is superficial. Can the teacher do anything? Is she necessary? Why not have a 'leaderless' group?

Most of the time it is not that the writer can't write, it's that she can't find out whether she can write or not. She can't get that far because she is held up by herself and her history, by the external and internal fears which crowd her as she puts pen to paper, standing in the way of real development. The teacher is an alternative or auxiliary voice, which helps the student make an arrangement with herself to continue despite her doubts, an arrangement which will let the student's natural abilities evolve without crippling inhibition.

Early on there was an exercise that appealed to the class. It wasn't something I'd prepared, but developed out of talking about writers who use alternative names, for instance Stephen King / Richard Bachman, Ruth Rendell / Barbara Vine. In the exercise you write under a pseudonym, as if you were someone else, or as if you were an actor 'freed up' in a mask. Who would you write like if you were liberated from the necessity of being yourself, if you could inhabit your strangest parts without believing you will turn into that person? In the spirit of Miles Davis's remark, 'There are no wrong notes in jazz,' it seemed important to encourage people to bring their worst selves to the page. Of course the idea of a 'second' or 'shadow' self is one which has been explored by writers as diverse as Poe, Dostoevsky, Stevenson and Maupassant.

'Remember, you are many,' was the note I gave them. Initially, people thought just 'the bad stuff' would come out, that their concealed desire would be abhorrent and they would discover only nightmares. One man began the exercise and immediately found his thoughts repellent, as he 'turned' into a rapist. His own 'darkness' was so agitating and his belief that once in it he'd never return so strong, he refused to continue the exercise and had to walk around the building until he calmed down. 'Saints can't write novels,' I said, unhelpfully.

For others, this disguised speaking of hatred, fury and longing had a surprising and considerable energy in it. Whatever their fears, most people seemed to feel that they had at least discovered something they could use – a new position to write from, for instance; something they would return to, and couldn't find any other way.

Ted Hughes: 'Writers have invented all kinds of "games" to get past their own censorship ... One thing such games have in common is a willingness to relax expectation, and to experiment, to let flow – a willingness to put on masks and to play.'

The writer here isn't attempting to find his voice, as if there were one such thing to find, but is discovering multiple inflections and the numerous attitudes it is possible to write from without wholly identifying with any of them.

When I set an exercise, I encourage the writers to read out the results. This can feel embarrassing and students are not compelled to do it. For some people, being heard can be harder than being ignored. However, it can be illuminating to hear yourself read in front of a small audience. The story will change as it reaches the light. If you are able to listen to yourself, you will hear the false notes and will, probably, stumble over them. The bad bits will leap out. As you go you will revise in your head.

The other day I read one of my own stories to the class, a story I thought, or hoped, was finished. To my surprise I received a good deal of criticism, most of which was helpful. Misunderstandings and the need for more detail were pointed out. Nothing holds up a story more than lack of clarity and this is not something you would always be able to notice yourself. I went home chastened.

There is a letter by Robert Lowell in which he says, 'I'd been doing a lot of reading aloud. I went on a trip to the West Coast and read at least once a day and sometimes twice for fourteen days, and more and more I found that I was simplifying my poems. I'd make little changes just impromptu as I read.'

The disadvantage of reading aloud is that it can encourage unnecessary irony and whimsy. The reader likes an instant response; he wants only to entertain and is afraid of a more subtle engagement with an audience. Reading aloud can also force writers to make too much sense of their ideas too early, foreshortening a productive mad rambling – an overspilling of ideas, memories, daydreams, night-dreams, images, fantasies, random thoughts and feelings – which might be more generative if continued.

A few weeks into the workshop I am aware of my own impatience. I'm beginning to wonder whether the work of this group is as good as that of other groups I've run and whether – and this must be any teacher's or writer's worry – other people really want that which is being offered. Of course, only parts, perhaps only a fragment of what you say will be important, just as certain parts of any work of art, or poem – perhaps only a section, paragraph or image – will resonate for a reader. But already I want them to be better writers. Why bother with a workshop otherwise? Or is it only certain sorts of writing that I like or want? Has my taste become too particular? Anyhow, I feel dyspeptic, sour and old. I remember seeing this in some teachers at school: for them, as a pupil, you were a failure already; just being a kid at all was a kind of weakness for them. I have to remind myself to be demanding without becoming destructive of hope. I don't want to be as hard on them as I can be on myself. But how can the teacher not reproduce with his students the relationship he has with himself?

There are lots of things I know and might pass on. But to have a chance they have to be said at the right time, when people are ready. This is something I can only intuit.

After a few weeks, something good is happening. All the students seem to be writing, both in the workshop and outside. At the end of each weekly meeting, they hand me more and more scripts and stories. Having read them I will sit with the writer, trying to say something which will make him want to continue, or which makes him see that he's found an idea or image that could be pursued further, which is a key to the way he sees the world. What interests or confuses me is the unevenness of their work – how they can write something shockingly compelling and original one day and hopeless and clichéd the next. I guess you couldn't have one without the other; perhaps one makes the other. It's odd, too, how sometimes they cannot tell the difference between the good work and the not-so-good.

Anyway, there are never going to be immediate results. Why should there be? A good deal of writing work is waiting, or gestation. The teacher and the writer both have to learn to wait, even when you're not certain that anything at all will turn up. Of course, in writing it's only yourself you're waiting for. That is the fantasy, or attraction of writing for some people, I believe; the fact there is no dependence on others.

Some people from my groups have become better writers; a few, ten years after they came to the group, have begun to make a living at it, having written successful first novels or plays. The point for me isn't to turn out writers in the way a technical college turns out bricklayers, but to use writing, as one might use anything else – drawing, say – to remake the world and think about the way one lives in it. Anyone can do this.

Usually, at the beginning of a workshop, I go around the circle and ask why people have come. I want to know why and how writing might be difficult – or how difficult they want it to be, and where that sense of difficulty originates – and whether there's a particular aspect of writing which bothers the students.

In this workshop the replies were intriguingly puzzling. Usually they're along the lines of, 'how should you write dialogue?', 'how do you get ideas?' and even 'how do you get out of bed and to your desk every day?' On this occasion, however, four people, in different ways, said 'structure'. A young man asked how he should 'connect' the various bits of his writing, saying he wrote different parts of a piece and then couldn't put them together.

These questions perplexed me because the 'structure' of a piece is often something that occurs quite late. Normally you can only decide what to do with what you've got when you can see what it is that's there. I assume that if the writer keeps looking at it, some sort of solution will occur, a solution that will be, that could only be, in the writer's own voice. However many books you've read or films you've seen, the piece you're working on will have its own peculiar problems to which you can only find a resolution according to the sort of person you are. The decisions you make can only come from you; they should only come from you and the characteristic way you think, otherwise the piece's form will only be conventional and something fresh might have been lost. First drafts are usually more original than finished work.

People's concerns about writing are also another way for them to talk about their lives. Daily writing, or the project of becoming a writer, can give 'structure' to a life, to people who feel their lives are unorganised. For young people in particular – and those who have recently left home – there can be too much experience and not enough understanding. While writing is a way of integrating unacceptable material into a life, the daily practice itself, the contract you have made with yourself to continue, along with the regularity of the workshops, will provide the form, framework and inevitability which parents and school once gave. Attending a weekly workshop can provide an important shape. You can only orient yourself in terms of other people. Nevertheless, it is the writing in between, that which people do outside the workshop, which matters most.

Of course, as every school kid and teacher knows, all classrooms are sexual sites. A writing workshop is always going to be more erotic than sitting alone at a desk, which can, for some people, be a way of avoiding bodies. Sometimes the students want to learn but sometimes they just want the teacher. Or they need someone in authority to make a demand on them. They need confirmation that what they want to do is worth the effort, and that they are not writing into a vacuum.

Their fear is of speaking with no one listening. Even worse is the common fear that others might listen but be bored, or turned off by what is being said. Of course, we know what this is like. Not only are we bored by others occasionally, but we are bored by having the same thoughts, fears and words in our minds for years. If we are to hear new stories, the old ones have to come into contact with reality. The question then becomes: can we do something with the past rather than have it merely haunt or oppress us? This need to create narrative and meaning – or new meaning – is not an indulgence or luxury, but an imperative for some people in certain circumstances, an alternative to various kinds of repetition or even breakdown.

One young man wants to talk to the group about his fear of being pretentious. He says his brother is an electrician whose existence seems to mock the young man's stated but shaky intention to write. Being an electrician is its own justification. You can't have enough electricians. A writer isn't like a scientist either, who has studied and passed his exams. Any old scientist has the right to call himself a scientist, but when do you earn the right to call yourself a writer? In my view, this doesn't seem to matter. It is the activity rather than the label which counts. I want to move on. But the group insists we discuss this for a while. It's important to them to worry about the circumstances in which you can legitimately call yourself, or 'come out', as a 'writer'. If others can recognise what you are, you're more likely to accept it yourself.

Behind this, I realise, is a certain amount of shame. It reminds me of the shame some actors feel at their profession and the feeling that what they do is really rather childish, not grown-up enough, and that people should grow out of their daydreams as, they believe, all adults do.

Any kind of writing is an act of faith. At first it is a 'relation' but not yet a relationship. The writer has to believe, somehow, that not only does he have something to say, but that he is of interest to others; that he can engage rather than bore them, that he can stimulate desire and curiosity in other people. He has to believe in the future, believe that writing this page today will, in the years to come, be sufficiently alive for others so that they might even pay to read it.

Any writer is more likely to believe this if she has had this experience before, if she has had a parent, teacher or carer who was convinced of the child's usefulness, who found the child's concerns appealing. If she lacks this, she will have to install or create this belief for herself, using others at workshops, for instance, as stand-ins for absent figures.

On the other hand, any sort of writer has to be able to bear the fact that other people will not be interested. They might be appalled, disgusted, indifferent. Then, like anyone facing criticism, the writer has to decide whether to continue in the same way, or modify what he does in order to suit the other.

To write seriously, then, a lot of things have to be in place and a lot will change as you go.

The question of who you write for can often be answered in this way. (In fact, you might as easily ask: who are you living for?) First of all you write for another part of yourself. And this other part of the self, this internal reader as it were, might be over-discriminating or have too confined a taste. There might be all kinds of possible work you could do (or possible lives you could lead) which are prohibited by the zealous internal reader. This scrutineer, who could become a tyrant or saboteur rather than an ally, might require an education – from others – in fruitful vulgarity. Workshop colleagues or a teacher might help you to be bolder.

Usually, at the beginning of each weekly workshop I ask what people have been reading or have seen. All the students watch films – commercial, American films mostly. Some of them go occasionally to the theatre. What shocks me is how little they read. While they mention some contemporary or fashionable novels, there are few 'classics' or philosophy, and little poetry.

I have always assumed that reading and imaginative writing go together. A writer's originality can consist of how he distorts or uses someone else's work. Even a failed plagiarist is an artist. What I'm trying to do, I guess, is get the students to read and look as writers, seeing how the author achieved an effect, being aware of what they can use or transform for themselves. If writing is the translation of feeling into language, I want to encourage a closer acquaintance with the language in order to increase the quantity and quality of expressed feeling. This is not reading for fun, and it is not literary criticism.

What I noticed as a young man at school – and it wasn't difficult to see, it was drummed into us – was that the well-behaved, the conformists and the compliant were, and would be in life, the most rewarded. What was disturbing was not only that the less bright would go down, but that the dissenters, the 'difficult' pupils, often the funniest or liveliest, would not only fail, but be excluded from approval. I suppose I saw myself like that. Luckily there were the Beatles and the Rolling Stones. Where I did belong, I discovered, was in 'pop', then a haven for non-conformists and the creatively odd. Around this time my friends and I began to use marijuana and take LSD regularly. Until then I'd been, I think, not unlike a lot of boys, educationally anorexic. Nothing would go in; I wouldn't let it in. One day someone gave me De Quincey's *Confessions of an English Opium-Eater*. I went from this to Hunter S. Thompson and after that never stopped reading. The dissipated writers, Bukowski, Henry Miller, Anaïs Nin, and then Roth, Salinger, Kerouac – artists who combined pleasure with art – seemed as self-destructive as pop stars. They were writers who eulogised wild, suffering young men in despair. This was both a picture of how I felt and a picture of who I wanted to be in certain parts of myself. I began to learn that literature was not respectable and didn't only belong to the teachers or upholders of culture.

Between the ages of fourteen and thirty I read novels, non-fiction, magazines, newspapers. I went to the theatre or concerts at least once a week. I listened to pop, classical and jazz music constantly, tapes, the radio, anything that was around or had been recommended. Later, I lay on the sofa reading *Remembrance of Things Past* in the afternoons, from three or six every day, until I finished it, making notes as I went. I read history, politics and philosophy too, in order to think about race, class and gender, notions which were being generally investigated at the time. There was a hunger or longing in me, during that confusing, semi-independent period after childhood and adolescence, for knowledge and comfort, for what I thought was wisdom, and for close contact with stories and writers. I was beginning to try to make sense of my childhood and parents; I required tools for understanding. At the same time I wanted the world but not too much of it. It was easier to bear mediated through books. Reader and writer meet but their bodies do not touch.

Later on I read to see what other writers were doing. This is still of interest to me, but less significant. I have my own voice and concerns as a writer. I'm less likely to learn from anyone else. I would like to read seriously and for long periods again, but there always seems to be something more important to do than remaining in close contact with the mind and feelings of a stranger.

My doubts about what I can offer as a teacher don't diminish. Although I've received much incisive and necessarily ruthless assistance over the years from directors, literary managers, editors and friends, I've noticed in other writers who teach an inability to see why their students might find it painful. If a writer can write it does not follow that he can understand what the problems of writing might be, or why someone else might find it hard or almost impossible to do. A writer might not want to look at how he had made himself. There could be mutual incomprehension.

Nonetheless I decide to continue with the workshop as long as people come. Sometimes the pleasure of the group seems to be its sole justification. After all, why a group at all when writing is so personal, so private, and may be a way of protecting yourself from various kinds of community coercion? You'd think it was the last thing people would want to do communally.

I was thinking this the other night, after setting an exercise for the group. If I ever wondered what the point of all this might be – my pathological scepticism, you might call it – the students' demands reminded me. They had come to the workshop in the cold winter rain believing there was something there for them. One man came from Exeter; another commuted weekly from Liverpool, and now fifteen people were working in a room next to the tube line. As I wrote, too, making these notes, I was aware of the quality of silence in the room, an extended, concentrated silence. The members of the group were lying on sofas, sitting on hard chairs, they were hunched in corners on the floor, but everyone was writing, separately but somehow together. I'd set a time limit for the exercise – so there would be time for a break, and then for participants to read work aloud – but it took me several attempts to interrupt them. Later we went to the bar for more talk about plays and writing, and some of the group exchanged email addresses in order to look at one another's work.

This was, it seemed to me, a productive way to spend an evening.

'Workshops' were used for group therapy by the psychotherapist Carl Rogers in, of course, California. This 'planned, intensive group experience' was, in his judgement, 'the most rapidly expanding social invention of the century'. Workshops were, in the jargon of the time, 'training groups in human relations skills'. The idea was that individuals would be taught to observe their interactions with others.

Rogers and others with Freudian backgrounds, like Fritz Perls (a German exile and Gestaltist, who began the Esalen Institute in Big Sur), knew already of the powerful feelings stirred in the traditional psychoanalytic couple – patient and analyst. They were curious to see what would happen if more people were introduced into the room, if you could, according to the democratic impulses of the time, attempt some kind of therapy with a group. If the usual social defences of 1950s America, which had begun to seem unnecessarily constraining – politeness, good manners, small talk and alcohol – were removed, the current of feeling between people ran with extraordinary strength. The intimacy, the quality of honesty, and of 'realisation' possible, was more illuminating and pleasurable – and painful – than a thousand conventional conversations. New, temporary communities could be formed when the old ones didn't work. These 'encounter' groups spread rapidly.

Workshops were taken up by dance, mime and theatre groups in New York in the 1960s and were used at the Royal Court Theatre in London in the 1960s and 1970s when actors, directors and writers would meet to talk, to experiment, and to improvise. These were not rehearsals of already written scripts, but loosely organised, intense meetings where nothing precise had to happen. This, I guess, was almost the opposite of education. There was no information to be conveyed, nothing which had to be put into the participants, only 'ideas' which might be discovered in a collective experiment.

'Workshops' – groups of people who meet in the hope of discovering something which might be of use – can be a powerful tool for emotional contact and learning, and can be adapted in many ways. Writing is a particularly good use for workshop time because despite their individuality writers have a lot in common and, in the end, all writers write to be heard by others.

You get to be a better writer not only by making more beautiful sentences, but by going deeper into your experience and finding a unique form for it. It is there, at the most fundamental level, that all human experience is similar and where you link up with others.

In writing at the moment, there seems to be a demand for instruction. Recently, in New York, where I hadn't been for five years, I visited the bookshops and headed for the 'writing' section. Up to ten years ago there would only have been a handful of writing guides, confined to the reference section, not far from the etiquette books. Now there was an entire shelf of them. There was writing from the body, heart, soul, unconscious, and, it seemed, from all the other parts of the anatomy, suitable or not.

In the 1970s my father would study the writing guides that were available – he was a keen self-improver, and loved 'wisdom' and 'guidance'. He came from a big family and, I assume, had to compete for attention. I read these guides too, though mostly the writers I'd look to for tips would be Somerset Maugham (*A Writer's Notebook*) and Henry Miller ('Reflections on Writing' from *The*

Wisdom of the Heart). There was also a little book of thirty-five pages by Ray Bradbury, published by Capra Press in 1974 (though I believe it was written in the mid-1950s), called *Zen in the Art of Writing*, which I still keep on my desk, with my father's signature inside, and the date, 19 August 1974.

The other book my father and I enjoyed was Herrigel's *Zen in the Art of Archery*, mostly because we were interested in sport and how its psychology might be applied to creativity. I remember my mother's puzzlement over our fascination with a book about archery. 'Who do you think you are?' she'd say. 'A couple of Robin Hoods?'

Collecting and reading these books is, for me, a way of finding inspiration and of wasting time when I could be writing, or of being close to my father, depending on how I'm feeling.

Most of them say similar things. They recommend free writing – free association by hand, you could call it – as a way of outwitting internalised censorship. This is an echo of Freud's most important request to his patients, which was that they say whatever came into their mind, however trivial, abhorrent or stupid. His only demand was that they speak as fully as possible, particularly if they found a thought trivial, abhorrent or stupid. This abandonment of consecutive or linear thought, the privileging of incoherence and verbal breakdown, in order to mine the realm of dreams and desire, became, for the surrealists, a style, and was the fundamental rule of psychoanalysis. It is still the basis of most therapies and 'talking' cures. From a Freudian point of view articulacy is not a virtue; one should be suspicious of those who claim to know what they mean. It's not that people aren't intelligent, it's that they deliberately, and with intelligence, hide the truth from themselves, and what is hidden dominates their lives. The hidden, which is raw, is of more use than the cooked.

Freud's first biographer, Ernest Jones, makes an intriguing claim for the origin of the idea of free association. He says that Freud may have been inspired by an essay written in 1823 by Ludwig Borne – one of Freud's favourite authors when young – with the excellent title of 'The Art of Becoming an Original Writer in Three Days'.

Borne states: 'Here follows the practical prescription I promised! Take a few sheets of paper and for three days in succession write down, without any falsification or hypocrisy, everything that comes into your head . . . and when the three days are over you will be amazed at what novel and startling thoughts have welled up in you. That is the art of becoming an original writer in three days.'

Such prescriptions reveal the proximity of writing to therapy, which is one of the things it can be used for. Certainly, at the moment, therapy seems to be the only progress myth there is to believe in. Therapy can help us endure and enjoy more; many teachers, healthcare workers and GPs are using writing in schools, prisons and hospitals in the way painting, drama, dance and music have been utilised in the past.

For me, writing is nourishing and a necessity, a place to commune with myself, to meditate and to be solitary without being lonely: 'a third space', as Winnicott calls it, between oneself and the world. For Winnicott, children's fantasy often involves aggression; playing is an expression of, and mastering of, the anxiety involved in this. The child requires it as a kind of self-restoration. I recall one of my sons saying, after a day out, 'but I haven't played today!' and he settled down, alone, with his cars, and played and talked to himself, until he was ready to be with others. Writers, too, can get irascible if they haven't put in a few hours with themselves at their desk.

Most human enterprises are more or less therapeutic – ultimately good for us in intended ways. It's hard to think of anything that couldn't be counted as therapy, if therapy is seen as the attempt to replace one state of mind with another, preferred state. For adults, to play is to 'do' something with one's anxieties, integrating them into the self, as opposed to leaving them frozen where they remain a dead area within the mind. In that sense writing is a release, which means not to think of those anxieties so much. No wonder writing is in demand as a vocation.

However, despite Freud's liking for Borne, there are vital differences between therapy and literature. Writing cannot replace what is unique in therapy; in fact it may enforce a dangerous solitude or narcissism. The desire to write can be a problem if it fosters a fantasy of self-sufficiency, omnipotence and withdrawal. At least in a workshop there's contact with others.

The Freudian patient's monologue takes place in the presence of another, a trained witness, an ideal listener who never speaks of herself, and whom one is paying. This is not self-analysis but an alliance which helps the patient through the locked doors of the mind that otherwise would remain unopened. In the absence of this, writing as therapy might become merely circular or obsessional; there's no other way out of the maze of ourselves. The therapist talks back to you in ways you can't talk to yourself.

One aim of therapy is liberating self-knowledge through contact with unconscious desire. You speak in order to hear yourself, to know who you are. The therapist helps you see what you are doing unconsciously. In writing, however, it often feels better to work in the dark. It is only later, in reflection after the act, that you will see what you have done, or begin to understand what you were really trying to say. But why, even then, would you want such knowledge?

Adrienne Rich: 'Without for one moment turning my back on conscious choice and selection, I have been increasingly willing to let the unconscious offer its materials, to listen to more than the one voice of a single idea. Perhaps a simpler way of putting it would be to say that instead of poems about experience I am getting poems that are experiences, that contribute to my knowledge and my emotional life even while they reflect and assimilate it.'

For me the workshop aims neither to produce significant work nor to 'cure' anyone of anything. (There's nothing wrong with them.) There's no anxiety of success, only the desire to work around the subject of writing. There is probably some benefit in this but I wouldn't want to know what it is in advance.

*

Sometimes it feels wrong to try to work out what a dream is 'about'. It seems like a reduction rather than an illumination. What you need to do is wander through its atmospheres, feeling what's there. Occasionally, in the class, when I'm listening to someone read, rather than considering the work as a literary construction, I let myself absorb it like a dream, encouraging my mind to move amongst the images and words, in order to see what they conjure up, returning some of this to the writer in the hope they can make something of it. Occasionally, rather than offering criticism or encouragement, I invite the group to free-associate around a piece of writing, offering lists of words, other dreams or any thoughts inspired in them, as if the writing, and the response, is one continuous piece.

I knew I liked Wallace Stevens's poetry but for a long time found him impossible to read, particularly as I've never read much poetry. He always made me think: how should I read this? I couldn't understand him. When I realised that 'understanding' him, as opposed to liking bits of what he did, or scanning through it until I found something which held my attention for reasons I could only discover, was not the best thing I could do with him, I found another way into his work.

In the end, it's the artist who is necessary. When you want sustenance, or pleasure, you're more likely to go to a poem by Eliot or Lawrence than you are to a piece of criticism by Leavis. Criticism erases the pleasure of reading, replacing it by understanding, which is a different sort of thing.

Occasionally I will ask the student to tell me what they were trying to say in their writing, in order to force clarity or focus. Mostly, though, it hardly matters what you say about someone's writing. It is the act of sitting there, of being present at all, which is of value. After having spoken and been heard, people's minds move on of their own accord.

Certainly writing is of benefit in the wider, political sense, particu-larly where there is a tendency for only the most acceptable or publicised voices to be attended to. The most impressive and influential writers of my youth were dissenters like Baldwin, Genet, Salinger, Fanon and De Beauvoir. It is the voices of argument, of dispute and disagreement, which can teach us the most about the position of excluded individuals and groups. Of course the young always feel like outsiders and this would appeal to them. The political effort of my era has been that of formerly suppressed voices, those of women, blacks, gays, the bullied and abused, the mentally ill and the addicted, to speak their history and to have it recognised. This is the struggle to uncover what was formerly hidden. There is also the struggle within each individual writer to believe that their voice is worth attending to. Confession, rather than irony, has become the modern mode. If party politics is banal, formulaic and uninteresting, and most of the media the same, it might be to something as old-fashioned as writing that we will turn to express and share our deepest concerns.

Since the arguments for equality of the 1960s and 1970s, these days the voices most neglected – probably because they are the most unsettling – are those of children. If the latest position for children is their use to adults as consumers – the exploitation of children's desire – writing freely can be an important implement for them, both in and out of school, enabling them to repossess their own thoughts. This can be particularly valuable for children in authoritarian systems, and most children live, to a certain extent, in authoritarian systems, called families.

There is also the sense in which writing, or anything creative, is 'counter-consumerist' in itself. When making something original from one's own life and feeling, we are not merely objects with wallets, but active and free subjects, the authors or artists of our own lives. Most of us know that when we are creative an authentic connection, or something particularly satisfying and original, has been achieved.

As a young man I didn't attend writing workshops. I didn't know of any, and would probably have been sceptical of them. I'd have wanted to impress everyone so much I wouldn't be able to get through the door. I'd have been standing outside, leaning against a wall with the collar of my jacket turned up, sneering, confused. I hated to learn from others. I think I was looking for something I could do on my own, or only with my father. I'm probably a better teacher than I am pupil.

As a child, and before I thought of becoming a writer, I envied talented children at school; I admired their ability and composure, envied the praise they received and, I guess, envied the envy I had of them. My mother had been to art school. Her portraits and abstracts were around the house. Sometimes she sketched. Mostly she didn't, though we liked her to. She preferred to demonstrate how much life you had to give up in favour of your children. At the same time my father was a published, part-time journalist.

Around the age of twelve I wanted to draw. Some of my friends at school were good at drawing, too, and would, eventually, go to work at one of the many advertising agencies which were opening in the 1960s. But the act of drawing itself wasn't enough for me. I was searching for a project, for some direction or meaning. I decided to become a painter, an artist. I did paint for a while, but without knowing why I soon became frustrated and gave up. After discovering the Beatles I began to play the guitar, but the same thing happened. There was a point beyond which I couldn't go. I didn't improve. I played the same thing over and over. I wasn't patient enough to see whether I could get beyond that point. At school there were a number of talented guitar players. Kids would bring their guitars to school and play at lunchtime.

I can see now that I wanted results – attention, the engagement of others, someone sitting beside me, interested enough in what I was doing to show me where else I might go. I concluded that playing guitar wasn't my thing. I remember the pangs of envy and self-hatred, almost erotic in their intensity, which accompanied my failure. That might have been enough for me, but I wanted a 'thing'. What was my thing?

No one I knew was writing. As a competitive kid, this suited me. I'd have hated to be up against any other kid. I'd have hated not to be the best: I could have given up, gone into a sulk, which finished me off. Writing, for me, was a private, if not secret occupation. Nevertheless, its point, in the long run, was to reach others.

My father was a good teacher; he lived with the dilemmas of writing and talked about them all the time. If I joined in his dream, he gave me a lot of attention. What I did do, under his aegis, as he sat in his armchair in the evening underlining phrases by Tolstoy, was write. I learned some discipline, developed a vocabulary, became used to arranging words into sentences in an order that seemed right, and then sentences into paragraphs. I always had a dictionary and thesaurus open on my desk.

I learned how slow and frustrating writing could be and, I guess, learned to get past this to other pleasures. I learned to use my experience of school, family life, friends, in my writing, and I learned how to remake that experience, in my imagination, into stories. I learned to see, from reading my own work, when it worked and when it didn't; when it sounded right or like me. I learned to think of writing when I wasn't at my desk, going over stories in my mind, testing them for potential.

I learned the habit of thinking as a writer and became acquainted with the usual doubts and fears, the isolation, self-belief and bloody-mindedness required. And from the rejections I received for my articles, stories and novels I began to learn something about the practical aspects and difficulties of making a living out of what I wanted to do.

In my mind or on paper, in various states of preparation – they might be notes, lists of words, character sketches, or scenes or paragraphs – I have numerous ideas which I poke now and again, for signs of life, to see whether I might get round to writing them, whether there's any urgency or necessity there. That is why, I guess, if I have an idea, I like to start on it immediately, whatever else I'm doing, when the ideas might 'run', and before I can persuade myself it's really no good. As time passes and I move away from the original impulse or inspiration, I'm less likely to write the idea. It no longer seems important. This way I can work a lot, which I like. But I often work too quickly and the piece might seem rough or unfulfilled, an effect which can have its virtues.

Of course, during the day, you write in different moods: sometimes intensively, unstoppably; at other times with self-hatred, or with bad concentration, indifference or boredom; sometimes an idea catches fire and there is an easy pleasure, and so on. These moods might follow in rapid succession. All you can do is sit through it all, knowing that different things are possible at different times, aware that the one thing you cannot do is find reasons to stop prematurely.

As with anything creative, so much of writing seems dilatory. What are you doing all day but dreaming, or dozing on the edge of boredom? Sometimes you follow whimsical or downright stupid ideas to see where they might go. You let pieces of work drift or hang about the house for months before abandoning them, or using them elsewhere; you worry, walk about your study, picking up books at random, leafing through art catalogues, hoping for something to occur. You think: if this was being filmed what would there be to see but a bored bloke doing nothing much? If you try to hurry up you slow down.

Sometimes all writing seems tiresome. You add something to a piece and the whole thing changes. Everything else has to be altered. It takes off in another direction, just when you were starting to get satisfied. Taking something out can have a similar effect.

A good deal of writing, most of it in fact, is craft: cutting and ordering and replacing material, trying it in different places, looking at it again, and going through this process repeatedly, alone and with others, until you think you're going mad. Most writing is mostly about giving the reader the right information at the right time. The reader's attention, like all attention, is sustained by withholding. This is partly an editor's skill and can be learned. What you're trying to do is to look at what you've done as objectively and coolly as you can, which is almost, but not quite, impossible.

Yet, somehow, eventually, things get done. People, fools usually, even say, 'But you've written a lot. You must be very disciplined.' I am still surprised that anything is finished at all.

It's as if I imagine there's another, ideal way to work, if only I could find out what it is. But this might be the best way to do it – haphazardly, in a sort of chaos hedged by hope, while waiting by the window to see my children's faces when they come home from school.

I wouldn't measure the quality of a day's work by the number of words written. The writing might be slow or slower but I'm more likely to see a good day in terms of fruitful ideas which take the piece forward. It is the idea which is significant. The writing itself becomes luxurious; I can enjoy messing around with words and seeing whether they lead to other words.

I have been a man who is always about to go into a room and write. That's where I'd rather be, most of the time. Sometimes I think everything else – and everyone else – is just getting in the way. I have, at least, learned to write anywhere and at any time: in cafés, on the train, in a car when travelling. Before, I could only write at my desk, with my 'ritualistic' objects around me.

My study is full of notebooks. My bag is full of notebooks. My coat pockets carry little notebooks. There are notebooks beside my bed. There are pens everywhere. Most of the notebooks are half-empty; in many I have only written on the first page. If I succeed in filling one I am delighted. Every time I buy a new one I want to write in it immediately. Clean white paper offends me; I want to scribble on it. My job is to turn white paper into half-dark paper.

Soon the notebooks are battered. I stick my wet umbrella on top of them. I write on trains or lying across the back seats of cars. I guess I like being a writer more than I like any of the other roles I have. If I take the notebooks with me, I can be a writer all the time; the further from writing I get, the flatter and more without purpose I feel, as if I don't know who I am.

317

Writing, or any imaginative act, feels sensual; it feels – perhaps it should feel like – a bodily act, rather than an intellectual one. The movement of the writing hand on the page reminds me of someone drawing a model, looking up, moving between inner and outer worlds. How you turn the page round as you go, how you add; the page with its arrows, additions, notes down the side, underlinings, circles and coffee rings, can look like a drawing. Ink on your fingers and jeans. Your materials matter; the whole thing matters. Fountain pens become a part of you, as the nib changes over the years. Love letters should only be written by hand. Children don't learn to write on typewriters or computers; you can't scribble with them. You can't write at an angle or turn the page upside down; everything turns out looking the same. They are for journalists.

Ray Bradbury says in *Zen in the Art of Writing*, 'The artist must not think of the critical rewards or money he will get for painting pictures.' It would be difficult to disagree with Bradbury here; you can never know in advance what people might want. The integrity of the writing itself has to be the important thing. But it cannot be the whole story. Even if it is unconscious, there is the desire to speak and, in any writer, that which he believes speaking will bring him, in the world, with others. What are you using these sentences to do? How do you expect them to reward you, both in the world and in your mind? Any working artist will have to have – at least – sufficient drive, motivation, energy or ambition which will make her want success more than almost anything else.

Freud, with characteristic good sense and a certain amount of condescension, writes of the artist's belief that his creativity will bring him 'honour, power, wealth, fame and women's love; but he lacks the means for achieving these satisfactions. Consequently, like any other unsatisfied man, he turns away from reality and transfers all his interests, and his libido too, to the wishful constructions of his life of phantasy, whence the path might lead to neurosis.'

This, then, is writing as a way of wishing, but of course it is not only that. (In other places Freud admitted his inability to understand the creative artist.) If the writing act remained at the level of internal chatter it would, indeed, be a 'neurosis' or even madness. But the 'phantasy' is turned into words for others, or into an extension of literary tradition – this is the difference between the phantasies of Flaubert and those of Madame Bovary – and is used to make an alteration to the world. The 'phantasy' goes on.

I've always liked to write every day, otherwise I get anxious. Though I rarely think of it consciously, what I'm doing is always with me and I want to take it further when I can. As a young man I took it for granted that becoming a full-time writer was my goal. I'm less certain now that this is the most fertile way for a writer to spend his life; anyone with a historical perspective will see that any number of writers have pursued other professions, which have informed and broadened their work.

The writer as 'artist', as opposed to professional craftsman, particularly during the period known as 'modernism', might have rendered fiction more solipsistic and less open to the pressures of the everyday world. In the end it is life rather than language which is interesting.

If writing is a profession as well as an art, sometimes I like to think of myself as a 'professional writer'. It's a craft, a job; just hard work. I do it to support myself and my family, and if I weren't paid would do something else. It feels better to be modest about such things: do what you can and shut up. At other times I want to be pretentious and consider myself an artist, a dreamer, someone with a unique vision. I can't make up my mind; I don't see why I should. I can be a different kind of writer on different days.

A few weeks ago I looked around at the young faces in my group and asked whether they wanted to be writers, working writers, as opposed to people who might write for pleasure, or as 'personal expression'. All of them put their hands up.

I thought: none of you have any idea what it's like to support three kids and run a house by writing. But then, nor did I, for a long time. When I began to write for the theatre I lived cheaply and thought little of how I might get by in the long term. The politics of the 1970s affected me; making money or a living wasn't the point: free expression was.

Turning a penchant for storytelling into a profession, into food you can buy in the supermarket, and how you might do this for a whole working life, is different for each generation. Not long after I started out as a writer, I did begin to write films, which a number of writers of my generation were doing. I knew this would be useful, and it subsidised my novels.

Not long ago I had dinner with a charming French novelist from Martinique, who writes in Creole. Mostly he works as a teacher, writing at weekends and during the holidays. He was surprised that I don't have to lecture or do journalism to make a living. He seemed to think there were not many French novelists who could do this. I said in Britain there were quite a few writers I knew who made a considerable living from writing, but that many of them also did other things, like writing for film, television and radio, partly out of choice, but also out of necessity.

Few of the writers I know teach much and the teaching I do myself is financially nugatory. These days writers are more likely to work in other areas of the media. As literature and academia have moved further apart, the profession of writing seems closer to the rest of the media: print, television and film. Most writers, these days, fancy writing and directing their own films, or at least having their work made into films, which is a good way of extending one's income and reaching a larger audience. Films can be lucrative and pleasurable, but they take a lot of setting up and can be a waste of time and hope, as so few of them are actually made. With a film there are usually two significant creators, the writer and the director. Occasionally, as with Bergman, say, this can be the same person. Usually it is not, as writing and directing are different types of talent. The writer does his work first, after which it is used in various ways by the director. The writer almost always receives less recognition than the director and often less than the actors. This can be a mercy, depending on the temperament of the writer and the quality of the film. He will be paid far less, too.

Around the time of *My Beautiful Laundrette* my life changed. There were trips to America, prizes, nominations, opportunities, praise, attention, and new girlfriends. I had to try to understand the way long-standing friendships shifted; there was envy and incomprehension. It was an 'accelerated' period, which made me fear who I was turning into, and made me want to cling on to a previous idea of myself. I couldn't integrate so many alterations; my identity seemed in flux. I didn't know how much I could change in order to enjoy what was happening, without turning into someone I didn't recognise.

My Beautiful Laundrette was a successful film, which took a lot of money at the box-office in relation to what it cost. I wasn't fairly rewarded and was told not to complain, since the movie had established my reputation and enabled me to get my next projects made. Yet others, who lacked my ability, made plenty of money out of it. I was keen for this not to happen again.

There are few more bourgeois professions than that of writer. The fiction artist is rarely a heaving volcano of dissent. It's the poets who are mad; they drink too much, bitch at one another, get into fights at parties and copulate with strangers. The novelists always leave early to relieve the babysitter. They want to be around for a long time; they think they'll get better and better. The novelist is someone with a solid, middle-class job, who can never be sure she will be making a living in five years' time. It's like having qualified as a doctor but being uncertain whether there will always be work available. Each piece of writing should be a risk; it would be worthless otherwise. But to what extent can you jeopardise your livelihood? What happens if you run out of ideas just as your house needs a new roof? How long will you have between your 'peak' and the beginning of your decline? Most writers, I'd guess, imagine at the beginning of their careers that their income will increase. But it's more likely to tail off, and there's not much they can do about it. A bad divorce and you could be down to nothing, doing rewrites on other people's films.

The other day I ran into a friend: we'd been young playwrights together; we'd shared awards and I'd stayed with him, discussing our work, directors and the theatre. He told me that last year he made only £1,000 from writing. Now he wrote proposals for television dramas or films, which were inevitably turned down by executives who'd never heard of him. He was, in fact, on his way home from a party where he'd met other contemporaries of ours who were complaining that their old work was no longer produced and they couldn't put their new work on. They were all less than fifty years old, already out of fashion and still with plenty to say as writers.

This mixture of security and uncertainty can be enlivening. It can also be depressing and discouraging, if you have a family. But unlike with other bourgeois professions, you have to endure regular criticism and advertise yourself as well as your books. It isn't imperative for doctors to appear in glossy magazines.

By the end of the 1980s, particularly after the publication of *The Buddha of Suburbia*, the commercial aspect of writing began to take up more of my time. If I wanted to have some idea of the financial possibilities of my profession, I had to learn fast about the nature of the business I was involved in. If I wanted to be an 'artist' I had to be practical.

Now, at least a third of my writing life is taken up with phone calls, letters, faxes, emails, business arrangements, interviews, readings, signings, travelling, seeing agents, accountants, students. In other words, it's like running a small business. All the working writers I know constantly have to make decisions about the proportion of actual writing to publicity they will do. The creative part soon becomes as hard to protect as it would be for someone trying to write while doing another job.

The modernist writers I admired when growing up – Joyce, Woolf, Eliot, Beckett, Burroughs, Genet – didn't expect to trade in the marketplace. They didn't work on TV series or do adaptations on the side; they didn't consider writing for Hollywood. They were artists and individualists, to say the least; they had integrity. Commerce was corruption. The second-rate writers made a living at it; the artists didn't care. Graham Greene seemed an exception: he wrote good movies and novels that sold. Otherwise, the world of the nineteenth-century novel – writer and large public in contact; writer to the side of, but part of the ruling class – didn't exist for serious writers. Storytelling in its crudest sense, as entertainment, as escape, had been taken over by the cinema, and then by television.

Yet Burroughs, Beckett and Genet did begin to sell, in the 1960s and 1970s, as did Sartre, Camus and Grass; when I was at university writers like Borges and Márquez were in most serious students' pockets. Publishers like Picador made hip books fashionable and sold them to the same people who would buy the Doors and Dylan. The expected 'break' between artist and mass audience never occurred. Just as in the cinema there are usually a couple of 'arthouse' hits a year, so it is with literary novelists, some of whom 'cross over'.

The sort of writer you can be is partly determined by the market and whether you want to sell books or not. If you want to make a living by writing, the kind of work you will produce might be different to that which you'd do if you had another job. Your relation to your audience will be different. By the end of the 1980s the nature of the profession and the opportunities available within it had changed considerably. Book publishing, with the rise of massive media conglomerates, became more dynamic. There was more media, more places to promote books and more 'profiles' of writers.

The intensification of publishing coincided with the rise of better bookshops – mostly Waterstone's, then, a bit later, Books etc. and Borders. Soon vast palaces of books were opening in London and other cities, where you could buy coffee and croissants, as well as CDs and magazines. These shops started to organise readings, where writers and their public could, at least, see one another. Each seemed curious about the other. The small independent bookshop – much idealised and often useful – could, at times, drive you mad. These shops were usually small and the selection narrow. In places like Waterstone's – if the past sometimes seems to have been expunged and you can only get the latest books – you can instantly get a good idea of what is in print.

I became aware of these imminent changes when a well-known American agent came to the apartment in which I was staying in New York. It must have been in the late 1980s, before I'd published *The Buddha of Suburbia*, and when, I imagine, I was still attending film festivals and conferences on the back of *My Beautiful Laundrette* and *Sammy and Rosie Get Laid*, which I did for months, travelling the world for the first time.

This thin, intense, black-suited man brought with him a calculator with a paper roll in it, which I doubt he still has. He sat down, set the machine up, and asked me what I intended to write in the next few years. As I reeled off the list of essays, stories, novels and travel pieces I'd been mulling over for years – adding a few extra, just for luck – he punched in figures. Finally, he came up with a figure so astronomical, with so many noughts on the end, that I couldn't believe my efforts could be worth so much.

Probably, going with him, I'd have made more money than I did eventually make. But it was a high-risk game. I might have moved publishers several times in the process, chasing the dollar, and been less well published as a result. I wouldn't have had such a productively quiet life. It might have been different if he hadn't reminded me so much of the bullying, loud-mouthed, suburban wide-boys I'd grown up with, selling socks and watches from suitcases on a pub floor.

Every celebrity these days, in whatever field, aspires to the condition of rock stars. Being 'good' at publicity might be as important for a writer as it is for a performer. But if writers are marketed in this way, their careers are going to rise and fall rapidly, too, and the pressure on them will increase. Recently a bookshop manager told me that the writers of the generation preceding mine, the writers I once wanted to be like, hardly sold now even as their reputations and advances increased. They had written neither literary classics nor popular novels. There were younger, more attractive, enviable and relevant writers out there.

There might be more opportunities to sell books, but you will have to work harder to get your work before the public, which includes giving interviews. As a kid I'd have read any interview with almost any writer to get an idea of how it's done, to find inspiration, and to increase my hunger and confidence. For me, writers have always had status as semi-sages. Where else do you go for insight, if not wisdom? Certainly not to politicians; and priests will give you only religious propaganda or morality. Perhaps you'd go to a therapist but there you're really only going to find out what you think. Writers at least think seriously about the world in all its aspects – emotional and political – and don't usually have a programme. They *think* for a living about the lives of men and women in all their aspects.

The writer who disappears behind his work or seems to dissolve into it, is almost impossible in the modern marketplace. The artist might want to discuss his work, but the journalist wants to know about the artist's life. The artist has attempted to capture some kind of complexity while the media caricatures and empties people out. The writer is stripped bare; no mystery can remain, unless he turns himself into a grotesque enigma like Pynchon or Salinger and will, therefore, be pursued and caricatured even more.

What can an interview do? There's usually a photograph and the name of the book or film you're promoting. This might be sufficient to get the work to an audience, to let them know it's there. You might also be invited to explain how you came to make the piece. Although some writers hate this – they're superstitious about how they operate; or, like conjurors, don't want others to see the banal workings of created wonders – it isn't uninteresting to talk about your work, particularly if you've just finished something. That is when you do want, maybe in exchange with a journalist, to get some idea of what has been achieved. You don't really know what sort of book it is you've written until someone else has read it. If you cook a meal you want people to eat it and tell you they liked it. Yet talking about a book after you've written it, when it's published, bears little relation to what you thought you were doing when you were writing it. The story of the book told in interviews becomes another made-up story.

Of course, as you promote a book or film in many countries, the questions are always similar and it is tempting to give the same replies. (This is odd and frustrating for an artist: how their work only stimulates certain kinds of questions.) It's exhausting, too, to talk to someone who cannot talk about themselves. You begin to hear your own voice droning on. It can be helpful to think of the questions as Zen paradoxes. Each time, if you empty your mind, you might hear yourself say something different, particularly if you try to think about what is really being asked.

Not everyone came to the workshop every week, but by the end there was a core of about fifteen. I withdrew after eight months, without quite knowing why. I wasn't convinced there was anything else I could give them, though why I felt I had to do more than listen and wait for something to occur, I don't know. Teaching can be draining. You have to put other thoughts and preoccupations aside, which is not something I'm used to. I wouldn't be able to do too much of it and continue to write.

As with some of my other groups, the workshop members continued to meet, at first in the theatre and later at someone's house, to read and discuss one another's work. Some students wrote together; one applied for writing jobs on soap-operas, and another found work writing erotic horoscopes. Two others gave up their jobs or went part-time in order to make time to write. Some joined or started other writing groups.

They were hard-working and committed. They knew that, despite its drawbacks, being a writer is a relatively free and rewarding life. Most of the group, by the end, were writing seriously and had embarked on substantial projects, whole plays, novels or films. Some were making films with digital cameras, using friends and out-of-work actors. Many of the friendships would continue; the students would send me work and invite me to readings and productions of films and plays.

Certainly many people attend evening classes and courses for some sort of community, contact and sustenance. Being an enthusiastic amateur is one of the most liberating ways there is of being an artist. Whether writing workshops are therapeutic, creative, good for making friends or useful in any other way, you can only ask the participants. There cannot and should not be any guaranteed outcomes. People meet to discover what they might do together, striving to get close to something that needs to be said, and to speak of difficult things in voices that have been muffled, ignored or silenced. There is always the need to speak and the need to be heard.

The Writer and the Teacher

First published in *The Reader* magazine, 2010

If it is true, as I have read somewhere, that at any one time at least 2 per cent of the population are writing novels, then many questions about 'creative writing' courses, and their recent rapid proliferation are really about what you need other people for.

Is writing something you do alone, or do you need others to help? You can have both useful and repetitive conversations with yourself, and you can have sex with yourself, though it might cause alarm if you claimed to be making love to yourself. Conversation and sex are generally thought to be more productive and unpredictable with others. Several of the most significant art forms of the twentieth century – jazz, pop, cinema – have been collaborative. Is writing like this or is it something else altogether?

Some people become writers because they want to be independent; they want neither to be competitive nor to rely on others. For them writing is an entirely personal self-exploration, a way of being alone, of thinking through their life, and perhaps of hiding, while speaking to someone in their head. And certainly, without a passion for solitude no writer is going to be able to bear the tedious obsessionality of his profession.

Yet that's not where the story ends, in solitude. Particularly when they are first beginning to write, some students like to show their work to their friends, and, sometimes, to their family, both as a way of informing them of certain truths, but also in the hope of a helpful reaction. Yet, however much the well-meaning reader might like the work, it doesn't follow that he will have the vocabulary to be able to speak usefully about it, saying something which might help the writer move forwards. Kindness may be comforting, but it isn't always inspiring.

Men and women have always searched for ways to enhance, modify or transform their states of mind, using herbs, nicotine, alcohol and drugs, as well as bolts of electricity through the skull, opium, baths, tonics, books and conversation. (Even 'pearl cordial' – powdered pearl – was popular in the eighteenth century, as a purported cure for depression.) There's no reason why the practice of writing can't help people see what's inside them, as well as helping them organise and deepen their ideas of who they are. Reading does this too, providing a vocabulary of ideas which you might utilise to view your life in a new way. But a writing teacher is not a therapist, listening patiently for the unconscious in a free association or dream telling, and the student would be surprised to learn the teacher saw himself as a healer rather than as an instructor.

When necessary, and it is usually necessary, the teacher has to teach, to pass over information about structure, voice, point of view, contrast, character, or the discipline of writing. But, particularly on those occasions when faced with a mass of work she can't understand, and doesn't know how to begin addressing – particularly horrifying for a teacher who might be under the misapprehension that she must understand, and quickly too – she might use something like a Socratic method. By asking numerous questions, the teacher will give the student her work back in a different form, making it seem both clearer and more puzzling.

Students are often at a loss when you ask them what a particular image or piece of dialogue means, and whether it is doing what they believe it is doing. While it might be productive to write from the unconscious where the world is weirder and less constrained, the work has also to be assessed rationally. Discussing it is part of this.

In a short film he'd made, a film student had stationed two young men on a park bench where he filmed them from behind – the backs of their heads – for some time. When I asked him why the shot was so sustained, he replied that the moment – to me a considerable moment – represented 'death'. He said he wanted the viewer, at this point in the film, to consider their own death. Always up for that, but trying to remain calm, and reminding myself of the nobility of teaching, I said it defeated me how he thought an audience would leap from the picture he presented to this thought. He seemed to see he needed more vivid and accurate images to convey what he wanted to say. It was also helpful for him to be told that he needed to develop a sense of story, rather than slamming scenes together in the hope the audience might notice some connection. If nothing else quite succeeds in a piece of work – humour, for instance, or the fascination of the characters – the story alone might still hold the reader's interest, as it does with soap-operas.

 This student might have also benefited from better authorities, from closer contact with other artists and dead poets, from whom he might learn more imaginative solutions as he strove to carry his internal world into the outside one. It is amazing that students are so rarely taught to see the connection between studying others and their own work. Borrowing a voice, or trying out new ones, isn't the same as acquiring your own, but it's a step in that direction. What you steal becomes yours when it is creatively modified. Since almost anything can usefully feed an artist, a broad humanistic education, a sort of foundation course involving religion, psychology and literature, would be a positive accompaniment to any writing course.

Conversations with a teacher should enable the student to get an idea of what an ordinary reader might make of her work, and how she must bear in mind that, in the end, she is writing for others. Writers are entertainers rather than exhibitionists. These exchanges should also give the student an idea of what she is striving to say.

The clarity a student might gain, along with new ideas, can also be obtained from writers working in groups. While concentrated individual teaching is usually preferable – most advice about writing is too general and is along the lines of 'write about what you know' – the advantage of the group is that each student has the opportunity to hear a range of criticism and suggestion, some of it mad, some invaluable. The students learn from one another.

Another version of this is for the students to work in pairs, reading their work to one another, though this is not easy with longer pieces, and difficult to keep going over the considerable period it might take to complete a sizeable work. What must be recognised is that the reader orients the writer, and the writer should understand he exists only in relation to the one whose attention is being solicited. The reader or spectator must be convinced by the competence of the writer, acknowledging that his work is credible, and that it's safe to believe it. What the writer wants is for the reader to feel as he felt.

When attempting to write there are some mistakes you have to make, mistakes which will yield good ideas, opening up a space for more thoughts. And there are other mistakes it might be worth avoiding, though sometimes it is difficult to tell the two apart. What might make it clear is when the writer gets blocked or stuck. A student of mine wanted to tell a story in the voice of a seven-year-old. As you can imagine, she was finding this inordinately difficult, and it was holding up her progress. (That which you most urgently want to say might not make the best writing.) By trying to inhabit a point of view it was almost impossible for her to see from, she was getting little work done and becoming discouraged. Good advice would have been for her either to see if she could get hold of the story from another position, or work on something else for a time, before returning to the idea.

She might then have to learn how to wait for the occurrence of a better idea. And this question of waiting, for a writer, is an important one. A good idea might suggest itself suddenly, but its working out or testing will take the time it needs. It might appear to acquaintances of the author that he's doing little but lying on the sofa staring into the distance, or going on long walks. (Clearly, Charles Dickens was writing when he was walking.) This might be when good ideas turn up – a book is a thousand inspirations rather than one big one – and the guilt of fertile indolence has to be borne.

Writing and life are not separate, though they can be separated, and, on the whole, it is the teacher's job to consider the writing as an independent entity. Often, though, a student will use writing to think about his life, so that what the student is showing the teacher is a problem.

A woman decides to write about her mother but finds herself overwhelmed with grief and heartache. She pushes on, but stops, terrified of what she might want to say. Eventually she must decide whether or not to drop this painful but essential subject. Perhaps she'd prefer to write something else. Or she might need to discover whether she can endure the difficulty of confronting the matter. And it might also occur to her: is writing a way of calming terror, or of creating it? We can see here that the writer *is* the material; the poem is the person. They are the same thing.

Following on from this, an anxiety in the writer will be a fear of what his words will do to others, and what others might do to him in return if he says what he thinks, even in fictional form. As there are certain ideas which are discouraged or forbidden in families, and indeed in all institutions, most adults – even if only unconsciously – are afraid of expressing their own ideas about what is going on. They fear they will be accused of betrayal and then punished – both of which are possible. They will have to wonder whether they are prepared to put up with this. A certain personal truth might, however, be what the writer most wants to reveal, thus creating an intolerable conflict which might lead to a block.

If a student can only write miserable monologues at the end of which the speaker kills himself, you might wonder, not only about the student's state of mind, but also about why there aren't any other characters in the piece, about the voices which aren't being heard. Obviously this student – who had been through the psychiatric system where he wasn't much listened to – was showing me something I had to take seriously and think hard about. It was worrying, and not easy for me to see how to proceed here.

Eventually I persuaded the student to bring in other characters to make more of a conversation of it. To his credit, after a few weeks, he was able to do this, though the suicides continued. I learned that when the unsayable was about to be broached at last, suicide was seen as the convenient way out. It was like a version of writer's block. But once his characters began to have exchanges – and the student saw the point of debating with himself, of opening up his own head – his work developed. The scenes got longer and the people spoke. His work became more available to others.

For a while at least, a measure of madness appeared to have been transferred from the writer to his characters. They were iller than he was. Certainly it's not the most healthy who are the most creative. As Proust reminded us, 'Everything great in the world comes from neurotics. We enjoy a thousand intellectual delicacies, but we have no idea of their cost, to those who invented them, in sleepless nights, tears, spasmodic laughter, rashes, asthmas, epilepsies, and the fear of death, which is worse than all the rest.'

It was my student's excitement and determination in his work which reassured me. Our meetings were a helpful structure. I think without a teacher to accompany him through this, he could have twisted in painful circles and become more isolated. As it was, his work was among the most imaginative and strange I've read, far removed from the dull realism and conventionality which most students think passes for imaginative work.

Some students have considerable fantasies about becoming a writer, of what they think being a writer will do for them. This quickens their desire, and helps them to get started. But when the student begins to get an idea of how difficult it is to complete a considerable piece of work – to write fifteen thousand good words, while becoming aware of the more or less impossibility of making significant money from writing – she will experience a dip, or 'crash' and become discouraged and feel helpless. The loss of a fantasy can be painful, but if the student can get through it – if the teacher can show the student that there's something good in her work and help her endure the frustration of learning to do something difficult – the student will make better progress.

In the end, the writer mostly teaches himself and will always want to develop, finding new forms for his interests. If he's lucky, along with learning to allow his imagination free rein, he'll mostly edit and evaluate his own work himself. Of course it doesn't follow that he'll never need anyone else. He might prefer to ignore others, but he will need to listen to them first, as he continues to speak.

The Rising Line

First published in *Zembla* magazine, 2004

A student came to me last week with a short film she'd made and we watched it several times on DVD, in my front room. I made suggestions and she said she'd go away and re-cut it. What I wanted her to do was get to the story quicker, to what I called the 'good bits', and she was rather bewildered by this, particularly when I said things like 'can't you put all the good bits together and hand it in?' She liked the other, slower, parts because she felt that to put the good bits in a sequence would make everything, as she put it, 'too sudden'. I knew what she meant and couldn't help but agree that the 'proportions' had to be right.

Under my sofa there are two novels written by former students, which I feel compelled to read. The first is about a girl whose father dies and her mother joins the Orange people, taking along the teenage daughter. There are, as you can imagine, some excellent sex scenes, full of hairy New Agers and embarrassment and sadness. The other novel is about a young man who joins a writers' group, not unlike the one I ran at the Royal Court at the end of the 80s, and that book is full of anxiety and competitiveness. If the writer does what I say it could turn out to be a decent comedy.

I wonder what I am supposed to give to these students, whether I can be any use. I could be a good parent, encouraging them to try new things, and I could be their first audience, telling them what I feel as I experience their work. I take this 'teaching' seriously, because they listen to me seriously and I'd feel guilty if I couldn't give them anything useful. Do they have anything in common, these three? It could be that the story they are telling isn't in focus, that there aren't enough 'good bits' in the right place.

Who am I to talk? I've just written a film which I've shown to friends. They think it's eccentric, weird and probably unfilmable. Also, I have hundreds of pages of a novel, (what Spalding Gray called 'The Monster In The Box', before he threw himself into the Hudson), which I am sure I will never be able to organise into a coherent whole.

On the floor of my study I keep finding words written on squares of paper. I bend over, pick up a bit of paper and it says 'horse' or 'scorch' or 'make' on it. My six-year-old and I have been making a 'wordbag'. If we find a likely-sounding word in the newspaper, in a book, or even said in the street, we write it down, cut it out, and stick it in a Christmas stocking. When we want to make a poem we haul out words at random and put them together, to see what happens.

I seem to remember William Burroughs doing something like this, which may be why his novels are memorable but unreadable. Others took this up in the 60s. When David Bowie was working on the music for the TV version of my novel *The Buddha of Suburbia*, and we needed a song, he asked me to bring in fifty words from the first half of the book. 'On one page,' he said. So I wrote down a load of words and was amazed when he made them into a good song which was played on *Top of the Pops*.

Faber have just published *On Film-making*, the writings of Alexander Mackendrick, who directed *The Man in the White Suit*. When he could no longer get his films made, Mackendrick became a film teacher in California and these notes are the book. One chapter is headed 'Exercises for the Student of Dramatic Construction' which I will read one day, because I know it will help me. There are ideas about how to make plots and create what he calls 'the rising line'. Mackendrick keeps the process alive by suggesting new, lateral, ways to proceed, as though he knows that at the slightest discouragement the artist will collapse and retreat to the pub.

Of course there are few things more temporarily satisfying than finding a rule or formula which one could follow forever, without the struggle or conflicts which characterise the creative enterprise. When I was researching *The Black Album* and *My Son the Fanatic* among young Muslims I envied the fact that, for them, there were no unanswerable questions. What could they have to worry about?

Of course it is common to suggest that writing cannot be taught. Despite this, there are now more books about writing than there are about learning to play the piano; some bookshops have whole sections devoted to 'creative writing'. Mackendrick's collection, full of excellent notions and exercises, is far better than most of the 'How to Write' books on the market these days. I've read a lot of them, which passes the time when one is supposed to be writing.

It's easy to sneer. You can't, however, forget that the foundation of Freudian therapy – the basic rule: free association, saying whatever nonsense comes into your head – was adapted by Freud from a self-help manual he read as a teenager, Ludwig Borne's 'The Art of Becoming an Original Writer in Three Days'. Borne suggested free association – on paper – as a method of evading internal censorship or what Freud would later call the 'superego'. It worked for Freud: he did become an 'original' writer by lifting this method, which is used in therapy everywhere today. Mackendrick's book is a variant of this.

So-called free assocation goes on all the time, but there are more unusual ways of doing it. Now I have an image: my three sons, all conventionally resistant to the written word, are on their knees on the floor, sticking their filthy fists into a bag, pulling words out, and making them into poems. At one point a fight breaks out: they all want the same word, which is ripped to shreds. Eventually something almost literary gets done. Here's one result:

Poem Five by Kier [aged 6]

Tomatoes gazed on
women flowers
books sound madly knowing
but tonight apples are
going
to
children.

Loose Tongues

Given as a lecture at Hay Festival, 2003

That exemplary dissident Oscar Wilde, whose punishment failed to erase his words but taught us something about where a loose tongue might get you, wrote, at the end of the nineteenth century, 'When people talk to us about others they are usually dull. When they talk to us about themselves they are nearly always interesting.'

This essay concerns something we are and take for granted: the fact we are speaking animals, full of words which have a profound effect on others, words that are sometimes welcomed, and sometimes not. I want to say something about words which seem possible and others that seem impossible.

It is no coincidence that the political and social systems which have dominated our era – communism, global capitalism, fascism, imperialism, the nuclear family, different varieties of fundamentalist religion, to name but a few – are marked by a notable factor. There are circumstances in which they don't want people talking about their lives. Tyrants are involved with silence as a form of control. Who says what to whom, and about what, is of compelling interest to authorities, to dictators, fathers, teachers, and officials of whichever type.

As Milan Kundera pointed out in his great novel *The Joke*, there are times when the need to be funny is so subversive that it can land you in jail. Isaac Babel, who was murdered in prison, and called a book 'the world seen through an individual', was himself not unaware of the ironies here, and said, 'Whenever an educated person is arrested in the Soviet Union and finds himself in a prison cell, he is given a pencil and paper and told "write!"'

338

What his interrogators wanted were words. But of course the meaning of 'corrupt' is to falsify, adulterate, or debase, in this case the language – that which links us to others.

In his short fiction 'In The Penal Colony', Kafka describes an ingenious machine for torturing to death a man condemned for disobedience. The device is equipped with ink-jets which inscribe the name of the crime on the victim's body, even as he bleeds to death. ' "This condemned man, for instance," – the officer indicated the man – "will have written on his body: Honour thy superiors." '

The whole process of writing as killing takes twelve hours. This calligraphy of colonialism might be called 'being killed by description', as the body is ripped to shreds by those who hold the pen. There is no question here of the victim having his own pen; he doesn't speak. His version of events, his story, will not be considered. Even his own body carries the inscription of the other.

Collective or shared stories, linked by implicit agreement about how the future should be, or about the sort of people who are preferred – heroes, leaders and the morally good on one side, devils, villains, the ignored and the bad on the other – can also be called ideologies, traditions, beliefs, ways of life or forms of power. After they've been told for a while, stories can turn into politics, into our institutions, and it is important that they seem to be just the way things are, and the way they have to go on being. It is always illuminating to think of those groups and individuals who are denied the privilege of speaking and of being listened to, whether they be immigrants, asylum seekers, women, the mad, children, the elderly, or workers in the Third World.

It is where the words end, or can't go, that abuse takes place, whether it's racial harassment, bullying, neglect, or sexual violence. Silence, then, like darkness, carries something important about who the authorities want others to be, something important about the nature of authority itself, and the way it wants to dehumanise others in the silence.

Of course different systems use different methods to ensure silence. From the cutting off of tongues to the burning of books, or the use of sexual morality as well as covert prohibition – like ignoring people, for instance – all are different ways of ensuring a dictatorship of voices, or of maintaining the single voice. If one person tells another who they really are, while denying them the right to self-description, certain kinds of self-doubt or inner disintegration will follow. People can be formed and also deranged by the stories others tell about them. When Jean Genet was told he was a thief, it was an idea it took him most of his life to escape.

The necessity of a certain interpretation of reality and the imperative that this idea be maintained couldn't be clearer than in families. Children are soon made aware of the force of a particular description, and of its authority. While most parents are aware that children develop when they are listened to, they don't always want to hear them.

On their side, of course, children are fascinated by language, especially when they discover that there are words which make the adults crazy or frightened, which make the adults want to slap them, or shut them up. Children can become compelled by any discourse which provokes terror in adults. Therefore children learn about the language community by discovering what cannot or should not be said. They learn about prohibition and limits, about punishment, about hiding and secrets, and about privacy. When they discover what cannot be said, they have to learn to lie or conceal their words, often from themselves. If they are lucky they become creative and use metaphor. If they are unlucky they go mad.

Depression, for instance, might be called a kind of slowness. It could be seen as a subversive refusal to move at the speed of the others, as the rejection of a banal, alienating consumerist world in favour of an authentic inner puzzlement. But, more commonly, without such an idealisation, it is a slowness which usually takes place in silence, beyond or outside language and symbolisation. The depressed, therefore, do not believe in language as the carrier of meaning. The dead cannot make friends. The depressed person, self-silenced you might say, feels far removed from the source of her words, which may well multiply on their own, and can seem to circulate wildly and without meaning, like birds trapped in an empty room.

The deliberately silent are at least making a point – to themselves – when they suppress or break up their own stories. The involuntarily silent, on the other hand, might feel as though they've had their words fruitlessly stolen from them. But this enforced silence on behalf of the powerful is not for nothing. The mythologising of those not heard is the opportunity for difficult and busy work. The silent other has to be called, for instance, a stranger, foreigner, immigrant or asylum seeker. She might be an exile, an interloper, the one who does not fit or belong, the one who is not at home, the one whose words do not count.

This range of denotions at least makes it clear that we can never stop wondering about our own alien, awkward or foreign parts, the elements which cannot speak except through the use of others. Racism might at least teach us that we are always strange – or other, or unwelcome – to ourselves, particularly when it comes to our need. We might even be aware that there is an odd but intriguing silent reversal here. The sort of capitalism we have has always depended on colonialism, and has always required both labour in the Third World and labour from the Third World – the immigrant, in other words. And yet our own need has only ever been represented in terms of their need, as their dependence on us. This is frequently manifested as an image of desperate people climbing over barbed-wire fences, eager to come over here and strip us of all we have.

The subject chosen to be strange has an important place. He or she has to be kept constantly in mind; worked over and worked on. It is a passion, this attitude to the threatening foreigner, the outsider, the one who doesn't know our language. Someone has to be kept in their place in order that the other can exist in a particular relation to them, so that hatred can flourish. I call this a passion rather than an opinion because these fictions have to be constantly reiterated. They cannot be stated once and for all, since the victim seems always about to escape his description. Unless he's constantly buried and re-buried beneath a deluge of words, and, of course, the actions which words entail, he might turn into someone like us.

If a plausible version of the twentieth century can be told in terms of silence and its uses, there is reason for optimism too. That period was also about people insisting on their own words and histories, speaking for themselves. The 1970s, as I recall, were about the formerly colonised, gays, women, the mad, children, putting their side of the story, telling it in their own words and being heard. As a result, in some places, there were significant social advances. It has been said that when Pinochet was arrested in Britain, things changed in Chile. The dictator wasn't sacrosanct; people began to speak, his mystique was penetrated at last.

Clearly, though, this description is simplified; there is an absence here. I have implied that on one side the words are there, ready and waiting to go, while on the other they are unwelcome or prohibited, that the only problem with the words is that the authorities don't want to hear them.

However, at the centre of this is something else: the person who doesn't want to hear their own words. This is the person who owns them, who has made them inside his own body, but who both does, and does not, have access to them, who is prisoner, prison and the law. Real dictators in the world are a picture, too, of dictators within individuals, of certain kinds of minds.

If we wanted to create an authoritarian system which was complete, in which there were no loose tongues – or, within an individual, no significant inner life – it would have to be one in which dreams were controlled. Even in prison, under the strictest supervision and observation, a human being can at least dream. Here he might, at least, represent, or symbolise that which cannot, or must not, be said. But how would these dreams be understood? Who would be there to receive the scrambled communications which might be his only hope?

342

In 1906 an English surgeon, talking to Ernest Jones, mentioned, with some astonishment, a strange doctor in Vienna 'who actually listened with attention to every word his patients said to him'.

What Freud realised was that because there are forms of speaking which are radically dangerous and unsettling, which change lives and societies, people don't want to know what those words are. But, he adds, in another sense they do really want to know, because they are made to be aware, by suffering, of a lack; they at least know that they will not be complete without certain forms of self-knowledge, and that this will be liberating, even though the consequences of any liberation could also be catastrophic.

Human beings leak the truth of their desire whether they like it or not: in their dreams, fantasies and drunkenness, in their jokes and mistakes, as well as in delirium, religious ecstasy, in babble and in saying the opposite of what they mean. It takes a rationalist, then, to see that rationalism can only fail, that what we need is more, not less, madness in our speaking. Otherwise our bodies take up the cause on our behalf, and bodies can speak in weird ways, through hysteria, for instance in Freud's day, the modern equivalent of which might be addiction, anorexia, racism or various phobias.

Freud invented a new method of speaking, which involved two people going into a room together. One person would speak and the other would listen, trying to see, in the gaps, resistances and repetitions, what else, in the guise of the obvious, was being said. He would then give these words, translated into other words, back to the speaker.

Great individualists though they might be, both Wilde and Socrates, like Freud, used dialogue as their preferred form. Indeed, in another essay, Wilde replaces the Socratic imperative 'know yourself' with 'be yourself', which might become, in this version of 'being' – that of the language community – 'speak yourself'. The therapeutic couple is one method of seeing who you are by speaking, and it is an original and great invention. But there would be something odd, to say the least, about a society in which everyone was in therapy. Not that there isn't something already odd in the idea that only the wealthy can buy mental health.

Fortunately there has always been another place where the speaking of the darkest and most dangerous things has always gone on, which we might call a form of lay therapy. We know that this mode of speaking is useful because of the amount of prohibition it has incurred. It is sometimes called conversation, or the theatre, or poetry, or dance, the novel, or pop.

What is called creativity or culture might remind us of Freud's method because many artists have talked about the way in which words have the knack of speaking themselves. The writer is only there to catch them, organise them, write them down. Even the prophet Mohammed, around whose name silence is often required, was visited by an angel who gave him the law. Mohammed didn't make up these rules himself; they were spoken through him but came from elsewhere. Another instance of the death of the author, or the author at one side to himself, as secretary or midwife to himself, you might say, making a divine Law that no human can modify or speak back to.

A culture is a midwife to images and symbolisations, a place where people speak to one another, where words matter and, because they are in the public domain, can be understood or used in a number of ways. It is also where one is forbidden to speak about certain things. It has, therefore, to be a place where the question of speaking and punishment is spoken about. The collective can have a conversation because artists like to loiter near the heat of the law, where the action is. If artists are considered to be on the edge, they are on the edge of the rules, close to punishment, and, like Beckett, not far from silence, where speaking has to be almost impossible if it is to be of value.

What Freud added, and the surrealists knew, along with the other artists who have formed our consciousness, Buñuel, Bergman, Joyce, Picasso, Woolf, Stravinsky, Pinter, was that if the unconscious was to be represented, there had to be new forms for it.

These artists knew that conventional talk, and the conventional art which accompanied it, had been turned into chatter. They knew that this worked as a block or filter to forms of knowledge which were essential if we were not to be silent, or if we were not to racially persecute, and kill one another, for reasons we couldn't understand. Therefore, if modern art and much of what has followed it has been the attempt to say the unsayable, some of these forms can only be ugly and disturbing. These forms have to be banned, dismissed and discouraged, partly because, like most forms of fantasy, they are subject to shame, itself a form of censorship.

To speak at all is to be aware of censorship. The first thing tyro writers come up against, when they uncap their pen, is a block – in the form of a prohibition. They may well find their mother's face floating into view, along with several good reasons why not continuing is a good idea. Freud, a prodigious writer himself, put it like this, 'As soon as writing, which entails making a liquid flow out of a tube onto a piece of white paper, assumes the significance of copulation, it will be stopped.'

This, you might say, is the imprimatur of good speaking – that there is a resistance which guarantees the quality of the utterance. There are, then, at least two voices called up here, the voice which needs to speak and the voice, or several voices, which refuse, which say these words are so exciting and forbidden that they are worthless. This is what makes any attempt at creativity a useful struggle. What makes it worthwhile is the difficulty, the possibility of a block.

Twentieth-century art has been fascinated by dreams and nightmares, by violence and sexuality, so much so that it might be termed an art of terrible fantasy. One begins to see splits, deep conflicts, terrors, hatreds and a lot of death in these art nightmares. These elements can be put together – somehow fused in a work of art – but they are not always reconcilable. However, irreconcilable parts may find a voice in some form of personal expression, which, partly, is why modern art has been so painful and difficult to look at, even now, and why any new art, to be of value, has to shock us. This is because it breaks a silence we didn't even know we were observing.

At least art brings us beauty as compensation for its message. But it is not, in the end, the favour it might be, because it can be an awful beauty, just as to tell the truth about sexuality might not be to talk about how good or hygienic it is for us, but to speak about how bad or painful it is for us.

Speaking, listening, being known and knowing others. We might say that at least, if everyone doesn't get much of a turn, we live in a representative democracy. This, at least, separates us from various fundamentalisms. We can vote; we believe we have politicians who can speak for us. Yet one of the reasons we despise politicians is that we suspect they are speaking on their own behalf while purporting to speak on ours. Our words, being handed on by our representatives, are not getting through and they never will. Our speaking makes not a jot of difference. One way of looking at globalisation, for instance, is to say that it is a version of certain Orwellian authorities saying the same thing, over and over, the attempt being to keep new words, or any human doubt, need or creativity, out of the system.

Surely, then, if politicians cannot possibly do the trick, artists might do it. Speaking from themselves and sensibly refusing to do advertising, they do nonetheless speak for some of us, and they take the punishment on our behalf too. In the absence of other convincing figures, like priests or leaders, it is tempting to idealise artists and the culture they make.

Nevertheless, in the end, there is no substitute for the value of one's own words, of one's story, and the form one has found for it. Sartre, in his autobiography *Words*, says, 'When I began writing, I began my birth over again.' There is something about one's sentences being one's own, however impoverished and inadequate they might feel, which is significant, which makes them redemptive. If you wanted to tell someone you loved them you usually wouldn't get someone else to do it for you.

If there is to be a profusion, or multiculturalism, of voices, particularly from the margins of expression, then the possibility of dispute and disagreement is increased. The virtue and risk of real multiculturalism is that we could find that our values are, ultimately, irreconcilable with those of others. From that point of view everything gets worse. There is more internal and social noise and confusion, and more questions about how things get decided, and by whom. If the idea of truth itself is questioned, the nature of the law itself is altered. It can seem conditional, for instance, pragmatic rather than divine, or at least subject to human modification or intervention, if not control.

There are always good reasons not to speak, to bite our own tongues, as many dissidents, artists and children will testify. It will offend, it is dangerous, hurtful, frightening, morally bad, others will suffer or they will not hear.

But the good thing about words, sentences and stories is that their final effect is incalculable. Unlike violence, for instance, which is an unmistakable message, talking is a free form, a kind of experiment. It is not a description of an inner state, but an act, a kind of performance. It is an actor improvising – which is dangerous and unpredictable – rather than one saying lines which have already been scripted. 'The thought is in the mouth,' as Tristan Tzara put it. It is not that we require better answers but that we need better questions. All speaking is a demand, at first for a reply, proving the existence of communication, but, ultimately, for an answer, for more words, for love, in other words.

You can never know what your words might turn out to mean for yourself or for someone else; or what the world they make will be like. Anything could happen. The problem with silence is that we know exactly what it will be like.

Telling Stories

Given as a lecture at La Villa Gillet, Lyon, 2009

From a certain point of view it's almost irrelevant who the protagonist of a novel is. What one wants as a writer when planning a piece of fiction is to find a position from which one can see. So what a novel does, for the writer, is to bring together the numerous notions that have been cooking in his unconscious for the previous weeks, months or even years. A book then will be a kind of imaginative diary, an account of what the writer wasn't quite aware of but would come to know as he proceeds.

When I wrote *Something to Tell You*, I chose to make the protagonist a psychoanalyst because writers and Freudians, though they may have presented themselves as rivals, were, during the twentieth century at least, interested in the same thing.

Modernism in literature and the discoverers of psychoanalysis were looking in similar places. So the three most significant works of the early twentieth century – which are Freud's *The Interpretation of Dreams*, Proust's *Remembrance of Things Past*, and Joyce's *Ulysses* – are all concerned with sleep, dreams, childhood, sexuality and jokes. They are, in other words, fascinated by all of that which cannot be apprehended and examined by consciousness. The mystery of the human subject, and its elusiveness, are common to both psychoanalysis and literature.

You might also say that the difference between psychoanalysis and literature is of course that psychoanalysis is therapy, that there is some notion of human good and the undoing of certain fixed ways of seeing the world behind the careful listening. But at the same time Freud would have considered it to be a very strange thing indeed if most of the population had decided to take to the

348

Freudian couch. The place where another, more extensive form of therapy takes place is in the culture. This is embedded in drama (Freud was fascinated by Sophocles, Shakespeare and Ibsen), in prose literature, and of course in conversation.

One of the reasons I may have selected an analyst as a protagonist is because for me analysis is an enviable profession. As I get older writing seems to me to be perhaps too solitary, and I require more the presence of others. So how can I not envy those who have the opportunity to listen to others all day? I think it is that curiosity that writers and analysts have in common. And of course Freud and writing always proceeded side by side: Freud won the Goethe prize for literature.

In the post-war period there has been a separation of psychology from psychiatry. The psychiatrist medicalises and therefore objectifies the human body, which no longer speaks as it did from the Freudian point of view in hysteria and in psychosis, but has become in the psychiatric idiom something like a malfunctioning machine.

To remain interested in psychoanalysis is an attempt to try and remember that primarily we are speaking beings and it's not only in our words that we speak. There's the great danger that much of the huge research done in psychoanalysis in the twentieth century may be forgotten or even buried, and the fact that writers today are taking analysts or their patients as subjects for fiction is a tribute to the desire to keep the human mind in the forefront of humanistic investigation, particularly when practices such as CBT, the spread of psychopharmacology and talk of brains and chemistry, may lead us away from the human being.

It is been said that Freud, his followers and their work are old-fashioned and have been superseded by other more successful and effective and more rapid practices. But there is something still startling in Freud's invention. The idea of two people sitting in a room with one another day after day, week after week, for as long as it takes for some clarity and understanding to emerge is an extraordinary innovation in psychology, because it places human discourse at the centre of understanding the human crisis. It is therefore not a matter of seeing what is ill or even wrong with the subject, but seeing what the person has made of his or her own history, or what they have turned it into as a matter of psychic necessity. It is a deeply humanistic insight that this necessity may be modified by conversation. And it is conversation, in the subject, in the culture and in colloquia like this, which is deeply important.

Introduction to *The Collected Stories of John Cheever*

First published by Vintage Classics, 2009

If you read John Cheever's *The Journals* alongside these stories, getting a sense of the man and what he made at the same time, you will be presented with a dark unease. *The Journals* themselves are one of the great confessional works, and I would rate them with Rousseau and Pepys as exemplifying the inner combat of a complex man never content with himself or others. As Cheever puts it, 'I've been homesick for countries I've never seen, and longed to be where I couldn't be.'

The Cheever of *The Journals* appears to be a thin-skinned loner who loved both men and women. This confused him and at times made him crazy to be with, since it was conventional, when he was a young man, to make a choice. But for a writer such a broad range of sympathy could only be an advantage.

Cheever wrote about the most important things. You might think, turning to the stories, that you would be hard pressed to learn much about a wider America, of black and Hispanic lives, of post-slavery trauma, inequality, political struggle, or poverty. But you do learn about the shabby hard lives of elevator operators, of janitors and the respectable poor.

In *The Journals* Cheever called his work 'confined' and worried about his limitations. And yet, far from being an elitist WASP with little knowledge of life outside of the evergreen and affluent suburbs, a wasteland of Saturday night parties and post-martini despair, where all the men are commuters and the women feel they have wasted their lives – not unlike the swimming-pool world satirised later by Charles Webb in *The Graduate* – Cheever's writing is right at the centre of things. His subjects are not freaks, losers or marginals, but children, work and the central idea of Western literature, what Cheever calls 'the bitter mystery of marriage', and the way marriage can make passion seem improbable, if not impossible. And while he is fascinated by what he sometimes describes as 'carnal anarchy', he is wise enough to know that it is status, self-respect and work, rather than sexual passion, which drives us: we live money, while dreaming of a complete love.

I guess you might want to characterise these stories as Chekhovian, if only because of Cheever's facility for capturing significant moments in ordinary lives with humorous compassion and without condescension, and because of Cheever's ability to write a breathtaking last elegiac paragraph which both encompasses and transcends the story, as though the whole thing at last is thrown in the air in a kind of bacchanalic celebration. You might also want to say that Cheever is less bleak than Carver, and more capacious, ironic and jaunty than Hemingway. But in the end he is always entirely himself, with every sentence weighed and balanced until it says the right thing and often more, rising until it unites the daily train with the wider political railway.

Cheever speaks of a society in which people are 'united in their tacit claims that there had been no past, no war – that there was no danger or trouble in the world'. How vast and important America was at that time, with his characters sharing a general American post-war hope for prosperity and peace while all the time undermined by the fear that it is all too new, and can be taken back. And with regard to the political scene, it is almost impossible to read these stories without some knowledge of what was to follow, that these shallow, narrow lives would be shattered by 'the 60s' – that uprush of excitement, cussedness and rebellion which changed everything. He makes us see it coming: his innerly divided people wish for ease and security, but they want love and unrepression too; they are engaged by desire of a very pressing kind, which breaks up most attempts at contentment and leads often to disaster.

You would, therefore, expect to find only ordinariness and the cleanest dull rectitude in the suburbs; that, presumably, is why people choose to live there. But on closer examination there are extraordinary human passions and weaknesses, an awful restlessness. At its most moderate this is sensible. 'In order to see anything – a leaf or a blade of grass – you have, I think, to know the keenness of love.'

But when was loving anyone simple? There are, as Bascomb the wise poet in 'The World of Apples' confirms, occasions when 'obscenity – gross obscenity – seemed to be the only factor in life that possessed colour and cheer.'

Further along then, desire becomes a destructive passion, a perversion even, which cannot be satiated. This is shown in 'The Country Husband', one of Cheever's best stories, and one of the finest ever written, where a man who narrowly escapes disaster in a plunging aeroplane returns home to find his wife and children not only indifferent to his narrow escape but perhaps to his entire being. Madly, he seeks solace with his young babysitter. As a result he goes to a psychiatrist, which was what many Americans did in the 1950s, where, after memorably saying to the doctor, 'I'm in love, Dr Herzog,' he finds more disappointment and a recommendation to take up woodwork. Where, then, might a suffering person turn, if not to the bottle?

The complexity of Cheever's own character – and what today would be described as a 'struggle with alcohol and sexuality' – enabled him to see that a good deal of his characters' misfortunes are due to their weakness and their history rather than to social forces or the malevolence of others. The eternal puzzle of why people do that which is not in their interest, and have a desire to lose what is most precious to them, makes Cheever fascinated by the deepest destructions.

Sometimes this is comic, with a gay man putting his head in an oven three times, only to be rescued by an annoyed homophobic janitor. But 'Reunion', a fine story only a couple of pages long, concerns a father who can only repeatedly sabotage a meeting with his estranged son, leaving both lacking the thing they most want, some connection and authentic exchange.

John Cheever was born in 1912 in Massachusetts. After serving in the army, he became a full-time writer in the early 1950s. In 1948 he wrote, 'We are as poor as we ever have been. I can write a story a week, perhaps more.' He succeeded, writing novels and stories until his death in 1982. He lived in Rome and wrote many brilliant stories set in Italy. Working in the commercial world, mostly for the *New Yorker*, Cheever managed to support his family with his writing. As half-artist, half-entertainer, his work is not only in the top range with that of Maupassant and Flannery O'Connor and the other great Americans, it is not conventional but experimental in the most interesting sense. In *The Journals* there is very little about his actual process of writing. Cheever is reluctant to talk to himself about what he is doing when he isn't doing it. Nor is he compelled to: this was before authors went on lengthy book tours, gave huge numbers of readings followed by signings, and were interviewed until their own voice horrified them. But he does give us something significant, once more in the *Paris Review*: 'Fiction *is* experimentation; when it ceases to be that, it ceases to be fiction. One never puts down a sentence without the feeling that it has never been put down before in such a way.'

The chief problem for the story writer however, particularly when it comes to a collection, is of variety, especially if the reader wants to consume the stories in one go; it could be like gobbling too many oysters, rather than taking them one by one at intervals, the ideal way. But there is immense range and variety here: this is a life's work, and it was a life of curiosity and renewal.

Oddly, Cheever never created a character as talented, intelligent or cultured as himself; these are all smaller people than he seemed to be, but they are scraps of him. The creation of character, the novelist's main work, wasn't his primary concern, but the putting together of it all at once. As he said, 'I don't work with plots. I work with intuition, apprehension, dreams, concepts. Plot implies narrative and a lot of crap.'

His ability to see and describe is startling: an 'unclothed woman of exceptional beauty, combing her golden hair' in the sleeping car of a passing train; a neighbour playing the 'Moonlight Sonata': 'He threw the tempo out of the window and played rubato from beginning to end, like an outpouring of tearful petulance, lonesomeness, and self-pity – of everything it was Beethoven's greatness not to know.'

To have written many stories that others can read with pleasure fifty years later, sentences which are intelligent and resonant, poetic and ineffable, is no waste of a life, and to read them, over and over, is to live better, and to allow the respect and admiration Cheever deserves.

Introduction to *The Graduate*
by Charles Webb

First published by Penguin, 2010

If the straightest places are where the weirdest things happen, then the American suburbs in the post-war period have good reason to fascinate American artists. From Cheever, Updike, Roth and Yates, to David Lynch and Mendes's *American Beauty*, the American ideal has also embodied the American nightmare. As John Cheever put it, 'Why, in this most prosperous, equitable and accomplished world, should everyone seem so disappointed?'

There are few characters in post-war fiction as disappointed as Benjamin. A brilliant and successful student with 'everything', as they say, ahead of him, one day in the early 1960s he returns home from college to find that nothing has meaning for him; he no longer wants what he is supposed to want. Who, in those changing times, should he become when his only desire is to flounder in his father's swimming pool on a rubber ring? But Benjamin is not entirely good for nothing. It is his good luck that someone does sense his dissatisfaction, and does want him. This is the wife of his father's business partner, the fabulous Mrs Robinson, who has been observing him closely.

The son of a doctor, Charles Webb was born in San Francisco in 1939 and was brought up in affluent Pasadena. At the age of twenty-four he wrote and published *The Graduate*, which received mostly indifferent reviews. It was picked by up Mike Nicholls in 1967 and made into a film which took £100 million at the box-office, though Webb had sold the rights for £20,000. Since then he has published seven more novels, some featuring characters from *The Graduate*.

There were many young disillusioned heroes being studied in the early 60s, Meursault in Camus's *The Outsider*, McMurphy in

One Flew Over The Cuckoo's Nest and Holden Caulfield in *Catcher in the Rye*. Like them, Benjamin is not a revolutionary; he doesn't want to make a new, more free or equitable society. That was to come: in the mid-1960s the American scene would brighten wonderfully before it darkened again. No, Benjamin merely wants to inform those around him that he hates the world they have made; it bores him, is stupid, and he cannot find a place in it. Like Melville's Bartleby, he would just 'prefer not to'.

This semi-teenage rite of passage baffles Benjamin as much as it baffles his parents. We see and hear this incomprehension in his very language, which is dull and inexpressive, as if he doesn't really inhabit the words he uses; like everything else around him, language appears to not quite belong to him and there isn't much he can make of it. Most of his speech consists of questions, few of which are answered, or even answerable.

But the triumph of the book, as of the film, is Mrs Robinson. If one essential quality of a good writer is the ability to make memorable characters which appear to transcend the work they appear in, then Mrs Robinson is one of the great monstrous creations of our time. Well-off, middle-aged, alcoholic, bitter, disillusioned, perverse, self-composed and yet to be rescued by feminism, Mrs Robinson's position is far worse than Benjamin's.

Nonetheless, she is the book's only potent character, a smooth, confident seductress, using Benjamin for sex while he is her more or less passive object. That, presumably, is how she likes them. Mrs Robinson, we know, will never consider her lover to be her equal. For her Benjamin is only of use if he is 'just a kid', and she always addresses him – with enraging superiority – in the firm terms of a mother to a child. 'That's enough,' she says to him relevantly and often, suppressing his curiosity with her constant scolding.

The couple may be able to make love, but as Benjamin points out, they cannot speak to one another. Their attempts at conversation are comically awkward and stilted, as if they are virgins at dialogue. Yet there is some progress even here, as he continues to question her. Having inducted him into the secrets of sex, she does eventually let him into a more complex and painful secret, the truth about marriage as habit, safety, and passionless comfort. She neither hates nor loves her husband, and that seems to be all there is to it. Once more numbness is preferable to unhappiness, frustration or worse, the madness of fury. This sentimental education by an older, experienced woman is, in the end, a pedagogy of disillusionment and failure.

When Benjamin decides he wants to break away from Mrs Robinson to begin the relationship with her daughter Elaine which the two families want so much – it is almost an arranged marriage – things turn nasty. The mother may not have much use for Benjamin herself, but she cannot let her daughter have him. Cleverly, she never lets him know why, thus banishing Benjamin into a whirlpool of self-doubt and bewilderment. Mrs Robinson would be happy to destroy Benjamin, and soon becomes a vengeful maternal succubus, the cold strict prohibitive mother who punishes for no reason apart from her own pleasure. Later she accuses Benjamin of raping her when it was, in a sense, the other way round. If the American male is on the road, it may be the mother he is escaping.

Benjamin's father finally intervenes, as he has to, and his solution is to threaten to pass Benjamin on to someone else: a psychiatrist. In the absence of other authorities, it is the white-coated contemporary expert, the psychiatrist, who is appealed to. Already invested with considerable power, the mind doctor might be 'the one who knows'. Certainly the father doesn't know what to do; the mother doesn't; Mrs Robinson doesn't, and the boy admits that he is lost.

A visit to the psychiatrist is the fate of other young dissidents of that period, of Holden Caulfield in *The Catcher in the Rye*, who tells his story to a therapist, likewise poor Portnoy with Dr Spielvogel, who famously says at the end of the book, 'Now vee may perhaps to begin. Yes?' Presumably the doctor will be able to straighten these boys out, rendering them normal by removing unnecessary eccentricities and individuality, an ideal of psychiatry which terrified Freud and is exemplified by *A Clockwork Orange.*

In the end Benjamin does act, doing both a conventional and rebellious thing by running away with Elaine, the one person forbidden him by Mrs Robinson. He has decided to become a teacher, thus fulfilling his family's wishes, though he takes the long way round, making into a choice that which was originally the will of others.

Charles Webb's *The Graduate* has long been eclipsed by the film, but in its deadpan quiet stylishness it is easily its equal, being that most rare and valuable thing, a serious comic novel which both exemplifies its time and continues to speak to us.

DOMESTIC

The Commitment to Pleasure

First published in the *New Statesman*, 2007

Last week I took my twin thirteen-year-old sons to see the Black Keys at the Empire Shepherd's Bush. The Keys are two American guys, one on drums, the other on guitar, and they make a mean, dramatic and impressive noise.

That evening my sons were tired from a day at school; they were worried about not doing their French homework, and whether they'd get in trouble the next day.

'Missing your homework for a rock 'n' roll band,' I grumbled. 'You'll have to do it in the morning on the bus.'

Then, as casually as I could, I asked one of them what he was best at, at school. 'Don't worry about it, Dad,' he said thoughtfully, 'I'm the best looking.'

The boys, who are uninterested in most adult things, were mesmerised by the show. They considered the evening to be 'sick', watching the guitarist and drummer carefully, talking to one another about what the musicians were doing.

It might have been the usual rock 'n' roll experience: sticky carpets, the toilet cistern leaking on your head, people taking your seat, the boredom and excitement of waiting for the band to appear, and a headache at the end.

But during the gig I recalled a quote from Jann Wenner, the founder of *Rolling Stone* magazine, who said something like, 'I recognised that the most talented of my generation were going into music, so I did too.'

Wenner was acknowledging the truth, something I've known since my teens. Music has been the most interesting, significant, liberating and sexually compelling cultural force of my time – and the most lively, gifted and attractive people went into it. Alas for the talentless and shy.

Now, nearly thirty years after *Sgt Pepper*, it is not only Tony Blair strumming his Stratocaster in the evenings and at weekends. A good proportion of the over-forty male population is learning how to master Samba TaPi. Well off and winding down, these lost men can now spend a lot of time in the music shops of Denmark Street, and with friends, practising their licks.

A successful writer pal of mine has been rehearsing with his band every Monday for ten years. He jammed with my sons, recently, teaching them Clash songs while they explained to him who The Feeling are.

For this man there is much to wonder over, and even regret. 'Don't you think', he says seriously, and almost plaintively, 'I could have been in a professional band – maybe as a bassist? I'm not Hendrix, but I'm as good a player as many of those who made it.'

Like most of my generation, I've spent more time listening to music than I have spent reading. Pop is the cultural form I have in common with most of my friends, and certainly, as I'm discovering, with the kids.

Luckily, after listening to hip-hop for a couple of years, my sons turned to American rock, and then to British pop and rock. I became interested in music again through them. Otherwise I'd feel a little embarrassed liking the Kooks and the Streets, as if I should have grown out of it.

When music hall died after the war, reappearing on television as variety, pop took its place on the stages of those old theatres. During the fifty years I've been alive, this country has continued to produce masses of high-class music, as well as absorbing and reinterpreting American music, and saturating its youth in the leery attitudes which accompany it.

Pop is the 'outsider's' cry – free speaking to a large audience – which has done more to remake British identity than any other form, and the spirit of punk still inspires it.

British music has always been mixed up in all senses. It is a democratic form, and it is multicultural; it has been black and Asian, working-class, middle-class, gay and lesbian. If I find myself talking to the kids about this, it is because this is their history too, and something they might like to know about, indeed probably should know about, as an alternative education.

The present commitment and fervency of religious believers is disconcerting, impressive and daunting, making us wonder what it is we believe. Our own lack of such belief might make us slightly ashamed. However, if such commitments are more or less unavailable to us, there are others which are, though they are less tangible and authoritarian, less of a programme, and more about feeling and self-expression.

But that which makes an identity – perhaps the most important part of it – might be something which, as the Who put it, you 'can't explain', that is put beyond the refinement of language.

Pop still represents the voices of those who are not normally listened to, and there remains something subversive and obscene about it. The odour of cheap sexuality, drugs and drinking, as well as desperation and people going mad, remind us that pop is, ultimately, about the deepest and most important things: anarchic enjoyment and bodily pleasure.

Unlike most art, which becomes over-sophisticated as it develops, pop remains simple and direct. As with music hall, its most important qualities are vulgarity, naivety and exhibitionism.

Fortunately, this is almost impossible to articulate or teach. Think of our recent passion to characterise 'Britishness', in order that we might impress it into the psyches of the potentially British, to stop them becoming terrorists. We could have newly arrived immigrants being forced to sit in booths wearing headphones, writing an explication of 'I Am the Walrus'.

The Britain of pop is the country I understand and like, partly because its music has never quite been domesticated. Neither parochial or patriotic, pop is an unusual identification, not one based on hatred, but on creativity.

Unlike identifications built on religion or on love of the state or the leader, it is forever shifting, still anarchic, cussed, rebellious, non-conformist. It is intelligent and witty, a running ironic description of contemporary British life.

A Great Leap

First published in the *Guardian*, 2005

'Dad, Dad!' is the familiar cry, the word I know I will hear most frequently this week. 'Watch me!'

To one side of the small shingle beach in Deia is a high rock with a flat top on which the more intrepid children gather, daring each other, and themselves, to jump. One older boy hesitates for two hours, but when at last he goes over, screaming, the entire packed beach, seemingly inert under the boiling sun, bursts into applause like the audience at a TV 'confession' show.

Much to my surprise, my first son, a twin of eleven, who traverses the numerous perils of Shepherd's Bush with caution, but otherwise has little contact with dangerous sports, leaps from the edge straight away. 'The only way to go,' as he puts it coolly, giving me five. But the other twin is up there for more than an hour, pacing worriedly, locked in his own existential panic, knowing he can't climb down without considerable loss of pride.

After he goes over, my wife decides she cannot be excluded from this carnival of courage, brushing aside the men and boys rather regally, and dropping into the water with her toes pointing down and arms up. This shows a level of bravery which eludes her entirely later in the week, when she sits on a horse as we drift past vines and red earth, weeping and shaking, as her harmless horse munches on a bush and the rest of us cowboys stare at her in bewilderment.

I notice Bob Geldof is standing on the beach, too, watching the boys on the rock. He doesn't mind a bit when questioned by a crowd of kids as to his mode of address to Snoop Doggy Dogg. ('Is it plain Mr Dogg, Mr Doggy Dog, or just Snoop?' 'Snoop is fine.' 'What's his real name then? Isn't it Curtis?' 'I don't think so, no.')

Deia is a quiet and cute little town, with good bars and live music, many restaurants and a fine bookshop selling rare first editions, and without a shred of advertising anywhere; all the colour is natural. It is where Robert Graves finally settled after the war, and is now said to be full of 'artists and writers', as though that might increase its allure. I think it's unlikely we'll find a Sky dish in Deia; we'll have to go elsewhere for football.

My children are unfamiliar with what we call 'the country'. When, one night, the hotel sprinkler system begins to hiss, they assume their room is being attacked by snakes. Their favourite place is anywhere with a mirror, and their idea of a good time is lying in a darkened room watching Sumo wrestling on Eurosport. They are capitalism's finest – perfect disciples and consumers: wishing, buying, envying: it is all aimed at them. I wouldn't want them to be excluded from the general orgy, nor for them to think it is all there is. But I know they will not want to miss the Manchester United–Newcastle match.

We drive along perilous coastal roads to the other, flatter side of the island, where, we have heard, the British gather; many of them have opened bars there. Many of them, I can see by looking along the beach, have read The Da Vinci Code.

In the car the twins are edgy and anxious, unimpressed by the precipitous views; next week they will begin at a new secondary school, an altogether bigger leap. If you have the misfortune to live with all your children, you won't know the pain of having them enter and leave your life abruptly and often. These long drives are a good opportunity for us to talk, and for them to hear me and what I want of them. They're even interested in what I might be writing next. They are surprised and not reassured to hear my theory that the worst bit of life is probably the beginning rather than the end.

We stop to eat at Es Guix, an old Majorcan property in the Sierra Tramuntana mountains, converted into a spacious restaurant. The lowest of its terraces has its own freshwater pool; after lunch the boys shoot down the slide into the freezing water, bobbing up under a waterfall, their bright faces howling in the natural shower.

The game has just started when we hurry into a British bar which has a large TV. The place is full of tattooed beasts in Newcastle shirts accompanied by robust pierced mingers in tiny bikinis talking on mobile phones. The staff are wearing England shirts with their black eyes; for some reason most of them have bits of sticking plaster on their faces.

'We're Manchester United,' one of my sons fatally announces, stripping off his hoodie to reveal his Man Utd away shirt. 'Only a little bit,' I say, in an extremely high voice. Unfortunately we win the match two nil, but are moving rapidly and soundlessly towards the door when I pick up a sun hat from a table, stuffing it into the front of my trousers, believing it to be my little boy's.

Outside, my progress is blocked by a large man standing in front of me. 'You got my 'at,' he says. 'Oh no, sir, surely not. I am hatless as well as quite ill.' 'What's that then, right down the front of yer pants?' 'Oh yes, this little thing,' I say, thrusting the hat at him, patting him on the back and legging it towards the car, the kids rushing ahead of me. 'It probably wasn't a good idea to tap on him like that,' one of them says, wisely.

'Never look back,' I advise.

'A paradise of tranquillity and relaxation,' as our present hotel – La Reserva Rotana, in Manacor – characterises itself. It probably was, until the Kureishis arrived. It has cavernous rooms, huge beds, old paintings, its own vineyard and golf course, and there's acres of space to chase chickens in; it has an outdoor chess set. Nearby there are monasteries, cathedrals, galleries, castles, gardens and lap dancers. We will be there for four days. This is some contrast to our first hotel, Ca'n Verdera, in the village of Fornalutx, which was compact, seemingly cut into the rock, weirdly and suddenly designed: post-modern in an old place. The Mediterranean, they say, is where all styles meet.

After this holiday I think the boys would want to go on a horse again, and they have even talked of taking up golf, after thrashing away with clubs one morning and shooting wildly across the course on a golf-cart. But kayaking wasn't something we'd have thought of doing ourselves. We couldn't even pronounce it. For me, usually, the point of a holiday is to be so indolent and bored that I can't wait to get home and hide behind the curtains. It had never occurred to me to go on holiday and *do new things*. But our outings were organised by Jane Stanbury – soon known as 'Indiana Jane' – of Balearic Tours – who knew the place well and is aware that a bored boy is a bad boy.

In Majorca the water is clear and warm: the kids lie in the surf for ages, or put on masks and snorkel. They've never been so close to a live fish before, or swallowed so much sea. We are taken out in a small boat, passing huge yachts and looking back at expensive houses on the mountainside, with kids sitting out watching one another, and impatient fathers in Speedos talking on phones.

We were put on even smaller boats – kayaks. This is like being strapped to a lolly-stick and thrown into a flushing toilet. The moment the three boys were put into the sea, they took off, digging madly into the water with an oar which resembled a double-ended shovel, looking at the caves and the rocks which ran down the coastline. For them it was like riding a bicycle without stabilisers for the first time.

To be a tourist is to be behind glass, of course, protected from the real politics and pressures of the place you are visiting. But unlike with some Third World destinations, in Majorca you are not locked into some sort of compound surrounded by wire, while the rest of the population roams around outside, looking as though they can't wait to get their fingers on your windpipe. The staff in the hotels are neither servile nor resentful. Majorca's narrow roads are often congested with huge coaches, and soon the island will have to make many decisions about how far to go with tourism – whether that is the only purpose of the place. But until then the place is sublime, with far more to do than on most sand-and-sun destinations.

I follow the yelling boys up the steep path of a challenging hill. They want to get to the top; I want to sit down. They want to wait for me, but I tell them to go on, ahead of me. Next year I'll be jumping off that rock, just watch me.

Venice in Winter

First published in the *Guardian*, 2009

This winter we thought we'd go to Venice by train, for the adventure. Having become averse to travelling, the Kureishi family had taken its previous holiday in Watford and we were home in twenty minutes; indeed we could have commuted. Not only that, on checking into the Watford hotel we discovered Ashley Cole, Frank Lampard and John Terry playing Scrabble in a side-room. The England captain charmed our ten-year-old son, asking him his name before giving him his autograph. The kid was smart enough not to let on that we were Manchester United supporters.

This time, after taking the Eurostar to Paris and the Metro to the Gare Bercy, we joined the night train. I took two sleeping pills and, wearing all my clothes, slipped under the thin blanket on the bunk bed, thinking how lovely it was to lie there watching the landscape and the lights speeding by. An hour later I woke up to find the train had stopped in a station and a crowd of French clubbers were staring into our cabin.

Every time I peered down at my partner in her bunk, her eyes were open and she was staring at the ceiling. The restaurant car had been splendid, but we did wonder at the level of hygiene in the tiny cabin; it was not unlike sleeping in a public toilet with a great view of the Alps. Indeed, if you did happen to peer into the train toilet, you could see the ground below.

But we did wake up in Venice, the train almost tipping us into the Grand Canal. I'd never been here in the winter, and it was a different beauty, stark and fresh. The sun was bright and near the Rialto, not far from one of my favourite shops, the Beatles' Memorabilia emporium, people were eating outside wearing sunglasses.

Luckily there was no sign of the worst flooding Venice had endured since 1966. Having watched the TV news in early December and seen a man canoeing across St Mark's Square and the rest of the population wading up to their gussets in sewage during a transport strike, I'd had to say to the Missus: that's where we will be spending the New Year.

The hotel we were put in, the Palazzo Barbarigo, was dark in the modern style – the modern style of the 1980s, resembling a smart Philippe Starck New York hotel, where everything straight was curved and you needed a torch to find your way around, even when the lights were on. But the floors were great for a ten-year-old Duracell-battery boy to skid across in his socks, and he could duck down behind the huge sofas when the need for discretion arose.

As I have a theory that you can eat almost anywhere in France or Italy and the food will be fine, that first lunchtime we picked a place at random. (Never try this in London.)

Opening a door into an almost deserted small place near the Rialto, we came across two old, frail women taking their morning cappuccino. Immediately they began to talk to us, telling us through gestures that our son Kier was both a genius and beautiful. Later, we learned what an impressive and relaxed café society there was in Venice: that local people, particularly older ones, gathered with their shopping in cafés in the morning, to gossip.

We had been anxious about whether our son would be sufficiently distracted during these few days in a drowning museum of a city. Fortunately he soon began to hop about happily in his Crocs. Since Venice combines shopping with water and boats, and in St Mark's Square the pigeons will still sit on a child's head, he adored it; and everyone in Venice seemed to adore him. Strangers on the water-buses – the vaporettos – and in the streets and cafés touched him and stroked his head as soon as they saw him. They wanted to give him stuff: roses, sweets, paper planes, pens, kisses.

What better company in the world is there than that of a ten-year-old boy who is curious and lively, retaining the charm and affection of a child without the sullen aggression of a teenager? He and I went to Harry's Bar for more conversation, where they took Kier's coat and brought him chips and ice-cream immediately. The bar was still chic and busy, with classic food, and it remains famous for the writers who like it. But these days a writer had better be accompanied by his publisher if he wants to afford it.

Years ago, a friend with incomplete English appeared to believe that there existed a useful book called *Men Are from Mars, Women Are from Venice*. But the women from Venice mostly appeared to be old women, widows probably, in fur coats, often with little dogs. There were babies too, but otherwise the city seemed bereft of young people or teenagers. While it can be a mercy to be free of the young and their exultation and hope, it was strange too. But without them what future could there be for a city which made a good living out of eternal decline? However, graffiti provided evidence that there were kids around. It wasn't until later that night that I saw them.

My friend, the painter Serena Nono, lives on the mainly residential Venetian island of Giudecca in the apartment her father, the composer Luigi Nono, wrote in. If St Mark's is crowded and claustrophobic, as it is for most of the year, it is easy to take a boat to Giudecca, just ten minutes away. Serena intended to show us a different side of Venice. She had said, pointing at the ground and then at the buildings, 'Never forget that everything is crooked in Venice; nothing is straight.' As Muriel Spark wrote, 'Venice is a city not to inspire thought but sensations.'

That night, at her urging, Kier and I took two vaporettos from the hotel to the Giudecca canal. It hadn't taken us long to get into the vaporetto thing. You can buy a limitless use twenty-four-hour ticket, and the boats are regular, run all night and are fun to ride on – you are on a bus on the water and the view is of ancient floating palaces.

But tonight it was dark, cold and desolate; the city tunnels were rancid and dripping, and Kier and I began to wonder if there really could be anything going on here, particularly when the only person around was a desperate Pakistani who jumped out of a doorway and sold us a laser pen and glasses which lit up. Still, at least I could see my son. And anyway, although Venice gives off a sense of menace and death – and one of the best things to do there is get lost – it is not violent.

At last, near the Zattere vaporetto stop, we came to a freezing toiletless squatted warehouse on the edge of the water. Venetians in overcoats were drinking mulled wine, smoking, feeding their dogs and playing table football. When a tight band began to do Elvis covers people slowly began to get up to do the twist, elegantly, while 1950s black and white movies were projected on a screen behind. My son, in his woolly hat and gloves, wandered to the front and stood and stared. I guess it was probably the first time he'd heard 'Heartbreak Hotel' and 'Hound Dog', and what better circumstances could there be?

Later, Serena's work was projected on to the screen, and a Venetian ska band started up. It had been so long since I'd heard a Venetian ska band complete with a Rasta saxophonist and trombonist as good as this that I started to dance on the concrete floor, though without moving my feet. Kier was still at the front of the crowd, which was jumping now, and a teenage girl took his hand and twirled him around. Just before midnight I had to drag him out of there; as I watched him watching those devil musicians I feared he'd been seduced for life.

Giudecca, once home to Michelangelo and Alfred de Musset, and now to Elton John, was beautiful in the day too. Serena took us to see her studio in a converted brewery, where a month before she had found her paintings floating. Now they were dry and stacked neatly against the walls.

Venice is expensive as everyone knows, particularly as all goods have to be transported by boat. But you can get by on a hot chocolate with whipped cream if you walk past the bleak women's prison to the almost deserted Hilton Hotel, where you can sit on the roof while contemplating the best view in Venice. From here you can confirm Jan Morris's remarks in her magisterial *Venice*, published in 1960, 'This is not a large city. You can see it all easily, from one end to the other. It is about two miles long by one mile deep, and you can walk from end to end of it, from the slaughter-house in the north-west to the Public Gardens in the south-east, in an hour and a half – less, if you don't mind shoving.'

It was important for us to get to know where the best pizza was. Fortunately ten minutes' walk from our hotel was the Campo Santa Margherita, in Dorsoduro, one of Venice's six sestieri, or districts. This square or piazza is lined by trattorias and shaded by trees; in the morning there's a fish market.

In a bar we ran into an actor, a man with the dignity of the great Fernando Rey. Though he didn't speak English nor I Italian, he invited Serena, and us, to his family house the next night, New Year's Eve.

We pondered this for some time. It seemed a little weird going to a generous stranger's house on the last night of the year. But what else would we do at midnight in a strange city? There was a dinner in the hotel, but it seemed a little impersonal. So we bought Prosecco and turned up at 'Rey's'.

It was a lovely, welcoming fish dinner; there were other children there, and we all sat around a small table. For entertainment we felt the bumps on the top of each other's heads. The actor and I couldn't speak to one another so he pulled out his albums from the 60s, put on a scratchy record by the Rolling Stones and we two strangers danced together. Later we found Kier outside, standing on the edge of the canal with sparklers in his fist, enraptured by a long-haired Italian girl.

As I got drunker, Serena Nono's Berkeley-born mother Nuria, whose father was the composer Schoenberg, told me stories of her childhood: of Thomas Mann making the children stay outside in the garden when her father went for supper, and the long wait for Brecht to visit – she was at school with his daughter Barbara.

Then, as though this had been staged for us, around 11.30 it started to snow. At midnight the fireworks in St Mark's Square began, and we had a perfect view from the other side of the city, the rockets firing into the snow, which was heavy now. Couples in the house began to dance and embrace – I don't mind hugging strangers if they're Italian. It was like a scene from *Fanny and Alexander*.

By now drenched and with white heads, we shoved into the loaded vaporetto, all the bells of the city ringing out at once. At the hotel bar I saw a waiter I knew hurrying towards me carrying a tray on which was a two-decker chocolate cake and a huge glass of vodka. After turning fifty, pleasures are harder to come by than at an earlier age; but they are more appreciated. I like to believe I woke up in the morning, still holding that glass of vodka.

It's a Sin: The *Kama Sutra* and
the Search for Pleasure

First published in the *Guardian*, 2011

'What a pity it's not a sin!' says a woman licking an ice-cream in a story by Stendhal, reminding us that the search for pleasure – and prohibited pleasure at that – is a primary preoccupation for most people a good deal of the time, even for those trying to hide from it.

Even reading the *Kama Sutra*, in a fine new translation by A. N. D. Haksar, feels like a guilty pleasure. In the mid-1960s, when I first heard of it, the *Kama Sutra* was, along with *The Perfumed Garden* and *Venus in Furs*, considered licentious and filthy, the very gateway to damnation. In the suburbs in the early 1960s, if a young man sought knowledge of sexual matters he had to traipse up to London to watch European films, and, if particularly desperate during a tiresome evening, might even be forced to turn to literature. My father owned copies of contraband like *Lady Chatterley*, *Lolita* and other such serious stuff, along with Harold Robbins. The real business, for me, was in the Robbins and I ended up never reading the *Kama Sutra*. And the longer I didn't read it, the more dreadful this famed carnival of desire and mayhem became in my imagination.

It turns out that *Kama Sutra: A Guide to the Art of Pleasure* by Vatsyayana is a compendium of advice about social and romantic behaviour, put together sixteen hundred years ago for wealthy young men about town. It contains information about hygiene and sexual positions, and advises how not to cause havoc in a harem, how to deal with courtesans, and how to behave towards 'the wives of others'. It suggests that the gentleman should keep away from lepers, malodorous women and anyone with white spots. It is arch, comical and amazing, less Byron and more the sort of thing that Jeeves would have said to a priapic Bertie Wooster had Bertie been Indian and P. G. Wodehouse without the sense to omit sex from his books. It states, for example, that 'intercourse with two women who have good feelings for each other is known as the "combination". The same with many women is called "the herd of cows". Apparently, if you bite a woman around the nipples, you could be quids in. Presumably, though, if you overdo it, you could find yourself on your way.

Although the *Kama Sutra* doesn't take pleasure seriously enough to be wise, whatever else it might be, it is certainly a reminder of the central place of sexuality and its pleasures in our lives – and pleasures, as every parent knows, have to be both limited and passed on to the next generation. They are, then, transmitted mostly by being forbidden, and it is this relation to prohibition that amuses and intrigues Stendhal. It is prohibition that makes serious recreation feasible, just as it is the rules that make sport possible. Without authorities or taboos there isn't more fun, but more nothing, particularly as we tend to treat ourselves more severely than even the authorities do.

The *Kama Sutra*, as a book of technique – a sexual self-help manual for the socially naive, a way for geeks to make it with girls – is fascinating, therefore, in what it omits, in what the author doesn't seem aware of. It neglects, for instance, one of the most important parts of love: that one can caress with the voice as well as with the eyes.

In fact, its routines appear to render any form of sensual trans-action uncreative, predictable and controlled, and the male omnipotent. If it turned out that the woman was also consulting a similar manual then the two characters in this drama would be playing roles that ensured they'd remain outside the experience. Both would be in a fixed place and the relationship would be merely an exchange of fantasies. The interesting question here is whether this is perhaps the truth about sex – whether a Clintonesque 'there is no sexual relation' seems to get it right, and there really is no touching, ever – or if this is wishful thinking. Like Alfred Kinsey's reports at the end of the 1940s and early 1950s, the *Kama Sutra* tries hard to turn passion into science.

One can see why. The minor pleasures may be satisfying and even fulfilling, but the major ones are serious toil. That sex is chaotic, mad, perverse, risible, enlivening and inspiring, and that in its awkwardness and self-consciousness there might be more real contact than in the simple following of positions, also doesn't occur to the author. If you'd never heard of sex until you read the *Kama Sutra*, you'd believe it was a trickle rather than a torrent, a conversation rather than an argument, a pastime rather than a life-saver. Certainly, pleasure can be valued or discouraged, and there are innumerable forms of it, of which, perhaps, sexuality, when combined with love, is the ultimate example of abandon, disarray and internal chaos. Or it should be.

It's easy to praise happiness. Apparently you can't have too much of it, and, like a lovely day, there aren't many people who have a bad word to say about it. Things look even worse for happiness now that even politicians have begun to take an interest in sponsoring, measuring and trying to roll it out to the public. Happiness resembles ambient music and writes white, they say. You won't find pleasure on the school curriculum; it comes, as Emma Bovary would have attested, in numerous dark shades.

About pleasure there is always, and should be, dangerous ambivalence. Too little of the devil's sport and life will seem attenuated, heavy and slow, if not dead. The negative of pleasure, or perhaps its antidote, is depression, the popular modern malady, an uncomfortably dull refuge from the question of pleasure and how much is the right amount for you. Most self-help books these days are either about depression, happiness or creative writing. Pleasure is barely a topic for the pseudo-shrinks, or for anyone, as if it's too dangerous to talk about – unless it's in the negative. After all, enjoyment might feel, as Baudelaire puts it, like this: 'The unique, supreme pleasure of love lies in the certainty of doing wrong.' Happiness is earned; pleasure is always stolen. We are more likely to envy others' pleasures than their happiness – in fact, pleasure is the only thing there is to envy.

The return of religious fundamentalism in its numerous guises is witness to the necessary presence of sin, the horror of pleasure and the desire for its strict regulation. Fundamentalism, and the obedience it enjoins, is an attempt to abolish the conflicts that pleasure involves. But in such circumstances, the pleasure of self-deprivation – religious obedience, dieting and other forms of abstinence – can come to replace genuine enjoyment. Pleasure can be slutty: it's a parasite that can attach itself to anything.

Whatever the manuals might say, and despite the rules of dating as laid down in the *Kama Sutra*, obviously there can't be a right answer to the question of the right amount, though there is much anxiety about the wrong amount. Certainly, if there is too much pleasure – if one hates or loves too much – there might be addiction, madness, violence, disappointment and the sacrifice of oneself and others. Pleasure can smash things up; you could die or kill for it, and people do so all the time. Where happiness is its own quiet end, pleasure creates consequences: it's where the moral stuff starts, and when the priests rush in with prayers and doctors make beds available.

There's nothing like a self-help book to make you feel a failure. But if someone really wants pleasure, and if they want obscene outrage more than they want contentment or safety or even happiness, the pleasure guru will have to act the minor Mephistopheles and let on that the price of the real thing could be high.

A genuinely useful self-help guide to bearing pleasure might have to contain advice about putting up with the envy, contempt and hatred of oneself as well as of others, along with any self-disgust, guilt and punishment that will follow, along with the inevitable loss. It would be an education in determination and ruthlessness and, to a certain extent, in selfishness and in forgetting. Inevitably, one of the lucky ones, a well-informed character in the Marquis de Sade's *The 120 Days of Sodom*, has the right idea: 'I hate virtue and never will I be seen resorting to it. I have no need to thwart my inclinations in order to flatter some god.'

He's fortunate enough to believe the law doesn't apply to him. But in Sade, as in all perversion, and to a certain extent in the *Kama Sutra* – despite the declarations of liberty – there's no freedom for the participants to escape the limited repertoire of roles their fantasies assign them, or to be altered by one another: the other doesn't exist. Pleasure is more contentious, difficult and subversive, both emotionally and politically, than these authors want to see.

However, the *Kama Sutra* does usefully demonstrate that sexuality is usually in excess of our ability to process or speak about it. Such enjoyment overwhelms, and we have to give ourselves up to it, forfeiting fantasies of control, which is why words fail, and literary descriptions can seem inadequate, amusing and foolish. Expressions such as Vatsyayana's 'the sparrow's frolic' and 'the bull's stroke' can hardly be expected to speak to us now, and pornography, of course, is incapable of describing the inner lives of sexual beings. Compared with the actual experience, words never seem to get close to the object, but stand around looking daft.

This may be because there is no mystery left in sex. We have seen everything at least twice and are jaded. But since most of the world is far more constrained than this little plot of land in Western Europe, the notion of sexual freedom, pleasure and desire – particularly for women, and in its more perverse forms – always deserves discussion. But for illustration it's the poets and sometimes novelists who can occasionally pin sensuality to the page. Nonetheless, portraying bliss is almost impossible work, and it is in soul music – in Billie Holiday, Marvin Gaye, Aretha Franklin and in some R&B – where you can see, and feel, how desire, longing, loss and fulfilment can be impeccably compacted, having a tangible effect on the listener, making them want to cry or dance.

It might be important to recognise that our pleasures have to be guarded from our own aggression, much as our freedoms are. You can make a cult of destructive pleasures, and you can devote your life to their daily deathly temptations, as many people have – 'You need a danger to be safe in,' writes Frederick Seidel.

But those who are afraid of the fire will want to value enjoyment as a source of illumination rather than as something that can be stared straight at. Kant defines pleasure as 'the consciousness of vital effort'. It is an afterglow, that which follows from something else, as one chases one's desire into solid, reasonable things – conversation, friendship, teaching, attending to others, and the erotic connections of creativity.

This is reassuring; however, the glow rather than the stare is not quite the real thing. But if you're reading the *Kama Sutra* you're not near the real thing either, nor is it likely to get you closer. Whichever way you like to take your pleasure, a faulty map will never guide you to your destination.